959.704   880288

Willenson, Kim

THE BAD WAR; AN ORAL HISTORY OF
THE VIETNAM WAR

THE
BAD WAR

AN ORAL HISTORY
OF THE
VIETNAM WAR

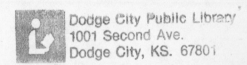

THE
BAD WAR

AN ORAL HISTORY
OF THE
VIETNAM WAR

by

Kim Willenson

with the correspondents
of Newsweek

A NEWSWEEK BOOK

NAL BOOKS

NEW AMERICAN LIBRARY

NEW YORK AND SCARBOROUGH, ONTARIO

Published simultaneously in Canada by The New American Library of Canada Limited

ACKNOWLEDGMENTS
"TIMES THEY ARE A-CHANGIN' " by Bob Dylan, © Copyright 1963 Warner Bros.
    Inc. All rights reserved. Used by permission.
"THE MOTORCYCLE SONG" by Arlo Guthrie, © Copyright 1967, 1969 by Appleseed
    Music Inc. All rights reserved. Used by permission.
"THOSE WERE THE DAYS," words and music by Gene Raskin. TRO-© Copyright 1962
    and 1968 Essex Music, Inc., New York, New York. Used by permission.

NAL BOOKS TRADEMARK REG. U.S. PAT. OFF. AND FOREIGN COUNTRIES
REGISTERED TRADEMARK—MARCA REGISTRADA
HECHO EN HARRISONBURG, VA., U.S.A.

SIGNET, SIGNET CLASSIC, MENTOR, ONYX, PLUME,
MERIDIAN and NAL BOOKS
are published in the United States by NAL PENGUIN INC.,
1633 Broadway, New York, New York 10019,
in Canada by The New American Library of Canada Limited,
81 Mack Avenue, Scarborough, Ontario M1L 1M8

Library of Congress Cataloging-in-Publication Data
Willenson, Kim.
    The bad war.

    (A Newsweek book)
    Includes index.
    1. Vietnamese Conflict, 1961–1975—Personal
narratives. I. Title.
DS 559.5.W55   1987   959.704'38   87-1679
ISBN 0-453-00546-2

Designed by Julian Hamer

First Printing, June, 1987

1   2   3   4   5   6   7   8   9

PRINTED IN THE UNITED STATES OF AMERICA

To the names on the Wall
And all the other names on all the other walls
That it may not happen again

Acknowledgments

I would like to acknowledge with gratitude the help and patience of the editors of *Newsweek*, Rick Smith and Maynard Parker, and the two senior editors, Steven Strasser and Melinda Beck, who conceived and executed the magazine's cover story on the tenth anniversary of the fall of Saigon. Without that base this book would not have existed. I am also indebted to senior editor Lynn Povich, who handles books and other special projects for *Newsweek*, for having taken the time to listen to the proposal and give it encouragement, and to *Newsweek's* agent, Rollene Saal, who had the persistence to sell it.

My special respect goes to my colleagues among the magazine's correspondents who conducted the bulk of the interviews that appear here. The native curiosity that is the hallmark of every first-rate reporter helped them to evoke from these conversations about events of ten and twenty years earlier an extraordinary portrait of a troubling time. In alphabetical order they are: Pamela Abramson, Edward Behr, Jeff Copeland, Daniel Pedersen, Martin Kasindorf, Patricia King, Allison Levin, Gerald Lubenow, Richard Manning, John McCormick, Ron Moreau, Richard Sandza, Debbie Seward, Steven Shabad, Vern E. Smith, and Anne Underwood.

Contents

Contents

Introduction

Victory has a hundred fathers;
defeat is an orphan.
—An anonymous aphorism

FOR almost a decade after the last American helicopter lifted off the roof of the U.S. Embassy in Saigon, the United States indulged itself in a great forgetting. A majority, perhaps a preponderance, of Americans agreed with Barry Goldwater, who remarked soon after the fall that he hoped the United States would learn *nothing* from Vietnam, because there were no lessons worth remembering. In the aftermath of the collapse, says Thomas Polgar, the CIA station chief in Vietnam from 1972 to 1975, the U.S. government never looked back. The CIA held no debriefings, asked for no after-action reports, prepared no summaries of mistakes made, established no patterns for future action. The same was true of the White House, the State Department, the Congress, the colleges and universities, even of the antiwar activists, who for the most part scattered to begin making ordinary lives for themselves. There would, after all, never *be* another Vietnam.

The military, which endured the brunt of the criticism and paid the bulk of the cost in lives and treasure, was better, but only by half. It assigned the task to its official historians and its war colleges. In the mid-eighties, very late but better than never, military men produced two works of genuine intellectual quality, *On Strategy*, by Col. Harry Summers, and *The 25-Year War*, by Gen. Bruce Palmer, who had been William C. Westmoreland's deputy and later commanded the U.S. Army briefly in Vietnam. Both of these books focused on the conduct of the fighting and the bureaucratic politics in Washington that produced the losing American strategy.

The tenth anniversary of the collapse, in 1985, brought forth the

Public Broadcasting System's televised recapitulation of the war, accompanied by Stanley Karnow's excellent written analysis, and a series of books and articles on the climactic fifty-five days in which the native army the United States had labored so hard to build blew away like a bamboo house in a hurricane. These were harbingers of a new and more rational scrutiny of the war—a healthy sign that the United States was finally coming to grips with its legacy to domestic politics and foreign policy. That is important, because a decade after the fall it is clear that the Vietnam experience deeply informs official and unofficial thinking in Washington about the uses of power abroad.

No generation could have gone through such a calamity without permanent scars to its psyche, and it was the Vietnam generation that managed military and foreign policy in the Reagan years. The legacy was visible in the U.S. decision to take its three hundred dead and go home from Lebanon rather than be dragged again into a situation it didn't understand, without a visible military objective. It could be seen in the decision to strike Grenada with enough force to settle the issue, even if clumsily, in just three days. It instructed a careful American campaign to develop a political alternative to the failing regime of Ferdinand Marcos in the Philippines, and then to get him out of the way without bloodshed, in sharp contrast to U.S. behavior toward Ngo Dinh Diem in 1963.

Even in Central America, where the White House and the CIA seemed ready to throw experience to the winds, the memories made the military and Congress reluctant to get directly involved. In El Salvador, they limited the U.S. presence, kept it well away from combat, emphasized economic as well as military aid, and fostered the rise of José Napoleon Duarte, a centrist alternative to the death squad rightists who had dominated the country's politics. In the case of Nicaragua, they provoked a first magnitude political storm. The Vietnam experience also became central to a running public debate between Caspar Weinberger and George Shultz over the uses of American military power, in which a dovish secretary of defense urged restraint while a hawkish secretary of state argued that the country had grown too timid about backing its word with bullets.

In a way, the Weinberger-Shultz debate was a high-level outfall of a campaign by right-wingers—most of whom had kept their brogans well clear of the battlefield—to rewrite the war's history. These latter-day hawks sought to restore an image of American omnipotence they believed had been damaged by Vietnam. In fact the decline of American clout in the late seventies was mostly in the eyes of Americans. As Congressman Stephen Solarz points out, the same period in which the right moaned about Soviet advances in Angola, Afghanistan, and Ethiopia was marked by the conversion of China, Egypt, and Somalia into American friends, by a turn to democratic government when Fascist regimes fell in Spain and Portugal, by a philosophical parting of ways between Moscow and the West European left, and by the emergence of Southeast Asia outside Vietnam as a pro-Western economic powerhouse.

Still, as Richard Holbrooke, a diplomat whose professional life was intimately bound up with Indochina for the better part of twenty years observes, Vietnam can be seen as the Civil War of the twentieth century. We will still be arguing about it, he says, on the twenty-fifth anniversary of the collapse, as we did on the tenth. By defining a political limit to the use of military force, the war disrupted the bipartisan consensus that had governed foreign policy since Pearl Harbor. By creating a focal point for dissent and protest, it spawned a social upheaval that transfigured domestic politics as well. It is the continuing campaign of the revisionist hawks to restyle the past that makes it worthwhile to give voice to people who actually participated in the event.

What is supremely ironic about the revisionism is that in hindsight, the defeat in Vietnam looks very much like a net plus for the United States. It deflated America's post–World War II hubris at a tragically large cost—but also at a price much smaller than we might have paid had we chosen Hungary, Czechoslovakia, Poland, or Berlin as the arena in which to toe a line in the dust. In a curious way, as retired Ambassador William Sullivan points out, the defeat made possible a geostrategic shift of cosmic proportion—the swing of China out of the Soviet orbit. That transformation, to be sure, was no fault of our own; it was created by political forces in the Eurasian heartland with which we had very little to do. But had we hung on in Vietnam, China might well have papered over its differences with Moscow, continued to support Hanoi in the name of socialist unity, and maintained a high level of tension with its neighbors. Instead, the shift fostered an unprecedented period of calm and of surging economic growth in Asia, and transferred the burden of preparing for a two-front war from America to the Soviet Union.

Any writer who claims to give a comprehensive account of the war in Vietnam does so at his peril. From beginning to end, Ho Chi Minh's rebellion lasted more than forty years, and involved the Chinese, the Japanese, and the French before the Americans appeared on the scene. Over the ten, fourteen, twenty-one, or twenty-five years the American role lasted—which number you accept depends on whether you believe it was Lyndon Johnson, John Kennedy, Dwight Eisenhower, or Harry Truman who got us involved—upwards of three million Americans served in Vietnam. Millions more were involved at home, either supporting and directing the conflict, or protesting and trying to undermine it. To their stories must be added those of the fifty million Laotians, Cambodians, and Vietnamese whose lives and countries it ravaged. If the hundred or so people who were interviewed for this book are any indication, every person who was there is an indispensable tile in an imaginary mosaic that comprises the story entire.

In truth, the war lasted so long, involved so many people, and was so complex in structure that no one person can know, nor can any one work reflect, its every facet. To some extent, we are all blind men trying to discern the shape of a strange beast from the feel of its parts. My intention in assembling this book was not so much to be comprehensive about the war as to convey the lasting impressions of some interesting people who lived the event. There is certainly some risk in this. Memories set down ten, fifteen, or twenty-five years later are bound to be both inexact and colored by personal feeling. Moreover, the recollections reproduced here were culled and consolidated from hundreds of hours of talk. While I have tried hard to be faithful to the subjects' meanings, some distortions may have crept in through the editing. If that has happened, I apologize in advance. Still, I think that from these conversations emerge a multitude of perceptions and at least in broad outline, some underlying truths about an event that recast the American perspective on the world.

The bulk of these interviews were conducted as *Newsweek* magazine prepared a cover story in April 1985 to mark the tenth anniversary of the fall of Saigon. Early on, Editor Maynard Parker, who had covered the war, and the two senior editors in charge of the project, Melinda Beck and Steven Strasser, decided to give voice to a number of people who had participated in the conflict, rather than to try to distill their thoughts into an essay. Since I had been involved from 1963 to 1975 in editing or writing stories about Vietnam, including six years on the ground in Indochina, I took on a substantial amount of the interviewing. As I listened, and later as I read through the material collected by my colleagues, I began to see a number of themes that seemed to shed fresh understanding on how the war came about, how it was mishandled in Washington and Saigon, and how it shaped foreign policy in the years that followed.

One is the notion, outlined by Clark Clifford, William Sullivan, Walt Rostow, and others, that going into Vietnam we believed we had both the responsibility and the power to stop the spread of Communism worldwide, and a well-defined strategic interest in doing so in Southeast Asia. These beliefs rested on the experience of the thirties and forties, when the West did nothing to stop Hitler's early advances, ended up having to fight World War II, and then, under the rubric of "containment," moved to limit the postwar Soviet advance. Kennedy's ringing inaugural declaration that we would bear any burden and pay any price in defense of liberty was a symbolic restatement of those beliefs—great rhetoric, as Clifford observes, but faulty logic and politics.

Kennedy's choice of Southeast Asia as the arena of test was dictated in part by events and in part by a belief that the two Communist giants intended, by seizing both Indochina and Indonesia, to put themselves astride the main shipping route from East Asia to the Persian Gulf and Europe. These were the "dominos" about which we worried, and given the Malayan, Burmese, Filipino, and Thai insurgencies of the era, and a Communist-inspired coup attempt in Indonesia in 1965, the worries were not nearly so irrational at the time as they may look in retrospect. It is true that outside of French Indochina, none of the dominos fell after the defeat. But it may be fair to argue, as Rostow does, that the U.S. intervention gave the others time to stabilize.

A second theme is that misapplied political science was responsible in large measure for our failed military strategy. The theory of escalation, developed by Herman Kahn, Henry Kissinger, Thomas Schelling, and others to provide a "rational" foundation for conducting limited nuclear war, was adopted by Robert McNamara as the intellectual underpinning for his effort to force North Vietnam out of the war with air power. McNamara believed that no rational leader would want his country bombed; therefore if the United States bombed him, Ho Chi Minh would do whatever was necessary to bring the assault to a stop. Schelling actually contended in an essay, notes Adm. James Stockdale—who led the air strike that followed the fake incident in the Tonkin Gulf in August of 1964—that this was a neatly packaged implicit transaction between Washington and Hanoi: a model for future armed "communication" between the American superpower and belligerent little adversaries. Of course it was nothing of the kind. That air raid and the subsequent campaign of escalation simply allowed Hanoi to develop other ways to cope—including the installation of an effective air defense in the North, and counterescalation on the ground in the South. The combination ultimately took a terrible toll of American lives and materiel.

Both Summers and Palmer argue in their books, as do many others, that the United States might have won if only it had had the courage to do what military common sense commended: to fully mobilize its reserves and move troops forward early in the war so as to demonstrate its resolve to win and its capacity to inflict permanent losses on Hanoi; if necessary, to invade Laos or even North Vietnam, cut the Ho Chi Minh Trail, isolate the guerrillas in the South, and convert the war into a frontal engagement like Korea—a kind of conflict the United States was better prepared to fight. But that course was considered often, and as often rejected. Lyndon Johnson thought he could avoid derailing his domestic programs if he maintained the fiction that Vietnam was only a small conflict. His key advisers were held in thrall by the memory of Korea. No one wanted to risk drawing the limitless manpower of China into a jungle where we were already unable to contain the forces of a nation so small and backward as North Vietnam.

That leads to a third theme: that we never bothered to study or understand the Vietnamese, Northern *or* Southern. When McNamara wanted to know how the bombing would affect Ho Chi Minh, argues Douglas Pike, the leading official analyst of Vietnamese Communist affairs during the war, in essence he interviewed himself. Rather than studying in detail the enemy's method of political and military operations, we practiced "vincible ignorance," a phrase borrowed from Aldous Huxley. We knew it was important, but we believed it did not matter. We thought we could defeat Hanoi with strength alone. In all the millions of official words written during the war, says Pike, there was not a single cogent examination of Hanoi's overall strategy. Even the postwar studies by Summers and Palmer ignored such subjects as the tactics North Vietnam used to defeat superior American force, or how Hanoi organized, trained, and motivated its troops to perform so well under the brutal battering of American weapons ranging from tanks and massed artillery to B-52 bombers. In large part, according to Pike, this was done by imbuing them with the notion of *dau tranh*, or "struggle," a concept with deep meaning in Vietnamese, whose emotional content cannot be conveyed in an English word or phrase. We knew about *dau tranh*, but we did not think it important enough to divine a way to counteract or defeat it.

Vincible ignorance applied to our vision of the South Vietnamese as well. We isolated ourselves behind a social barrier of post exchanges, commissaries, private clubs, and walled compounds, as though the people, the culture, and the country existed in another dimension that only obliquely intersected with our own, says former AID-man Gary Larsen. Although the State Department made a concerted effort to teach its officers Vietnamese, the CIA and the military did so much less. And those who did learn the language and gain some real vision of the Vietnamese mentality were most often younger officials whose opinions carried little weight with those who fashioned policy.

Of all the things we failed to understand about the South Vietnamese, perhaps the most important were their sense of dependency and their overweening self-concern. They were willing to fight so long as they felt we were standing by to protect them. When we said in the early seventies that we could no longer endure the domestic price being exacted by our military sacrifices, the Vietnamese professed both to understand and to be prepared to soldier on alone. But when the crunch came, they fell prey to fantasies that we had some master plan and would stage a grand rescue. And when it was clear that we were *not* coming back, that no rescue plan existed, they abandoned the struggle in an instant and ran to save themselves.

There were abundant signs of these attitudes all along, which for the most part we chose deliberately to ignore. We knew that thousands of young Vietnamese were evading the draft; they were visible in the streets and the nightclubs of Saigon and other cities. Yet we calmly sent thousands of young Americans to fight and die in their places. It was plain to all that the military men who took power in the coup against Ngo Dinh Diem had neither popular appeal nor the will and skill to create a non-Communist alternative to the nationalist charisma of Ho Chi Minh. Yet we were so shaken by the revolving door governments of 1964 and 1965 that once Nguyen Van Thieu was able to stabilize the generals, we dared not demand that he proceed with genuine political reform, though that offered the only hope of creating a government with a popular base. Instead we gave lip service to the vague goal of creating a nationalist democratic system, and hoped in vain that Thieu might one day develop enough magnetism to lead. We failed to understand that no one who appeared to be our puppet could have popular appeal, and that we had created conditions under which no leader of South Vietnam could be seen as anything else.

We knew that corruption was endemic not just to the civil government but to the police and the military as well. Though some Vietnamese officers were genuinely dedicated to fighting the war, many others spent their time plotting how to turn a dollar by selling their supplies, or how to get themselves back to safe and lucrative positions in Saigon. Yet we persuaded ourselves that this could be remedied by piling in more supplies, and that the lack of leadership it betrayed did not matter. In the success of the secret preparations for a nationwide offensive at Tet of 1968 we saw that hundreds of thousands of Vietnamese could be party to a vast conspiracy against us, and not one would give us warning. We knew also, as Palmer and others observe, that the Vietnamese government and military were shot through with people in important positions who kept a foot in the other camp and regularly betrayed our military plans to the enemy. Yet we never stopped pretending that the Vietnamese were good and faithful allies whom we could not desert. We saw in the collapse of the northern defenses and the pell-mell flight of civilians from Hue during the Easter Offensive of 1972—an onslaught staved off only with American air power—a precursor of how it would all end. Yet we chose to ignore what this said about the will of the Vietnamese to fight for their own future.

And this leads to a fourth theme, which is that we did not understand *ourselves* well, either. If there was a half-conscious inclination in Saigon to look away from unpleasant facts in the name of keeping the applecart upright, there was a deliberate conspiracy of silence in Washington. Before the first U.S. combat troops ever landed in Vietnam, says Alexander Haig, Gen. Harold K. Johnson, the Chief of Staff of the Army, reported that it would take many years and perhaps a million men to win with the strategy on which the Administration insisted. Yet in the interest of preserving an appearance of military unity and of not giving advice they knew their masters did not want to hear, the Joint Chiefs of Staff watered down his report to a useless piece of paper, instead of sending on to Lyndon Johnson a clear warning of the immense cost of the course on which he was about to embark.

Just so, the Army never believed that air power would win. It opposed the bombing of North Vietnam because of the political cost in the United States and the battlefield cost in Vietnam, says Morton Halperin. But it kept quiet because the campaign was an Air Force program, to which the Army leadership had agreed in order to get Air Force support for other things the Army wanted. The nature of deal-making among the services so as to support each other's programs was a mystery to the civilians then, and is only dimly perceived outside the defense community even today.

By the same token hundreds and perhaps thousands of officials as well as military officers recognized that bombing the Ho Chi Minh Trail was a futile enterprise. We had already seen in Korea that air raids could not effectively shut off the flow of supplies to an enemy's front. By 1966 that was also visible in Indochina. When American planes destroyed bridges, the North Vietnamese brought in ferries and pontoons. When we broke up paved roads, Hanoi reconstructed with dirt. When we destroyed one truck, two came behind. Simply by pouring more in at the top of the funnel, Hanoi could always get enough out at the bottom to sustain operations no matter how much we destroyed on the way. But the U.S. Air Force could not admit the failure without risking a hard look at the utility of air power per se. Its very *raison d'être* would be open to question. So we ignored the evidence and continued the campaign at an ever-increasing price in men, materiel, and political condemnation.

At least as important, observes Halperin, a nearly complete silence was enforced on the civilian as well as military bureaucracies by Johnson and McNamara. They did not want the truth spoken openly, even within the secret councils of government, because that would require them to make decisions they wanted to defer—either to cut their losses and get out, or to escalate to a level that would assure the enemy's defeat. Johnson and later Nixon continued the war not to win, but in the name of not being the first to lose, and the United States found itself, as Georgia Senator Richard Russell once put it, in the same predicament as a cow hung up on a fence. It couldn't go forward and it couldn't go back, and all the time the pickets were hurting its belly.

As the war progressed, the hurt in the belly was amplified many times over by the carnage on the screen, the biting commentary in the press, the mind-bending battlefield ordeal of hundreds of thousands of GIs and the rise of a potent resistance on the home front. It was the combination of those factors with the fiction the government was forced to maintain about its indefensible goals in the war that finally injected the Vietnam poison back into the American political bloodstream and caused the war effort to self-destruct. The fatal implement, in the end, was Watergate—an event that seemed on the surface to have no relationship whatever with Vietnam. But as Halperin, Holbrooke, John Lindsay, and others observe, the burglary of the Democratic Party headquarters in Washington grew directly from a pattern of illegal actions ordered by Richard Nixon and Henry Kissinger in a futile effort to stem a tide of leaks about war policy.

The first of these was news of the secret B-52 bombing of Communist base areas in Cambodia, which led to the wiretapping of journalists and Kissinger aides, including Halperin. Then came the plan to firebomb the Brookings Institution, part of a plot to retrieve a Johnson-era paper on the discontinuation of the air war. And finally Daniel Ellsberg's leak of the Pentagon Papers caused Nixon to create the infamous Plumbers' Unit—led by the same characters who later were arrested at the Watergate—to break into the office of Ellsberg's psychiatrist in a vain effort to find material that could be used to discredit him. The concern about these leaks stemmed not from military secrecy—the Communists could hardly be unaware of the bombs being rained on them in Cambodia, and the Pentagon Papers were three years old when they surfaced—but from their domestic political impact. These were matters to be kept secret not from the enemy but from the American people.

It was, of course, the need to hide the pattern of wiretaps and black-bag jobs ordered from the very center of the American government that led Nixon and his aides into that fatal, tape-recorded conversation in the Oval Office during which they hatched the Watergate coverup. Two years later, Nixon disappeared into his own domestic quagmire. And, with a marvelous circularity, that sealed the fate of South Vietnam by removing from office a President who might yet have tried to strike back at Hanoi's transgression in 1975, replacing him with one who had no inclination to see his own political future sink in the Indochina quicksand.

But what no discussion of the American policy dilemma can explain is why we were unable to motivate the South Vietnamese to fight for themselves, as the Northerners clearly were willing to do. The answer to that, I think, also relates to our failure to understand ourselves. It lies in the way the historical context of the war shaped our approach to the Vietnamese as people. We went to Southeast Asia, after all, as the winner of World War II, developer of the nuclear weapon, possessor of the world's most powerful military and its dominant economy; in short, as a big, white superpower that could not possibly lose to sixteen million underdeveloped Orientals.

And that made it unnecessary for us to explain our purposes. Just as we were never able to articulate at home a clear reason why Americans should sacrifice their sons and their treasure to preserve South Vietnam, we never took the trouble to provide to the Vietnamese a clear reason for them to resist the Communization of their own country. The United States had not then—perhaps has not yet—developed a distinct voice for its own philosophy. Rather, our policies were founded on a negative: anti-Communism. We could enunciate what we were against, but we could not say precisely what we were *for*. We did not successfully educate the Vietnamese about the practical effect on their lives of the Communization of their society, or press them to make the changes in their behavior that would have laid the foundations for a switch from postcolonial feudalism to a genuinely democratic and capitalist society.

Instead, we were transfixed by the idea that security came before all else, and that we, rather than the South Vietnamese, had to take charge of providing it, because *only we* could deal with an enemy who was superior to them. We accepted that the country's lackluster economy had contributed to the peasants' discontent, but instead of fostering a capitalist remedy, we simply provided the civilian economy with the fruits of capitalist bounty. In essence, we considered the Vietnamese too ignorant to comprehend an argument based on first principles, and tried to buy them off with artificial security and an artificially inflated standard of living, rather than making clear to them that it was their country and that their future depended on pulling together to prevent it falling into the socialist trap.

The truth is that we treated the South Vietnamese like children, while the Soviets and the Chinese treated the North Vietnamese as adults. We insisted on being the big kid who goes out to defend his little brother. Moscow and Peking said to Hanoi in effect, "You are grown up now. Here's a slingshot and some rocks. Go fight your own battles." Even ten years after the fall, the last CIA station chief, Thomas Polgar, thinks of the United States in Vietnam as the parent of a handicapped child: We couldn't have expected him to become a senator or a college professor, but we would have been happy if he could make a living as a counterman.

Douglas Pike likens the South Vietnamese to his child learning to ride a bicycle. Although he had been riding successfully, when he realized his father was no longer holding him upright, he fell over, because he *thought* he couldn't ride alone. Diplomat Lionel Rosenblatt says he and a colleague, Craig Johnstone, went AWOL from the State Department in the final days and flew to Saigon to rescue their friends, because the U.S. Embassy said it would tell those Vietnamese it couldn't evacuate by air to go to sea and be picked up by the Seventh Fleet. To them the notion of city-dwelling Saigonese getting themselves to the coast, let alone on boats and into the ocean, was incredible. And yet as Saigon fell seventy thousand Vietnamese did just that—and in the decade since, a million others have made a more perilous journey still, to places as far away as Thailand, the Philippines and Indonesia.

There was in our behavior toward the Vietnamese a powerful element of the colonial mentality described by George Orwell in *Shooting an Elephant*. As a British district officer in Burma, Orwell went one day to deal with a rampaging elephant that had trampled a child. By the time he arrived, the elephant was tame and back under the control of its master, who pleaded for its life. Nonetheless, Orwell shot the beast because he believed that was what the natives expected a colonial officer to do. We were big, white, rich, well-armed, and felt in every way superior. We thought the Vietnamese expected us to behave like overlords, and that is how we behaved.

In short, we went to Vietnam bearing the white man's burden. We regarded the Vietnamese as our little brown brothers, with the emphasis on little and brown. We called them slopes and gooks and showed by word and deed that we believed them inferior, and in the process we convinced *them* to believe it, too. We sent out twenty-two-year-old boys to hold forty-year-old province chiefs and battalion commanders to account. When Nguyen Cao Ky proposed a military counterpunch against the southern panhandle of North Vietnam—a perfectly logical idea for a nation under attack—we laughed off the project not just as unthinkably pretentious, but as one that involved issues larger than Vietnam and that we could under no circumstances permit. When in the wake of the Tet offensive we finally decided it was time to talk with Hanoi, we sent *ourselves* to the bargaining table, rather than the South Vietnamese—an explicit recognition that we were the masters and they merely the puppets that Hanoi had always called them. Small wonder, then, that when they realized we no longer had our hand on the strings, they collapsed on the stage.

The final theme that emerged from these interviews is a question, really: Will we make such mistakes again? It would be comforting to think not, but on the record of the Reagan years it does not seem beyond the realm of possibility. We have clearly learned *some* lessons from Vietnam. The effects were visible in Lebanon, Grenada, El Salvador, and in the Philippines, where two primary American goals, in addition to replacing Marcos, were to avoid the involvement of American troops and to promote a speedy economic recovery.

We seem to understand that we cannot police the world—that, as Defense Secretary Weinberger puts it, we ought not to involve our troops where we do not understand the local circumstances, where we cannot define our objectives in terms of achievable military goals, where we cannot deploy adequate force to win quickly, and where the issue is not so visibly important to American security as to create a solid political base for action. We seem also to accept for the most part that while we can assist people who are motivated for their own reasons to resist external domination—as in Afghanistan or Angola—we cannot create political will and military skill where none exist naturally, as in Cambodia. We have even moved gradually toward the notion that our primary objective must be to promote *something*—individual freedom, democratic political systems, capitalist economics—rather than simply to pursue the negative of anti-Communism.

And yet, there was one arena of foreign policy in which the Reagan administration seemed in the eighties to be pursuing an opposite course. That, of course, was the struggle with Nicaragua. The parallels were by no means precise. Nicaragua was two thousand miles away, rather than ten thousand, and it was a Marxist-ruled Soviet client, making the security implications more visible. Its language and culture were Western rather than Oriental. And in a strictly military sense, it could be isolated from military resupply in a way that was impossible in Vietnam.

But the similarities were uncanny. The United States was unable to state an objective, because overthrow of the Sandinistas had no popular appeal either at home or among the allies most directly affected in Latin America. The U.S. sought to build a military force in the absence of popular leadership, a cogent political program, adequate control and discipline of the troops, or an attempt to create a nationwide political foundation within Nicaragua itself. The guerrilla force it created looked as much like an American puppet as did the Army of South-Vietnam. As a result the Administration had to strong-arm money out of Congress, and pursue a course of incremental escalation that appeared, as in Vietnam, to produce a result opposite of the one intended. Five years into the operation, the Sandinistas were militarily stronger in relation to the Contras than they were when the so-called secret war began.

But perhaps the most telling parallel of all was the Administration's effort to conduct the war covertly. That allowed the CIA and a handful of National Security Council aides, operating without adequate political oversight, to concoct an embarrassing series of hare-brained schemes. Acts such as the mining of Nicaragua's harbors, raids on its airports, and the publication of a CIA-sponsored "assassination manual" led Congress to cut off all funding for the Contras in 1984–85—and that, in turn, led to an even greater inanity. A cabal within the NSC, led by Lt. Col. Oliver North, contrived a plot to fund a "private" support effort for the Contras, with the profits from secret and possibly illegal sales of arms to Iran. The revelation of that scheme in late 1986 created an uproar in Washington rivalling that of the Watergate scandal, and it seemed likely to put an end to official American sponsorship of the effort. Once again, the poison generated by a secret and unpopular military involvement abroad had filtered back into the domestic political bloodstream, with profound consequences for the war itself.

If all this sounded distressingly like many of the same foolish errors that bedeviled us in Indochina, the comparison was inescapable. Yet even Congressional opponents of American support for the Contras refused to commit themselves to putting a final end to the effort. And so it remained to be seen, as the Reagan presidency entered its home stretch, whether good sense would prevail, or the United States would put its foot into quicksand once again.

A Vietnam Chronology

1945

June   The World War II Allies agree at Potsdam to postwar occupation of Vietnam down to the 16th parallel by Nationalist Chinese troops.

August   The Viet Minh, with which the U.S. has maintained relations during the war years as part of the anti-Japanese front, proclaims its own rule over an independent Vietnam.

1946

March   The Viet Minh agree to a temporary restoration of French colonial rule, largely to end the possibility of a permanent occupation by China.

Autumn   French-Viet Minh agreement breaks down. Viet Minh evacuate to countryside from Hanoi. Guerrilla warfare against the French begins.

1950

February   New Communist government in Peking formally recognizes Viet Minh as government of Vietnam.

May   President Truman authorizes first U.S. military aid to French in Indochina war. By 1952 400 U.S. advisers and supply personnel are serving in Vietnam.

1954

Spring   Siege of French troops at Dien Bien Phu begins; France asks for American intervention. President Eisenhower, concurring with Army Chief of Staff Gen. Matthew Ridgway, declines.

April   Geneva Conference to negotiate an end to war begins.

May   Viet Minh defeat and overrun the French at Dien Bien Phu, effectively ending the war.

July   Geneva Agreement partitions Vietnam at 17th parallel, pending a nationwide election to be held in two years. Laos and Cambodia become independent. Ho Chi Minh takes control of North Vietnam; Ngo Dinh Diem becomes Prime Minister of South Vietnam.

Summer/ Autumn   U.S. Navy ships and French planes begin moving massive flow of mainly Catholic refugees from North Vietnam to the South.

1955

July   Diem government refuses to prepare nationwide election scheduled for 1956 on grounds no free ballot could be conducted in Communist-controlled northern half of country.

October   Diem deposes former French puppet Emperor Bao Dai and proclaims South Vietnam a republic.

1956

April   Last French troops leave Vietnam. U.S. Military Assistance Advisory Group (MAAG) begins expansion that will take it up to nearly a thousand people by the end of the Eisenhower years.

1957

Diem succeeds in bringing a variety of warring sects under control, largely pacifies South Vietnam, makes a start on restoring economy.

1958

Spring/
Summer
Guerrilla incidents in South Vietnam begin to rise, U.S. becomes aware that North Vietnam has begun infiltrating cadres to the South by way of Laos. U.S. advisers in Laos arrange for Col. Vang Pao, a Meo tribesman by origin, to organize guerrilla harassment of North Vietnamese troops occupying border areas east of the Plaine des Jarres.

December
North Vietnam openly seizes the Laotian town of Tchepone and a series of tiny nearby villages in Laotian panhandle, to guard infiltration route around the western end of the Demilitarized Zone (DMZ).

1959

Spring
U.S. secretly opens a military mission in Laos headed by Gen. John Heintges and called the USAID* Program Evaluation Office. Its function is to strengthen Laotian Army against Hanoi-backed Pathet Lao, and to continue to organize guerrillas to harass infiltration.

1960

January
Viet Cong fight first battalion-sized engagement with ARVN† troops. Diem shortly thereafter declares a state of emergency and asks for increased U.S. military aid.

January
U.S. replaces Program Evaluation Office in Laos with White Star Mobile Training Teams of Army Special

---

*The United States Agency for International Development.
†The Army of the Republic of Viet Nam.

Forces troops. Harassment of North Vietnamese infiltration is stepped up, and so is the war between the Pathet Lao and Laotian government forces.

1961

January   Kennedy is warned by Eisenhower during ride to inaugural that Indochina is a growing problem.

Impressed with a report by counterinsurgency expert Edward Lansdale and Gen. Maxwell Taylor, Kennedy orders an increase in the nine hundred man MAAG in Saigon.

February   Kennedy says that U.S. advisers in Vietnam will fire back if fired upon.

March   Kennedy announces he has sent Marines to Thailand and will intervene in Laos if need be.

May   Geneva Conference on neutralization of Laos begins work.

June   Kennedy and Khrushchev agree at Vienna summit to support neutralization of Laos, but Khrushchev tells Kennedy bluntly he will support "wars of national liberation."

September Kennedy sends Taylor and Walt Rostow out to report on deteriorating situation in Vietnam. They recommend more aid and possible dispatch of U.S. troops.

Autumn   Diem and his brother Ngo Dinh Nhu adopt a program to set up *agrovilles,* or strategic hamlets to protect rural population from guerrilla raids.

December First load of U.S. helicopters and warplanes, together with pilots and maintenance crews arrives. U.S. troop total reaches 15,000.

1962

February   Saigon MAAG is converted to Military Assistance Command, Vietnam (MACV) and Gen. Paul Harkins arrives to command it.

July   Geneva conference agrees on neutralization of Laos. U.S. White Star teams withdrawn. CIA, using Special Forces troops as operatives, recruits *montagnard* tribes to try to control infiltration routes in from Laos.

1963

Throughout year war goes badly. ARVN troops suffer numerous defeats. U.S. armed helicopters begin playing a major role. Montagnard tribesmen rebel against being forced into strategic hamlets.

May   Buddhist revolt in South Vietnam begins with a grenade thrown at a Buddhist festival. Spreads to Saigon with self-immolation on a Saigon street corner by a monk using a can of gasoline.

August   U.S. Ambassador Frederick Nolting, a strong supporter of Diem, is replaced by Henry Cabot Lodge. Secret police organized by Nhu raid Buddhist temples.

October   U.S. gives final go-ahead to generals to oust Diem in a coup.

November Diem is ousted and he and Nhu are murdered. Three weeks later, President Kennedy is assassinated in Dallas.

1964

A period of political instability begins, in which the generals conduct coups and countercoups and seven separate governments hold power in Saigon over the next two years.

May   U.S. says it is bombing in Laos, in support of government troops resisting Pathet Lao takeover.

June   Maxwell Taylor takes over as Ambassador from Henry Cabot Lodge, who has returned to U.S. to run for Republican presidential nomination. William C. Westmoreland becomes MACV commander.

July   Republican presidential candidate Barry Goldwater accuses Lyndon Johnson of being soft on Vietnam.

August   Tonkin Gulf incident occurs and Johnson uses it as an excuse to order first U.S. air raid on North Vietnam, and to get Congress to pass Tonkin Gulf Resolution.

November   Viet Cong mortar Bien Hoa Airbase in first major direct assault on U.S. unit in Vietnam.

December   Terrorist bomb blows up Brinks BOQ* in downtown Saigon just before Christmas, inflicting severe casualties.

1965

February   Communist troops mortar Pleiku airfield, destroying large numbers of U.S. aircraft and inflicting serious casualties. U.S. conducts a second air strike on North Vietnam. A terrorist bomb blows up a U.S. military barracks in the port town of Qui Nhon—and afterward, the U.S. begins the steady bombing campaign against North Vietnam called Rolling Thunder.

March   First U.S. combat unit, a battalion of Marines, lands at Danang, ostensibly to provide security for Danang airfield, from which some of the air strikes against North Vietnam are being conducted.

May   First U.S. Army unit, the 173rd Airborne Brigade, arrives in Vietnam.

July   Johnson approves a U.S. combat presence of 175,000 men in three and a half divisions in South Vietnam, and gives Westmoreland the right to maneuver and use his troops as he sees fit.

Summer   U.S. troops fight first big-unit engagement with Communist forces at Ia Drang valley near Cambodian border.

December   American troop total reaches 184,300 by year end.

*Bachelor Officers' Quarters.

1966

A major buildup of U.S. forces takes place, heading toward an eventual presence of more than a half-million American troops. One by one U.S. divisions arrive and take up positions in the north, the Central Highlands, the Saigon area, and the Mekong Delta. In addition, the U.S. persuades several allies to contribute troops. South Korea sends three full divisions, Australia one, Thailand one, and the Philippines contributes a brigade. South Vietnamese forces are relegated largely to pacification duty.

Westmoreland begins in early 1966 the first of what becomes a lengthy series of massive search-and-destroy operations, such as "Manhattan," "Junction City," and "Allenbrook." The operations disrupt the lives of millions of rural Vietnamese, and refugees begin to crowd into the cities. Eventually Saigon swells from a half-million to 3 million, Danang from 300,000 to 1 million.

The U.S. Air Force also extends its air war in North Vietnam to heavy concentration on infiltration routes through the Laotian panhandle, but with little effect.

May U.S. forces begin firing into Cambodia against sanctuaries.

June American planes begin bombing Hanoi and vicinity.

Summer Another Buddhist rebellion, this time in conjunction with Vietnamese troops of the northern command, breaks out in Danang and Hue. It is put down forcibly.

December U.S. troops number 385,300 in South Vietnam, 60,000 Navy offshore, and 33,000 in Thailand.

1967

March Johnson summons Nguyen Van Thieu and Nguyen Cao Ky to a grand conference at Guam, where he introduces them to his new team—Ellsworth Bunker as Ambassador, Robert Komer as chief of pacification, which is to be placed under the overall command of Westmoreland.

The Americans dismiss out of hand a proposal by Ky for an invasion of North Vietnam.

April   Westmoreland makes the first of two trips home to help Johnson generate political support for the war. He addresses a joint session of Congress and predicts victory.

Spring   After a year of heavy combat along the DMZ, U.S. Marines are sent to occupy Khe Sanh, below the western end of the zone, to try to block a major infiltration route.

Spring/   U.S. domestic protests and dissent begin to rise, dem-
Summer   onstrations occur. The Administration begins to feel political heat.

Summer/   Marines lose control of hills near Khe Sanh, and the
Fall   airstrip there becomes unusable. Airdrops begin.

November   Westmoreland again comes home to generate support for the war effort and says in a speech to National Press Club that he thinks U.S. forces will have situation well enough in hand within two years to begin major withdrawals.

1968

January   Tet offensive opens at end of month with Viet Cong penetration of U.S. Embassy, and open combat in forty cities including Saigon. The offensive stuns both U.S. command in Saigon and Johnson administration in Washington. Although bulk of fighting is over in a week, it takes twenty-eight days of heavy, bloody combat to recapture Hue, giving the impression of prolonged resistance country-wide. Siege of Khe Sanh begins in earnest.

February   Clark Clifford replaces McNamara as secretary of defense, launches immediate sweeping review of U.S. war policy.

March   Sen. Eugene McCarthy comes within an ace of beating Johnson in the New Hampshire Democratic presidential primary. Bobby Kennedy decides he, too, will run against Johnson, who looks increasingly vulnerable.

March   LBJ, persuaded by Clifford that the U.S. should cut its losses and get out of Vietnam, decides not to run for another term, to declare a partial halt to the bombing of North Vietnam, and to seek negotiations with Hanoi. Hanoi agrees to talk—but only about ending the rest of the bombing.

April   LBJ announces Westmoreland will be replaced in Vietnam by his deputy, Gen. Creighton Abrams. Siege of Khe Sanh is broken—and shortly thereafter, Marines withdraw, leaving it unoccupied.

July   Hubert Humphrey is nominated by a riotous convention in Chicago. Richard Nixon wins Republican nomination and campaigns on the strength of a nonexistent "secret plan" to end the war.

November   Johnson halts all bombing of North Vietnam and Hanoi agrees to four-power peace talks just before the election. Nixon wins a cliffhanger victory.

1969

February   Communist troops launch another Tet offensive, but it is much smaller and does not take U.S. by surprise.

March   Secret bombing of Cambodian sanctuaries used by Vietnamese Communist troops begins.

April   U.S. troop strength peaks at 543,400.

May   The New York Times reports secret bombing of Cambodia, prompting Nixon and Kissinger to launch wiretap program to stem "national security" leaks.

July   A military scandal erupts, with reports that Green Berets have been murdering suspected double agents. Nixon announces the first withdrawals of American troops.

November   Nixon announces "Vietnamization" policy and intention to gradually withdraw all Americans over a period of years. Antiwar demonstrations peak with a march of a quarter-million protestors in Washington. Reports of a more serious military scandal, the My Lai massacre, begin to surface in Washington.

Through the second half of the year, as troops are affected by rise of antiwar feeling at home and by the announcement of troop withdrawals, morale begins to decline. There is a sharp rise in use of narcotics. "Fraggings"—grenade attacks—aimed at officers, and "combat refusals" (in effect, mutinies), begin to occur.

1970

March   Cambodian General Lon Nol ousts neutralist chief of state Prince Norodom Sihanouk in a coup.

April ✗   Nixon orders U.S. troops to invade Communist sanctuaries in Cambodia in a futile search for Communist headquarters called COSVN (Central Office for South Viet Nam). Antiwar demonstrations break out, and National Guardsmen at Kent State University in Ohio open fire on students, killing four. To restore political calm, Nixon promises to withdraw troops from Cambodia within two months.

U.S. withdrawals continue, and troop level is below 400,000 by year end.

1971

February   ARVN, at U.S. behest and with American air support, launches invasion of Laos to block Ho Chi Minh Trail. It is so badly beaten that troops come out clinging to skids of helicopters, while wounded left behind beg for guns to kill themselves.

June   *The New York Times* begins publication of Pentagon Papers. On Nixon's orders a "Plumber's Unit" is assembled to try to get evidence to defame Daniel Ellsberg, who has leaked the papers, by burgling the office of his psychiatrist.

December   U.S. planes conduct five days of intensive air raids against North Vietnam in retaliation for alleged violations of agreements made in exchange for the 1968 bombing halt. These follow months of so-called protective reaction air strikes in which fighter bombers carry out bombing raids whenever the reconnaissance planes they are accompanying are fired upon. U.S. withdrawals continue, and by year end the last full division has left the country, and the total of American troops is down to 140,000.

1972

February Nixon goes to Peking for a historic visit reopening ties with mainland China.

April North Vietnam, in "Easter Offensive," invades directly across the DMZ with a massive offensive that destroys one ARVN division and panics two others. Population of Hue flees en masse. U.S. planes resume bombing of North Vietnam, including Hanoi and Haiphong, and in early May, Nixon orders mining of Haiphong harbor.

June The Watergate burglary of Democratic National Headquarters in Washington begins the unraveling of the Nixon Presidency.

August Last U.S. combat troops leave Vietnam.

October/ November Kissinger reveals he has been conducting secret talks with North Vietnam, that an agreement is near—and just before the election he says "Peace is at hand." But North Vietnamese at last minute refuse to go along, possibly because U.S. announces a rush program to load up South Vietnam with huge new supplies of arms that can be replaced under the agreement.

December Nixon orders another round of "Christmas bombing," this time using B-52s to hit Hanoi itself.

1973

January At end of month, Paris Accords are finally signed, calling for a cease-fire in place in South Vietnam—and leaving

North Vietnamese troops inside the country. Meantime U.S. government ends the military draft.

March   Last U.S. troops leave South Vietnam.

April   Hanoi releases 590 prisoners of war.

June   Congress bans further bombing in Indochina by act of law.

July   Congressional hearings reveal the U.S. conducted 3,500 secret B-52 strikes into Cambodia.

November Congress overrides Nixon's veto of War Powers Act.

1974

May   House Judiciary Committee opens impeachment proceedings against Nixon.

August   Nixon resigns. Gerald Ford sworn in.

October   U.S. intelligence acquires Hanoi politburo's COSVN Resolution for 1975, calling for renewal of warfare against South Vietnam.

December North Vietnam launches probing attack against Phuoc Binh, capital of Phuoc Long province, one hundred miles north of Saigon.

1975

January   Phuoc Binh falls and neither the United States nor the Saigon government reacts. Surprised, North Vietnamese begin moving into position for a larger assault against Central Highlands.

March   Hanoi's troops assault Ban Me Thuot with two divisions against a single regiment, and overrun it in one day. Thieu convenes a conference of his top commanders at Cam Ranh Bay and indicates Saigon may have to abandon the

Highlands. His commander there, Gen. Pham Van Phu,
orders an immediate evacuation that becomes a disastrous rout, and the South Vietnamese Army begins to
collapse. In late March, the defenses at Hue and Danang
in the north also fold without a fight.

April   Yet another U.S. military mission takes a look and flies
home recommending $650 million more in aid, but Ger-
ald Ford delays sending the request on to Congress,
where it is sure to be killed. The Americans begin a limited evacuation by air of Vietnamese who may suffer
under a Communist takeover, and Thieu flees the country at mid-month. Phnom Penh, the capital of Cambodia,
falls on April 15 after Americans have fled by helicopter. In Vietnam, a struggle ensues to get Thieu's old
and half-blind Vice-President Tran Van Huong out of the
way for Gen. Duong Van "Big" Minh, who it's thought
might be acceptable as a face-saving compromise. But
Minh holds power for only twenty-four hours, and as the
Americans flee by helicopter from the Embassy roof, he
tells his troops to lay down their arms.

May   A North Vietnamese tank smashes down the palace gate
on May Day. At mid-month, Cambodian Communist
patrol boats capture the freighter *Mayaguez,* provoking
one last spasm of warfare as U.S. planes level port of
Kompong Som to get the crew and vessel back.

CHAPTER ONE

Beginnings

THE use of pretexts to justify the beginning of combat has a long and dishonorable history, but nations really go to war for reasons buried deep in their collective political psyches. Early in August of 1964, just after the start of the presidential campaign between an incumbent "dove," Lyndon B. Johnson, and a hawkish challenger, Barry Goldwater, the U.S. Navy reported two armed encounters between North Vietnamese torpedo boats and a group of American destroyers on patrol in the Tonkin Gulf. The first of those episodes was real, and American forces reacted by sinking two of the attackers and sending a third scuttling back to port. The second, two days later, was a phony: a product of fevered imagination enhanced by stormy weather, false radar readings, and misinterpretation of an intercepted North Vietnamese military radio message. Still, the Johnson administration chose to use this second "incident" as the excuse for its first major air strike on the territory of Hanoi. "The other side got a little sting out of this," Secretary of State Dean Rusk remarked in a memorable phrase, as officials described (there were no pictures) a three-mile column of smoke rising from what had been a fuel depot in the city of Vinh.

In truth, the sting was the one inflicted on the United States by its own leaders. The Administration had been told immediately and in no uncertain terms by its commanders on the scene that there was no second attack. Worse, the President and his men were well aware that even the first PT boat assault was a response to American provocation: The United States had been conducting a secret program of commando raids on North Vietnam's coast. Nevertheless, the second "incident" also became the basis on which to obtain from an almost unanimous Congress the Tonkin Gulf Resolution. The resolution was touted as a simple show of solidarity in the face of an "unprovoked" attack on the U.S. Navy at sea—an act of a type that had justified half of America's foreign conflicts since the War of 1812. But it was much more than that. Whatever the Congress may have intended, the resolution amounted to, and was used as, an open-ended license to conduct a general war in Indochina. In retrospect, it seemed to many—including some of the people directly involved—to have been a political con of epic proportion worked against a gullible and trusting country.

One can fairly ask why honorable men should have felt compelled to do something so dishonest in order to obtain a political goal. The simple answer is that they were trying to prepare the country for a war it was clearly reluctant to enter, but that they honestly believed might be necessary. American troops had already participated in the Vietnam conflict for almost three years as suppliers, advisers, pilots and secret combatants, with precious little success. In the summer of 1964, South Vietnam seemed in danger of losing the war fairly soon, and a genuine fear developed that the ring of "containment" was about to be broken. Yet another huge chunk of Asia—Vietnam and many of its neighbors—seemed ready to fall under Communist control, and just as with China fifteen years earlier, it was happening on a Democratic watch, with potentially disastrous domestic consequences. It was that deeper complex of beliefs, perceptions, and fears about the lessons of failing to respond to aggression and about an emerging geostrategic threat in Asia that lay behind the Administration's behavior.

———————◆———————

It is given to few to be the point men of history. ADM. JAMES B. STOCKDALE *is one who was. On a stormy night over the Gulf of Tonkin in August of 1964, he became the unwitting pawn of an Administration looking for an excuse to start a war. Stockdale took off from the carrier* Ticonderoga *to provide air cover for two American destroyers whose crews thought they were under attack in the so-called second Tonkin Gulf incident. Though he concluded—and reported—that no attack had occurred, he was ordered the following day to lead the first major American air strike against North Vietnam, in "retaliation" for the alleged incident. Shot down thirteen months later, he spent seven and a half years in prisoner-of-war camps—an experience that turned his thick shock of hair snow-white and left him with a permanent limp. Stockdale, now retired from the Navy, is a senior fellow of the Hoover Institution on the Stanford University campus. He and his wife, Sybil, have published a book,* In Love and War, *about Vietnam and its effect on their lives.*

The thing that sticks in my mind ten years after [the fall of Vietnam] is the fact that the decision-making processes that precipitated the war are still in place. In other words, the fact that we continue to conduct foreign policy with a very intricate, heavily politicized bureaucracy, with only cursory reference to on-site observers twelve thousand miles away, could put us into equally disastrous situations tomorrow.

You cannot reproduce reality on paper twelve thousand miles from the scene. In Washington what comes in over the teletype is that there are North Vietnamese PT boats in such and such an area of the ocean. But it's one thing to accept that as a fact and another to be on the scene listening to hesitant, heavily qualified, stammering people on radios trying to disabuse themselves of a hell of a lot of doubt about the reality of the situation.

That was Tonkin Gulf. There was understandable confusion. *I* was confused for a while, and I had the best seat in the house, orbiting a few hundred feet above the two American destroyers, clear of the surface haze and spray that their crews' eyeballs and radars had to penetrate. And when, after a couple of hours, it came to light that no American eyeball, from the air or from the destroyers, had ever detected a PT boat or a wake or a gunflash, a steady stream of messages emanated from that same destroyer commodore who had sent the first [alert of a possible attack]: "Wait, there may have been a mistake, take no action until we have proof. Hold your horses." Then messages about those messages started racing back and forth across the Pacific. They were still coming in and going out twelve hours later, when I blew up the oil tanks at Vinh.

The whole scene was loaded for misinterpretation. You had people in Washington who had passed up the opportunity for a show of force two days before. You had a frustrated President who was getting heat on the back channels from Maxwell Taylor and the then-current head of state in Saigon—heat for passing up that chance. You had a President who felt inferior and ill at ease in the office, and who had bearing down on him from behind in a hot presidential campaign, Barry Goldwater, whose main plank was that Johnson was soft on Vietnam. And so when the messages started to come in saying that there *was* a second Tonkin Gulf event, he was elated because here was the reprieve: "My God, two days ago I made an ass of myself and now I can recover and win the election and happy days are here again."

They had started getting enemy radio intercepts that could be indicative of preparations for an attack. Specifically what the messages came down to was that they ordered two older non–torpedo boats to make ready for operations, to be joined by a single PT boat if it could be made ready on time. This was the one torpedo boat that had made it home from the Sunday raid two days before. God knows what the mission was. But little things like that suggested they were coming out to get us again.

Now there was a book written by the doctor on the *Maddox*, and until I read it, I didn't realize the state of mind on the destroyers. They felt they were trapped in this body of water that is surrounded mostly by Communist-held land. And they were attacked two days before in a half-baked effort by three little PT boats, so the mood was one of anticipation of more trouble. And combined with that, we had peculiar weather of a kind that made radar give false targets. They got what they call "ducting." The electronic beams actually bend and you get strange targets from way out of normal range. So they're getting spooky things on their screens and they were convinced that they were being shadowed by boats. Combined with that there was faulty sonar equipment on the *Maddox*, and combined with that, a shortage of trained men. The best sonar man on the *Maddox* was also a great gun operator, and he took the gun job that night, thinking it was more important under the conditions he anticipated. That left his striker, a young sailor of comparatively little experience, to become the most important man in the government decision-making process that night, because he was telling the captain torpedoes were out there—when actually the sound was reverberations off the ship's rudder at the high speed they were making, and there *were* no torpedoes out there.

There were lightning flashes and thunderstorms and high winds. At one time the North Vietnamese shut off the lighthouse they were using for their fixes. And at first the destroyers thought they were under attack. There were no sightings, there were no firings. No destroyer ever saw a boat or a wake. But they said, "We're heading south. We're getting out of here. We're being surrounded." And that message came in [to Washington] at about the same time as this message that said two boats prepare to get underway for possible operations.

But nothing happened. The visibility from the deck of the destroyers was nowhere near as good as it was for me circling around at a thousand feet, surveying the whole area. They later found sailors who claimed to have seen sparkling things in the water, but most of those "sparkling things" sightings were dreamed up a couple of days later, when re-debriefings were conducted after a message from Washington demanded "proof." I know of no responsible person who considers them anything but bunk. Two days before, I'd led the attack against real boats in the daytime and I saw my bullets hit them and even in bright sunlight I could see sparks as they glanced off. I could see their wakes were wider and more pronounced than the destroyers' wakes. Their guns flashed. People say, "Wasn't it a dark night?" Yes, it was dark as hell and that's why I could see so well. The wake would have been luminous. The ricochets would have been sparkling, the gunfire of the PT boats would have been red and bright. I'm sure I'd have seen anything within five miles of those boats during the hour and a half that I was there. No question about it.

No boats were there and when I got back to the ship, the commander of the destroyers had come to the same conclusion. He [cabled Washington] "Please don't take any rash action until you verify this." In other words, a plea to disregard the [earlier] messages he'd been sending—that weather conditions, the sonar operator's lack of skill and other things had rendered the question wide open and not to take action on it. These cables were part of the same three-hour continuum. And Washington had those in their hands for twelve hours and I'm sure that important people were seeing them. They had twelve hours to change their minds and it still went on.

I went to bed laughing that night. I was very tired and I was laughing in relief. I'd nearly flown into the water and killed myself trying to find these boats. It was the third flight I'd had in one day, it was after midnight, and on the way out there I thought we were going to war and I'd said, "My God, I'm going to be telling my grandchildren about this night." And I finally realized there was nothing to find and came back and they read me the messages that had passed from the destroyers to Washington saying the same thing. And they also sent in my reports. Everybody was saying "Well, that was the goddamnedest mess we've ever been in. Let's have a cup of coffee and forget about it." If this had happened in the nineteenth century, before radios, that would have been the end of it.

And then I was awakened about two hours later by a young officer and told that they have received word from Washington that we're going to retaliate. And I said, "Retaliate for what?" And he said, "For last night's attack." He didn't know any better. Well, I sat there on the edge of the bed realizing that I was one of the few people in the world that realized we were going to launch a war under false pretenses. And sure enough, the next day we did.

I led this big horde of airplanes over there and we blew the oil tanks clear off the map. Forty minutes after the last jet was catapulted, we were descending in formation and radio silence, cutting in and out of cloud layers and intermittent rain to our rendezvous area just southeast of Vinh. Rain, and we had prop driven planes and they were up ahead of us and we had to get the jets rendezvoused and get behind this hill where we'd have a radar shield. This was just pulled out of our behinds. We were just doing it by instinct. There's no great science to it.

[*Reading from his book.*] "Forty minutes. . . I was growing apprehensive because it was looking more and more like our rendezvous was going to be touch and go. I thought of those Japs going into Pearl Harbor. I had to do this right the first time. If I didn't find those Spads* and get this flight together and coordinated, they were going to get their asses shot off. This flight was a history-maker and I felt like the load of the world was on my shoulders."

Now it is very important to understand that there was a tinderbox situation in the Western Pacific that was probably going to precipitate war, and a person might say, "What's all the fuss about. It was going to happen anyway, what is so wrong about picking the opportune time to trigger it? No big thing." But there is such a thing as moral leverage, which tilts the argument in the other direction. The Communists have a great nose for moral leverage. Any good bargainer knows the balance of authority has tipped when the other guy has performed some act of which he might be ashamed. And in the case of starting wars it is very, very important that you have that moral leverage behind you.

A leader who starts a war must face the fact that there will later be many times when he wishes he could get out of that war. Because as the caskets move by and grief emerges there is going to be a great temptation, unless he is just an Adolf Hitler, to get out of that. And "to get out of that" that way is a worse mistake usually than getting into it, because it lets everybody down, just like McNamara and Johnson bailed out and left a whole generation of Americans over there to pick up after them.

I'm a warrior and you can see I'm a hawk, but I'm going to tell you that when you get into a war you've got to be very sure that you are on honest, solid rock foundations or it's going to eat you alive. In a real war, you just cannot risk losing moral leverage, which he [Johnson] did. There was no question that Washington knew what they had done and not a lot of question about them knowing it as they did it. Johnson always made light of those things. He once said as he slapped somebody on the back, "Those sailors are probably shooting at flying fish. We will never know what happened out there."

Well, I am the guy who rose from the ashes, and twenty years later telling you I saw it, and there were no boats. And I didn't have all the appreciation for the importance of moral leverage until I was in the jails of those people and I realized how much their resistance

---

*The prop-driven A1-E Skyraiders.

and tenacity depended on this absolute conviction of moral supremacy. And we brushed that off as kind of an old-fashioned idea that
didn't have much to do with modern technology.

And you couldn't do anything to stop it?

I could have sulked or resigned but I didn't. I would have been ground
up like an ant. There would have been no satisfaction in being a
martyr. Anyway, I told them what the truth was. A message went
out from the ship to Washington right after I had landed, saying that
I had seen no boats. But it was a great learning experience. I was
forty-one and growing up. I had always thought the government
worked just like Poli. Sci. One and Two said it did. And now I realized that this was a goddamned fiasco and I was a part of it. And I
thought, "Well, live and learn. This is the way the ballgame is
played."

So away we went, and there's another subtlety that doesn't come
through back in Washington—that this was a "retaliation." There's
a piece written by a great economist named Thomas Schelling in
'66, before he knew the truth, about what a neat package of tacit
negotiations this had been: The boats had attacked and we went
back and retaliated against the boat facilities. And this was a great
transaction that had taken place—not too many people had been
killed—and that was really the modern wave of the future and the
way we must negotiate and save lives. And it was bunk.

What he thought was a neat little package of a certain number of oil
tanks blown up, translates quite differently when you're up there
and they are in a city of forty-four thousand people. Our marksmanship was uncanny. The bombers got the bombs down into the
tanks and nothing outside the fence surrounding it, but there were
still people around. And when you see flames shooting up ten thousand feet from the middle of a big city, you know that's not a signal, that's war. And I said to myself, "There's no question about it.
We are committed. All options are canceled." I thought "Well, here
I am, a little boy from the Midwest, right here with the best seat in
the house to watch this parade of human foibles colliding in the drama of the twentieth century."

I told some Stanford Business School students the other day a story about my graduate student adviser at Stanford. His name was
Anthony Sokol. He was Austrian and he spoke with a German
accent, and he was an admirer of Clausewitz, the German philosopher of war. He asked me one time what I was reading that quarter.
And I said, "I'm reading books about national strategy by Kahn
and by Schelling," and a whole group of names rattled off my tongue.
And he turned beet-red and said, "I do not read those books. Those
books are written by economists, and in the world of strategy econ-

omists suffer a great defect because their whole discipline depends on rational choice. Two products of an equal worth, the cheaper one would be the one he'd pick up. Don't you remember Clausewitz—the two equal sides, objective and subjective?" He said, "They think that by means of economically derived processes—by economics, I don't mean money—that they can play games with people."

And this was prophetic. The dodge that we will signal them with this bombing raid against these oil tanks that we won't tolerate any more of this became an infection with us that carried on throughout the war. The Tonkin Gulf resolution passed on August 7. That was two days after the flight I'm talking about. And the State Department said that was the functional equivalent of a declaration of war. But it passed on the coat-tails of the second—the false—incident. And McGeorge Bundy later said that Johnson was so much a child of Congress that when he got the resolution he thought the war was over. If Congress was behind him, then it was just a matter of waiting for the curtain to fall.

He signed that thing on August 11. And that day we read at the breakfast table that the Harris poll showed LBJ's popularity jumped fourteen percentage points. And just before noon that same day I was sitting at my desk doing paperwork when suddenly the ship's yodelhorn blared the welcome-aboard honors appropriate for a vice-admiral. I remember wondering how that happened out there in the middle of the ocean. And then the phone rang. It was Captain Hutch Cooper. He said, "Jim, a couple of guys just came aboard and say they want to talk to you. I'll send them down with an escort." There were two guys in sports shirts and slacks, one about my age and the other younger. The older one introduced himself as Jack Stempler, special assistant to Secretary McNamara. And he said, "The day before yesterday, I was down with my family at the cottage at Nag's Head. About four in the afternoon I was walking back to the beach and what do I see but a government staff car in the driveway. I was to go right to Washington. So I picked up a bag and away we went. We were sent out here just to find out one thing. Were there any fuckin' boats out there the other night or not?" And this is four hours after they'd signed the "declaration of war."

The cloak of secrecy that was kept around this whole thing was bound together by these intercepts and the fact that we had on the destroyer a special van in which there were receivers with Vietnamese language speakers listening to the radios ashore. And they wrapped this in great secrecy. In fact, you asked me why I didn't mention this for twenty years. When I came back from Vietnam, this had been on my mind the whole time. I thought the Vietnamese would find out I was on that raid and they would torture out these facts.

So I went to see some of my old Navy friends who by this time were retired admirals and I said, "Jesus, did we ever luck out on that one. You know I was in the Communist prison knowing all about the fiasco of that Tonkin Gulf thing." And they all reacted the same way. "Well, now you've gotta understand that we've had big arguments about that and it's been decided that there were boats out there." "Well," I said, "I don't mean to be pushy, but there weren't any. I'm the guy that was there."

They said, "But you didn't understand. You've got a lot to learn. And there were some secret messages that prove it beyond a doubt." Well, these "secret messages" remarks deterred me from talking about it until everybody else started talking about it. Later I became a friend of a guy who was very high in the CIA during the Tonkin Gulf days and later went on to the State Department, and I said, "Listen, I know about these intercepts. They're all written up in the unclassified report of the McNamara hearings. Is that all they're talking about, these 'secret messages?' " He said, "That's all."

It's the obfuscation of the event that's been their major protection. The major part of McNamara's proof rested on the intercepts and actually, sadly enough, the things they used in the hearing three years later to prove there was Communist activity afoot were replays of messages sent by the Communists during the battle I flew in two days before. These messages reflected not anything like reality on the night of the fourth, but I could recognize their descriptions as being exactly what I was doing two days earlier. This happens because people rebroadcast action reports. It's like listening to other people's telephone conversations. You don't know whether they're telling what just happened, or reading a letter they got two days ago.

———————

SEN J. WILLIAM FULBRIGHT (Democrat, Arkansas) *was chairman of the Senate Foreign Relations Committee when the Johnson administration contrived to hustle the Tonkin Gulf Resolution through Congress as a legal basis for making war in Indochina. It's still a matter of considerable pain for him. He is now a lawyer in the Washington firm of Hogan and Hartson.*

When the Tonkin Gulf incident happened we had a meeting with the President with all his assistants—and General Wheeler and McNamara, Rusk. We went to the White House either the first or the second day, and we all said, "Well this is an outrageous attack on us, an unprovoked attack. We just couldn't take that," and so on. And they intimated—and we thought—that this was a way that we could show unity behind the President. Congress supported Lyndon Johnson not only on this occasion but on most occasions of controversy. He'd have the leadership down and get them committed, if he could, before there were any hearings, and sort of foreclose any debate on the subject. And nobody raised the question "Are you sure it's happened?" Why they were so sure, it would have been very bad taste to question their veracity at that stage.

They just repeated and repeated that it was an unprovoked and outrageous attack upon our ships on the high seas where they had a right to be, just patrolling in a regular manner. And later on McNamara said he hadn't anything to do with any sort of provocation, the so-called 34-A,* which came out later, much later.

When I look back on it, I couldn't have made a greater mistake. I consider that as my greatest mistake in the Senate, to believe what they said and not take it skeptically and examine it. They made it appear that this was very important to support the President and that if he had the backing of this great country, that we could make North Vietnam understand that the United States couldn't be pushed around in this fashion and that they would in effect sue for peace, and it would end the thing there. That was the main reason for the urgency, to create the psychological impact. They would see this was going too far, and they would have to give up and accept the division [of the country into North and South]. It would be so impressive that a little country, undeveloped, with no resources, couldn't possibly see that it could stand up to us.

And they urged immediate consideration without any hearings or amendments. They particularly urged not to accept amendments, which would require a conference between the House and the Senate and delay it and in the meantime all this psychological impact would be lost. The House voted unanimously, and they urged us not to have prolonged hearings and not to accept any amendments, no matter how innocuous. It was very important to proceed immediately. Even Wayne Morse,† who liked to talk at length, though he voted against it, asked for two hours, that's all. And for Wayne that was like nothing. And so he only spoke for a couple of hours and then he and his friend Gruening‡ voted against it.

---

*A program of covert attacks on North Vietnam's coast.

†Morse, an Oregon Democrat who had begun his career as a Republican, was the Senate's certified maverick in those years.

‡Sen. Ernest Gruening was an Alaska Democrat who often sided with Morse against the party leadership.

Gaylord Nelson* offered an amendment and it was a reasonable one and I just simply rejected it because I was under the impression it was very important not to accept *any* kind of an amendment. And there's no excuse for my stupidity in going along with the Administration. I shouldn't have. It was a mistake, that's all. And I've said it time and again, and if you want me to say it again, well I will. I was mistaken and I'm sorry and that's all I can say. I've said it at least fifty times.

And when did you begin to suspect you'd been hustled?

It first came to my attention that it was cockeyed about a year or two later when I got a letter from a retired Admiral True in California. He wasn't there, but he said, "I commanded a destroyer for twenty years and that's not the way destroyers [operate]. It didn't happen." And that's what started my idea we'd been deceived, and then we had the hearings. The hearings resulted primarily from that, although there were several other little incidents. One fellow approached us, a junior officer in the flag plot, and he said it hadn't been that way. He talked to Norville Jones,† and the next thing we knew they'd picked him up and sent him to a psychiatric ward.

———◆———

Former SEN. EUGENE MCCARTHY *(Democrat, Minnesota) launched the political challenge from the left that played a major role in the fall of Lyndon Johnson. White of hair but still sharp of mind, McCarthy has a certain dreamy quality to his manner of speech, but the underlying thoughts cut to the core of the issues that concern him. McCarthy is a director of Harcourt Brace Jovanovich Publishing's Washington office.*

I wasn't on the [Foreign Relations] Committee at the time of the Tonkin Gulf Resolution, but the testimony of Rusk and the statement of Fulbright to the Senate were that "this doesn't give 'em anything." I listened to the debate, and a few bells rang. I asked Humphrey "What the hell is this all about?" We had got into the habit of passing resolutions—you know, Quemoy and Matsu, Formosa and Taiwan, and so on—it was like a garden club. And Humphrey said "It doesn't amount to anything. Give him [LBJ] the vote."

---

*Senator Nelson, from Wisconsin, was in the left wing of the Democratic Party, and his suspicions about the Administration's course had been raised by an aide, Gar Alperovitz, who pointed out the needlessly broad language of the resolution.

†Fulbright's chief of staff on the Senate Foreign Relations Committee.

It'll make him feel good. He needs a little encouragement." Frank Church was standing there, and even Frank didn't say anything. But that was the general attitude. "It's just something they want, so don't vote against it and make them mad."

And then later on, when Johnson began to use it, and especially Rusk, I said "Well, even if it did mean what it says, it didn't mean we were committed forever to whatever you guys wanted to do." But that was their attitude. It was passed and I think Rusk had had in mind all the time to use it. I'd asked Dean Acheson before he died "What about Korea—did you think about a Resolution?" And he said "Well, it was proposed and Truman didn't want it. He [Truman] said 'This is my responsibility. If they want to criticize, let them, but I'm not going to try to get off the hook.' "

And finally, when fifteen of us or so signed a letter to Johnson about the bombing, and there was some criticism in the course of the Fulbright hearings, McGeorge Bundy came up and tried to silence us. He called George McGovern and me off the floor of the Senate and gave us the word. "Now don't pressure Lyndon because he's under real heat from the hawks, and if you doves carry on like this, the hawks will just get stirred up." And I think he was telling the hawks the same thing. "You hawks take it easy, because if you don't, those crazy doves will get loose."

There were two lines running through our policy. One came from John Foster Dulles who laid down these ideological lines—Communists versus free people. It was like justifying a religious war. He said "Well, we don't have to raise any question about the right to attack them or destroy them." The other part, credit it or blame it on McNamara and LeMay, was "We can do it. We have the military potential and the military plans and we know the tactics in order to win *any* war, *especially* one like this. You just lay it out for us and tell us what you want and when you want it, and we can do it." They said "We did it in Europe, and we did it to the Japanese. We don't really have to worry about the opposition, because we can do it." And when the two came together, they said "Well, they are Communists and we have the power. We'll do it by Christmas." If Lyndon had said to McNamara he'd like to have Peking by Easter, McNamara would have said "Well, maybe a couple more weeks. I think I can make it for you by the first of June," or something like that.

———————•———————

CLARK CLIFFORD—*a Washington attorney, power broker, and Democratic sage on politics, war, and diplomacy since the Roose-*

velt years—became Lyndon Johnson's secretary of defense shortly after the Tet offensive in early 1968. His searching review of U.S. policy revealed the bankruptcy of American strategy and was the key to LBJ's decision to leave the presidency and seek negotiations with Hanoi. But Clifford's unique vantage point gave him a commanding view not merely of the immediate events but of the broad sweep of history that led the United States into the war.

I lived Vietnam and I slept Vietnam for a very substantial part of my life. It is very clear to me now that we entered the conflict in Southeast Asia for the noblest of motives. We were coming to the rescue of a beleaguered South Vietnam, which was resisting aggression from North Vietnam, supported by the two great Communist powers. We felt that if we could defend South Vietnam, we could stop this Communist aggression from spreading throughout that part of the world. You recall the domino theory: If you let South Vietnam go, then Cambodia and Thailand and Laos and Burma and the rest of Southeast Asia would go, and the Philippines would go, and Australia and New Zealand. And I accepted that for a while.

Later on, we got into it more and more for the purpose of defending the freedom of these brave people, and also looking out for our own national security. I concluded after a while that I could no longer accept the relevance and the accuracy of that theory. And so I turned against the war, and I did all in my power to try and persuade our country's leaders to get out of it. And now as I look back on it, it is quite clear to me, despite the splendid motives, that we misunderstood and exaggerated the situation. I do not believe our national security was involved. I do not believe that had we not intervened, the rest of Southeast Asia would have gone. The fact is, in my mind I knew it was untrue.

When we did go in, it was not a theory held just by a few people. All you have to do is look at the Gulf of Tonkin Resolution. It was a virtual declaration of the President's right to use military force in Southeast Asia. That was the feeling of all of us at the time. I accepted it. And for quite a long time I continued to believe in it because I was being told that our policy there was a success and that we were prevailing, that we could see the light at the end of the tunnel. One time we were told that our boys were going to be home by Christmas. And had that all occurred it would have been construed as a successful enterprise on our part.

I would say, as President Truman said, "Those with hindsight have twenty-twenty vision." I have hindsight. And I see really quite clearly what was in the minds of all of us then, whether conscious or not. It all goes back to the failure on the part of France and England to face up to the threat of Hitler and the Third Reich, in which the United States, it seems a little more clearly, might have supported and helped them make a policy. When we got into the late thirties, Hitler in violation of the Versailles Treaty was building up constantly his military strength. He finally decided that the time had come when he could test the attitude of the rest of Western Europe.

And over the objection of the German general staff he moved into the Rhineland. France and England didn't challenge him, and so he waited a little while and he moved into Austria. And France and England did nothing and we did nothing. We all said "Well, maybe it will go away." And then he moved into Czechoslovakia. And Chamberlain went to Munich and came back and said he had accomplished peace in our time. Now, the next move was into Poland and that triggered the Second World War. It's just as clear to me as if I could see it on a blackboard, if Hitler could have been stopped, the Second World War could have been prevented, with the millions of men who lost their lives and the trillions of the world's treasure that was destroyed.

And after the Second World War was over and the Soviets started their aggressive stratagems, Mr. Truman and others had before them the clear example of what happened if you didn't face up to the threat of aggression. So Mr. Truman stepped up to Soviet aggression with the Truman Doctrine and then with the North Atlantic Treaty Organization, in which he said to the Soviets "Attack any one of our allies in Western Europe and you attack the United States." And then came maybe the greatest of all, the Marshall Plan, Point Four, and the manner in which he handled the Berlin Blockade. All of those stopped Soviet aggression in its tracks.

And as we got into the early sixties, the country's leaders had those two dramatic illustrations: We could have prevented the Second World War had we moved; and after the Second World War the Soviets started their expansionist period, and we moved and we stopped it. And you learn from success. And then years go by and we see another movement start in a different place, backed by two great Communist powers, perhaps conspiratorially. And they begin to move in Southeast Asia. And the theory was "By God, we're not going to make a mistake this time. We're going to step in there and excise this cancer before it spreads throughout the body politic in that part of the world." That was the kind of reasoning that went into it.

And we did it honorably—we followed through on what we thought was right. The whole country thought it was right from the very beginning. And nations make decisions of that kind for laudable purposes. Men agree on what the right policy is. But as time goes on other factors intrude, and that's what happened to us.

———◆———

He is a stocky little man who wears thick eyeglasses and speaks excellent English in a thick Mittel-European accent. He is voluble, opinionated, just a shade short of garrulous; far likelier to be a professor of Slavic studies than a spy. But THOMAS POLGAR *came to the United States in 1938 to go to school, joined the Office of Strategic Services during World War II, and was co-opted by the CIA at its founding in 1947. He was the Agency's station chief in Saigon for the three and a half years leading up to the fall of Vietnam. Retired in 1981, he is an international security consultant in Maitland, Florida.*

The United States at times says glorious things, but the whole truth isn't quite there. The words sound beautiful. Read President Kennedy's inauguration speech—no sacrifice too great and so forth. Read what various Presidents were saying about Vietnam. But the fact is we got tired of it, just like a child who gets tired of his toy and throws it away. It became a painful nuisance and a reminder of our own inconsistency.

We didn't go into Vietnam as a result of a single, considered decision. We drifted into it over a period of maybe fifteen years. The real American commitment—I can tell you exactly when it started. After the 1954 agreement in Geneva, it was decided between North and South that people who want to live in the other side can move freely, and you had three or four million people, mostly Catholics, who lived in the North who decided to go South. And how they got to the South? Most of them were carried by the U.S. Navy.

At that point the South became the apple of the eye of the U.S. Catholic Church. Cardinal Spellman in New York embraced the cause of Catholic South Vietnam against the Communist North. Spellman and a bunch of the other articulate bishops and archbishops started a tremendous propaganda drive. And of course, Ngo Dinh Diem, the head of South Vietnam, was a devout Catholic and his brother was the Bishop of Hue. And gradually an emotional attachment formed. Catholic Relief sent their people to Vietnam, and a tremendous push started to shore up this Catholic country in pagan Asia. That was the root of the American involvement and then, like a gambler who's losing, we throw good money after bad.

In Truman's day we had already four hundred people there. When

Eisenhower left office we had maybe a thousand. When Kennedy died we had fifteen thousand. And when Lyndon Johnson left office we had five hundred thousand. [There was] never a clear decision how much is this thing worth? Can we achieve with ten thousand or fifty thousand more what we haven't achieved with what we got now? What are the limits of our liability? In 1964, I was in Vienna and Senator [Richard] Russell came through on a trip. I was invited to a luncheon in his honor and Russell was then chairman of the Military Relations Committee of the Senate and he said that to his way of thinking the United States was hung up in Vietnam just like a cow on a picket fence in Georgia. You couldn't go forward and you couldn't go backward and the whole time the picket was hurting your belly.

It seems to me once you decide what your policy objective is, then you've got to calculate reasonably what do you need to do it with and don't go in there with less than you think you need. I mean don't get yourself caught in a position where you say, "I want a car but the price is a little too high so instead of four wheels, I'll just take three." Maybe you can cut your objective, but your decision to commit your assets has got to be sufficient to do the job required and if you feel that that is not the case, then you have two choices. Either lower your objective or up the ante. We simply do not have the luxury of waging gradual war and committing our forces piecemeal. If you want to win, you got to go in there to win but be clear in your mind what is it you want to win.

I was talking with Kissinger one day about this. He says, "Did you read *The Best and the Brightest*?"* and he thought it was about ninety percent accurate. Kissinger would never admit that anybody was a hundred percent right, so ninety percent coming from him is pretty good. And he says, "What I can't understand, what is it that they had in mind?" He could understand what happened and how they got from one place to another, but what he can't understand is what they originally had in mind. How did you get yourself into that situation?

———————⬩———————

Retired AMBASSADOR WILLIAM SULLIVAN, *a career diplomat, was involved in the Indochina conflict from beginning to end. At Geneva in 1962, with Averell Harriman, he helped negotiate the "neutralization" of Laos. Later he was U.S. Ambassador in Vientiane while the Central Intelligence Agency and an army of thousands of*

---

*A 1972 book by David Halberstam about the policymakers brought to Washington by John F. Kennedy who led the country into Vietnam.

*Meo [Hmong] tribesmen led by Gen. Vang Pao conducted a "secret"
war that paralleled the open conflict in Vietnam. After Laos, Sullivan helped direct U.S. war policy from Washington. In the seventies, he was ambassador to the Philippines when thousands of
Americans and Vietnamese landed there after the fall of Saigon.
Still later he was the ambassador in Teheran as the Shah went down.
He headed the American Assembly, a foreign policy group in New
York, for several years. He is now retired and living in Cuernava-
ca, Mexico.*

My first brush with Vietnam came in '47, when I was out in Bangkok and the Viet Minh made contact. They wanted some friendly
sympathy from the United States in their fight against the French.
They had a mission there, headed by a fellow named Tran Van Dinh.
He later showed up here in the United States in the sixties as a
free Vietnamese democrat. In those days the Viet Minh had a number of democratic parties that had agreed to stay with them, and
very shrewdly in their representation to Bangkok, they sent the
non-Communist ones. They did propaganda and intelligence work
against the French, and a little gun smuggling into Cambodia. And
sort of loosely associated with them were the Laotians that I knew
at that time—Prince Souvanna Phouma's older half-brother, Prince
Phetsarath and his bodyguard, Phoumi Nosavan, who died recently.*

I was looking for information on crude drugs and medicinal herbs
to answer a questionnaire from the Department of Commerce. I discovered that the Anglo-French Drug Company was the primary
source, but the telephones weren't working in those days so I went
down there and walked in. There was a *métis* [Eurasian] recep-
tionist and I spoke to her in French and she just ushered me into
this room to see *monsieur le docteur*. And when I got in, there was
a meeting of the French intelligence types and their maps spread all
over the table. This was 1947, and we had just created the CIA, and
they assumed I was a CIA officer. I wasn't, but I guess word spread
that I might be and that's how the Viet Minh looked me up.

I got more seriously into it in '61. When the Kennedy administration came in, they said anybody who had fresh ideas on policy, drop
them in the basket. So I wrote up two, one on moving toward recognition of China, and the other on the neutralization of Laos. The
Laos paper got adopted and led to the Geneva conference. I did not

---

*Souvanna Phouma became the neutralist prime minister of Laos after the 1962 Geneva
Accords; Phoumi Nosavan, later both a general in the army and sometime minister of defense,
led the political right.

go at first, but when it turned into a long proposition they sent me, and I ended up as Harriman's deputy.

In '63 I ran a special interdepartmental group dealing with Vietnam, attached directly to the secretary of state. And there were several moments of truth. When General Lyman Lemnitzer, who had been chairman of the Joint Chiefs, was retiring, he gave as a sort of a farewell effort a briefing in the secretary of defense's office. He brought in his charts and he made a plea that United States forces could not effectively fight a counterguerrilla jungle war ten thousand miles from home, and that if U.S. forces were going to be sent they should be used at the things they were best at. In other words, not to go into the jungle way the hell out in a place that was not susceptible to American-style warfare. Instead he proposed that we put forces across the beach at Vinh in the southern part of North Vietnam, run them up against those limestone escarpments which are north of the passes onto the Ho Chi Minh Trail, and thereby block the North Vietnamese [supply line].

This rang some bells with me, because at that time a number of retired French military had taken the trouble to come to the United States to talk about their own experience and to make a plea for exactly that type of strategy. It struck me as a very logical thing. It was rejected because everybody had memories of Korea. The 17th parallel was taken as being comparable to the 38th parallel: If we went north the Chinese hordes would come in and the whole thing would turn into a war against China which nobody wanted. Of course, knowing what we now know, it's somewhat questionable whether the Vietnamese would have wanted the Chinese to come in or the Chinese would have come in. I've asked this, incidentally, of some old Chinese generals, and the general answer is to smile and pour you another mao-tai.*

Anyway the trouble was the Joint Chiefs were all split at that time. Curt LeMay was gonna bomb them back to the Stone Age. "Just let me go, just let me loose." And he came up with a plan. Then I was put in charge of a group to select targets. We came up with nine targets in all of Vietnam that we considered useful for strategic air. Curt insisted we sabotaged him, but then he never directly challenged that he had any more [targets in North Vietnam whose destruction might have made a difference].

From '61 to '75, I suppose I saw the war from more different perspectives than just about anybody in the United States government. And I came to a number of conclusions. One, that the Lao Dong, the North Vietnamese Communist party, consisted of a group of

*A potent Chinese liquor.

ambitious leaders who had a totally warped perspective and were perfectly prepared to sacrifice millions of their young peoples' lives to the pursuit of their ambitions. Second, that the strategic purposes that the United States had in 1962, '63, and '64, had significant merit. But thirdly that one conclusion we didn't draw was that much of that purpose was altered by the failure of the Chinese-sponsored coup d'état in Indonesia. Our real strategic concern [before the war] was that with Communist control of both Indochina and Indonesia, there would be a pincer that would cut off Japan's supply routes, isolate Australia and New Zealand, and work strategically to the United States' disadvantage in the far reaches of the Pacific.

The real prize in this was always Indonesia. And it was the countercoup against the Communist rebellion in 1965 that eliminated that piece of geography from the equation. The Communists came within a hair's breadth of winning, and if they had gotten General [Abdul Haris] Nasution [the defense minister] and one or two others, they might have succeeded. But the army took over and three hundred thousand Communists, including D. N. Aidit, the party boss, who was in Peking when the coup took place, were slaughtered.

That raised a flag to people like Chou En-Lai,* that this was a grasp not within their reach. They also began to get fed up with the Cultural Revolution back home and some of the more practical people, particularly Chou, decided that all this futzing around was counterproductive. Now that might not have happened if we hadn't also at the same time visibly committed ourselves in Indochina. That caught them by surprise. The Chinese were beginning to believe their own words that we were a paper tiger. They had thought the lesson of Korea would keep us out. And when it didn't, the Chinese threat diminished.

We also failed to appreciate the degree to which the schism between the Chinese and the Soviets was real and could be exploited. That became apparent to those of us who were in Geneva in 1961–62, but when we came back to Washington and suggested it, the Communist experts in the Department of State [insisted] this was all play-acting to entrap us guileless types. In fact the Chinese began to feel that Indochina was a place that had better be balkanized. Vietnam itself did not worry the Chinese, but I think they concluded that balkanization was needed to keep the Soviets from acquiring a significant base on their southern flank. So the United States was very slow in reacting to those changes. Had we done so, it would have made an enormous difference in our ability to handle North Vietnam.

---

*Then the premier of China, and principal operator of the Communist government's foreign policy.

WALT WHITMAN ROSTOW *was chairman of the State Department Policy Planning Council from 1961 to 1966, and then became Lyndon B. Johnson's national security adviser. An unreconstructed hawk, he teaches economics and history at the University of Texas at Austin.*

You may scoff at the domino theory today, but a lot of people believed it in the early sixties. And Hanoi did take over Laos and Cambodia, but the critical issue was always Thailand. In a war halfway around the world, the United States could not afford to diffuse its power. That was why Kennedy didn't want to fight in Laos, and it was why we chose Vietnam as the place to make a stand and save Thailand. And the policy worked. I am sure that if Lyndon Johnson had not acted in 1965 in Vietnam, then Thailand could not have been saved. By the same token, I don't think the Indonesian military would have stood up to Aidit if President Johnson hadn't made a commitment to put troops into Vietnam.

We were not by any means the only people who saw the danger. The attitudes in Australia, New Zealand, Thailand, and even among Laotians like Premier Souvanna Phouma were very much the same. No one doubted that if the United States failed to act decisively, the dominos were going to fall. In 1977 Howard Beale, who was the Australian Ambassador to the United States during the Kennedy and Johnson administrations, published a book called *This Inch of Time*, which makes the point exactly. He wrote:

"It is now said that there is no foreseeable threat to the security of Australia within the next fifteen years. . . . The scene was not at all like that when Australia gave assistance to the United States in Vietnam. What seemed much more likely at that time was that had there been no intervention, South Vietnam would have collapsed and so would Laos and Cambodia, as they have now done." And Beale goes on to make the point that the most important factor for Australia was Indonesia, that Sukarno was trying to do a balancing act between his Army and the PKI [the Parti Kommunist Indonesia], that the PKI might well have won, and that the installation of such a regime in Djakarta would have made life very uncomfortable in Australia. And that was why Australia joined the United States in putting troops into South Vietnam.

Now, the fact is that even when South Vietnam fell, the executive branch [of the U.S. government] did not walk away from Asia. The fall of Vietnam might have had a totally different impact in Southeast Asia if President Ford had not said, in effect, "I don't agree with what Congress is doing." The *Mayaguez* affair* made a substantial difference to the Southeast Asians. If it had been the President of the United States who had put the knife in their backs, it would have produced a much different reaction than that it was the Congress. They were skeptical about us, and to a certain extent they still are. But we have not gone away, which is what they feared.

———————————•———————————

GRAHAM MARTIN *was the U.S. Ambassador in Saigon from mid-1973 until the collapse of Vietnam. Earlier he had been ambassador to Thailand during the buildup in Indochina—where he was credited with having helped to defeat a budding insurgency by* avoiding *the introduction of U.S. troops. A tall, spare man who didn't much like the press though he was once a newspaperman himself, Martin seemed to many who knew him in Southeast Asia at once arrogant and a burnt-out case. He is retired and lives in North Carolina.*

I was on the other end of the cable in Paris for eight years from 1947 to 1955, during the whole French experience in Vietnam, and fascinated by it. In 1960 I was in Geneva as chief of mission to the European office of the United Nations. I saw Rusk there and a little later the Kennedys yanked me back to Washington, at first to be deputy coordinator of The Alliance for Progress and then on the Counter-Insurgency Committee, which was looking for ways to fight this new kind of war. And I kept telling both Bobby and Jack that we simply were not equipped either intellectually or with the materiel to do it. But they were adamant, so we went down to Fort Bragg and ended up vastly expanding the Special Forces. Now, what often happens in institutions is that if you don't like a new policy, you change it back to something you do. And the Special Forces were really being taught not to deal with counterinsurgency, but how to be insurgents.

The great difficulty is that no one ever really commands an army. It operates on a doctrine in which it has been drilled, and for which it has been equipped. To the degree that it has been drilled to operate almost with automaticity, it will be successful if it has the proper tactics and proper equipment. We went into Vietnam with a doctrine of conventional war, and also an older doctrine on the admin-

———————

*In which the new Khmer Rouge regime in Phnom Penh intercepted a passing U.S. merchantman on the high seas and held its crew until U.S. warplanes started bombing the port of Kompong Som.

istration of occupied areas [that grew out of] postwar operations in Germany and Japan. When we tried to marry the two and apply it to insurgency in Vietnam, you had the prescription for disaster.

Now, come to Thailand. The Kennedys were very concerned over what they had inherited from Eisenhower in Southeast Asia. Without anybody paying any attention to it, Kennedy sent a whole division of Marines into Thailand up on the Lao border, announcing the decision before the Thai were even consulted. Then, since the Kennedys knew much of what I had been doing, they sent me to Thailand to take a hard look at what it would make sense for us to do.

Unfortunately, three weeks later my president was dead and I had Lyndon Johnson in. I had known him since we were both secretaries to congressmen. But that was not any asset really. Johnson looked at things with kind of a Tex-Mex attitude. He really didn't know that you don't ever ask the U.S. Army what needs to be done because they will tell you "Move over." And for fighting some little brown guy with a rusty rifle and a bag of rice it's just ridiculous. They had before sent out a mission to organize the South Vietnamese into a regular army for plain old conventional war. But the other side just wasn't playing fair. They weren't coming down in divisions.

And in Thailand I didn't see any white faces on the other side and I didn't see how we could ever tell a good Thai from a bad Thai, a good Vietnamese from a bad Vietnamese; only *they* can do that. So if you get in there, you're going to end up hating everybody. Now the Thai had already organized to get health, national development, education, and a military presence out in the northeast, where the insurgents were growing. They hadn't been oppressing these people, just totally neglecting them. The area was wild country; it wasn't worth much, they hadn't spent much time on it, so it was open to subversion.

I remember one senior military officer said the only thing we were doing in Thailand was chasing the insurgents up and down the Phu Phan mountain range. He was right, but what he did not understand was that we were not letting the insurgents stay to provide the parallel infrastructure in the villages that is essential if they are to move like little fish in the broad stream of the people. I had read Sun Tzu and he had not. I had followed what had happened in China under Mao, he had not.

Meantime the buildup was going on in Vietnam and there was nothing any of us could do to stop it. We would say "We don't believe this makes sense," but nothing much happened. [Defense Secretary] McNamara, who is a good and decent man, really had a great handicap. If you could not convert what you were talking about into binary nomials that could fit into a computer, he was not intellectually prepared to cope with it. It was his insistence on statistics, statistics, statistics, that drove everybody nuts. I once wanted some additional trucks for the Thai and he said "You can't have any because their truck maintenance is far below our standards." Now we may take a truck fifty thousand miles and junk the damn thing. But they don't have any Detroit in Thailand and a bad truck is better than no truck, so they patch it up. It's totally irrelevant, you see, to try to apply these bloody statistical standards.

Then McNamara put down this enormous billion-dollar line of sensors.* You know, a little North Vietnamese feed company bedding down would trip the sensor, which triggered something up in Nakorn Phanom, and this is the way you could tell how many were coming down. I said this is fine, but I could spend a billion dollars a little bit better.

Westy [Gen. William C. Westmoreland] saw himself as the CINC-SEAsia [Commander-in-Chief, Southeast Asia]. For example if the Chinese came in, it wouldn't do to be exposed in Vietnam, so Korat in Thailand would be a proper place for the [alternate] seat of CINCSEAsia. And I encouraged that, so we had a great port built at Sattaheep, we had a road built up to Korat, and I extended that on into the northeast. We opened the damn country for development. You got that highway in, you didn't have to do anything else. And you could fly over that thing, you could see the buffalo carts and the rice began to spread, on each side of this highway.

People ask me what the hell we think we accomplished in Southeast Asia. It was never really an anti-Communist thing as such. It was I think so far as Rusk and others were concerned simply remembering what happened in the thirties when the Japanese invaded Manchuria and the Germans went into the Rhineland and nobody did anything.

But one of the consequences of Korea was that in Southeast Asia when you started the damn fight, there was a great caution that you didn't have [another] MacArthur try to get up to the Yalu and get smothered by the Chinese. So the U.S. wanted to fight a wholly defensive war, or attempted to, to contain it in the South. That may have been a mistake. All the military people tell you it is, and they're probably right. But I can understand the reasons. Statesmen who have the responsibility of seeing we *aren't* incinerated can be a little cautious on those things.

---

*A little-known project in which the Pentagon seeded virtually the entire length of the Ho Chi Minh Trail in Laos with listening and sensing devices whose radio signals were fed into a vast computer system at Nakorn Phanom airbase on the Mekong River in northeast Thailand. The computers tracked movement on the trail and automatically passed on target information to American fighter-bombers and gunships overhead.

DOUGLAS PIKE *went to Asia during World War II as a U.S. Army journalist, ended up in Tokyo during the Occupation, then went to Korea during the war there. He joined the Foreign Service in 1960 and was sent to Vietnam. A communications specialist, he became fascinated with Communist propaganda and eventually became the U.S. mission's premier analyst of captured documents. By a whim of bureaucracy—he had overstayed his time abroad—he was ordered home in late 1974 just in time to save his collection of eighteen thousand books and two and a half million pages of documents. After the fall of Saigon he served on the State Department's Policy Planning Council, and later was the Pentagon's resident expert on Indochina. Since 1981 he has headed the Indochina Archive at the University of California at Berkeley.*

A lot of people, even a lot of people who were there, have a kind of *Apocalypse Now* memory of the place. You know, a place of alarms and excursions at night, of terror and killing and bloodshed. That was there. But somehow it didn't dominate our lives. I remember the overthrow of Diem and people in the street dancing and burning the flag. I remember also taking some artillery shells. They were shelling the Palace Guard barracks, which was two blocks from my house. My wife and I were in the stairwell and a hundred and five-millimeter shell landed across the street. A piece of it came buzzing in and hit the wall. Like a dummy I picked it up. The goddamn thing was a red-hot hunk of metal and now, Jesus, I had wounds of war and I can still remember instantly thinking, "What a dumb thing to do."

I think of those as good years, actually. I think there's a considerable myth about them, even with veterans. You talk to veterans and they say what a bloody nightmare it was. But you're drinking beer, and they say "I remember that time in . . . " They start telling you war stories. And the next thing you know they're like the song "Those were the days my friend, We thought they'd never end." I have that. Of course I was insulated. But I saw considerable combat. And I would argue that most GI's did not see combat. Even those who did see combat didn't see very much of it. It was a quiet war. When it erupted, it would be sudden and then it would be gone.

Most people have an image of Vietnam being like a no-man's land, a lunar landscape devastated from bombing, defoliation, death, and destruction. But it wasn't like that. There was hardly anything visible. My memory of Korea is of village after village leveled. Not one brick on top of another. Or Tokyo in 1945. Christ, you could go from downtown Tokyo to downtown Yokohama and it was level as far as the eye could see. Hiroshima the same. The thing is I brought to Vietnam much more of a memory than most people.

When we first got to Vietnam, we got very attached to the place. We led a Great Books discussion group. You discuss the Declaration of Independence. I thought, "This is a very good way to get inside Vietnamese minds." You say, "Do you have a right to overthrow the government or not? Did Jefferson know what he was talking about, or not?" "Yes," the Vietnamese say, "if the ruler disrupts the harmony of the universe then the mandate of heaven is withdrawn and the people can replace it." Pure democracy, but it's also Confucianism.

So we got very emotionally attached, and we really hated Diem. I was an activist, a Kennedy type, pay any price, go anywhere, do anything. And what was impelling us in Vietnam was the desire to help put things right. We didn't really agree on what "put things right" meant, but it was a kind of general sense. Then Diem was overthrown and it seemed to me things were going to improve rapidly, and it would be all downhill from there.

I can remember, we were in Tokyo on leave and we were at the Sanno Hotel [an American military club in downtown Tokyo]. This is one of my strongest memories. We were having lunch with some friends who'd been in Saigon, and we came out to the front entrance talking, my wife is at one end and I'm on the other. I look up at her and tears are coming down her cheeks. She's staring, and I look around to see what she's staring at, and it's the headline on *Stars and Stripes*: "Coup d'État in Saigon." It was the coup that overthrew Big Minh.* I looked and I had about the same feeling. "Oh Christ," you know. "Shit. It's all back to square one," and "How the hell could this happen?" Then almost immediately a second reaction, which was "Why am I getting so emotional about this? I mean it isn't my country, it isn't my responsibility. It's their country and their responsibility." And even though I like the place, I don't do them any good by getting emotionally committed.

They tell you this, of course, in Foreign Service indoctrinations. The danger of "going native." You're there to represent the United States, not to represent X country. You're there to explain X country back to Washington. Remember what side you're on. A lot of Americans didn't do that. The result was those who really got committed got torn apart by Vietnam's defeat, and they're down the tube.

---

*Gen. Duong Van Minh, who took control of South Vietnam in the aftermath of the coup against Ngo Dinh Diem. His ouster a few months later, of which Pike speaks here, was the first ominous signal of what became two and a half years of political turmoil.

GEORGE BALL *was undersecretary of state in the Kennedy and John-*
son administrations. Afterward he returned to the practice of law
and investment banking in Wall Street. A prolific writer on foreign
policy, he is one of the Democratic party's leading doves.

I hated the war from the beginning. It seemed to me that it was an
aberration and that we were getting into a situation where all experience and prudence told us we should never be. From the day President Kennedy first reacted to the Taylor-Rostow report,* which I
think was in September of 1961, I felt a distinct distaste for the whole
enterprise.

I thought we were undertaking something where we could not succeed. I had known a good deal about the French experience in Vietnam, since I had been a legal adviser to the French government.
And I had a feeling that for us to be drawn into this mire would
mean extending our resources in a futile effort to try to accomplish
something of which we weren't capable. And in the process not only
would we lose a lot of American lives, but we would distract our
country in an endeavor which was very peripheral to American
interests.

And that's why I told President Kennedy at the very beginning, that
if we went down this road it would be a great catastrophe—that we'd
have three hundred thousand men in the rice paddies and jungles of
Vietnam in five years' time. I was quite wrong. It was five hundred
fifty thousand in about three years' time. But Kennedy said "George,
you're just crazier than hell. That isn't going to happen." And he
was rather a little bit hurt.

I have wondered sometimes if Vietnam was not inevitable in the
sense that we seemed for a while to be successful at playing a role
which was clearly at some point going to push us beyond our competence. This was a result of the fact that after the Second World
War, the United States found itself the undisputed leader of the non-
Communist world and we had a feeling we could do anything and
everything. All one has to do is look at the expansiveness of Kennedy's inaugural address. Well, sooner or later I suppose we had to
come up against the hard reality that that just wasn't the case. If
only we could have done it in a less costly way.

---

*Kennedy sent Gen. Maxwell D. Taylor, a former Army Chief of Staff who was then his
special assistant, and Walt W. Rostow, then head of policy planning at the State Department, to survey the situation in South Vietnam in the fall of 1961. Their report recommended
the dispatch of American advisers and military hardware to help the government of Ngo Dinh
Diem fight off a growing Communist insurgency. The first increment of American aircraft and
pilots arrived in December.

CHAPTER TWO

Grunts and Generals

IT is sometimes said that old men vote for war because they know it is the young who will have to fight. There is a fraction of acid truth in that. There is also truth to the notion that democratic countries cannot tolerate long wars. When it comes to combat, out of sight is truly out of mind. The suffering of sons and brothers can be endured only so long as it is confined to distant battlefields.

Through most of American history the gulf between the home front and the fighting front didn't come close to being bridged. Soldiers went away to war and did not return until it was over; the means of mass communication were so primitive that they could not begin to convey the mud and dust, the blood and smoke, the terror and disgust of the killing grounds. Even as recently as World War II, the government had sense enough to withhold from public view until years later combat footage of places like Tarawa that showed whole boatloads of Marines being shot to pieces on the beach.

But all that began to change in Korea, and it was transformed with a vengeance during Vietnam, both by television and by the fact that legions of young men served one year and brought their memories home. The country at large was exposed to a kind of carnal knowledge once reserved to the troops alone, and it found the experience so revolting that it turned against both the war and the warriors. It is worth hearing some soldiers' tales, if only because they convey so plainly the feelings of the times.

———◆———

KEN BEREZ *grew up in Brooklyn and southern New Jersey outside Philadelphia. He went to Vietnam as an infantryman and came home with one leg paralyzed by a spinal wound. He is associate director of the Vietnam Veterans of America Foundation.*

My generation came of age totally post–World War II. We were the savior of democracy, the policeman of the world. Dwight Eisenhower, a national hero, was the first President I consciously knew of. And of course then came John Kennedy, who really personified my generation. "Ask not what your country can do for you," and so forth. It sounds jingoistic today, but we took it seriously back then. And we didn't question our political leadership. The opinion-making institutions of that time pushed the line that Vietnam was good and we should get involved. It wasn't until we ran up against it that we started to ask questions. But for most of us that was too late.

I was twenty when I got drafted. I liked to think of myself as an intelligent person and I began to question the war before I was drafted, in '67 or '68. However, all that said, I was a second-generation American in an ethnic family and I was bred to believe that when called upon you served your country. And when push came to shove, I just couldn't see myself going off to Canada or Sweden.

Initially I didn't think about the fact that I might be going to Vietnam. The total flip-flop from a middle-class, civilian existence was enough. It was not until I got into advanced infantry training that I realized where the pipeline was going. I flew out of McChord Airbase in Washington. It was a bit of craziness. We flew on civilian airliners. Mine was a Seaboard World Airways 707, and we already had been issued our cammys—camouflage, brand-new, pressed fatigues at Fort Lewis. It was a twenty-hour flight. We got fine meals on the plane, we had pretty stewardesses. We were going off to war first class. And then we stepped off the plane at Cam Ranh Bay, and two things hit you—the heat and the smell of dead fish.

Twenty-four hours later I ended up with the 82nd Airborne in Tay Ninh, the Parrot's Beak-Angel's Wing area, on the northwest approaches to Saigon. They gave us first a week of physical training, to get us used to the heat and the humidity—a hundred degrees heat and a hundred percent humidity can knock the hell out of you—and get us used to the rifle again and the tools of war. Most of us had been on leave for three or four weeks. They would take us out on mock patrols beyond the perimeter. And one day we were be-bopping along outside a village and there was some fire. And the training sergeant said "That's just part of the training." Not until we got back to the perimeter did they tell us it was hostile fire. Because we literally were just there a few days in country, they did not want us to panic.

After that, I went into a rifle company. I was no different than a lot of other guys. The two or three years leading up to that time, I saw the war on television like everybody else. And then one day you're there, sloshing through a rice paddy and you're looking for the TV camera to pan, and you realize you're not watching television. This is it. And it's, you know, that total cultural shock, that time warp of the fact that within literally hours or a couple of days you could be on the West Coast of the United States and then sloshing through the paddies. We were a leg unit, and when we were out of the firebase, which was anywhere from ten days to two weeks at a time, we slept on the ground on your poncho liner. And then if you were lucky enough you got back to the firebase for a few days to clean up, take a shower, get some hot food and live in a bunker. That was the basic rotation—a couple of weeks out and three or four days in.

You didn't think politics when you were out there. It was just basically survival. I knew I was there for a year. I knew what date I was going to be coming home. And I basically looked at myself as "I'm dead now, and I have a year to work my way back to life." And after a month and a half, two months went by and I saw my share of action, you build a self-confidence. It's "I'm doing my job well. I'm surviving ambushes and actions that we've seen, large or small." And you really think you are gonna make it. Mentally that's how it worked for me. And I think most of the others were the same.

People out there didn't talk about the war much at all. You look at pictures in magazines of that time, and see guys with peace symbols on their helmets and so forth. But for whatever reason, the 82nd was a rather professional unit, and I don't think they would have stood for it. The commanding officer, if he saw a beard growing, said "Shave it off." To the extent that combat troops in swampy terrain can look professional, we were.

I do remember that just after I got there the Vietnam casualty toll hit thirty-two or thirty-three thousand and I remember the headline "Vietnam Passes Korea." I spoke once or twice with others, maybe, about "What are we gonna do? The argument is we can't pull out now because all these men would have died in vain. But then again if we stay, are we just gonna prove that ten or fifteen thousand more can die?" And in a sense that was prophetic, because another twenty-five thousand did die, and what was accomplished? But the reality was survival, keeping warm, keeping dry, getting your mail from home, going on R and R,* and that's about it.

I was there about three months before I got hit. It was the rainy season already, and the only way you could get around was by helicopter or by river boat. That afternoon, we marched down through the swamps to a river and got into these flatbed boats, two of them, a squad in each boat. And we were just turning a blind bend in the

---

*Rest and recreation—a one-week leave from the war zone granted to each soldier who served in Vietnam.

river, just like in the movies, and there was a VC ambush waiting
on the banks. They opened fire, and I remember somebody yelling
out "VC in the tree," and instantly fire opened up. I fell on somebody's legs, and somebody fell on my legs. I remember trying to
get my rifle up over my head, over the side of the boat, to get fire
out. You're taught that if you get into an ambush, the first thing
you do is simply fire to make him duck his head. And I guess I just
lifted myself up on the side enough to give a profile, and a bullet got
me right in the back, in the spine. I thought my legs were blown off,
because I remember losing instant feeling in my legs. It was just
total numbness.

There were a few others hit in the boat with me. And I remember
us taking off with the boat and returning fire as we were heading
upriver back to this makeshift firebase. I was conscious most of the
time, and I remember saying to myself "Keep calm and don't talk.
Save your energy." Then I was taken out of the boat and there happened to be doctors at this village. They worked on me, trying to
get an IV in. They tried in my neck and my arm but my veins were
collapsing. And they finally found a pulse and got an IV into my
ankle. And in another ten or fifteen minutes a medevac* came and
picked me up, and I was told that within forty-five minutes I was
being operated on. I have no doubt that's what saved me.

———————•———————

JOHN DiFUSCO *served in the U.S. Air Force in Central Vietnam.
After the war he conceived, directed, and acted in* Tracers, *a play
about Vietnam that opened in Los Angeles and played later in Chicago, England, and Australia. It was performed at Joseph Papp's
Public Theater off-Broadway in New York City in 1985.*

There have been many times when I wanted to forget the war. I
was talking to my uncle over the Fourth of July, whom I was named
after. He was in World War II. I said, "Do you still think about
the war?" He said, "Yeah, sometimes it seems like it was yesterday." Then he proceeded to tell me a couple of experiences about
a few guys that he lost. I have a brother-in-law who's getting out
now. He's in his second hitch in the Army. And he read the script of
Tracers one day. He's essentially been in a peacetime situation,
but he says, "You know, a lot of the things you bring out are scary,
but I'd like to go."

---

*A term for the ambulance helicopters that were used to evacuate wounded troops from the
battlefield.

I volunteered for Vietnam. Part of it was that I was trained to fight, and I felt like I was wasting my time stateside. I had been stationed in Amarillo, Texas, for a year and a half. I also have a very distinct memory that this was going to be a major event in world history, and I wanted to be able to say, "I was there."

I arrived in Cam Ranh Bay, and the first thing that hits you is this place is really different. It's like prehistoric in some ways. And I got on the C-130 to fly up to Phu Cat, and it kept getting shot at all the way up there. You think, you don't know where you are. You've been in the country a day and a half and you're getting shot at.

Fun place. I was in the Air Force Security Police. I sat on a tower with a machine gun every night. My job was to keep the VC from infiltrating and blowing up airplanes. It was a medium situation. It wasn't real bad, but it wasn't Saigon either. During the Tet offensive and towards the end of my tour, I started to see more and more action. It was curious because the first thing they would do was mortar or rocket. What they were really after were the airplanes, so if you were out on the perimeter, the rockets would be going over you. Then they'd try to come in behind. That was maybe where you'd have actual contact.

Once we were out in a security alert team, it's like a SWAT team really, and twelve of us on the back of a truck had to come in because there were five or six VC blowing up airplanes. Everybody was shooting everywhere. There was nothing to hide behind. That's the memory that's most vivid for me. And the feeling of a bullet coming right past my ear. You could feel the wind and hear the slight whistle and if I'd just cocked my head this way I might not have come back. And I was real short at the time, I had about a week left.

I used to see Puffs* all the time, every night. I volunteered to work at night. When nothing was happening, I would find myself wishing something would happen, and one of the things that would make me feel that way was watching Smokey† and Puff in the distance where some shit was going on. And I'm sitting there with this machine gun and all these grenades and nothing is happening. And yet I'm seeing all this stuff go on. A strange experience.

One night I had to guard a napalm bomb dump. We got hit with rockets and mortars. In the morning, we had to go around and count the holes. Right next to my tower there was a rocket embedded in asphalt that didn't go off. If that thing had gone off, not only would I be gone, but it would have easily done in a couple hundred people.

---

*Twin-engined C-47 Dakota transport planes of World War II-vintage armed with high-speed Gatling guns fired out of side-ports in the fuselage to strafe enemy positions.
†Another type of aerial gunship.

The Bob Hope show came to Phu Cat while I was there. It was the day after Christmas. And there was a Huey helicopter coming in from some place where there was a lot of heavy stuff going on. They were on their way in for relief. It crashed just fifty yards from where the show was. Everybody on the chopper was killed, and on the side it said, MERRY CHRISTMAS. Some guys had spray-painted it on there.

We had a guy that needlessly shot a kid about twelve years old, walking a water buffalo. Most of us had seen the kid from day to day. Maybe he was some kind of VC observer, but nobody really knew that for sure. He just seemed like a farm kid. Then one day this guy shot him down. I don't know what became of him, but for the first few days afterward, he was ostracized socially. No one spoke to him 'cause most of us knew this kid, and something didn't seem right about it.

I've heard other vets say you didn't really know—that eight-year-old kids could blow you away.

In this situation, that wasn't quite the case. It was more the case out in the bush. We were surrounded by a couple of small villages. One night we had a firefight with the ARVNs. It was ridiculous. There was a whorehouse in Phu Cat that was supposed to be just for Vietnamese. Some of our guys went. The next night, we started getting fired on. About half an hour into it, somebody figured out it was the ARVN camp firing because they were pissed off that we went to their whorehouse.

The nearest city was Qui Nhon. But Qui Nhon was like a small version of Saigon, a real sin city if you got in there. The first few times I was with prostitutes, I could not have an orgasm to save my life. You'd just go on and on forever and they'd get pissed off: "Here, take your money back. Get out of here." You always had this fear that you were going to catch something. They had rumors of the black sift—a disease that if you caught it they would send you off to an island that was like a leper colony. You would never be seen again. I doubt it was true, but the superiors would start these stories to keep you from going out.

The Dear John letter, I'll never forget. That was a trip. I think it's affected my relationships with women ever since. I seem to only go so far with women. When I got there guys would say, "Got a girlfriend?" "Yeah" "Forget about her. You're going to get a letter. Jody's going to get you." Well then, one day I got this letter. I'd only been there about two months, maybe three. Every letter I'd received always began, Dearest darling, Dearest something or other, Dearest this or that. Then the letter came. It started, "Dear John." Total cliche. She went out with my best friend. When I came back from Vietnam I bought a car in Massachusetts, the first car I ever owned. I drove it cross-country. I still had more time to do, I got stationed in California. And I stopped in Amarillo, Texas, to look for her. I just had to see her, but I couldn't find her.

I don't hold it against her. I do wonder what happened to her. It wasn't a first love for me, but she was the first woman I'd slept with for any length of time. It was pretty painful. At that age you don't like to show your pain. I read the letter, I was just sitting on my bunk, and I had this kind of disbelief. This guy walked by, a great big black guy named Edgar Lewis walked by, and he just stopped for a second, and without even asking me anything, he just said, "Come on. I'll buy you a drink." And it was like, another one down. Everyone got them. This war in many ways was the war of breaking down myths, and one of the myths was that the girl back home was going to wait for you, especially because we were all eighteen and nineteen years old. It wasn't the same as World War II.

———————•———————

JOSH CRUZE *joined the Marines at age seventeen with the somewhat unusual hope of thereby avoiding Vietnam. His war experiences sent him into a long bout with post-Vietnam syndrome before he became an actor and joined the cast of* Tracers.

I had a feeling that when I turned eighteen, I was going to be one of the first ones they called, so I said to myself, "Let me join one of the armed forces and get some type of an education and cut my chances down of having to go to the front." When I went to the recruiter, he had told me, "Yes, there is a good possibility that you can get some type of occupation. If things get busy, you could see some action."

My dad did not want me to go into the Marines. I fought him every inch of the way. I brought the recruiter up to the house to assure him everything was going to be alright. My mother got to the point where she just was fed up and said, "Sign the paper." So my dad said, "OK, I'm washing my hands in front of you like Pontius Pilate. If anything happens to him, I didn't want him to go." The morning that I was leaving, he wouldn't talk to me. He was eating his oatmeal, and I said, "Pop, I'm going." And I kissed him on the cheek and I left. I wrote letters. He was proud of me at graduation [from basic training]. He came down with the whole family but I could see that he was frightened.

It was a very big change. My first night in boot camp, I cried. I played the trumpet, so I auditioned for the Marine Corps Band, but they said the quota was all filled up. My MOS* when I graduated was 0331, which is a grunt. I figured, "Well, maybe things will change. They can't send me until I'm eighteen. I've still got six months." So they took me to Hawaii with a number of guys from that platoon. We stayed there and had maneuvers and jungle training from September to January.

And when they gave us the orders that we were going on a Pacific cruise, we thought, "This is going to be great." We get out on the middle of the Pacific, and this guy gets on the PA system and says, "This ship is now en route to Danang, Vietnam because of a crisis." This was when Tet took place and they needed reinforcements 'cause they had a lot of casualties. When we landed the unit went in and all the seventeen-year-olds stayed behind.

And then we were shipped to Okinawa, and as the birthdays came up, they woke us up and said, "OK, pal, Happy Birthday. You're leaving tomorrow." They put me on a commercial airliner to Danang. That was an experience in itself to get off that commercial plane and see all these guys screaming that they're going home. "Your turn." A jeep came to take me to my battalion area. We're driving, and it was strange, because I'd never been in a foreign country before, to see these people with the conical hats and the kids on water buffalos and rice paddies.

When you first arrive, you see them sitting around in that squatting position and talking, and you think, "What an odd way to just hang out, squatting like this." And you see the women with betel nut in their mouth, and their teeth are all black and you think, "Ooh, they don't take care of their teeth." Then you see the men holding hands, and you think, they're all faggots. But it's a custom. It just goes to show you that when you're coming from an environment like I was you think, they're wrong because they're doing things we're not accustomed to doing.

There was something very frightening about it. I might not come home from this adventure. But then there was the excitement of being with my buddies again because we'd spent five months in Hawaii together, we'd spent Christmas together, my first Christmas away from home, and New Years we partied on Waikiki.

When I got there, some of the guys were on patrol. I just saw a few old faces, and some new faces. They gave me some jungle gear and they put me up on one of those lookout posts with a starlight scope on my first night. I was shitting. I was seeing things that weren't

---

*Military Occupational Specialty—Pentagonese for a soldier's job category, designated by a number code. Cruze's MOS was infantryman—or in the parlance of the Vietnam years, "grunt."

even there. I was thinking, "If I shoot and there's nothing there, I'm going to be embarrassed." Something I thought was a person with one arm up turned out to be a tree stump. I said, "Boy, I'm glad I didn't make a jerk out of myself by shooting a tree stump." The next day they gave me my M-60 [machine gun] and I felt great. "Now, I'm one of the guys."

They flew us up to Phu Bai* in a C-130. They packed in about two or three platoons. A C-130 has a door that comes down at the back and everybody piles in, and then the door closes up. You could hear the propellers starting and all you could see was this mist inside the fuselage and it was like we're all going on this adventure. I'll never forget that feeling. I get flashbacks when I'm on the subway, the IRT.

A director I did a film for said to me, after World War II that generation of kids came up very secure in the way they were trained to think about things. Everything on TV was nice. The John Wayne flicks. We were invincible. So when we were taken into this to the war, everyone went in with the attitude, "Hey, we're going to wipe them out. Nothing's going to happen to us." Until they saw the realities and they couldn't deal with it. "This isn't supposed to happen. It isn't in the script. What's going on? This guy's really bleeding all over me, he's screaming his head off."

The first guy I saw hit, I was just shaking and chattering and trying to tell him everything was all right, and my hands were shaking. I was trying to put a bandage on this guy. I never knew there was so much blood in the human body, all sticky. How do you tell this guy who's screaming, "My leg is gone," "It's going to be all right." You're trying to keep it together yourself.

The whole John Wayne thing went out the window when I saw my first experience. After that it was day to day and hoping that if you did get hit it wasn't that serious. I was in a hospital nine months. And a guy's in bed, and then all of a sudden you see, no legs, or you try not to notice the [missing] arm but it bothers you. And you wonder, what's he going through? And for the guys who take it well, man, I want to cry because that takes character. Some guys couldn't deal with it. They're very bitter. Those guys that did, I don't know how they mustered up the courage. There's no way you can make it up to them.

Easter Sunday. Every Easter I remember we were in a very big firefight. We lost fifteen, sixteen men. That's also the first I had any encounters with Phantom jets. I volunteered to go to this schoolhouse with my M-60. And one of my friends says, "You're crazy.

---

*An airfield and base area just south of Hue.

You're out of your mind." I said, "Okay, I won't do it." And this jet comes around and starts firing fifty-caliber bullets. And he drops this canister, I swore it was going to fall on the schoolhouse. All I remember is seeing it whirling right over my head. Finally when it blew up it was like a dragon, with all this smoke going straight up for fifty or sixty yards. I said, "That's powerful. That's power." It was the first time I saw napalm.

One night we went out on an ambush. Full moon. We go into this rice paddy. We're being very quiet and I'm trying not to slip on the dikes. I'm sure they could see our silhouettes. We left the rice paddy and came to these mounds, and the corporal had a starlight scope, and he said, "Get down." So we all got down and he looked in the scope and he said he saw two or three figures. So he told the guy with the M-79 to shoot up a flare and catch them 'cause the first thing when light goes up, everybody freezes to see what's going on. He said, "When I shoot two or three rounds, everybody get to work." So everybody just opened up, That thing went off, and there was this pop, pop, pop-pop-pop. In that direction we saw these two silhouettes and they went down. We waited. Nothing.

Then we had to find these bodies. We went out there. We found one body. "I got one, I got one. He's really messed up bad." "Find the other guy." says the corporal. "We've got to find the other guy. I know I shot another one." We were all looking. And all of a sudden this black fellow says, "Here he is, here he is. I got him." This guy was begging for his life. I said to the corporal, "What do you want to do with him?" I said to myself, "We'll take him prisoner of war. We'll take him back and interrogate him." But the corporal said, "Waste him." The guy said, "What?" He says, "We're not taking any prisoners." So he put it on automatic and pumped twenty rounds into this guy and all I have in my mind is this body rattling.

So I said, "All right, just leave him there. We'll go back to where we were and we'll stay there and wait for the sun to come up and wait to see if anybody else comes behind him." So we waited there till dawn. The sun came up. No contact, no nothing. The corporal called up the base camp and asked the lieutenant, "What do you want us to do with these guys?" He says, "I want to confirm them." Only an officer could confirm kills. So he said, "All right, we'll bring them back." So he goes, "You and you, take them back." I said, "They're falling apart." He says, "I don't care. Just get them together and take them back." So I said, "Look at this guy." He was a mess. He was almost unhuman. So I put my poncho down and I asked my friend to help me. "Just roll him over. Be delicate, it looks as if his arms are going to come off." I had to hide his face. I couldn't look at his face 'cause he had bullet holes in his head.

I covered him up and started dragging this guy. All I can remember is I had my M-16 on a sling, and my helmet was hitting my M-16 and I'm dragging this guy. When we got back to the base camp, everybody was like, "Oh, wow! We got two guys!" They propped him up on the side of this stone wall and everybody was taking pictures. Of course, I had to get in on it too. Then we dumped the bodies into this ditch. That happens to be one of the most horrifying experiences I went through—spitting on it, kicking it, and throwing it into a ditch. I lived with that for the longest time.

And something inside of me said, "What we did is wrong. Somehow this guy's going to haunt me, all of us." So that afternoon, some guy from the village came on his bike. We raised our guns and said, "Where are you going?" He said, "No, no." He took his ID card out. Then he went over to the ditch and said, "VC, VC." He made a face as if to say, "You really got him good." Then he got back on his bike. That night, we got mortared—dead hits. About four in the morning, boom, ba-ba-ba-boom, boom, boom. The lieutenant lost his eye, it was nothing but a hole. The sergeant got hit, and some other guys. I said to myself, this guy must have paced it on his bike. He must have said, "That's one turn of the wheel, two turns of the wheel." All he's got to do is count the turns, see the mark he made on the ground, and he can tell how many feet it is to the base camp. And he said, "I'm going to get you son-of-a-bitches tonight."

Some of the southern boys were very trigger-happy. If they saw an old man, and he didn't stop when they said, "Dung lai," they'd blow him away. We went through search-and-destroy missions that I felt very guilty about. We used to go into these hamlets and go into their personal belongings and tear pictures of relatives down, turn furniture over, break their dishes and pots and pans, set fire to hootches. I thought, "This is so un-American. This is not what we're supposed to do. These are all people." Little kids were crying. My friend shot some woman that was innocent. You think, "This guy's going to get paid back," and he did. We were on a patrol and we got sniper fire from this treeline. We called in rockets from the Hueys. Who do you think got hit? I thought, "They're paying him back for blowing away that old lady."

I was hit. We had just come from Hue, and we went down to Danang to get involved in Operation Allenbrook. We were supposed to make contact with a large body of the enemy. Guys were just tripping mines all morning. We'd have to stop, get a chopper in, and medevac them. I was so pissed, 'cause they told us we were going to get a couple of days rest, have some beers, have showers, and they just put us out into the field again. I was carrying all this gear. I was a machine gunner. I was just so pissed I said, "If I get blown up, whatever happens, happens."

I was talking to another gunner, Vincent Stamato. We were kidding around so I said to him, "Why don't you take a hundred rounds from me, 'cause this heat is killing me, and I'm just getting tired of this bullshit." And he said, "No way. You want to be a machine gunner, that's what you've got to do." So I turned around and told him to fuck himself. Kidding around. Then I heard someone give a command to spread out, we were getting too close together. I took three steps to my right, and the next thing, this explosion.

My first thought was that I was dead 'cause I looked up into the sky and all I saw was this black smoke. As the smoke cleared, I saw the sky, I thought I was going up into the sky and I thought, "This is it." Then after the initial stun, I heard screaming, my ears were ringing and I felt dull pains where I was hit, and I felt a scratching sensation on the back of my flak jacket. My back was real hot. Then I realized what happened. I looked to my left and I saw my friend Vinnie, whom I'd just spoken to. He was in shreds. My immediate reaction was anger, that these guys wouldn't come out and fight us, that they had to use tactics like this, and they killed my friend in the process. I wanted to get up and take my machine gun and just run out to the field and start shooting. But I couldn't move. Then I relaxed a few minutes and looked at my arms. And there were big chunks of metal in my arms, my flesh was burning. I was cursing. A corpsman came over and said, "Relax, you're not too bad. I'm going to take a look at Vinnie." And then he came back and said, "He's gone."

Some other guy got wounded pretty badly and was taken to the hospital and died on the operating table. Another guy lost his ear. I just lay there. They hit me with morphine and I started to feel very nice. They threw us all onto this chopper and we took off. As we took off I saw this line of men, and I said to myself, "I'm finally leaving this hell." But even though I was leaving with a sense of relief, there was also the sense, "Gee, I'm leaving my buddies behind." There was a tug of war. Yes, I was happy I was going, but I wanted to be with them because we were so close.

When we landed in Danang, it reminded me of *M*A*S*H*, when they run towards the choppers and take all the wounded off. I can't watch the beginning. We were taken towards this building. You could see choppers coming in one after the other, and them running in, taking more wounded. Another would come right behind. It was a mess. They were all full of blood and torn apart.

I went right to x-ray and the operating room. Everything was clean and so different. Fifteen twenty minutes ago I was in the bush with all this shit going on. Now I'm in this secure area, and I'm going to an operating table. The guy gave me some anesthesia and left me there. I saw this clock on the wall—one of these big black clocks with the second hand that's red. It was 1:10 and all I could think of while I was going under was different things that people were doing all over the world at the same time—people making love, people starving, people getting blown away, people going out in New York.

Next day the sergeant came in and started putting Purple Hearts on everybody's bed, opening them up. He said, "The general's going to come and give you Purple Hearts." The hearts stayed there for a good four or five hours. I'm wondering, "When is this guy going to come?" Finally, the guy comes back and starts closing all the cases. I said, "What happened?" and he says, "The general couldn't make it. You'll get your Hearts some other time."

[A few days went by.] The guy next to me says, "Sarge, what is that tag on the end of my bunk?" The sergeant says, "Oh, that means you're going home." So I couldn't see if there was one on the end of my bed. And I said, "Sarge, do I have a card down there?" He pulled it up. He said, "Yes, you do. You're going home, too." And my eyes filled up. "My God, I can't believe I'm really going home. This is what I wished for the last three months." I'd developed a nice relationship with this Vietnamese—I guess it was an ARVN. He had lost his arm right from the shoulder. I used to play cards with him. He comes over and I said, "I'm going home! I'm going home!" And he says, "Ah, very good, very good" in broken English. He was happy for me. And I looked at this guy, and all of a sudden I said, "Where is this guy going to go?" And I started crying for him 'cause I said, "Shit, this guy's got to stay here. He's got no arm. I'm happy because I'm going someplace, and this guy's got to deal with this shit for God knows how much longer." And he was happy for me and I was sad for him. What an experience. Happy and sad at the same time.

From Danang, we went to Guam. One thing that happened to me in Guam was one of the corporals who got hit says to me, "Cruze, you know who tripped that mine?" It was as if he was inferring that I was careless. And the guilt of me being pissed off because we didn't get those two days off made me feel that maybe I killed my friend. I lived with that guilt for the longest time, that because I was only thinking of me that I did him in, wounded myself and another guy. I cried for this guy. I tried to call his family in South Philly. His mother and father, they broke up. Some guy told me they had problems when he died, they were fighting over the money they got from the government. I wanted to tell them, "I'm sorry. I might have killed your son. I didn't mean to kill your son." All the time what I really wanted to do was go down to Philly and have his mother say, "Look, it's Ok. If you did, I forgive you." The image of him smiling at me. Those four seconds, then I told him to fuck himself, like giving him the big send-off.

They didn't ever receive a telegram at home that I was wounded. It wasn't until I got a free call from the Red Cross that I spoke to my Uncle Jim. And it was five o'clock in the morning in New York. I said, "Hi, Uncle Jim. It's me, Josh." "Hi, how you doing? How's everything going?" I says, "All right. I'm just in the hospital, I've been wounded. I've got shrapnel in both my legs and both my arms. But it looks like I'm going to pull through. Didn't you receive a telegram that I'd been wounded?" and he said, "No." I said, "Well, just break it lightly to my dad. Let him know that I'm all right, that I'm in a hospital in Guam." Well, the shit hit the fan because my uncle went upstairs. My dad was getting ready to go to work. This was all told to me by my mother. She was in the kitchen making coffee and she heard the footsteps 'cause they lived on the third floor, and she thought, "Jesus, who's coming up the stairs so early?" And my dad was in the bathroom and there was a knock on the door, and it was my uncle. And she says, "Jim, what are you doing here so early?" And he says, "Is Peter around?" My father heard that I was wounded, and he closed the door and started crying. Jim says, "It's all right."

My parents wanted to fly to Guam. But the Marine Corps said, "Look, he's going to be coming home in a week's time. It doesn't make any sense for you to go out there. You can see him in St. Albans hospital." It was just hard to see my father react like that because we had such a hard relationship, And he came and all he said was, "See, I told you not to go, I told you not to go." And he was hugging me and kissing me. And he said, "I didn't want this for you." And I said, "It's all right, I'm fine. Look at these other guys." There was one guy who had his whole forearm blown off. He had his arm sewn to his stomach so the skin would grow onto it and they could do a skin graft. I said, "I'm not as bad as that guy. I'll be out of here soon." Our whole relationship changed.

———————◆———————

CHARLES LITEKY, a Catholic U.S. Army chaplain, won the Congressional Medal of Honor during his first encounter with serious combat in Vietnam. A longtime supporter of the war, he grew gradually to question and finally to hate it. Eventually, he left the priesthood, married, and became a militant antiwar activist. He came to Wash-

ington in 1986 to campaign against U.S. involvement in Central America. By autumn he was so angry with the government's course in Nicaragua that he had turned in his Medal of Honor by depositing it at "The Wall"—the Vietnam Memorial—and, in company with three other veterans, begun a hunger strike on the steps of the Capitol.

I served grunts. I was a Catholic chaplain, and I was about thirty-five when I went. My father was a thirty-two-year Navy chief petty officer, so I was raised in the service and lived on the East Coast and the West Coast and spent five years in Hawaii. Service came easy for me and a sort of an inbred anti-Communist attitude was part of my culture. I was very much against that kind of total control over people's lives—what they would choose to do and what they would choose to read and the terrible kind of confinement that Soviet Russia, from all that I read, would levy upon their people.

When the Korean War came along and I was thinking about going into the seminary, that was very much on my mind. I actually started the seminary in 1951, so those years from '50 to '60, I was almost in a cocoon. I went to a place called Holy Trinity, in Alabama. We were very isolated. It was out in the country, and we didn't even read newspapers or magazines. It was with a little order called the Missionary Servants of the Most Holy Trinity, sometimes called the Trinitarians.

I was ordained in 1960, and sent to New Jersey to do retreat work. Later I went down to Virginia and did three years of mission work in a parish of about twenty-five square miles with three of us to cover six mission churches. I was getting a little bit dissatisfied with my life as a religious, and I thought maybe I'd go into a different kind of priesthood for a while. I asked my superior about that and he said, "Well, have you ever thought of going into the service?"

This was about 1965 or '66. The Vietnam War was building up and there wasn't a whole lot of resistance to it. The military ordinarian at that time was Cardinal Spellman, who was a friend of Diem's and very much in favor of what we were doing there. Vietnam had started to come into my consciousness about 1964 or '65, just from reading about it in the paper and hearing that they were very short on chaplains in the Army. In fact, Cardinal Spellman made a plea to all religious orders to send a few men into the Army. And since I wanted to make a change anyway this was an out for my Superior.

So in 1966 I went to the chaplain school and then to Fort Benning, Georgia. And after about six months I volunteered for Vietnam and was assigned to the 199th Light Infantry Brigade, which had been formed up in Benning and preceded me there by about six months.

My first impression of Vietnam was this was like stepping off onto another planet. I was given a tent with wooden pallets as floorboards and a cot and a field telephone and that was it. I came in during the dry season so it was very dusty, and I can remember watching these old ladies that looked to be in their sixties or seventies move rocks and bricks around to make way for more permanent buildings. And they were bent over, carrying tremendous loads on poles balanced on their shoulders. I just couldn't fathom that. I thought of American women and our great concern for fashion and all that, and how physical labor was not a part of our culture, and here these ladies were carrying tremendous burdens.

The brigade had four battalions and I was assigned to the Fourth of the Twelfth. The commanders did not object at all to the chaplains going out on missions—in fact, they thought it was good for morale. But the 199th's mission at that time was light pacification work around Saigon and Bien Hoa. The biggest danger was booby traps. Very seldom did we actually see the Vietcong, and the NVA* were a long way from us. It was sort of a breeze, just going out and taking hikes through the paddies. I don't think we ever felt great danger until the end of 1967, when we began to hear about the big offensive that was to come up in '68, and which turned out to be Tet.

One day in December of 1967, my battalion suddenly was air-cavved† about twenty miles northeast of Bien Hoa, an area we had never been before, and it was pretty heavily wooded. The intelligence said the NVA was in there. We moved a little over five hundred men into the area, set up a base camp, and built bunkers all in one day. Well, that night they threw in about ten mortars on us. We'd never been mortared before. There was a certain amount of excitement, and fortunately nobody got hit.

In the morning the colonel sent this captain to go check out the site of that mortar. So he takes a platoon and I went along. Okay, so about fifteen men in front of me and fifteen men behind me, we go off into the woods following the [compass] azimuth from which the mortars had come. Well, we got about maybe three quarters of a mile out and we found a path going up a hill and three, what looked like VC, darted across in front of us. The point man and the dog handler took off after them.

The captain and everybody comes up there, and initially they lie down. Then he took half the platoon to go into the woodline after these guys, and he had them stand up and start walking. They got about ten yards into the woodline when they went on automatic and

---

*North Vietnamese Army.

†A term derived from air cavalry, or heliborne assault troops.

started firing. That was supposed to establish fire superiority. They got about five more yards and just all hell broke loose, explosions, rattatattat, machine guns. I was back with the reserve squad and I started hearing these cries "Medic," and, "I'm hurt." I went over to the captain and said, "Well, what can I do? What do you want?"

He wasn't even paying attention to me. He was on the radio back to the base telling them he needed some help—gunships or whatever. I could see he was busy so I just went on into the woodline and began to see all these young soldiers who had been hit. The medic had had his leg blown off so he couldn't do anything. So I just started going around checking. The first guy I came to, Penny, a little red-headed boy from Iowa or someplace, had a big hole in his back. He was breathing, and I didn't really know what to do so I just took him in my arms and held him. I could see the light was leaving him. I gave him the last rites finally, when he stopped breathing, and then started moving on. And it was just a series of this going from one to the other.

I remember crawling up to this one fellow and he was just face down and his weapon was right there. And after anointing him, I reached over and picked up the weapon, because I didn't ordinarily carry a weapon and I looked out in front of me. I was laying down, and I couldn't see anything, it was very thick in there and I just put the weapon aside and said to myself "This would be a hell of a way to go: 'Priest Tries To Shoot Cong.' "

Four or five of the other guys had found a ditch and I went and talked to them for a while. And about that time, a machine gun started firing again. At first I thought it was warning fire to tell us to stay away from them, but then I saw two guys fly up in the air. They came down and they were still alive and they were hollering for help so I crawled up there. And I looked over and there was a round Chinese Claymore* about fifteen yards away. It was round, maybe ten inches in diameter, and I could see it sitting there on a tripod. So I just grabbed one of the fellows and started getting him out of there—put him on top of me and started using my elbows and my feet and got him back to a clearing where they had called in the medevacs.

So the captain then tried another assault and the same thing happened.

You mean after he'd gotten ambushed the first time, he walked back into a second ambush?

He tried to go in with another group and we got hit again. By that

---

*An antipersonnel mine loaded with thousands of steel pellets like a giant shotgun shell.

time help was on the way. The APCs* started coming in with their fifty calibers and gunships started coming over and two companies were airlifted in, one on one side of the NVA, one on the other. What we had run into was a base and we didn't know it.

Anyway, they seemed to be willing to settle down for a battle. It went on until nightfall—four and a half, five hours, and we lost eighty men wounded and twenty-five dead. And while this was happening I didn't have anything else to do but to anoint the dying and get them out of there. I got slightly wounded in the foot, but it wasn't anything serious, so I stayed that night with the group. We formed a circle in that clearing and they kept pounding the NVA all night long.

The next morning we went in there and found that it had been a battalion-sized base camp. We had walked into the side and up close, maybe five or six feet away, you could see firing ports, a foot or so off the ground. It was a very neatly constructed series of bunkers and trenches, zigzags, heavily fortified. Even after a lot of pounding most of those bunkers were intact, and they were very well camouflaged and beautifully constructed. And we found two of our people that had been caught and hung up and really mutilated, cut and stabbed.

Did the troops feel like there was something wrong with the captain who led them into that place?

No, I don't think so. It was their first encounter with the NVA and so, I don't know that the captain really knew what was in there. It didn't make a lot of sense to me to see anybody going in against fortified positions standing up, but of course he didn't know that at first. When those guys continued to do that afterwards, I said, "God, that's crazy." I mean I'm not a tactician but I just couldn't understand that. The following week I was with another company and another captain and we got into the same thing only this time we had a whole company.

We were walking along a path a couple miles west of there, and I think the enemy actually began to fire on us before we broadsided them, this time a regimental-sized base. It was a good, well worn path and we could see commo wire going up the trail, and I didn't think it was too smart to walk on that path, but he put out some flankers maybe five or ten yards out on each side going through the jungle. When we got close enough they opened up and got the point men. This time the captain was a West Pointer, and as soon as we started receiving fire, he got his people down and then we waited

*Armored personnel carriers—tanklike vehicles armed with machine guns, mainly used for moving troops on a battlefield.

for the artillery and the gunships to soften them up, and find out what the helicopters could see from above.

So this went on for about an hour. There we are laying on the path and beside the path and our artillery's coming in, and the shrapnel is falling all around us. None of us got hit but it was raining pieces of metal and you'd hear it falling around you. I was thinking "Well, thank God we're not in *there*." And I'll never forget this top sergeant who had been in Korea, said, "Well, boys, just relax now because when this is over we're going to be going in there, and" he says, "all hell's going to break loose." And I said, to myself, "It sure is."

And so we did. This captain had his men stand up and he had his lieutenants up there, and they got on line and started going in and, boy, sure enough, the same old thing. I was really frightened because I knew what was going to happen, but I couldn't say anything. On that first wave he got about five people killed and then he stopped and pulled them all back. He realized that despite the softening up they were still dug in. So, to his credit, we pulled back maybe two hundred yards to a cleared area. He left a few people in there just to, I suppose, confuse them so that they wouldn't think we were retreating, and they kept firing from safe positions.

He radioed for help, but this happened about two or three o'clock in the afternoon, and by the time we finally got all the dead and wounded back it was dusk. They didn't like to do night evacuations, but they kept pounding that place with artillery and at dark they brought helicopters in to evacuate us. And as we were piling into them I heard machine guns and I thought, "God, this is it." But they were actually on the helicopters shooting protective fire into the woodline. They pounded that place all night and they called in a B-52 strike the next day.

It was two weeks before we went back in, and when we did it was just sort of like the moon—huge, huge craters, maybe a hundred and fifty feet across, one after the other. And all the foliage was gone. There was just nothing there. It looked like you were walking on the moon. We began to get a lot of contact then because it was one of the big staging areas for Tet, so the NVA was there in force. And like I said, we were just a light infantry brigade. We weren't supposed to be fighting people like this.

Well, I had decided to extend and take a second tour. If you extended, they would give you a thirty day R&R, so I went home right after Christmas and missed the Tet offensive. I was somewhat of a hero as a chaplain because they had recommended me for the Congressional Medal of Honor by that time, and I was going around speaking. I gave one speech in Jacksonville, Florida, and I was explaining the situation in Vietnam, and I said I couldn't understand why we weren't using all our vast military power to wipe those guys out and get the job done. That's how much of a hawk I was.

My experience was that in my brigade we were very limited in the use of our power. I mean you could call in a B-52 strike, but there were many areas you couldn't touch. In order to establish a free-fire zone, this was a long procedure. You had to go to a village and check out the people, the leaders, let them know nothing was to move in this area, and so on. And all of that took time and I felt we were very restricted. I was thinking like a military person. My position was "Listen, war is hell and we can't talk about gentle ways of killing people." There was a group back in the states, Clergy and Laity Concerned, talking about the immorality of the M-16, and I said, "What the hell are you talking about? Are there humane ways of killing people?"

And in this speech I said, "Why aren't we fighting this war at its source? Why don't we go up and bomb the harbor? Why don't we bomb the dikes?" At that time the president was contemplating whether to bomb or not to bomb North Vietnam. And the Jacksonville paper came out with an article that said "Liteky disagrees with the President about the use of U.S. power." And the next thing I know I get a letter, and I'll never forget it, which said, "Well, Father Liteky, I think you've taken the church militant just a little bit too far." I was so angry I just tore the thing up and I said, "This guy doesn't understand what we're up against."

———•———

Rail thin, confined to a wheelchair by a bullet through the spine, but so full of energy that it's sometimes difficult to keep pace with him as he shuttles himself around his office, BOBBY MULLER *is consumed by passion about the war and the injustices done to those who fought it. The founder and president of Vietnam Veterans of America is so persuasive a spokesman for his cause that in the spring of 1986 he managed to convince Sen. Jeremiah Denton, (R-Ala.),* a former POW, not merely to withdraw his objections to, but to actively endorse a congressional charter for his organization.*

Back in late '66, early '67, everybody was very rah, rah, Vietnam. I was in business school at Hofstra, and in the last part of my junior year I was doing very well, dean's list, management as a specialty, and my professors said many times, "You better have military expe-

---

*Denton was defeated in 1986, in a bid for a second term.

rience on your resume, or people will think you're a queer or you shirked your obligation. And by the way, it's an inside track: there's a fraternity on Wall Street that welcomes leadership. If you were an officer and had combat experience, that's a real ticket. It's a good punch." And maybe more important, it was obviously very significant as a generational experience and I felt uneasy over not being involved.

So it was clear I was going to do it. Then the question became did you want to risk winding up under some nincompoop who gets you killed, or did you want to be the one to call the shots? So instead of letting myself be drafted, I thought, "I'm going to enlist." And one day on campus they had a Marine recruiter at the Student Center. And, no bullshit, the guy was a classic—six feet two, built like a stud, dress blue uniform, sharp as a tack. And I said, "Dammit, if I'm going to do it, why not do it all the way?" I had a fiancé, who I went home to and said, "I want to join the Marines." She said, "Join the Marines and I'll never see you again." Next day I joined the Marines. We stayed together, but the fracture in our lives because of the war, ultimately, years later, wound up still being the breach that we never healed from.

That's pretty tough.

Yeah, I was kind of determined. I went in saying, "Yeah, I want to be a Marine." I was honor man in my training session. I demanded infantry and I demanded Vietnam. Out of fifty officer candidates in my platoon, six or seven of us chose infantry. We ran all the tactical problems, learned how to issue orders, how to read a map, how to call in supporting arms, everything. The rest of the guys in the class used to laugh at us: "You're infantry. You're going to die." But every single lieutenant went to Vietnam and had to take over a rifle platoon for at least three months in the bush. And the pucker factor for these guys who were laughing and didn't bother to pay attention was extraordinary 'cause they didn't know the first fucking thing about what was going down. I was good, but even *I* felt totally unprepared for the reality of Vietnam.

I got out there in the fall of '68, right after Khe Sanh. I landed in Danang, was there for maybe thirty or forty minutes, and caught a flight up to Phu Bai. It was absurd from day one. I had orders to join Second Battalion, Third Marines somewhere up in Northern I Corps. Somebody said take a flight to Phu Bai. When I got there they said the unit is up by Dong Ha or Quang Tri. So I said "Fine, how do I get there?" They said "Well, catch a truck convoy going up the road, whatever." I wound up working my own way up to my unit.

When I got up there, I met this black guy, Sergeant Ernie Edwards, seventeen years in the Corps, previous tour of Vietnam, good guy.

He had come out of the field to go to the dentist. And I knew he was going to be my platoon sergeant. That evening we did a little drinking. It was a great night because he said, "With all due respect, I hate second lieutenants." I said, "I can't disagree with you, Sergeant." We talked and I said, "Look, you know more than I do about fighting this war. So when we're out there together, I'll want you to be giving me some advice and telling me what to do." And he said, "No sir. You're the lieutenant, you make the decisions. You determine what you want done, you tell me and I'll get the men to do it. If you don't like something, you tell me and I'll straighten it out. If you make a mistake I'll come up and suggest you may want to consider doing it some other way. But you're in charge. That's what you're paid for, that's what the men expect." And I have to say, that probably is the best thing that happened during my entire tour, him telling me, "Whether you know what you're doing or not, those eyeballs are going to be looking your way, so make the decision."

The next day, I went to get a chopper out to the unit. A guy comes out and says, "Take your pack off, Lieutenant." "What's the problem?" "Your unit's in contact." So I waited a while. Finally he said, "We'll try and get you in." I got on the chopper and I remember, we circled the mountaintops and I kept looking for a landing zone, but there was nothing there at all. Where it was, I don't know exactly, but out in the mountains south of Khe Sanh, toward the A Shau valley. And it was just fucking crazy when I got there.

Welcome to Vietnam, right? The tail end of the chopper touches down on the mountain. Front end of the chopper is hovering. I didn't know it, but we'd landed in the battalion CP,* where they had the eighty-one-millimeter mortars. We start coming out of the chopper and they pop some mortar rounds off, I guess for suppressing fire. We had no idea what the fuck was coming down. All I know is that a guy jumped over me, we go tumbling down the mountain and he ripped his asshole on a root. Before the chopper left, he was back on as a medevac. I'm fucking holding my head down. A guy comes over, taps me on the shoulder, "Hey, Lieutenant, it's okay. They're our mortars."

I get up and hi-diddle-diddle we start walking down the trail. I see some bodies alongside the trail. First time in my life I ever saw a dead body. Said, "A-ho." Hook up with my platoon. My guys had, I think three killed and eight wounded. We had to get medevac ships in to lift them out.

Before the medevacs come in, we called in supporting arms. In train-

*Command post.

ing they give you the "Mad Minute," which is very impressive but doesn't hold a candle to the real thing, when you walk in your artillery and call in your jet strikes just beyond your perimeter. It was awesome. Awesome. And I got so pumped, I said, "Ain't nobody going to fuck with us. Not when we can do what we've just done to those poor sons of bitches."

So in come the medevacs, throw in the dead and the wounded, the chopper lifts off, maybe fifty meters off the deck. And all around us all of a sudden Prrow! Prrow! Prrow! Fucking chopper starts to wobble. Boom! It goes down in the valley. Everybody on board is killed. I said, "Holy shit. Batten down the hatches." That was my first afternoon. I said, "All right. A little reality therapy right off the bat. I am your new lieutenant, guys!"

Next day I take out a patrol. Guys leaving the perimeter cross themselves. Each one looked at me and right off the bat, I understood that it wasn't a game. Lots of fear and very, very intense. And it was my introduction to the absurdity of it all because we were out in no-man's land, and they didn't have the helicopters to lift us out, so a couple of days later they had us walk out. We had to go down to the valley and walk along the river bed. There were supposed to be NVA regiments in the area. For three or four days from sunrise to sunset we walked, sometimes along the bank, sometimes in water up to your waist, with the banks coming in vertical drops right to the river. I kept saying to myself if there *was* an NVA regiment in the area, forget it, we're dead. They could have set up an ambush any one of countless places. All I remember thinking from the get go was the absolute stupidity of this entire fucking war. I waited three days from sunrise 'till sunset to get blown away.

But that was the Marine Corps, and I got to tell you something. I'm not passive. I'm not indifferent. I hate the Marine Corps. It is a stupid branch of the service. It should be eliminated. We were less than one twelfth of the troops in Vietnam and we were more than a third of the casualties. I'll never forget one of the last classes at basic school, they brought us out to a fortified bunker and they said, "Remember if you ever see one of these, you can always send some guys around back with grenades. You don't have to hit it head on." Why? Because they had a lieutenant that had recently graduated, who had his Marines assault a fortified bunker head on, because their basic mentality is "Charge!"

In November I was up at Alpha Four. The edge of the base was literally the southern boundary of the DMZ, and we'd sit on top of the bunkers, watching truck convoys come down the other side of the DMZ, headlights on, all night. I'd say, "Hey guys, right there is where the bad guys are." And there was this humongous NVA garrison flag that we used to see flying right across the DMZ, and I used to take patrols in there. And every time we got a little bit too close to that flag, they'd pop a couple of mortar rounds and back us up.

There was supposed to be neutrality in the DMZ, but one day they wanted to send some recon teams in there to capture some North Vietnamese soldiers. We were briefed that they want to ship them to Paris and bring them out at Peace Talks and say "Look we captured this guy and you're violating the neutrality of the DMZ." I had a reinforced platoon and I was the reaction element. If the recon teams got into shit I was supposed to get them out. And since this was a top-priority mission, I had all the guns in Northern I Corps in support, had the battleship *New Jersey,* and they said to me, "You got carte blanche, kiddo, anything you want."

Well, the recon team had eight guys in it and three guys were hurt, and we went in to help them. But these fucking idiots said they wanted the original team to stay and they wanted the reaction element which was me and my guys to come out. I had spent the afternoon blowing up the DMZ so bad that they knew in Hanoi Muller had landed. And this kid corporal says, "If they take you out, we're dead." I said, "I can't argue with you." And to his credit, this corporal got on the hook and told the colonel, open mike, "I ain't John Wayne. I'm getting the fuck out of here," and he threw the headset down. The colonel gets on with me and says, "I expect you to have that man stay there." I said, "Sorry, if he's not going to listen to you, he sure isn't going to listen to me and I ain't about to shoot him so I think you better expect he's coming out with us."

Tell me about getting dinged.

I went to Vietnam with six other lieutenants, and I lasted the longest, eight months, which is considered good. The irony is, the afternoon I get dinged, this Army lieutenant comes up to me and says, "You Lieutenant Muller?" I said, "Yeah." He said, "They're going nuts. They want you in the rear ASAP. You're supposed to take the next chopper out of here." I said, "I'll be right with you. I just got to finish something up."

That afternoon I had something like five hundred ARVN and ten US Marine tanks. It was a combined operation and it was a rock 'em sock 'em day, just a little bit south of Con Thien, a heavy-duty afternoon. We had I swear to God, it wasn't more than fifteen or sixteen NVA dug in on a hilltop. We had a unit up north and we were trying to close them in. And before we even started to take the hill, we had four jets drop their payload right on top of them. We had over an hour of heavy artillery, 155-millimeter guns, pounding it. Of the ten tanks, eight of them were gun tanks and two of them were flame tanks. I had one of the flame tanks burn the hill. The eight gun tanks expended half their ammunition.

And at the end of all that a tank came in on the radio and said, "You know, we still can see these guys popping their heads up out of holes. They're bleeding from the nose and the ears from the concussion but goddammit, you still got to dig them out of their holes," which means you got to go in toe to toe. And in the middle of that I got dinged.

Getting dinged was like being inside a bell—a big gigantic bell, bong! you know, brrrr! or like the windshield of a car just shattering into a thousand pieces. I caught a bullet through the chest. It went through both lungs, severed the spinal cord. Your spinal cord has all those nerves, right? Boom, when something goes through that sucker, that rings a bell, and it was just stunning. I felt like I was in a kaleidoscope and everything was fragmented and multicolored and boom. I'll never forget the sequence of thoughts: "Oh shit I've been hit. I got it right in the gut. My girl, she's going to kill me." Then I said, "I don't got to worry about that, I'm going to die."

Then I was just on the ground looking up at the sky and I just felt a warm glow, very mellow, and I felt like a balloon that was deflating. I just felt, blubbbbbb, I was going down. Nothing I could do about it at all. "Okay," I said, "I don't got to worry about it, I'm going to die." And my last words were, "I don't believe it. On this shitty piece of ground, I'm going to die. I don't fucking believe it."

Well, we already had medevac ships coming in and I got literally instant evacuation to Quang Tri, and from there right to the hospital ship *Repose,* off the coast. And they put in the medical records that had I arrived one minute later, I'd have been dead, because both lungs had collapsed. All I know is that I woke up with tubes everywhere. But I was stunned, amazed, overwhelmed and ecstatic over the fact that I woke up at all.

The doctors came and said, "You're probably going to be paralyzed for the rest of your life." My reaction to that was, "So what?" I can say to you honestly that I've never been depressed, remorseful, whatever over being paralyzed. While I was in the VA hospital a psychologist was hammering away at me, saying, "You know what your problem is? That you've never grieved over the loss of the use of almost three-quarters of your body. You've got to go into a corner and cry." And I said to her, "You don't understand. You look at me in terms of what I've lost." But to me to be given a second chance was a miracle. I couldn't believe I didn't die. I said to the doc, "That's okay, I'm here."

MAJ. GEN. GEORGE S. PATTON III *is the son and namesake of "Old Blood and Guts" of World War II fame. The younger Patton fought in both Korea and Vietnam, where he served three tours between 1962 and 1969. His last assignment there was as commander of the 11th Armored Cavalry Regiment, which his father had led during its horse cavalry days. Retired from the service, Patton raises produce, blueberries, and cattle on a piece of land he inherited from his family in Hamilton, Massachusetts.*

I've got to say the soldiers in Vietnam that I was associated with in my three tours, who were pretty much front-line troops, were the best I'd ever seen on any battlefield. The soldiers were up against incredibly difficult rules of engagement.

I'll tell you a story. It's a real good story. We had some villages to run civic action and medical help in. My engineer company built a school. We were in the village of Binh My, and we got some lumber to rebuild a schoolhouse. We were about two thirds of the way completed. We had a teacher hired who was a cripple. My engineer company was bringing in supplies in an armored personnel carrier along the little road up to the schoolhouse and they hit a mine. Luckily nobody was seriously injured. Well, the engineers went out there and fixed the armored personnel carrier, and then continued right on building the school. I went up to them and said, "You all are pretty complacent about this." And they said, "Sir, that's our job." That shows the nature of the men in Vietnam. They did their job. There's no way of telling who laid that mine, but it was someone who didn't want us to build the school. They knew we used that little trail. But we just went right on.

The trouble is the goal was never clear. It changed under the Johnson administration from time to time. Our overall goal was pacification, but it didn't work because of lack of strategic direction from the United States. I want to make sure you understand this. The national leadership, the President, did not bring the country into the total scene of the war. There was a lack of unification of the American people. A manifestation of that lack was the failure to mobilize the National Guard and Reserves. In my opinion, one of the great criticisms that will be placed against the leadership will be that failure to mobilize. The point is, when you mobilize the Guard and the Reserves, you also act toward mobilizing the people, because some guy gets called out of a drug store and called to active duty, so the burden is not just placed on the career services, who were stretched to the breaking point.

Do you see what I'm getting at? You can do all kinds of things to this testimony and make me look like a goddamn nut. But I'm talking about strategic direction plus violation of the fundamental principles of war—of which there are nine. Those were violated, not all of them, but most of them. We could have won by more correct adherence to those principles, such as the principle of objective, the principle of unity of command, the principle of surprise and security, all of which were violated. The United States can never afford again to allow itself to be at such a vast strategic disadvantage as we were in Vietnam. I sincerely hope we've learned. We were defeated by an eighth-rate power.

You've been described as "utterly fearless."

Who me? Who the hell said that? Everybody's afraid, but to do your job you have to put your fear down. If you're not afraid in combat, you're either a fool or a liar. I'd go back to the Army tonight if I could. I loved the people, the life, the fellowship, the travel. There was nothing about it I didn't like, except my tour in the Pentagon. I liked my tours in Vietnam because I felt I served my country in the way I had been trained to do. Let's put it this way, a violinist who doesn't have a violin is going to be a lousy violinist. A soldier who does not participate in his country's wars is not a very good soldier.

I didn't realize we were going to lose until I was well at home. You've got to understand that I came home in '69. But in May '75 I sat in front of the television set and watched all that fighting along the Saigon Bridge and the final death throes of the South Vietnamese, and the pictures of them throwing the helicopters off the carrier, and I bawled. I cried.

———————◆———————

MAJ. GEN. ROBERT MOLINELLI *served two tours in Vietnam, the second of them during the 1971 invasion of Laos by South Vietnam with American assistance. A much decorated helicopter commander, his mission was to destroy North Vietnamese units along the Laotian border—without leaving South Vietnam. He was commanding general of the U.S. First Army in Europe for a time and now directs Army research on combat support systems.*

I would give my eyeteeth to go back. I would love to meet the commanders of certain regiments on the other side. I have the names of some of them. I would like to see, without being shot at, some of the places I had been. I would love to go back and talk to the people who were there, North and South Vietnamese. I'd go back if it were combat—go back in a flash.

I didn't find combat difficult at all. It was a very intense activity, something that I could do and do as well as or better than most people. I must admit after both tours I found normal conventional life a little dull. I would read and listen to and do everything to find out what was going on from whence I came. I have to admit I missed it.

During '71 my mission, in a normal sense, was to find an enemy unit and pin it down if I couldn't kill it myself. If it was larger than I was, then the division would jump on it. That was the cavalry concept. We always had a company on thirty-minute alert. You were supposed to get a battalion and an artillery battery to help.

One day I did need some help. I called the division for assistance. Nothing happened. Finally the division said "You'll have to get yourself out." It took till three in the morning. We had twenty-four aircraft shot up that night. I went and saw the division commander, and we had some words. This was the whole turnaround for me in the war. The bottom line was that he couldn't afford to commit infantry at that time. They were being pinged on casualties. That kind of changed our way of doing business. I began to realize that we were having a hard time and probably weren't going to make it.

I took a lot of things in a personal sense. We took a lot of losses. We lost sixty-three or sixty-five out of a hundred and eighteen aircraft. We recovered most of them but probably twenty or thirty percent went down that we didn't recover. Some of them are MIAs. That's always bothered me. I can remember one day, one of the Cobras* in front of me was hit. It went straight into the side of a mountain in the middle of an NVA unit. I just declined to go on the ground trying to find those bodies. It would cost me more killed. These things come back and I think about them a lot.

The one experience that stands out more than anything else in my last tour is this Lam Son 719 operation—the invasion of Laos. It's probably the most key thing I did in either tour. The Army today is still benefiting from the lessons we learned. This operation was the first time a helicopter had killed a tank. It was a real turn for Army Aviation when they found they could kill tanks.

Some things bothered me a lot. I had indications of Soviet helicopters and some fixed wings. They sent a team up from Saigon to tell me I was crazy. One night I chased one of these things about forty miles into Laos trying to get permission to shoot him down. I couldn't ever get permission. I said to myself, "What are we afraid of? Why not admit the thing is there and go after it?"

---

*A helicopter gunship.

CLARK CLIFFORD

We didn't operate well in Vietnam. We weren't prepared for what we found there. We had no expertise in jungle warfare. Well, who did? The French were colonials for centuries and they didn't do any better. By Dien Bien Phu they'd had it. And our military boldly moved in there with our enormous firepower. We were going to prevail, and it wasn't going to take us forever. We could bomb them from the air. We could block their ships from getting into their harbors. We had a ten- or fifteen-to-one firepower advantage and it wasn't going to be much of a struggle. But it was the first time we had ever fought that kind of war, and it wasn't what we thought it was going to be at all.

Once we conducted a great sweep through the A Shau valley. Fifty thousand picked troops, wonderfully prepared and all. It was looked upon as possibly the seminal event of the war—it would break the back of the opposition. It took ten or fifteen days to move through there, and I'm not sure we killed even two hundred of the enemy. They just weren't there. They knew all about the planning, the day we were going to start and all that. It was a sieve over there.

One time I heard a general coming back from an aggressive campaign say, "Goddammit, they won't come out and fight." And I thought at that moment that some British general during the Revolutionary War, when the American squirrel rifles were knocking the red stripes off the chests of those Hessians from behind the rocks and trees, must also have said when he got to his tent at the end of a day, "Goddamn 'em, they won't come out and fight." There was a lot of that in Vietnam and we were not prepared for it. The things we tried, all of which should have had a great impact, didn't work.

CHAPTER THREE

The Politics of War

IN the early years, when Vietnam was merely a small brushfire in a faraway place, hardly anyone in Washington paid it much attention. Recognizing that it would be hard to find political support for a major conflict, the Kennedy and Johnson administrations pretended from 1961 until well into 1965 that it was a problem well in hand. Soothing statements emanated from officials: the country's internal politics had stabilized; the Vietnamese Army was getting better. American boys, asserted Robert McNamara in the autumn of 1964, would begin coming home by Christmas. And these statements were, in the main, taken at face value by the people and their elected representatives. Nowhere was it acknowledged that the country was plunging into an open-ended combat that would cost tens of thousands of casualties and tens of billions of dollars.

Only when the size of the effort became too large to ignore, when the bodies began to come home in quantity, when the dates of predicted success passed, one after another, without perceptible progress on the battlefield, did it begin to dawn on Americans that their government might not be telling them the truth. Then came into the language phrases like "credibility gap," which expressed the thought that officials were telling falsehoods, though without impugning their honor by actually calling them liars. But it was not until well into the war—really, until mid-1967—that the gulf between the official line and the obvious facts began to generate enough political unrest to interfere with the government's ability to manage the conflict. The result of the prevarication was a rise of domestic unrest, the Eugene McCarthy challenge for the Democratic nomination, and two months after the Tet offensive of 1968, the political demise of LBJ.

But there was in addition an invisible and far more insidious effect of this propensity for untruth. As the comments of Alexander Haig,

Bruce Palmer, Morton Halperin, and others show all too clearly, for reasons of bureaucratic politics, the U.S. government lied not just to the public, but to itself. In the name of preserving an appearance of military unity and of supporting the political direction of the war, the Joint Chiefs of Staff under General Earle G. Wheeler deliberately watered down what should have been a warning to the President in 1965 that he was embarking on a perilous course. As the war progressed, again in the name of interservice unity, the Army suppressed its critical views on the use of air power. And later yet, Johnson, McNamara, and others imposed a conspiracy of silence on lesser officials, because they did not want to be offered unpleasant advice that would have been difficult to ignore.

To be sure, lying about wars is nothing new. War is an act of politics, and the mass warfare of the industrial age touches so many lives and reaches so deeply into so many pocketbooks that it cannot be sustained without a popular political base. At least since World War I, when Great Britain elevated "propaganda" to the level of public policy, governments in time of conflict have made it a practice, as Churchill once said, to protect the truth with "a bodyguard of lies" so as to sustain their political support. We have got used to the practice. This is an era in which the U.S. government feels free to distribute calculated "disinformation," to deny its obvious connections with clumsy privateers in Central America, and to send out "spin masters" to try to make the public believe that a failed summit was in fact a grand success.

But whatever the government may say in public, its practice of lying to itself is truly frightful. If truth cannot be spoken even within the sanctums of the policymakers, there can be no rational basis on which to proceed in war *or* in peace. That is the hallmark of a system in train to fail.

———————•———————

J. WILLIAM FULBRIGHT

It's hard to remember the earliest stages. I didn't pay that much attention to it. I was put on Foreign Relations as a junior member, but I unexpectedly became chairman of the Banking and Currency Committee, which took up most of my time and attention aside from Arkansas. When you're chairman, you know, you have to go to all the meetings. Nobody else comes to many of them.

See, what you forget about senators is you've primarily got to look after the water systems and the agriculture of your state. Being on Foreign Relations is a very unprofitable political activity. I became

chairman very unexpectedly because of defeats and deaths, and politically that was a great burden for me because in Arkansas they didn't
appreciate your interest in foreign relations.

Anyway, we were mostly concerned about Europe. Vietnam was a
minor sideshow way off there where none of us knew anything about
it. Nobody on the committee except Mike Mansfield had ever been
in that area. I had reservations about our intervening pretty much
anywhere. I still do. I'm not for the United States throwing its weight
around except where we appear to have real interests.

We had no previous political or economic interests of any consequence in Vietnam. We had no troops over there. It was a French
colony and the first I guess I ever heard of the damn thing was in
the Geneva Accords. The aid to France for Vietnam was relatively
small. Europe seemed to be much more important. The possibility
of war, of trouble with Khrushchev over Berlin was the big issue.
And I don't recall being particularly interested in or concerned about
Southeast Asia. We were concerned about the stability of France
and I think the main reason they gave aid was not so much [because
of] Vietnam but they were afraid that France *in Europe* was going
to go Communist by elections.

I don't remember what I thought about the Geneva Accords. See I
became aware of this after we got involved and I got books and I
started to study the record of *why* we were there and so on. I didn't
pay much attention to it in the beginning.

EUGENE McCARTHY

Johnson used to invite us down to the White House, ten or fifteen
senators for a night, and he'd have the cabinet people come in and
speak to us. The minor ones would get five minutes, but the big
ones, like Rusk and McNamara, would get ten. And sometime in
1964, at one of those sessions I asked Rusk "How is this government—is it stable?" And Rusk said "Oh, we've really put it together now. The Catholics and the Buddhists are getting along and General [Nguyen] Khanh is in good shape. We've really stabilized it."
That was on a Wednesday night. On Friday morning, the headlines
said "Khanh Thrown Out." Rusk wasn't trying to fool us. He just
didn't know what was going on over there. They were trying to run
a war when they really didn't understand or have control of the political situation.

And the next year, '65, when I went on the Foreign Relations Committee, I began to watch McNamara more closely, too. He visited

Vietnam ten or twelve times and almost every report he ever made was in error. When they started the bombing, he told us it would stop the North Vietnamese from infiltrating more than forty-five hundred men a month. Six months later he was back testifying and his report was that they were infiltrating seven thousand a month. And when I asked him to explain the difference, he said "What difference?" He tried to tell me that they had *always* been able to infiltrate some number larger than forty-five hundred a month, but the bombing was holding it down somewhere between forty-five hundred and the larger figure. But when I asked what the larger figure was, he said he didn't know. And you had to conclude he really didn't. And I suppose that was when I first began to realize that it was out of control.

In November of '67 we began to challenge them. That was before the Tet offensive and I said I was going to run in four or five primaries. It's curious about Tet. They still say it was a victory. Rusk said we decided to ease up on the bombing because we'd won this great victory. And I guess technically they had, but you know the cost. And I sort of understood Rusk and Lyndon better when I read that they thought not just that they had won technically, but that this would be understood in the country as a great victory—just the numbers that were killed. They said, the kill ratio in Tet was twelve to three or twelve to two. But Americans didn't care how many Vietnamese were killed. It was just about then that *Life* magazine ran pictures of all the American servicemen killed in one week. It was when it got to the point where they were reporting [American casualties] in the county seat newspapers and everyone began to know the people who were being killed, that I sensed something political was happening.

[There were several other things that helped shape the decision.] One was [Attorney General Nicholas DeB.] Katzenbach coming up and saying "The Senate really doesn't have a right to criticize this sort of thing." And Rusk talking about how the Tonkin Gulf resolution had silenced us—procedural things that I couldn't accept, and that had to be challenged, apart from the particulars of the War itself. That's what sort of fed into my decision. I didn't think we could win the election, but we could certainly raise the issues and make them answer to what they wouldn't answer to before, when we had used a reasonable, orderly approach.

The Washington you describe must have seemed terribly corrupt.

It was a strange kind of corruption, a sort of preserving the institutional interests of the party, that commitment above all else. You were given this stuff about "You gotta be loyal to the President of your party," and "You know, it's a Democratic President." I didn't

realize until later just how strong that force is. They never really
forgave me—not even people who turned on the war after Nixon's
election. I don't think I've been invited to a national party thing
since '68. The only one who tried was Bob Strauss. Somewhere in
'69 or '70 he invited me to a telethon in California. I went out there
and hung around for two days and two nights, and I never got on.
They put on Teddy and McGovern and a lot of others. They interviewed the governor of Kentucky and the governor of Minnesota.
But they never got to me. I think it was the party people, the labor
guys who blocked it. Bob never explained anything. And in '72 I
wasn't asked to speak at the convention, which was four years later.

———————————◆———————————

GEORGE BALL

I defended the Administration in public because that was required
if I was going to stay in the government, and I felt I was serving a
purpose as a counsel for the defense. The President was listening to
me. I was forcing a discussion of the issues and that seemed worth
doing. After Johnson came in, I had an increasingly sad feeling that
I was fighting a rear-guard action. I was giving President Johnson,
every few weeks, a long memorandum telling him to cut our losses
and get out because we couldn't win. And while he seemed affected and concerned and quite prepared to discuss it at length, nevertheless, my colleagues were on the other side and I found myself
isolated.

Did you ever visit Vietnam?

No. I never did, and for a very clear reason: It was impossible for
me to go to Vietnam without being captured and brainwashed. There
was no way that I could go out and form clear impressions of what
was going on, because I would be taken into camp and surrounded
by the entourage in Saigon—the Embassy, the military, everybody.
I saw no purpose in it. I knew what their line was. All I'm saying is
that it was just impossible for a high official by visiting the place, to
get any counter-impression other than what was coming through the
normal channels anyway. So I relied for my impressions on talking
with practically every newspaper correspondent that had a chance
to go out there.

Later I was appalled by what was going on on the campuses. It
seemed to me that the students were tearing their institutions apart
for juvenile reasons. I had no patience with those excesses because
it seemed to me that their leaders were just taking advantage of a
situation to raise hell with no particular purpose. I was sympathetic

with their problems in being forcibly dragged off into a war they regarded as immoral. But the manner in which they reacted, I must say, I found rather distressing. And I was constantly distressed by the loss of life, not so much on the American side, although that was bad enough, but that we were in effect saying to Vietnam, "We're going to make you free, to save you from Communism, if we have to kill everyone to do it."

———•———

ALEXANDER HAIG *was a military aide to Secretary of Defense Robert S. McNamara and Deputy Secretary Cyrus Vance during the Vietnam buildup. He commanded a combat battalion in Vietnam, and then returned to become a trusted aide to Henry Kissinger on Richard Nixon's National Security Council. Nixon made him the White House chief of staff after the departure of H. R. Haldeman. Gerald Ford elevated him to four-star rank and made him the Supreme Allied Commander in Europe. In the early Reagan years he served as secretary of state. He harbored presidential ambitions, but they came to naught. He is now a consultant in Washington.*

Maybe my foremost recollection is from the mid-sixties, when our intervention was on the increase, and it's about the conditions under which that came about. I happened to be right in the middle of it, between MacNamara and Vance. I was the deputy special assistant to both the secretary and the deputy secretary. I was greatly concerned that we were pursuing an incrementalism in which incentives for the enemy upping the ante were inherent in our approach. That was underlined by the fallacious belief prevalent in the Administration that we could have guns and butter too. I was only a lieutenant colonel at the time, but I made those arguments vigorously. And had our military leaders been more courageous I think we'd have been much better served. Before we made the decision to engage our troops, there should have been some associated actions to engage the problem at its source—to mobilize American military assets and to convey to the instigators that it was a matter we regarded as one of America's vital interests.

What I'm talking about is the process we went through in preparing recommendations to the President in the spring of 1965, to justify landing the Marines in Danang. Before those recommendations went over to the White House, the Army Chief of Staff, General [Harold K.] Johnson, went to Vietnam to look the situation over. Johnson came back with a wish list of thirty-five recommendations, and they included mobilizing the Reserves, moving forces to the West Coast to demonstrate that we were willing to bring the battle to Hanoi, and putting the Soviet Union on notice that we would do that, as we did ultimately when we bombed Hanoi and mined Haiphong. What we really needed in '65 was a series of credible steps that showed our determination.

And I felt that if these issues had been brought to the highest level of the government, then the President would either have had to go ahead and make a real war out of it, or to recoil from what he was doing and choose another course. But in fact they were never brought to him that way. Instead, those recommendations were purged of every item that would have given a meaningful indication of our will to see things through. It was done in a bureaucratic process that showed not only a lack of courage by the military leadership, but also the shortsightedness of politicians who were much more interested in the Great Society, and who were fearful as well. There was a deep-seated conviction in the establishment in 1965 that that kind of threat to Hanoi would have resulted in a Chinese intervention. History shows that was false; in fact even at the time it should have been obvious that there were differences between Moscow and Peking we could exploit.

You have to remember that we had been through Korea in the fifties, and through the Cuban missile crisis in the sixties, and particularly the second of those had imposed a real psychic drain. Our basic desire was to do everything to avoid a superpower confrontation—and that gave us the wrong instincts. In such cases if you do just enough to demonstrate that you have a degree of will, but not enough to prevail, the incentive to the other side is to hang in there and keep on notching things up. In a nuclear age you cannot be trigger-happy, but if you are unwilling to take risks, it is best to stay out of conflict entirely. The result was that we ended up by 1968 spending twenty-eight billion dollars a year, and an awful lot of American blood, and what's more, starting an erosion of American military power that contributed a great deal to the problems we are dealing with today.

———————◆———————

GEN. BRUCE PALMER, *now retired, was William C. Westmoreland's deputy and later commanded the U.S. Army in Vietnam. Subsequently Vice Chief of Staff in Washington under Westmoreland, Palmer is the author of* The 25-Year War, *a book regarded by many as the single most authoritative account of the American involvement in Indochina. Palmer lives in Alexandria, Virginia*

Before I went over in '67, I'd been the Army DCSOPS—Deputy Chief of Staff for Operations. The DCSOPS of the services sit in with their chiefs at JCS meetings and they meet with the Director of the Joint Staff once a week at what is sometimes called "the little JCS." So although I wasn't part of the JCS, I knew a lot about its operations. And it is true that for the sake of appearances the chiefs under General Wheeler, who didn't want split recommendations to go forward, often gave the impression of agreement when they were fundamentally in disagreement.

At the time Haig was referring to, in March of '65, the air offensive was just underway, and the air power proponents said, "Just give us time and we'll bring those guys to heel." The Army never believed that, but the Chiefs didn't want to give an impression of pessimistic gloom. The attitude was "Well, we don't want to upset the President and Secretary of Defense too much." If air power had been applied the way the chiefs wanted to—as heavy as we could muster, sustained and hit them with everything but the kitchen sink before they could build up an air defense and condition their people, that might have been a different story. I still don't think it would have shaken that regime, but as you know, we went at it very piecemeal and gave them time, and that just aggravated the problem.

But the real feeling was that if we submit a split recommendation somebody's going to say, "My God, here the top professional people in our armed services don't agree," and they'd be right back to square one and nothing will happen. Therefore, Wheeler was always talking the other chiefs into waffling their differences. I take just the opposite view. I think when it is a fundamental disagreement and has such far reaching consequences then the split views should go forward. The President and the Secretary of Defense should know.

You see the civilians were just as split on this question except they were looking at things in terms of the effect on world opinion. And they could see that the picture of this great big superpower picking on this little country would lose us what little friends we had. And this was one of the basic reasons we didn't do well. We didn't have anybody supporting us.

It happens that I overlapped with [General] Johnson's trip. I had gone over earlier and visited all four Corps areas, and I'd reached the same conclusions: The ARVN was demoralized, going down the tubes and the only thing that would save South Vietnam was the intervention of U.S. ground troops. And that begged the question of whether you want to do it or not. As we found out later, Hanoi was going all out. They were hoping to knock them out before the United States intervened.

The civilians thought the air offensive might dissuade Hanoi from

intervening with North Vietnamese troops. What they didn't know
was that it had already occurred. Hanoi was playing two scenarios:
a short one, hoping they might get a quick knockout before we intervened, and a prolonged one in case we did come in. They could see
that the United States was getting ready, and in late spring or early
summer of '64 the first NVA troops started down the trail. By the
time of [General] Johnson's trip in '65, they'd already made up their
minds that if we did send troops in, they would escalate to keep the
ratio of forces even. So I think Al is right in saying that when it
came to committing ground troops, we really never debated the basic
question of should we do it in the first place. Would it work? And
what essentially was the commitment? [General] Johnson used to
try to tell them that if you weren't going to go in all the way, you
better not go in at all. He could see no halfway once we committed.

Do you remember when Hanson Baldwin* wrote a story that said
he'd gotten somewhere that it would probably take a million men to
do this? That was the kind of thing [General] Johnson had in mind.
With the geography, and the strategy of fighting defensively in South
Vietnam and putting pressure on the North instead of physically
cutting off their route of infiltration, with that long border, it would
take all the armies in the world to seal that thing off. Your only chance
was to cut the trails—my alternate strategy—and try to get something like we did in the Korean War. But our decision was to let
them come down to us. Well, we were dancing to their tune. [General]
Johnson saw that that was a loser. His real regret, he told me this
before he died, was that he hadn't turned in his commission.

As I understand it the Chiefs were very close to resigning en masse
in the fall of '67 when they were turned down again on the question
of mobilizing and really getting into the war. General Wheeler talked
them out of it. I've changed my mind over the years, but at the time,
I agreed and the rationale was something like this: First it would be
taken as disloyal to the President—even as a mutiny. Second, there
was this strong "can do" syndrome. The military guy is trained to
carry out his mission. And third, there was a feeling that "all the
president has got to do is accept our resignations and put someone
else in there who will do what he wants."

[General] Johnson felt it's best to work within the system. And most
active duty men would probably still agree with that. Whenever I
talk to a military audience and tell them this story they say, "Oh,
you can't do that. That would be disloyal. You've got to do what
the law says and obey your orders." The American military man is
very much imbued with the idea that the civilian is the supreme

---

*The military correspondent of *The New York Times*..

authority, and that's not only the law, it's the tradition of our country, back to the days of King George and his redcoats.

J. WILLIAM FULBRIGHT

It seems that McNamara, General Johnson, and others were aware as early as the beginning of '65 that it was going to take five hundred thousand or a million men.

That was not made clear at all. Remember McNamara said the troops would be home for Christmas. There was an admiral out there at CINCPAC who made very optimistic statements. After Pleiku, when the President announced that he was gonna send some Marines, Mike Mansfield and I raised at a meeting in the White House, a question about getting deeply involved. And he can speak for himself, but on one or two occasions or more he, being the Majority Leader, would make a speech and I would agree with him about not getting further involved. And all this business later made me employ two people as special representatives to see what the truth was, because we believed we were being given wrong information.

WALT ROSTOW

I think perhaps the single most important moment would have been in early February of 1968, when it was quite clear to us that the maximum Communist effort at Tet had failed. There was still plenty of fighting but it was clear they had a maximum objective militarily and politically, and we knew within a matter of days they weren't going to achieve it. And then the question became whether U.S. public opinion would hold up.

And then, in the curious way that history has, there was a tragic failure of communication and understanding. Why was Tet so misunderstood in the United States? And it'd be fun if I could say it was all the media's fault. It was half the media's fault and it was half our fault, or LBJ's problem. The media misinterpreted it grossly, as Peter Braestrup and Don Oberdorfer* documented painfully. But also President Johnson, as he himself says in his book, should have gone to the people in the State of the Union message and

---

*The authors of two first-rate books on the Tet offensive and its impact on American war policy. Interviews with both appear in Chapter Seven.

explained the military realities. The reason he didn't was that there is very strong pressure on a President not to reveal what he knows via intelligence.

The point is the people wouldn't have been as surprised by the headlines. They'd have said, "The president said they're going to make a maximum effort and let's see how it comes out, boys." And they would very soon see how it was going. But I think that a lot of people after Tet said "Well, we didn't lose the war, but we're not going to act decisively." The real defection at that stage was the hawks, not the doves. The doves stayed stable, about twenty percent who didn't like the war from the beginning. But the hawks said, "Well, if you're not going to win the war, to hell with it. Get out." And that was the attitude of a lot of people, and it's understandable.

CLARK CLIFFORD

When did you first realize we had lost the war?

In the late summer and fall of 1967 President Johnson sent General Maxwell Taylor and me on a trip out to the Pacific and Southeast Asia, to all of the troop-contributing countries, to see if we couldn't get them to send more men. We couldn't get any of them. And I came back unsettled and uneasy. We saw the top people every place we went, and they didn't accept the argument even though they were much closer to the danger than we. It shook me badly.

But what overcame that uneasiness was the constant reiteration that we were prevailing and the thing would be over soon. And then came Tet. We thought we had seen light at the end of the tunnel, and then all we saw was more tunnel. The impact on me was that first month in the Pentagon when I had complete access to all personnel, military and civilian. I am a trial lawyer, and a trial lawyer has to get the facts. And I used that month to get the facts. I spent days with the Joint Chiefs and with the civilians, everybody who had been through the war. I went through a long process of attempting to evaluate what our theories were, what our plan was for victory. And it didn't take me very long to find out that we didn't have any plan; that we were just going to go on and fight and ultimately attrition would catch up with our enemies and they would capitulate. And I could see we were no closer to that in 1968 than we had been in 1963 or 1964 or 1965. I reached the absolute deep conviction that we weren't going to win the war. And if we weren't going to win the war then the thing for us to do was to get out, and get out as quickly as we could.

President Johnson went through a terribly difficult period, as did my relationship with him at that time. But he showed a lot of courage. Here he'd been gung ho. I'd been with him at Cam Ranh Bay when he said "I expect you men to nail the coonskin on the wall." He wanted a victory. He wanted it so bad he could dream it. And finally at the end of March 1968 when I said "Let's be realistic about it," in these long, arduous sessions we went through day after day after day, he faced up to it. In effect, on March 31, he said "I'm not going to send any more men." And that was it. He was saying "I don't expect to win. I'm going to find a way to get out and I'm going to get a negotiated peace."

There are those who thought we should have kept on with the war. I think they were very, very wrong. When the Nixon administration came in in 1969, during the interregnum I had three long meetings with Henry Kissinger. I thought I had persuaded him and Mr. Nixon of the unique, rare opportunity to render a great service by declaring that we were going to get out of Vietnam. I later learned that he did not support it and either did Mr. Nixon. They continued on in Vietnam for another four years.

Mr. Nixon said we must fight on in Vietnam or the rest of the world would consider us a pitiful helpless giant. That was terribly wrong. The rest of the world did not consider Vietnam a test of whether we were a pitiful helpless giant. The rest of the world really was mystified about why we continued on in Vietnam. We went through a series of NATO meetings when I was at the Pentagon, and as I got to know other defense ministers they would get me off in a corner and say "Tell me why the United States is in Vietnam." And I'd give them the stock response, and they'd say "Well, I just wondered if there were large supplies of crude oil. All those ports are being deepened. You can't be there just for the reasons that you give. There's got to be some other reason."

So this theory, repeated over and over again, that unless we continued, the rest of the world would lose confidence in us, was terribly, terribly wrong. We stayed there for six years under Nixon. We were still there under Ford. And we didn't get out until Congress turned the spigot off.

And let me tell you something else. There were those who felt not only should we not get out, but we should greatly accelerate our presence there. Mr. [Walt] Rostow urged that we should plan an Inchon type landing—go up about halfway into the North, and cut North Vietnam in two. It could have been done. We had the naval power. We had the firepower. But North Vietnam had a mutual assistance pact with Red China. Every Southeast Asian expert we talked to said if American troops are placed up there, the North Vietnamese

are going to trigger that assistance pact. Our relationships with the
Red Chinese were extremely hostile at the time. We considered them
a bitter enemy, and they had about the same regard for us. And I
don't believe I'd have the imagination to think of any other course
of action so damaging to my country, as to involve it in a land war
in the jungles of Southeast Asia with Red China that had a billion
people and could pour men in there in limitless numbers while we
tried to support that war from eight thousand miles away. I guarantee to you, that if we had the staying power, we'd still be in the war
if we'd done that. It'd be like cutting a vein in our wrist and we'd
still be bleeding.

————————◆————————

ROBERT KOMER *ran a special office on Vietnam in LBJ's White
House, and in 1967 went to Vietnam with the rank of ambassador
to run the pacification program. He served as deputy defense secretary in the Carter administration. A dapper, diminutive man, he's
sometimes called "Blowtorch Bob" for the rising crescendo of his
voice when he launches into an argument. It isn't that he's angry,
a listener soon discovers; it's just that his volume turns up along
with his enthusiasm to persuade. He is now an analyst at Rand Corp
in Washington, D.C.*

People who argue that we should have invaded Laos or North Vietnam completely misunderstand the constraints on limited war in a
nuclear age. We did not think that Vietnam was worth an appreciable risk of a larger war with China or the U.S.S.R. Now at no time
did we regard these risks as being fifty-fifty. We always thought the
other guy would not respond if we escalated. But there was enough
risk of an escalatory spiral, with at the end the awesome possibility
of nuclear confrontation, that even when we had a nuclear monopoly as in the Korean War, we always operated under limited war
constraints. We were trying to win the war in the South with the
minimum adequate force. Were there ways to do it? I'm one who
thinks there were. Bill Colby is another. And that way was pacification—real counterinsurgency.
    We really didn't get off the ground with pacification in '67. I was
fooled by my own statistics, the HES—the Hamlet Evaluation Survey. Not a Komer creation, a McNamara creation out of CIA. I
protested some bad features of HES, and McNamara gave me the
back of his hand. But you mention HES, and people think Komer
and Colby. We inherited it, we improved it. And as measurement
systems go it was a hell of a lot better than the body count. At least

it was an honest, reasoned evaluation. Well, I'm not going to say with all the wisdom of twenty-twenty hindsight that pacification was going well by the end of '67. I thought it was and I learned differently in something called the Tet offensive.

What really surprised us about Tet—and boy it was a surprise, lemme tell you, I was there at Westy's elbow—was that they abandoned the time-tested Mao rural strategy where the guerrillas slowly strangle the city, and only at the end do they attack the seat of imperial power directly. At Tet they infiltrated right through our porous lines and attacked some forty cities. They abandoned the countryside where they were doing very well, and boy did they get creamed in the cities. For once, the enemy, who we could not find out there in the triple canopy jungle, who could control his losses by deciding to cut and run every time we got after him, for once we could find him. He was right there shooting at us in our own headquarters, and the cost to him was enormous militarily.

I always felt that the Tet offensive was a desperate gamble on the part of Hanoi. They saw the American presence going up and up and up, they saw us beginning to get a pacification program going, and they decided they better go for broke. And they did dislocate us. It cost them enormously. They had snuffed out the best of the southern cadre by sending them into the cities. We had a startling success in pacification after the Tet offensive because the enemy had sacrificed the core of his guerrilla movement. After Tet it really became an NVA war.

But he had also fatally weakened us at the center of our political structure. I mean Washington panicked. LBJ panicked. Bus Wheeler, Chairman of the Joint Chiefs, panicked. We didn't panic, mainly because we were too goddamn busy. But after the first day we knew we were back on top. The one place where after three days we were still out of control was Hue. Now that was two North Vietnamese divisions. And that was a big problem. They really had to be dug out, and we didn't finish it until February twenty-sixth [nearly a month after the offensive began].

It was the Tet shock to the American psyche that made me first think we might lose. And the shock in Washington was materially increased by the fact that the top command—Bunker and Westmoreland in particular—had come back in late November and reported confidently to the President that "Boss, finally all this stuff you have given us is beginning to pay off, and we look forward to 196C ˙.s a big year of success for us." Westy has great plans for pushing back the NVA. Finally we have an elected government even though it's Thieu and not Ky, and so on.

We were not engaging in deception. We genuinely believed at the end of 1967 that we were getting on top. Hell, I was there in the top three or four Americans in Saigon. Westmoreland believed, Abrams believed, Bunker believed, and I believed that finally, with five hundred thousand goddamn troops and all that air, and pacification finally getting underway, with the Vietnamese having set up a constitution and elections, we really were winning. We couldn't quite see clearly how soon, but this wasn't public relations, this wasn't Lyndon Johnson telling us to put a face on it. We genuinely thought we were making it.

And then boom, forty towns get attacked, and they didn't believe us anymore. Bus Wheeler with his three dwarfs, [Phil] Habib, [George] Carver, and [Gen. William] DePuy, comes out about the twelfth of February. The Chiefs have decided, because they too panicked, that we're losing. Besides which, there's the *Pueblo* incident in Korea, and maybe there's another Berlin crisis brewing. We have no strategic reserve; it's all either out in Vietnam or on the way. The Chiefs want to go to the President and say "We've got to call up the reserves, because if we get a second front in Korea there's not a goddamn thing we could do about it."

Wheeler comes out and asks Westmoreland "What do you need if we call up the reserves and the wraps are off." Westmoreland says "Look, if you call up the reserves and we've got five hundred thousand more men to play with, I would like two hundred thousand more." He pulls out of the drawer a request he had made in the spring of 1967, which was turned down, and has his guys burn a little midnight oil to update it. He gives it to Wheeler and he says "Look, this is to speed up the pace of victory. We think we have creamed them at Tet. They are on the run now. By God, if you'll give me the resources I'll chase them back into Cambodia, Laos and North Vietnam." He also has some plans that he tells Wheeler about: A hook around the DMZ at Cua Viet and go up there north of Dong Ha. Go into Laos. Go into Cambodia. He wants to hit the enemy in his sanctuaries. He says "We've got them on the run. They're going to retreat to the sanctuaries, and by God let's follow them in there and we'll win this war." Nothing big like taking Haiphong or anything like that. It's a conditional request. Westy is saying "If you're going to call up reserves and the other theater commanders are bidding, I too am going to put in a bid: two hundred thousand more men in two tranches, a hundred thousand in '68 and a hundred thousand in '69. I'll win your war for you in three or four years."

And then they decide not to do anything about the *Pueblo*, and the Berlin crisis proves evanescent. By the time Wheeler gets back, the whole case for calling up the reserves, which the JCS have argued for since the day we entered Vietnam, has disappeared—except the Vietnam case. But the fact that Westmoreland's conditional requisition, which is based on A. calling up the reserves and B. letting him use these troops to go into the sanctuaries, none of that is ever mentioned by Wheeler to either the President or to McNamara. By God they would have thrown him out on his ear. Can you imagine? So the perception in Washington is that we have just suffered a massive defeat and here's the commander saying "Boy, I've just won a massive victory. Give me some more guys and I'll clean this thing up fairly quickly."

So the three gnomes, Habib, Carver, and DePuy, go and talk to the President with Wheeler's patronage, and they say "Those guys in Saigon are smoking opium. We think the situation is much worse than they do. We have just been out there and we disagree with Komer's optimism, with Westmoreland's optimism, with Bunker's optimism and Thieu's optimism. Those guys just got surprised. Who wants to listen to them? We are in deep trouble, and that's why we need more men—not to insure victory but to stave off defeat." And of course this is leaked by some civilian who knows nothing of the conditionality of the request. The Chiefs never tell anybody anything. The goddamn Chiefs of Staff. Wheeler's the evil genius of the Vietnam war in my judgment.

One of the most interesting signs of the times was that before Tet when I went back to Washington every couple of months I was one of the lesser lions of the hour. McNamara wanted to talk to me, Rusk wanted to talk to me. The President was mad if I didn't call on him as soon as I got back, and then call on him again before I left. He kept saying "What can I do for you? You're doing great." I was due to come back the week of Tet, but when the offensive started I put off my plans, and I didn't get back until the middle of March. And when I did, it was all the other way. The feeling was palpable. You could tell they felt like "You guys have lost the war." The President saw me only because I asked to see him, and nobody else wanted to talk to me. They were all too busy. Now I wasn't born yesterday, and I knew in one day that whatever had happened out there, Tet had changed absolutely everything in Washington.

———————◆———————

Morton Halperin, *a colleague of Henry Kissinger on the Harvard faculty, went to the Pentagon in the mid-sixties. Initially a supporter of the war, Halperin soured on it as he watched the inner workings of the Johnson administration. Nonetheless, he supervised production of* The Pentagon Papers, *and was recruited into the*

National Security Council staff by Kissinger. He stayed only nine months—just long enough to become one of the first victims of illegal behavior by the Nixon White House. Halperin was one of several people whose telephones Kissinger ordered tapped after a leak to the New York Times of word that the United States had begun using B-52s to bomb Cambodia. Halperin is now director of the Legislative Office of the American Civil Liberties Union in Washington.

I would say that the system under LBJ was characterized by what Richard Neustadt* calls "reticence." That is, very little of what anybody believed was said to anybody else, except for some of the private memos that went back and forth between McNamara and Johnson. In the formal system, nothing was ever said. One of the things that happened with the Clifford review in March of '68 was that for the first time we were allowed to say nobody knows how many men and how much time it will take to win the war. Which everybody knew nobody knew, but it was never put in a memo to the President. That was one of the things that I think turned Clifford around, and some of the others.

That the system worked that way was partly normal procedure and partly Lyndon Johnson. Johnson, from what I could tell, did not want to be told things that would be difficult for him to deal with. I think Johnson knew, but he would not have wanted a piece of paper saying that, and would not have wanted anybody formally to tell him, because he had to do what he had to do to prevent losing and he didn't envision winning and didn't want to be confronted with something that would make it politically difficult to go forward. So to some extent, everybody knew everything, but nobody said it.

And to some extent people didn't know things. I don't think people understood that when the Joint Chiefs said that stopping the bombing would be disastrous to the safety of American soldiers in the South, that merely meant there was a deal among the military services that nobody would criticize anybody else's programs. The Air Force was bombing the North because the Air Force came out of the tradition of strategic bombing. The Army believed that bombing the North was contributing almost nothing to saving lives in the South and that redirecting the bombing to the South would indeed save lives. I don't think many people knew that.

I actually discovered it, to my astonishment, when I was interviewing military officers for my staff and the Army turned up a guy named Herb Schandler, who later wrote a book. I asked him a question: "If you could change one thing about the conduct of our policy in

---

*A well-known political scientist who has specialized in studying the presidency.

Vietnam, what would you change?'' And he said without hesitation "I'd stop the bombing of the North.'' And of course this was at the time when McNamara was getting creamed by Stennis and everybody. And I said "Why?" And he said "Because if we redirected the bombing we could save lives and it would reduce the controversy in the United States.'' And I then asked a very naive question. I said "Is there anybody else in the Army who agrees with you?" And he said "Everybody agrees with me," and he then proceeded to explain to me what now seems obvious but wasn't at the time. But my understanding is that senior Pentagon officials didn't know it and I'm not sure the people in the White House did. Certainly when I dealt with people in the White House on other issues, they didn't understand the Pentagon at all.

People don't understand—you can say it now; it has become public information which it wasn't in the sixties—that when the Joint Chiefs unanimously say "We need the M-X missile," or "We need a nuclear-powered aircraft carrier," it doesn't reflect anybody's view except the service whose weapon it is. It's hard for people to believe that there's a log-rolling system. What seems to people as a very momentous thing—that the Joint Chiefs of Staff believe X—all it means is that they made a deal.

When Schandler told you this, what did you do?

I began looking at the whole system with different eyes, and I left the government and wrote a book about it, but I didn't do anything about it in the system. There was really nothing I could do. The bombing of the North was an issue being handled in the stratosphere. It was not something that I could have done at my level.

Later I was very heavily involved in NSSM One* at the beginning of the Nixon administration. The whole point of that was to expose to the President the deep divisions within the government about what was going on in Vietnam, how good the South Vietnamese army was, what our options were, and how deeply people were divided. That was the first piece of paper in the history of the war in which the deep differences on what was going on, let alone what *should* be going on, were laid out.

In a way that's very disturbing. We outsiders always assume that no matter what front the government puts on, there's open debate behind the scenes.

People always pick their spots carefully because you use up a lot of capital by provoking fights. Particularly if you don't win them, but depending on how you win them, even if you do win them. If you

---

*National Security Study Memorandum, a term for documents prepared by the National Security Council staff to help set policy.

can demonstrate clout, you can get more influence—or you can use up credit. It's not always easy to tell.

———————————•———————————

ALEXANDER HAIG

I have always thought that had we been able to conduct the bombing at the level we did at Christmas of 1972 for another six weeks, we could have gotten a commitment from Hanoi to withdraw. In the early stages of the war, bombing alone would clearly not have done it. We needed a far more solid demonstration of our resolve. But by 1971, Hanoi had already suffered major losses at Tet, and it was clear that China was no longer a reliable rear area. They had to depend on the supplies that could come in by boat through Haiphong, and that gave the Christmas bombing a leverage that was unnaturally strong.

But you have to remember that the President was juggling with Congress right through that period. The issue really boiled down to the possibility of an impeachment vote, or a vote to cut off *all* the bombing. Faced with that, Nixon opted to take the high-risk course at the negotiating table. But we failed to understand that to keep the peace accords, we needed sanctions to enforce them. That was how I sold the peace treaty to Thieu—by telling him that Congress and the American people would certainly support the clear right of an aggrieved party to respond in force. I don't suggest for a moment that I myself wasn't racked by doubts and uncertainties. By that time it was always a delicate calculation of how far we could go before the President was disemboweled by Congress. But in finally supporting the treaty, I concluded that we had not yet lost our national manhood. I was wrong, of course, and what contributed to that was Watergate. The constraints enacted by Congress in the spring of 1973, where any sanctions for violation of the Paris accords were stripped away and simultaneously we took away from the Vietnamese army the resources that were necessary to sustain its operations, inevitably resulted in a victory for Hanoi.

———————————•———————————

GRAHAM MARTIN

You once said when they first approached you about going to Vietnam, your response was "Hell no, I won't go."
There was really no way to win with what was going on here in this

country. There was a great question as to whether we would continue to get the resources. I'd spent forty years in government service. I had this little farm up in Italy. I wanted to spend about half time there and half time here. My greatest ambition was to graft an olive onto a juniper tree so you could have an olive to put in your alcohol and get automatic gin. I would have liked to have written, to have explored, just to have lived. But you get caught up in things. I resisted for a year and finally they said "We really think you're the only guy that can pull the whole thing together, who has the background on the development side, and knows the military side and has a reputation with the Asians and will be respected and who will keep internal discipline on the American side. You've simply got to go."

Thieu still had "The Mandate of Heaven"* in '73 when I got out there. If you could have had an election, supervised by anybody to make sure it was fair, he would have carried eighty percent. There was no effective opposition to him. And it wasn't because it was repressed either. He did what all the politicians do here. He got on a bicycle, rode it around. Kids loved him and he obviously loved children. It sounds corny but it's the meat of politics everywhere. And his ambitions for the country were not really all that bad. He wanted to reverse what had happened under the French, the centralization of everything in the government, and return to the classic Vietnamese village democracy. I've never known of a dictator who gave arms to all his people. He did—armed the villages so they could protect themselves against the Vietcong. And it was working.

Now, the Vietnamese are energetic, hardworking, largely intelligent people, and from the beginning they could have done more. When they got pushed aside they said "What the hell, let 'em fight if they want to fight for it." But when they were on their own they went down in the Delta and cleaned out the Seven Sisters mountains— things that we'd never been able to clean out. All along the line, the military initiative was on their side.

But bad things had already begun to happen. I've seen very little of this written, but the Yom Kippur War was the greatest single blow to South Vietnam. The price of oil, which is an essential not only to run things but for fertilizer, went up four times. And without something to compensate, you reduced the aid by seventy-five percent right there. And secondly the enormous military shipments to replace Israeli losses cut down what was available. They took money and material earmarked for Vietnam and used them to replace stocks in

---

*A Confucian phrase expressing the ruler's right to remain in power so long as events remain favorable to his country.

Europe. They didn't want to go back to Congress for what had been used up to support Israel.

When we left Vietnam, our commitment under the '73 accords was that we would replace lost equipment on a one-for-one basis. The Vietnamese logistics organization was tied in by computer directly to some shipping point in Pennsylvania. Suddenly their requisitions began to be kicked back without explanation. My defense attaché, General John Murray, began to raise unshirted hell, since these were bought, paid for, appropriated. In the latter part of 1973 Murray warned me what was going on. I told Thieu this. He had to slow down, but coming from him it didn't make the military feel the Americans were pulling back. But Murray got so mad he finally retired with some remarks about "the fiscal whores" in the Pentagon.

————————◆————————

THOMAS POLGAR

In 1971 as I was doing my orientation in Washington, I went to see Mel Laird, who was the secretary of defense, and I said, "As a father of three children, I really have to consider the advisability of accepting permanent assignment in Vietnam." And Laird says, "Oh, don't worry. We are going to have a residual force in Vietnam for thirty years, just like in Germany."

I went out to Vietnam and Laos on a visit in October and I came back fairly optimistic. I thought Vietnam was by Western standards a miserable place, but compared to ten years before, considerable progress had been made. It was a handicapped child, and once you have a handicapped child no matter what you do it ain't going to be normal—maybe he will never be a professor or a senator, but you are plenty happy if he can make a living as a counterman. And it seemed to me that South Vietnam could stand on its own feet as long as we give it aid and above all we continue [to keep] Hanoi under the impression that if they attacked they are going to be punished.

Bill Colby had spent a lot of time in Vietnam, and naturally, being chief of station going out, I went in and called on him. Colby's a great talker and he was telling me how we were emphasizing too much the military side and not enough the grass-roots democratic development. We talked for several hours, and at the end Colby says, "Now don't take anything that I have said too seriously because I have been concerned with Vietnam affairs for twenty years and not a single thing that I have ever predicted has come true."

I got there in January of '72 and my baptism to fire was the Easter offensive. That was the first time the Vietnamese forces on the ground stood by themselves. Of course, they still had American air support, which made a very big difference. In '73 we had the Paris Agreement, but in fact, we never had a *cease*-fire. What we had was a *less* fire. Violence was continuing but at a level which both sides could absorb, and generally speaking, the South Vietnamese government controlled eighty-five percent of the population, and you could drive to any part of the country during daylight hours. I know I permitted the CIA people to drive to resort towns like Dalat and Vung Tau. It was basically an acceptable situation. The skirmishes took place on the far peripheries.

Until Nixon's resignation, the North Vietnamese thought they had to be patient. Some of their phrases out of our intelligence reporting that I remember were that "Our struggle has lasted now for thirty years and it may last another thirty years"; and "The Paris Agreement was a necessary step to permit us to rebuild, and this rebuilding may take some time." But the station also did a situation appraisal on the eve of the Paris Agreement where we said "Bear in mind that the tiger hasn't changed his spots, and the moment they get the impression that we are no longer backing South Vietnam, they'll be back again." It caused considerable dismay in Washington, because Nixon was saying "We won," and Kissinger was saying "Peace with honor."

CHAPTER FOUR

American Views of the Vietnamese

IT can fairly be said that although America was deeply involved in Vietnam for fifteen years, the Americans never quite got the Vietnamese into focus. There were many reasons for this. At the higher levels, U.S. officials often based their political judgments on their own backgrounds and values, rather than on a thorough understanding of the local dynamic. Frequently their information—as well as their intuition—was wrong. Often, as in the ouster of Ngo Dinh Diem, they chose to act simply because it seemed that action was required, rather than because they had thought through the consequences and plotted a rational course into the future.

At lower levels, most Americans went to Vietnam on short tours, which gave them little incentive to spend the time and make the intellectual effort required to get into real contact with the Vietnamese. Few took the trouble or had the talent to learn the language. Most relied heavily on a huge establishment created to provide American-style food, housing, entertainment and services, which left them effectively isolated. Critical pieces of information, such as the degree to which the Vietnamese were prisoners of superstition, or the existence of nationalist admiration for Ho Chi Minh even among supposedly loyal Southerners, were simply beyond the ken of many Americans.

And if few understood the South Vietnamese, fewer still bothered to study those from the North. Once the United States had entered the war full scale, it was almost as if the Vietnamese themselves were irrelevant: American power could and would prevail, whatever the local circumstance. Given our predilection at the same time to fib to ourselves, it was almost as though we had set out with deliberation to ignore that most famous piece of advice from the classic Chinese military philosopher Sun Tzu in his *Art of War*: "Know the enemy and know yourself; in a hundred battles you will never be in peril. When you are ignorant of the enemy but know yourself, your chances of winning or losing are equal. If ignorant both of your enemy and of yourself, you are certain in every battle to be in peril."

———————•———————

WILLIAM COLBY *was "one of the very few Americans," as he puts it, "who went through the entire experience. Most people had about a two or three year, max, exposure. I was there at the beginning of it with Diem [as the Saigon CIA station chief from 1959 to 1962]. Then I came back here and I was chief of the Far East division of CIA for the next six years, and I was running back and forth to Vietnam two and three times a year in the mid-sixties with McNamara and all the rest. Then [Robert] Komer [the special ambassador for pacification] asked for me to go be his deputy and so I went out in '68, right after Tet and stayed until '71. I became the director [of the CIA] a year or so later and I was still the director at the time of the fall." Colby now practices law in Washington, D.C.*

Max Taylor, who became the Ambassador in '64, believed that if a paramilitary operation got big it should be turned over to the military, so we turned the Vietnamese one over and its orientation changed. Our direction was you organized these villages for their own defense, and that expanding defense then excludes the enemy. When the military took over, it was "You take these forces and use them on offensive missions." They sent them up on the Cambodian border and they chased around in the woods and it never had a damn thing to do with the overall strategy.

In the early years I had been involved with Ngo Dinh Nhu in getting the Strategic Hamlets started. It began well but then the bureaucracy put up one strand of wire and counted it as done. Nhu and Diem were sort of beating on it to make it work better. Nhu made one serious mistake, I think. He wanted to make a massive grab for the country rather than a very careful buildup. That's arguable. It produced some of the fakery but it also seized the initiative and the Communists themselves said that 1962 belonged to the government. Nhu's point, I remember, was always that you put the stakes so they're pointed out. You don't put up barbed wire to hold people in; you put the defenses so they protect the people. He was no democrat, don't get me wrong. But that was his concept of the war and it was right.

But the Buddhist thing interrupted all that and led to the overthrow of Diem and Nhu, at which point that whole program went under. The guys who were the heads of the Buddhist movement, I assure you, were just as flaky as the Ayatollah Khomeini. I talked to Thich Tan Chau after the coup against Diem and I couldn't get a straight statement out of him. We went round and round for an hour and come to the end, I tried to write it down and I couldn't figure out what the hell he said and I don't think he knew either. A typical religious zealot: "Don't bother me with logic." Diem was a very strong Catholic. Clearly he was trying to lard his government with non-Catholics. I mean, you need that, so long as they behave and do as they are told. He had a prejudice in favor of Catholics as being "more reliable," which was a weakness on his part. But the Buddhists didn't have any sense at all.

I thought we should stay with Diem. I thought he'd provide a better government than anybody else would offer. He was an autocrat, but a noncorrupt autocrat. He seemed to have a concept of how to fight the war and our interest was in winning, not making a perfect democracy. But his failing was that he never felt the need for an active political base. We had a big battle all that summer [of 1963] between State and the National Security Council. State's position was that you cannot hope to win with Diem because he cannot generate popular support. That was an honest appreciation. The other side, people at Defense and in CIA who'd been there, believed you weren't going to get much different government from anybody else. Actually, I think we got worse. And during that entire period I don't remember one sensible discussion as to who would succeed him. That to me typifies the entire blindness of much of the rest of our approach to Vietnam.

———————◆———————

RICHARD HOLBROOKE *joined the Foreign Service in 1962, straight out of college. He had been best friends in high school with the son of Dean Rusk, who by then was Secretary of State. He served in Vietnam as a province advisor and later as an executive aide to Ambassadors Henry Cabot Lodge and Maxwell Taylor, worked in the White House under Robert Komer in 1966–67, wrote a volume of the Pentagon Papers, and as Jimmy Carter's assistant secretary of state for East Asian and Pacific Affairs from 1977 to 1981, negotiated with both China and Vietnam on normalizing relations. He is now an investment banker in New York.*

I spoke a little French and I had asked for a non-European assignment. I wanted to see a part of the world I wasn't familiar with, Asia. So they assigned me to Saigon, and they detailed me to AID. I went to Berkeley to study Vietnamese for a season, and then back to Washington. I remember coming into the State Department and getting a briefing that the war was going very well. And I remember thinking two things. I was astonished there were ten thousand Americans in Vietnam—it seemed like an awful lot. And secondly I hoped the war would still be going on when I got there. I thought war is one of mankind's most basic occupations, and I didn't want to be like Stephen Crane and write about it and not have ever seen it. But according to the briefing it might all be over before I finished language study.

When I got to Vietnam in May of '63 there were still only ten thousand Americans there and about forty people had died. When I left in June of '66, there were five hundred forty-nine thousand five hundred dred Americans there and American casualties were already up in the tens of thousands killed. I was assigned first to AID's office of Rural Development—pacification—headed by a young man named Rufus Phillips who was a protege of Ed Lansdale. It was supposed to be a very glamorous office that was going to change the nature of the war. I worked in Saigon for a while, and then a crisis developed in Ba Xuyen province in the Mekong Delta. The province governor had gotten into an argument with the AID representative and they weren't going to send a replacement. I went to Phillips and said, "Send me down." He said, "You're just a kid." And I said, "If you're not going to send anyone, what's the difference? I want to get out of Saigon and see all this."

So at twenty-two, I found myself in charge of the Strategic Hamlet Program in Ba Xuyen, a province of six hundred thousand people, where the Bassac River meets the South China Sea. The capital was Soc Trang. There was an American military advisory group there, and a division advisory group with the 21st ARVN in Bac Lieu, another big town. At the time it seemed quite normal to me to go into the office of a lieutenant colonel in the South Vietnamese Army with a sheaf of vouchers and say, "I can't sign them unless you will certify them." We'd sign the stuff together. I was representing the United States. This province governor must have been about the same age as I am today [forty-four], and I think if somebody twenty-two years old came into my office and said, "You can't have your money unless I sign it with you," I suppose I'd like to kill him, but if he had the authority I might have to deal with him. It's a very strange world.

About a third of the province was controlled by the Viet Cong, about a third was controlled by the government, and about a third was gray area. I remember this vividly because following the chain of reporting down to the province level, you kept getting different perspectives on what was actually happening. In Saigon it was reported that Ba Xuyen had three hundred twenty-four strategic hamlets completed. And these three hundred twenty-four *completed* hamlets were very critical, because the amount of money dispensed to the province was dependent on the number of hamlets. So I asked for the exact locations, and I couldn't get them. And I said, "Well, I can't sign these vouchers unless you tell me where these hamlets are." Finally they gave it to me—and the first thing I discovered was that about forty of them were simply wards in Soc Trang and Bac Lieu.

And of the remainder I said, "Let's go visit this one." And they'd say, "That's pretty hard to get to." And it would turn out they'd done nothing more than erect a picket fence or put a few punji stakes in a moat, which could be easily jumped. So the first thing I discovered was that the chain of command had somehow converted this combination of urban wards and inaccessible, insecure hamlets into three hundred twenty-four completed hamlets with X percent of the population under government control—and that wasn't true. There was a profound gap between what Washington had been told about this province, listing four hundred thousand people under government control, and the real situation, which was *far* shakier than that.

The reporting system was perverted, and I raised questions. I was quite outraged by it. Some people in Saigon understood. Others thought I was making trouble. But I did *not* draw the conclusion that something was wrong with our effort; I only drew the conclusion that there was something wrong with our reporting, and that you have to seek truth from facts as Chairman Mao might say. I was *very* surprised that the leadership of the U.S. government could be making policy based on false information. And yet there was Bob McNamara back in Washington talking about body counts, weapons capture ratios, and percentage of population control. And all the figures were wrong. I thought that was a profound failing, but it never occurred to me in the year 1963 that the United States could lose a war. How could it?

———◆———

BRUCE PALMER

You said in your book that a number of key ARVN officers were actually Viet Cong.

It was disheartening to me to realize that the whole country had been penetrated, from the palace down to the platoons. The Vietnamese could not put out their orders the way we would. They did not trust their own chain of command. They wouldn't tell the troop commanders where they were going until the last minute. And I think that when we went in there, we didn't really realize the extent of the subversion. I guess it was ignorance and failure of intellect on our part to figure that out. It was difficult for Americans to understand that kind of thinking. It seemed to me the Vietnamese could switch sides so easily. I wonder even now about these people that surfaced and said they were Vietcong agents all the time. You wonder how many times they switched sides as they tried to figure out which one was going to win. I guess that's human nature, but they're different from us. It's difficult for me to imagine in our Civil War, for example, Yankees and Southerners being ambivalent about whose side they were on. In Vietnam there was an ambivalence that to this day, I don't understand.

————◆————

WILLIAM CORSON *enlisted in the Marines during World War II and soldiered across the Pacific from island to island. Like a number of other Marines, he was coopted by the OSS and later the CIA. He was given a direct commission in 1949, and early in 1950, before the outbreak of the Korean War, made the first of many trips to Indochina. He retired as a Marine colonel in July 1968 and is now a Washington editor for* Penthouse *magazine.*

In '62 and '63, as part of what the Agency was doing we were finding our people, the U.S. types, as well as some of the other fellows and ladies working for us were getting the black hand—being fingered. And we're looking around, "Jesus Christ, how did that happen? What kind of security do we got in this goddamn lashup?" I was back here then, and complaints were coming in from the field that we're penetrated. So there was established a CI [counterintelligence] element in the Station. And McCone sent a guy from Jim Angleton's staff out.*

The guy who went out there was top-drawer and had had good time on the ground in Asia. He started up and they began to spot some of these fellows who were in the improved and expanded ARVN. And now they were going on up and this guy's dirty and this guy's maybe not squeaky clean. And they were successful in turning some Vietnamese in the ARVN and in the GVN† to our side.

So here was a CIA officer running a net of spies in the government

---

*John McCone was director of CIA under Kennedy; Angleton ran the Agency's counterintelligence division for many years.
†Government of Vietnam.

of Vietnam, targeted against some of the people that we knew belonged to the Communists. And when I made a trip out there in 1965, he comes over to see me at the Majestic. I know this fellow because he had been in Cambodia several years before and he had been a very competent professional. He had worked in straight security as opposed to counterintelligence in some of our stations. And I said, "What's up?" And he said, "I'm going home." And I said, "What the fuck you talking about? You just got here a couple of years ago." And he said, "I'm going home and we're all going home and we're closing the shop down." And he said, "Colby has ordered that we cease and desist and the function can now be carried out by the counterintelligence division of MACV. It's now an Army problem." I said, "Those guys will be lucky if they can find somebody selling goods out of the PX. What's going on here." And he says, "We are now co-belligerents and this is the sovereign nation of South Vietnam, Corson. We don't spy on our allies."

And therein ended any opportunity we had to know who the bad guys were. From then on it was MACV that handled it. They had a brigadier general and a bunch of "misters" with strange ID cards. I did a little bit of lobbying to say this is crazy when I got back here. People got all over my case and then I realized that I should have known better. I was warned and I was told about it and I tended to dismiss it because I thought it was too fuckin' incredible.

I'm told you know of a South Vietnamese intelligence officer who turned out to be a Viet Cong.

Well there were several. One was a colonel named Trinh, Vo Bac Trinh as I remember it, a tall, very good-looking fellow. He was the intelligence liaison officer between the U.S. forces and the Joint General Staff, a very critical position. When U.S. forces were going to start an operation, they had to let the ARVN know where we were going and when, which units and how many guys, so they wouldn't shoot up the wrong people. And quite literally the warning orders were in the hands of the Communists in many cases before they were even in the hands of the U.S. units. And after Saigon became Ho Chi Minh City, Trinh turned up as a major general in the NVA.

In practical terms let's say that you got a LRRP [pronounced "lurp"]— a long-range reconnaissance patrol] out there, and they see these bad guys, and if the bad guys want to *di di* [escape] it's gonna take them time. So the patrol comes up on the air and says "Bingo." You got reaction forces ready to go, but you got this constraint: It goes to ARVN and goes through Trinh and his crowd, and gets to the Communists. This system got set up in 1965 after some GVNs got caught in the middle of a Marine operation. Now in reality it wasn't just one single colonel. There were people throughout the

ARVN system feeding us disinformation and misrepresenting the enemy situation. Sometimes where you expected to encounter a platoon you ran into a reinforced company. And other times you'd come into an LZ* you expected was gonna be hot, and there wasn't anybody there. And consequently our troop leaders began to use the "Jesus factor," which is that if the G-2† tells me there are fifty enemy, I better go prepared to encounter a hundred and fifty, even though I may not encounter any.

In 1967 I was in the Pentagon, in charge of evaluating intelligence in Vietnam, and I did some multiple regression analyses on how often we were able to find the enemy when we had valid intelligence that showed he was there. This was confirmed intelligence because we were getting it from the other sources *after* the fact, or from their communications, and cross-referencing it. And the analysis showed that they were able to accept or decline combat based on whether or not it was favorable to them. The correlation on this was about .92 or .93—when you had confirmed intelligence that the enemy was there, .92 times they declined combat if you went with enough to defeat him. Now in terms of game theory, if one side has all the information and the other side doesn't there's no way you can defeat him. And that's precisely what occurred. They were able to bleed us at very little cost to themselves.

When you discovered this, what did you do with it?

Nothing. I knew what was happening, and I knew who the who was, but I had no means to be able to raise this about this sovereign ally.‡

BOBBY MULLER

Probably the first two months I was there, I spent out in the bush. Out there the war was easy in a way because there was no ambiguity. Anybody you met out there was hard core NVA regular. No "good guy, bad guy" problem. Later, when we came back to work the coastal area where there were villages and refugees, that's when things started to go "wait a second." Cam Lo, which is one I remember very well, was a refugee village where people had been taken from another place called Gio Linh, ten or fifteen miles away. I didn't understand it then, but for Vietnamese, villagers, their rice paddy

---

*Landing zone.
†The intelligence staff.
‡Meaning he knew who among the Vietnamese was leaking U.S. war plans, but could do nothing about it.

and their little ancestral burial ground defines their universe. You take them away as we did and you've totally disrupted what they relate to. And in Cam Lo what I experienced was just hatred in the eyes of people.

The Vietnamese did not like us and I remember I was shocked. I still naively thought of myself as a hero, as a liberator. And to see the Vietnamese look upon us with fear or hatred visible in their eyes was a shock. The only thing we were good for is to sell us something. And frankly every time we operated around Cam Lo we got fucked with. Any patrol, any operation, any convoy passing by would get a smack. So the people that I thought would regard us as heroes were the very people that we were fighting, and all of a sudden my black-and-white image of the world became real gray and confused.

Then I came into contact with the ARVN and that was all the more absurd. First there were some joint operations and then I went with MACV as an advisor and worked with three different ARVN battalions and that's when everything just went screwy in my head. Every night I slept with the battalion commander. We had personal bodyguards and the reason was that a good percentage of the guys in the ranks were VC or even North Vietnamese. The bodyguards were to protect us against getting blown away by the guys we were fighting with. We went out into the A Shau valley for what was supposed to be a ten-day operation and it wound up being ten weeks, and we lost a good number of guys not because of firefights but because they took as much rice as they could carry and they split. The A Shau was badlands. It was not a friendly place. And when you leave your unit out in the A Shau you ain't leaving to go bring in the crops back at the farm. You're leaving because you're joining the other side.

It was a joke. The enemy was a tough, hard, dedicated fucking guy, and the ARVN didn't want to hear about fighting. It was LaLa Land. Every, every, every, *every* firefight that we got into, the ARVN broke, the ARVN fucking ran. I was with three different battalions and the story never changed. I almost fell over laughing once. I had an Australian I was working with, and this NVA unit had just ambushed us. We had two companies of ARVN, and finally they got on line to counterattack, and the company commanders give the order to move and nobody moves. And they have to run up and down line with little sticks, beating these guys and kicking them in the fucking rear end to get them up out of their holes. And the Aussie and I look at each other, and we know then and there that this ain't going to work.

LIONEL ROSENBLATT *worked in the U.S. pacification program in South Vietnam from 1967 to 1969. In 1975, with the country crumbling, Rosenblatt and a colleague, Craig Johnstone, went AWOL from their assignments on the Washington interagency task force on Vietnam and flew to Saigon on an unauthorized rescue mission to evacuate two hundred Vietnamese friends. Rosenblatt is now a legislative management officer at the State Department in Washington.*

I arrived in Vietnam several months before Tet, when the Americans were saying that we had turned the corner. Like everybody else I was surprised by the pervasiveness of the Tet attacks. On the other hand, realizing, as most people in the States never did, that basically Tet was a military defeat for the Viet Cong and the North Vietnamese, I went on from that initial baptism to leaving just after the first American troops had begun to leave in June of 1969, with a feeling that we might not win.

Leaving was a hard decision. Like so many others who served in the field in Vietnam, it was in my blood. The responsibilities I had in the countryside were sort of like what a British district officer might have done in colonial days—a little bit of everything. I thought we were working well with the Vietnamese, and I felt I was having an impact. And then I went back to Saigon and worked as an advisor with the Vietnamese side rather than in an American office in Saigon.

But the bottom line was, I had to ask myself, "Where is the country going?" And I came to two fundamental conclusions. One is that basically most people did not want the Communists to win, but that both governments were still quite ineffective. So I made a conscious decision not to stay, not because I felt that our side was wrong but because I felt that we would fritter away a chance to win. And I felt that because I could see we did not use our political leverage very well. Using our leverage well would have been primarily from unvarnished field reporting about where the difficulties were and a willingness then to get at that: military and civil service reform, land reform, stopping corruption, replacing leaders at fairly high levels that simply weren't effective. One of the things that told me not to stay was when the same policeman said to me on several occasions, "We could win this war. We are not a pro-Communist society, but why the hell can't you Americans give us a decent leader?" My standard response was, "You guys have to pick the leader. It's your country," the standard Embassy answers to this point.

Did you believe that?

No. No. I believed very strongly that with five hundred thousand men on the ground and all sorts of material support, we had an obligation to also fight the political war. But having been burned by the Diem experience, we were unwilling to use political leverage, almost as if you had a brawny, hulking giant unwilling to use his brain. Now if you're going to use leverage right, you've got to be well informed; you can't have the reports get progressively optimized as they go up the chain of command, which I think happened in Vietnam. So the policymakers neither had good enough information or, above all, the will to intervene on the political front. So I left out of potential frustration. I left because I was afraid that given the need for fundamental reform and the ineffective use of our strength, we were going to end up being outwitted.

There was also a question of our patience. It occurred to me after Tet that we might end up having all but won, only to find that American patience had run out and that there wasn't going to be anything left in the supply line. One Vietnamese general put it so well—I think it was Tran Van Don—when he said, "You Americans trained us to fight in your style and Americanized our armed forces and then you pulled the plug on the support necessary for this kind of army." And I think there's a lot of truth in that. It was more the psychological scare than that the lack of supplies had by then *really* hurt them. So knowing it was going to be a near thing and that we weren't going to really optimally use our strength, and that we couldn't count on American patience to stay the course, I left.

———————◆———————

GARY LARSEN *worked in Vietnam as a Foreign Service officer from 1969 to 1973. For nearly two years, Larsen, who speaks fluent Vietnamese, was the American counterpart of a corrupt Vietnamese district chief in the Mekong Delta. He is now chairman of the board of International City Bank in Long Beach, California. He has traveled to Vietnam and Cambodia since the war, representing an international relief group, "Operation California."*

The thing I remember most vividly is how little we knew about Vietnam. It was as though the people, their culture, their country existed in another dimension which [only] obliquely intersected with ours. To be sure, we made the obligatory gestures. We had our linguists, our culture specialists, our orientation studies. Yet for the vast majority of Americans the Vietnamese were puppets and their country a stage on which we pulled the strings and rearranged the props at our whim.

This is not surprising when you consider that we had no consideration of Vietnam as an ancient civilization. What was surprising was that our efforts to learn were so meager and so late. Very few people ever realized, for example, that the streets of Saigon were largely named for kings, heroes, and poets rather than for trees, flowers, and places. Or that Vietnam had a flourishing civilization when Washington, D.C., was only a swamp. Ironically, Vietnam's literary masterpiece, Kim Van Kieu, which occupies a place in Vietnam analogous to that held in the West by the masterpieces of Chaucer and Dante, never appeared in this country until 1973, the year we finally declared peace and withdrew.

Our ignorance was reinforced by our inability to communicate. There were, of course, some people who spoke the language, read the literature, and invested the time to pierce the veil. Unfortunately, they rarely made the decisions, and when their comments were at odds with accepted policy, they were dismissed as having "poor attitudes," or as having "gone native." In the absence of English-speaking counterparts, the only people [most of us] felt comfortable talking to were our interpreters, who often unknown to us, seized control of the dialogue and while our interest waned, put forth their own ideas—or ours as they understood them—and in the process promoted themselves.

We compounded this infidelity to competence by vacations, short tours, and our own enclaves. In fact life in Saigon was so complete, and the circle of office, PX, and clubs so secure, that one could go for extended periods of time meeting only Vietnamese who served as drivers, secretaries, maids, and bartenders. And when the occasional ceremony or meeting brought us into contact with other Vietnamese, we retreated into small talk, cliches, and drink, which isolated us from any deep awareness of where we were or what we were doing.

This ignorance nourished our arrogance. For if we were not aware of the consequences of our presence, we could proceed blissfully with actions based on our own one-dimensional view of the country and the people. And proceed we did, getting no smarter but simply overwhelmed. As somebody once said, "We did not have twenty years of experience. We had one year twenty times." In the end we made peace and withdrew with the same arrogant disregard for the people and their country which had characterized our whole involvement. And the lessons were buried under self-praise for a noble effort and guilt-expiating succor for tens of thousands of refugees. Fortunately, there is ample blame for all involved.

———◆———

MICHELL JACOB *of Minneapolis went to Vietnam with a private aid group, International Voluntary Services, in 1967 and worked in a Mekong Delta village for three years helping farmers raise an improved breed of pig. Now an agricultural consultant based in Washington, he has worked with hog-raising projects in Haiti and Mali in recent years.*

I first went to Vietnam with the idea of seeing if I wanted to work overseas. Also, being an American, I felt responsible for what was happening, and I wanted to contribute in some way to help the Vietnamese people. I knew I did not want to be a soldier. When I got on the plane all I knew about Vietnam was that Vietnamese are Asians and Asians are inscrutable. Once I learned the language, I never had a problem. In the village I made lifelong friends, and a totally new world opened up for me.

The villagers were extremely sensitive, very philosophical, always willing to talk about human relationships. They taught me things I never would have learned elsewhere: how to be sensitive, how to observe, how to be kind, how to put yourself in another person's place, how to listen. They did this in a style that was very classy. If your father wants to teach you something, he'll stand over you and tell you to do it a certain way. The Vietnamese taught me with infinite patience and persistence, but always with a smile.

When you are working in rural development you learn it's best to pick leader-farmers, and work with them first. The village chief introduced me to a farmer with whom, he said, it would be easy to work. The guy was great, his whole family was great. One day a strange farmer dropped by my friend's house. We had a little light, get-acquainted conversation. Then he left. My farmer friend asked me if I noticed how the other farmer lacked patience, how he asked another question before I had answered the previous one. The man simply hadn't acted with courtesy, the farmer said.

I agreed that he had rushed things and had been arrogant for a Vietnamese. For example, he was sitting back in his chair rather than politely leaning forward to listen. I realized that he was the type who would just try to get something from me. Yes, agreed my farmer friend. Thus, I had got my daily lesson in human relationships. No one said that I shouldn't work with that farmer. My friend only hinted that I should look at him closely. That's a Vietnamese trait: They are extremely observant and sensitive.

Another trait is the personal and cultural strength of the Vietnamese. It was a terrible war in terms of the bomb tonnage dropped, the amount of lead flying in the air, the number of civilians killed, and the widespread destruction. But the people in my village, who were living in the middle of a war zone, were strong, with such identity, with such strong cultural roots, with such pride that I don't believe the war ever got to their soul.

That discovery taught me a lot: that as bad as things can get, you don't have to let it get to your soul. I never doubted the Vietnamese would preserve their culture and would continue to function as individuals despite the war. In fact, there seemed fewer crazy people in Vietnam than you would expect to find on the street in the U.S. or in an African town. The Vietnamese are a disciplined people who learned to handle what was coming at them. That's unique.

You know what would happen if I went back to my village? I say "my village" because I was part of it; I was even on the local school committee. I believe that if I walked into the village tomorrow, we would pick up our relationships exactly where we left off. We would go out and *nhau* ["drink"] and talk in the local coffee shop which was just like my office. I think they would still accept me. There wouldn't be much of a ripple. I think they would still feel comfortable with me. They would probably come up to me and say, "Remember Farmer Bao's pig? Well, it's still sick."

———◆———

CHARLES BENOIT *went to Saigon in 1967 for the U.S. Agency for International Development, and seldom left the country until it collapsed. He ended up as chief of the Ford Foundation office in Saigon. He was fluent in Vietnamese and his assessment of events was so pessimistic that U.S. Ambassador Graham Martin once called him "a known peace activist and Hanoi apologist," and vigorously asked for his removal. He now works for a computer importer in New Hampshire.*

The Vietnamese had a sense that anything that happened in Vietnam happened due to the planning of the American government. I would hear some of the most grandiose concoctions to try to explain [events]. The Vietnamese felt there was always someone behind the scenes, pulling the strings. Their speculation was not that the ARVN were getting the pants beaten off them, but that somebody had a larger plan. And people spent an awful lot of time trying to figure out what the United States was up to. Somehow, we held the key to the puzzle. They believed the United States was invincible, and we were going to pull this out because we couldn't afford to lose.

It took a long time for them to realize that we weren't in charge—and when that realization struck, there was nothing left to sustain them, and things really started to unravel. When it was finally clear the Americans were leaving, a Vietnamese said to me: "I couldn't believe how you came here. You came lock, stock and barrel; you came with refrigerators; you came with everything imaginable and you built these big empires out of wood, scrap lumber. I also can't believe how fast you're leaving." You see, there was this assumption that we really knew what we were doing and that they were the lesser factor, so to speak.

———————◆———————

THOMAS POLGAR

There were all sort of factors in the makeup of the South Vietnamese fighting force which the American army really should have known and calculated. It's hard to believe this, because many of the officers were highly intelligent, university-educated people, fluent in French and English, Chinese and Vietnamese. But sometimes even if the order called for an offensive they wouldn't move because the constellation of the moon to this star to that star wasn't right. And to superstitious people morale is even more important than with nonsuperstitious ones. Once they get the feeling that the signs aren't right, they haven't got the restraining force of discipline and rationality that you could perhaps exercise with an American unit or a British or a German unit.

Even Thieu regularly sought the advice of a Chinese geomancer. You know what a geomancer is? A geomancer translates astrological signs to figure out which is the optimum location of a building on a given ground. And this is all very much involved with the Chinese mythology. Thieu once had bought a big house for his mother and afterward the geomancer told him this house is sitting on the neck of the dragon, according to the signs. And Thieu had the house torn down and rebuilt facing in a different direction. I don't know whether it would have been possible under any circumstances, but we had trouble revamping this people into our world.

Another thing that was really troublesome was that in the Vietnamese culture, it was impossible to give a simple negative answer. When I was first speaking to General [Creighton] Abrams who commanded the troops when I got to Vietnam, he said, "In your job the most important thing is to be able to differentiate between a yes that means yes and a yes that means no." And I remember even in our home in Vietnam, I asked the maid, "Did so and so call? "Did a package arrive?" And if the answer was in the negative she would say, "Yes, sir. No." This, of course, contributed to our misreading the Vietnamese and the Vietnamese misreading us. I think it worked both ways.

The South Vietnamese were good people, hardworking, industrious, but they were very different from us and I don't think that we ever really understood them. The culture is totally different. They are a lot more fatalistic than we are, but even among Americans, intangible things make a very big difference in performance. I go back to my own experience. When I was an infantryman in the 78th division and they took us out on a thirty-mile hike my morale got very bad. And literally thousands of soldiers gave up the march after ten or twelve miles and sat on the road and sighed and waited until the trucks came to collect us. But when I transferred to the OSS and thought I was in a very good outfit and my morale was high, on a thirty-mile hike, I had no trouble travelling the distance.

And in South Vietnam in '72, their morale was good and they fought like hell and successfully because they knew that the Americans were in it. In 1975, when they had the feeling that the Americans are no longer backing them then their morale gave out and they did not fight. It's like your children—don't they need the feeling that you are going to support and you are going to protect them? It's an absolutely essential feeling. And it has to be a very strong person who can carry on when he feels abandoned.

I was in the room, third of April 1973 in San Clemente, when Nixon kept promising Thieu that if the North Vietnamese attack our retaliation is going to be instant and brutal. We took the Seventh Air Force, and moved it to Thailand and rechristened it the United States Special Action Group, but it was still the Seventh Air Force headed by a four-star general and we told everybody that the purpose of this Air Force is to punish the North Vietnamese if they should make an incursion. But they never did. And Nixon also told Thieu, "You can count on a billion dollars of aid every year as long as I am President." Now that was fine, but nobody knew that in another year Nixon wouldn't be President.

———•———

DOUGLAS PIKE

In 1975 there was the battle of Phuoc Long, up north of Saigon, an unimportant battle, but Hanoi won the whole province just like that.

Nobody could figure out how the hell they did it. Telegrams went back and forth. "It was a fluke." "They didn't expect it." "One of a kind." "It won't happen again." Then Ban Me Thuot fell and the explanations wouldn't wash. And actually it turned out Ban Me Thuot was the last battle of the war. They just started pushing down Highway Fourteen to the coast and down the coast to Saigon, and things crumbled in front of them. We had picked up high-level, top-secret electronic intelligence intercepts from Hanoi [to the Communist commanders in the South] saying "You're moving too fast. They're sucking you in." And they reported back, saying "No, they're really just crumbling." The South Vietnamese had stood and fought under far worse conditions in the past. Now they weren't standing and fighting at all. And soon the disarray was so great that even if an individual soldier wanted to stand and fight, he couldn't. It was all chaos.

Now, why was that? It's one of the major unanswered questions of the war. The best explanation I have for it lies in the Vietnamese psyche. The Vietnamese, unlike other Asians, have a sense of dependency. All Vietnamese political movements of the twentieth century have had a kind of umbilical cord to outside support. If you compare them, say, to the Congress party in India, it had connections with the Left in London, but the whole sense of Nehru and Gandhi was that "We are going to make this on our own here in India." But the Vietnamese have always had this sense of needing support from an outsider. Ho Chi Minh spent forty years trying to get somebody to deliver Vietnam to him. He tried the Japanese, he tried the French Left, and he tried the Americans. The Dai Viets had their connections to the Japanese, the VNQDD [Viet Nam Quoc Dan Dang] to the KMT in China, the Buddhists to Sri Lanka. Even today there is a Vietnam totally dependent on the Russians.

The meaning of this is that if you cut the umbilical cord, things wither and die. Looking back on it, I didn't go into that far enough. I would say to South Vietnamese in the '74 period, "Do you think you people can make it by yourselves? You've got air power, they've got a few more tanks; you've got more fire power, they've got more long-range artillery. It sort of balances." And we cut that umbilical cord, saying to them, "In objective terms you can now stand by yourself; we have got to do this. You must understand what this war is doing to us in the United States. We just can't go on any longer being torn up by it." And they'd say "Yes, we can do it. We *must* do it. You've carried us too long."

I believed them, and in a sense they believed it themselves. But in their heart of hearts, every man-jack of them knew or thought "We cannot do it alone." I'll tell you where this realization came home to me. In '75, I was in the back alley in Cleveland Park in northwest Washington teaching my son, Andrew, to ride a bicycle. And he said, "You hang onto the saddle. Otherwise I'll fall over." And I said, "Okay." So I was running up and down the alley and after he'd get going, I'd take my hand off the saddle, but I'd hold it just a little behind and he did fine. Suddenly he looked back and saw that I wasn't actually holding on, and he fell over. I said, "There's no reason at all that you can't ride alone. You were riding alone for a long time. You just didn't know it." And he said, "Yes, but when I saw you weren't holding on, I didn't think I could do it by myself."

We were doing to the Vietnamese the same thing. "You're equal to these guys. You can stand up to them. You don't *really* need our help." And they would say, "Yes, that's absolutely right. We agree one hundred percent." But in their heart of hearts they knew if we let go they'd fall off the bicycle. Analogies are dangerous, but that comes as close as anything I can uncover. All the other explanations as to why it ended the way it did just don't hold up. They did not run out of ammunition. They would eventually have run out of ammunition, but the fact is they had six billion dollars worth of hardware left. So much that they're still using it on Cambodia.

The thing that bothered me most about Vietnam was that we did not understand. If there is an epitaph for the war, it is that we lost because we did not understand. It's what Aldous Huxley called "vincible ignorance." It's something you do not know, and you know you don't know, but you don't think it makes any difference.

The most important thing we didn't understand was the nature of the strategy the other side used against us. It was full of odd terms and it didn't *sound* like a military strategy. But it wasn't all that complicated. Every Viet Cong recruit understood it and was drilled in it. It was called *dau tranh*, which simply means "struggle," but is a golden word in Vietnamese—what psychologists call emotive or emotional. Struggle doesn't have that meaning in English, but a Viet Cong says "I fight. *Dau tranh* is my whole life. I live and die for *dau tranh*." It doesn't square with the English translation if you just say "struggle."

There was armed struggle and political struggle. Armed struggle could be either big unit warfare or guerrilla warfare; it also included things like assassinations and kidnappings that you don't usually associate with armies. The other kind of struggle is political *dau tranh*, which is not politics but is the gray area between politics and war. It's what you might call politics with guns. There are three types of action within this: action among the enemy, meaning the people controlled by the enemy; action among the people, meaning the people they controlled in the liberated areas; and action among the enemy's military. The South Vietnamese knew about it, but they were as guilty as we were of vincible ignorance. You know it exists. It's not a secret. But you just say "So what? It doesn't make any difference." In many ways it remains inexplicable to me. I've gone to West Point and to Army historians' conferences. At one point I really took off on these guys and I said, "You didn't understand the war then and you don't understand it now. What really drives me up the wall is that you know you don't, and it doesn't bother you." It's like Harry Summers' book *On Strategy*, a best-seller. He doesn't *deal* with Viet Cong strategy. I said, "Harry, how can you write a book on strategy in Vietnam and not have one chapter in which you talk about the enemy?" He said, "Well, that is very hard to do, hard to understand. Anyway, this is about American strategy." Well, would you write a book about fighting Rommel in the desert and not go into what Rommel was doing and thinking? Doesn't that escape you, the logic of it?

Doing some research recently I realized that we have tons of stuff but nobody ever wrote a book about the other side. Nobody. We had five hundred and fifty thousand Americans there. They were writing every other goddamn thing you can imagine, but nobody sat down and said "Who are these guys? How are they recruited? Where did they get their officers? What training do they get? What is their history? What's their military science? Is it Marxist militarism or what?" That's vincible ignorance, you see. We knew we didn't know it but nobody thought it was necessary.

McNamara wants to know what will be the effect if we start air strikes in the North. What did he do, in effect? He says "Well, if I were Ho Chi Minh I would not like to be bombed. And if I am bombed extensively then I will do whatever they want me to do to stop the bombing." Does he research it? No. He interviews himself. Well, unfortunately for us, he wasn't Ho Chi Minh. Ho Chi Minh's reaction to the bombing wasn't the same as McNamara's. Yet McNamara was aware, I'm sure, that he didn't know *what* the reaction was. He just thought it didn't make any difference. "I'll pretend that I'm the North Vietnamese and answer this question."

You can go through the whole *Pentagon Papers*, which I did in researching a book, and at the end of fifteen volumes and taking out everything said about North Vietnam, I had about a half-page of notes. That was it. It really comes home to you that we have all these studies on Vietnam and nobody ever took the effort to look at the other side.

The real irony of the war, the paradox almost, is that we addressed ourselves fully to armed struggle, and we absolutely blunted it. The American army won every major battle it fought—a record unparalleled in the history of warfare. The war should have been over in '68, by logic. But we were never successful in addressing ourselves to the political *dau tranh* thrust. That is what did us in in the end.

CHAPTER FIVE

The War from the Vietnamese Perspective

THE sense of helplessness and dependency felt by so many Vietnamese was shaped in large measure by experiences that taught them they were in the grip of forces beyond their control. For the common people, the war was a dreadful random infliction that on any given day or night could disrupt their lives, destroy their homes, wound their loved ones, or kill them outright. For many Vietnamese, life became so nasty, brutish, and short that it is somehow surprising the society held together as long as it did.

Do Duc Cuong begins to know war during the French occupation, when he is only five. In the sixties his village is visited several times by battle, and ultimately taken by the Communists. His house is blown up, his sister killed, his mother captured, his farmer father forced to flee the land, and at a tender age he witnesses a killing so gruesome it hardly bears description. He comes to think of life in the war zone as something "really crazy . . . The father pawned the gun to the son, and one they loved the Communists, one they love Nationalists, and they kill each other." Ultimately, he joins the army, which is perhaps the last constant in a world of instability.

Others of his generation react quite differently. The family of a young man, La Anh Tu, pays ten thousand dollars to buy his way out of the draft, and he spends the war making music. Khe Ba Do's parents and family are compelled to flee their village near My Tho in the Mekong Delta; if they stay, either the Communists will take them away or the government will be suspicious. A young woman of good family, Mai Pham, is at once enthralled by her chance to work with Americans and dismayed to see her countrymen—and women—sell out to them. Ultimately, she is dispirited by Henry Kissinger's pro-

124

nouncement that "peace is at hand," because its inner meaning is that the Americans are leaving—and consigning her homeland to a socialist hell.

To the elite, who were perhaps more insulated from the brutality, the war was not so much a personal struggle as a mere extension of the greater East-West conflict—the battle between capitalism and Communism, between the United States on one hand and the Soviet Union and China on the other. That vision was reinforced by Washington's insistence not merely on conducting the war with American troops under American command, but on dictating political and bureaucratic behavior in Saigon.

Requests for aid to pacify the country, says former Gen. Tran Van Don, were brushed aside by American officials who "wanted to make a big war." But Nguyen Cao Ky's proposal for a military counterstroke against North Vietnam was also dismissed out of fear that it would make the war *too* big, by bringing on a Chinese intervention. Meantime American advisers seized administrative control of the country by using senior bureaucrats like Khe Ba Do to undercut the power of cabinet-level politicians. Small wonder, then, that hundreds of bright young Vietnamese like Nguyen Van Hao, who might have created a capable governing cadre, took themselves out of the country in the late sixties and early seventies. Like a man who grieves the loss of a wife he mistreated, they can now only lament their failure to pull together to defend what they once had.

Listening to these stories, which represent only an infinitesimal sample of what the Vietnamese endured, one is struck by the fact that even Americans who spent years "in-country" could have had only the most constricted idea of the human desolation the combat wrought. It was even then more than a century since a conflict of any kind, the Civil War, had devastated their own homeland. The impact of the fighting on the Vietnamese was the subject of brilliant essays at the time by, among others, Jonathan Schell and Frances Fitzgerald. And in a conflict that was so directly fought for the loyalties of individuals (recall that awful phrase "hearts and minds"), it merited much more attention than it got. On the evidence, American men of affairs concerned with the grand strategy of "stopping Communism" paid too little heed to warnings that a plague of high-level violence over a long period of time could only create a people alien to everything but immediate personal interest.

———————◆———————

DO DUC CUONG *was born in central Vietnam's Quang Ngai province, son of Do Duc Thanh, a civil official who eventually held a* ·

high rank in the Phoenix assassination program aimed at Viet Cong cadre. Cuong studied medicine for two years, but his school was shuttered when the students joined street demonstrations. He switched to engineering at Phu Ta Technical University in Saigon, got his degree and was offered a civilian job at a power station. But his fiercely anti-Communist father persuaded Cuong to volunteer for the ARVN. He trained at Tu Duc military officers' school, served in the ARVN Green Berets, later as a Ranger, and in the last year of the war as a captain in intelligence. Cuong and his family escaped Vietnam by boat in 1978. He now lives in a modest stucco apartment building in Santa Monica, California, a half-block from his job as a mechanical engineer for an aerospace firm, with his wife, Nam, and his eight-year-old son, Freedom.

I first know war when I was about five years old. Then the French were still involved. I born in central Vietnam and that they call the Fifth Corps of Communists at that time. I recall in my mind when I was six years old or five years old, doing everything at night and in day we go underground because we avoid the air raid. And at night I saw what they call the Peoples Court.

This the Quang Ngai province. Before 1954, before the Geneva Cease Fire agreement, from Nha Trang to Hue belonged to the Communists. At that time they put my father in jail. He was teaching French in high school so like most of people who could speak the French and have a higher education, he had to go to the camp. But he break out of the camp and he goes to Thailand. So he left the family about five years before 1954, around 1949.

After the Geneva Cease Fire Agreement had been settled he came back to work in my village, Pho Quang, in Duc Pho county. After 1954, in my area the Communists start operations around 1960. The reason is the 1954 Cease Fire Agreement, they withdraw just a part of their members. Most of them are still there so they begin the Civil War from central Vietnam. So my first experience about fighting with Communists in my area is about 1960. That's the first time it happened after President Diem. Diem, he tried to isolate the Communists by pulling the country people to one area, and let them defend themselves by building strategic hamlet. And that cause a problem for the Communists in my area.

Before 1960, I heard in my village about the Communists ask support to build the underground for them because my village is far away from a city. The big problem with them is they got isolated from the people. They needed support from people. But this program caused a problem getting support from people. So they start attack to try to break down. So the first fighting I experienced was around 1960.

I lie a whole day in the bamboo porch, you know? The fight is just around me and at last, my father, my mother tried to get all the children out, you know, and at that time my uncle, he tried to go to local force defense for the South government. He the first family— was the first member of family who got a gun. They were a very old model from France and they called calib douze or calib twelve. And we were yelling at him, "Put the gun down!" He said we had to fight because we cannot let them burn the village and I saw the people fighting with Communists but the Communists got support more than non-Communists so the Nationalists they lose the village.

At the end of the day, very dark, my mother, she tried to pull all the kids, you know, my brother, my sister and myself, and tried to run out of the area. And they asking me to go back to house to grab some of the blankets and suddenly the house is burned by mortar and my sister, she got wounded. The family carried her to the river and when we come to the river, it's after midnight, I think around two o'clock a.m., and my sister died. Her name was Lan. And my mother decide to stay back with my sister dead body, and at that time my uncle and my father coming. They asking me took all my family and run, so I tried to swim across the river.

And I could remember that very cold night. Almost the Chinese New Year, so very cold and I tried to swim and at last I lost the family but luckily, I crossed the river about five a.m. and I tried to run about one kilometer and I got captured by Communists. A lot of people got captured. They question us, but I am too small so I saw them hit some people but not me because I am young boy. So they asking each person carry some weapon they took from the Nationalist force, carry some food and I saw some man carry some wounded for them and all we go to the jungle.

After that they put me into their base in the jungle, and they let me take care of some water buffalo and stuff like that. I with them half of the year. Because they let me took care of the water buffalo every day they'd give to me one sweet potato for whole day's food and I save some and let them dry, and I save up until I think I got enough and then I run away. I know if I go east, I will get home. That took me five nights and four days.

I go back to the county city, Duc Pho. When I come in there, I just found my father and my uncle. My older brother Luong, he decided to join to the Army. He got sent to the south and he fight until he lost his arm in the Delta I think around 1966. Then he come back to

Saigon and quietly he build his family in the outskirts, you know and go to work as a laborer. He's still in Vietnam. My mother was still in village, earlier they took control. And I think about six months from that time, the Nationalist forces recaptured my village. My father start working for the government because before he just tried to build a farm for the family and he don't think he will get involved to the politic, but after the incident people decide if they like the Communists, they will go directly to hold the gun with them and those who don't like Communists, they go to working for the government.

After that I have about five years go back to school. In my school, sometimes they are no national force around there, and the Communists they come to teach us. They come tell the students "You have to go home. Don't go to school. Have to do this, do that."

After they killed President Diem, that affected us right away. On my right leg I still have a tattoo for 5-11-63. That's five days after the coup. The result of the coup is some of the main defense force like the 25th Infantry Division, withdrawn to the south so they leave the whole area undefended. So the Communists took it all over. From that day I never see my village again. I did that tattoo when I was twenty-two year old when I go to the Army Academy for training and am very sad because I never come back to my village from that day.

That was most terrible fighting because the infantry force it withdraw and in that area is only the local force, they hold these very old guns, you know? They're still using calib twelve. I separate with my mother and my other sister, Sao Huu, two years from that time because I am the boy so I could run longer and my mother and my sister they got captured. So they stay over there working for the Communists in the rice field or go to build for them the bunker, underground tunnels, something like that. I saw them next time in 1965. We recapture the area again and luckily my mother, she can get out of this area and go to the refugee camp.

Me, I decide to go looking for my father. He was in Saigon at that time, working for the government. I had no money to go to there so I go to work for the family at the city and try to get enough money to pay for bus and went to Saigon. On the bus, I have no money to buy the food and a very nice lady, she gave me a little money and she talk with me and I told her everything. After the bus stopped, she promised she try to help me to find my father and she asked me, "Do you have somewhere to live?" So again I work to help with cleaning the house, cooking and go to school at night until I finish the high school.

And I didn't know but my father, he went back to the province. He became an official in the north.* I didn't know until I tried to come back to see how my mother doing and I find out he a top official over there. So I join him, and he wanted me to go to school. I go back to school in '67. I got an exemption from the Army because the age and the education. At first I would like to learn the medical, not engineering. I got two years for that one and then the situation come badly because all the student they go out every day into the street for demonstrating. I tire with that and I decide to go to technical school. And after I get out of there, I join the Army and become intelligence officer.

If I think back about that, something's really crazy. The family come completely apart. The father pawned the gun to the son and one they loved Communists, one they loved Nationalists, and they kill each other. When I'm young, I don't know what the Communists, what the Nationalists, even I just heard about U.S., United States of America. I have seen some of the magazine named "The Free World." That's the first time I saw very nice pictures, something that looked like it did not belong to the earth.

So I started thinking, why are people like my mother or my father, he do nothing, but when I was born, I never saw him and always my mother said, he in jail. So I'm thinking a lot and the fighting starts. And the big question in my mind, "Why?" I saw the Communists, I know them because they are the local people. I met them every day. They are look normal with me but under the fighting they are acting like the devil, like they're blood thirsty. Especially when I go back to school and sometimes I got stopped by Communists or they sneak into school and some of my friends they decide to join with them, but I do not like it. I decide myself not to belong to them. I think the reason because what I witness when I was young and because of the bloody battle that happened in my village.

Something unbelievable, I tell you. I saw some lady die the worst, I don't think they could kill that lady that way. She the wife of village chief. And you know, uncle, the village chief he do nothing. And especially his wife. Absolutely an innocent woman, she never did anything that made the people get mad or something like that. But terrible. You know the iron stake that they using for the fence, the triangle bar? They pushed through her hip up to the mouth. That happened in front of my eyes or I won't believe it. I saw it and when they are gone, I run over. She's still alive, she's still breathing and

*The northern part of South Vietnam.

warm and it looked like she tried to tell something to me and that was terrible. I don't believe it.

And her son, a friend of mine, about my same age, he went crazy because I told him how his mother die. He joined the local force and he tried to kill the Communists. But the way he killed the people, I don't like it also. You know, they sneak to the river. Beyond the river are Communists, and with the guns he kill anything moving. But after that they kill him too, so I think that's the game of life and death and the people sometime are not decide to become part of this game but something pull them to play.

————◆————

One of the most galling aspects of wartime Saigon was the visibility in the very heart of the capital of hundreds of draft-age young men lounging about in bars and cafes while American GIs the same age were killing and dying in the jungles. For their habit of wearing jeans and riding motorbikes, they were known as Saigon cowboys. Though the government often denied it, Americans suspected that the cowboys had bought or influenced their way out of the war. LA ANH TU a slender, youngish man with a reddish cast to his dark brown hair, is a case in point. The son of a man who worked for a CIA radio station in Saigon, he spent six years dodging the draft while he, a brother, Tuan Ngoc, and four sisters, Thuy Anh, Khanh Ha, Uyen, and Lan Anh, ran a rock band called The Uptight. They mainly played the GI clubs at Long Binh, the sprawling U.S. Army headquarters twenty miles east of Saigon; after the Americans went home in 1973, they shifted to downtown Tu Do Street nightspots, and to the Officers' Club at Tan Son Nhut, where they performed for hundreds of cheering Hungarians, Poles, Indonesians, Canadians, and later Iranians—members of the International Commission for Control and Supervision (ICCS) established by the 1973 Paris Accords. At the end, Anh Tu and eight members of his family were smuggled out of Vietnam by his sister's fiancée, Larry Pope, who managed the Tan Son Nhut club. Pope is now a hotel executive in Chicago. Anh Tu and his family have put The Uptight back together, and the band now plays California nightspots.

In 1961, when my sister Bich Chieu left Vietnam for Paris, we knew a lot of people can help us get out of Vietnam easy. My mother does not think war is going to last that long. I was eleven. So we stayed Saigon. In 1970 war was still on. We know sure we will not be able to win the war. My mother said she knows the Communists, they never give up. So I change my papers, even to a Chinese name, and I have to study Chinese.

We had no car. Most of the money we make goes to my papers, even to borrow at high interest for my draft evasion. It cost us ten thousand dollars. We got the papers through the wife of a guy in police headquarters. She said she wanted to help us leave. Men couldn't get out, though it was easy for girls. He found a Chinese paper from Danang. I put my own picture on it and a different name. He removed my Vietnamese papers at police headquarters. I was a People's Republic of China citizen. With that paper I was almost going to leave.

Khanh Ha and me and Thuy Anh started the Blue Jets in 1969. We played for American soldier clubs for three years. The band broke up and we formed a new one. It was our agent who gave the name The Uptight. In '73, after the cease-fire, we played for Vietnamese audiences. In Danang I played for Americans the last day before they left Vietnam. We never want to get out of Saigon too far, never want to stay away from home. But the agent said in Saigon there was not enough business, so we had to go to Danang. There were still a lot of Americans. We were supposed to spend one month there. When we were there only fifteen days everybody left.

Then we start to play for the ICCS. Communists, they like American songs, too. One Hungarian came to my house, too. He says, "Your family have so many girls. Tell your mother to give me one to bring back with me." They give us a tape and we learn a Hungarian song for them. We played at the Tan Son Nhut club, Larry's club, the old American base. There were three or four hundred people in the audience, five nights a week. They liked "Aquarius" and "Let the Sun Shine In." The Canadians liked "Snowbird." The Hungarians liked this song "Amicor," ("Friends"). We sang one Indonesian song, but not one Polish song—it was too hard to pronounce. They were crazy about us. Every night ended with "Aquarius." We went into the audience and they make a conga line behind us.

I got caught and drafted in August 1974, eight months before the end. The draft age was eighteen. I was twenty-four. Later on we try to find people to make veteran's papers. They were cheap, eight hundred thousand piasters, on condition that I cut my two toes off. I said no. If it's just the money, okay, but not the toes.

After three months basic training I moved to base. They sent me to the field, to bunker. We avoided the area assigned to look for Viet Cong. We would hide all day from the helicopters. Officers, too. One day I was walking in the middle of a field. We saw some VC. They just fired a few shots and ran. We didn't follow them. We may get in a trap. Nobody wants to fight, even the VC.

I played at Christmas, holidays or parties, or the colonel's party. They had big party at headquarters. Big bosses were there, and Khanh Ha was there, brought by two friends of mine. They asked Ha to sing a song for them. They tell me to sing one song. The colonel knew I was in the troop. "Now you form a band for me," he says. "Once in a while play for me." He was very good man, likes music.

Though she never saw the United States until she was evacuated from Saigon at age twenty, MAI PHAM *looks and sounds like an Asian-American who's lived in California all her life. A morning news anchor woman and reporter at KXTV in Sacramento, she speaks English without the slightest trace of an accent. She's a journalism graduate of the University of Maryland, where her father settled the family after 1975.*

We are from Saigon. My father, Pham Van Xuan, was the number two man in the Vietnamese CIA. I am the third of four kids. I was one of the well-known "two sisters" active in communications. My sister, Denise, was very famous as the voice of House Seven, the CIA clandestine radio station. She was a disk jockey trying to convince the Communist soldiers to defect.

Denise was on the air as Mai Lon. She was also the first one to do an English-language show, broadcasting to the American soldiers in 1969. She got a scholarship to NYU. I stepped in for her at sixteen in 1971, and never left. I did that show, then went over and co-hosted a show with a navy journalist. It was "The Mick and Mai Show," a Saturday top-forty radio show where I would chat on Vietnamese customs and culture.

Because I was doing this show, I had a good opinion of most American people. I knew officers in Saigon. I thought they were okay. I was supposed to help Americans understand the country they were helping to protect from Communism. But it was sad to see Vietnamese cluttering around military bases. Bars were springing up overnight, kids selling cigarettes in the street. To this day whenever I see a GI in a movie with two girls, like *An Officer and a Gentleman*, I get upset. I reminds me of the aspect of Vietnam that I'm not proud of.

We had a big three-story house, a beautiful home my parents had built with savings from my father's diplomatic career. It was in the heart of Saigon, fifteen blocks from the palace. He had been a military attaché, mostly in Thailand, working with SEATO, and also in Taiwan.

Then I became interested in news. I pitched ABC as needing someone with Vietnamese perspective and language. As a tryout, I analyzed the impact of the [1973] cease-fire in villages. I talked to
peasants and gave ABC a twenty-page report. Two weeks later they
asked me to work as vacation fill-in. I did, and began attending military briefings and going to the PRG* at Tan Son Nhut. I was doing
little color stories on the Viet Cong there.

Being with the American news media in Vietnam was like being a
spy. There was something very romantic about it. At the Continen-
tal Palace I would eat real butter and French bread and talk about
stories with my friends, learning things you ordinarily couldn't learn.
And also to be among the excitement. And to work with people who
are today big, big shots. I researched for Ted Koppel, Dennis Troute,
and Steve Bell. I was hired by Kevin Delaney, who now is the *ABC
Closeup* producer.

After '73 I was still a DJ, for ARS, the American Radio Service, a
civilian station serving the Embassy. We were all hanging onto something that just wasn't there any more. I worked one hour a day from
two to three p.m. A couple of songs always remind me of Vietnam.
We would always play that Beatles song, "The Long And Winding
Road," and my U.S. press friends liked the *Woodstock* album.

The single most demoralizing event for us was Kissinger's "peace
is at hand" remark, which was on TV and in *Stars and Stripes* headlines. It meant the Americans were out, the whole war machinery
stopping, and the tanks rolling in. As long as you didn't have the
Americans there, you didn't have anything. Because the Vietnamese
weren't fighting, and they certainly weren't going to fight without
the weapons. Everybody said, "Maybe they will come back."
Nobody thought the Americans were leaving for good. And maybe
other Free World troops would come in. We were so used to having *somebody* there. The withdrawal was very traumatic for our society. Sixty percent of the civilian employment revolved around the
Americans. People got mean then. The *beggars* were mean.

To me, the fall of Saigon was never an if, it was a when. I had been
convinced since a couple of years before. To fight a war you need
tools. So long as you are depending on another country to supply
the tools, one of these days the other country is going to stop supplying them. Unlike others, I knew of the antiwar movement.

My father thought I was pro-Communist. "If you don't believe in
the Saigon regime, you're pro-Communist!" he would tell me. I just
didn't believe the regime would *survive*. I knew of the North Vietnamese commitment. They had the political maturity to make it suc-

*Provisional Revolutionary Government—The political arm of the Viet Cong.

cessful, and we did not. We were trying to have a democratic state, but we could barely count the ballots. All the elections were rigged. It's hard to ask somebody to believe in a system like that. I felt caught in the middle.

———————◆———————

KHE BA DO, *who holds a Ph.D. from the University of Southern California in higher education administration, was vice-minister of education in Saigon from 1971 to 1974. Then he founded and became president of Thu Duc Polytechnic University, eight miles outside Saigon. He was brought out of Vietnam by the Americans in the last mad dash for the exits. He is now dean of the science and health faculties at American River College, a two-year school in Sacramento, California.*

In '54, when the country was divided along the seventeenth parallel, I was already working at the College of Science at the University of Saigon and finishing my degree there and also teaching in a private high school. I have never been in the military because even though people of my age at that time were drafted, there's some deferment clause for people that government feels are necessary to run the offices. And I was one of the rare Vietnamese working under the French professors at the College of Science and so every year I got that deferment.

Before the war there was only one university for whole Vietnam and it was in Hanoi, the University of Indochina. And only after World War II the French, under pressure of the people from South Vietnam, established a branch of the University in Saigon. I was the first one employed to help the French perfect it, to establish the physics lab in Saigon. I worked for the University and starting as a lab technician and then as an assistant actually and then as a professor and an administrator later on. I was with University of Saigon until 1975, when I left Vietnam.

My father was a farmer and a village official in My Tho province in the Mekong Delta. I consider 1958 and '59 one of the best periods for South Vietnam under President Diem. The country kind of raising after President Diem has defeated those factions like the Binh Xuyen, and there's some lack of fighting between the Communists and the Nationalists. In 1958 or '59 we still can go back to the village for a short period. We dare not stay overnight, but traveling in the daytime, it was all right. In 1960 my parents they have to leave their land and move to Saigon completely and to stay with family, especially my older brothers and my younger sisters.

The fighting started there, and it's not safe at all, because if you stay there, you're either forced by the Communists to go with them or you are suspected by the Nationalist government. As a matter of fact all of my greater family, extended family have to move to Saigon from My Tho. Then before the Diem assassination things got worse because besides the fighting against the Vietcong, there's those Buddhist demonstrations and we felt that there's some crisis coming. I tried to avoid the crowd then because it is very dangerous. And you see many people in uniform, military trucks, and if you drive from province to province at night you can hear the bombardments. Most of the time it's safe to travel in daytime but you can see sentries posted along the road so very clearly this country's at war.

Right after the assassination we have a long period of instability. At that time also I was what they call in French *chef de cabinet* of the Ministry of Education. The cabinet changed many, many times. One time it survived just one hundred days. The minister change every few months and the American education advisors were concerned about the continuity of American aid to education so they urged me to stay in cabinet. It happened that the ministers were mostly not educators. They were lawyers or pharmacists or medical doctors and they did not have much experience in education. And the new minsters always brought with them a whole new staff, but in my case every time, the American advisor came and said, "Well, okay. I want you to stay in spite the fact it's so difficult for you to adjust to the new staff, in order to insure the stability of the whole thing." So I stayed *chef de cabinet*.

As the *chef de cabinet* I also supervised the whole foreign assistance to education. And at that time, it was very important because with American money we were building the teaching hospital for Saigon University and the College of Education and at least, as I remember, eighteen technical schools across the country and also around 1961–62, in the Strategic Hamlet program we build fifteen or sixteen thousand classrooms and I have to work out all those plans. Without American money we could not have the model facilities for education at all levels.

After I survived about seven ministers I got tired and a lot pressure also. So in '65 I left. I went to California and I came back in '70. When I came back there were a lot of changes. The face of Saigon different because more and more military trucks, more and more GIs, more and more hotels and buildings around and Saigon is more crowded especially. I was amazed by the number of Honda motorcycles, motorbikes, those things. The country is fighting a war but still it looks like the economy is okay. The Americans pouring money in. And I found that I was maybe one of the poorest among my friends because most of them, I don't know, they go out to deal with some black market, but it seemed that all of them have houses and have cars. My wife woke up in the morning and ask the maid to go and buy something for our breakfast, and she have no idea of the value of money. For example in the past a bowl of rice and noodles cost lets say, one piaster; now it cost something like fifty piasters. And my wife was giving to maid ten piasters for the breakfast and the maid is just smiling but she didn't say anything. Finally, she just explained, "No, you can't do anything with ten piasters here."

Business people are always making money, but the people who suffer most, I think, are the workers and the government employees with fixed salaries who cannot keep up with the price. My wife found a job with a regional organization for education development in Southeast Asia, and she earned more than me because they pay what you call a third-country salary in dollars, so converted into Vietnamese piasters it's not bad for a couple. We have a government apartment, but even with the money we earn we could not afford to buy a house or a car. The prices going up so fast that we cannot keep up.

In 1970, really, I didn't see anything bad yet, but I know there's something wrong for the South from the Paris negotiations. In 1971 Thieu won the reelection, and that year it seemed the Saigon government was still strong. Only after they cross the seventeenth parallel in '73 did we see the end is coming. But we're still fighting, and the South Vietnamese government is still fighting furiously. Talking to the American advisor, I felt the aid to education especially and for the economy in general was cutting down, down, down after the Paris Agreement. That worried us, but we still believed, or for myself at least, I still believed what the government officials say. They sound optimistic, and they deceived people I think. Until the last minute, during the invasion from the North in '75, we still believe that the South, with the help of the Americans, could fight back.

———•———

TRAN VAN DON, *sixty-seven, French-born and-educated, was one of South Vietnam's key military and political leaders. As a senior general, he was a leading plotter in the successful 1963 coup that overthrew President Ngo Dinh Diem and resulted in his murder. He left Vietnam in the U.S. evacuation on April 29, 1975. Now living in Fairfax, Virginia, where he operates a travel agency, he has published two books about Vietnam, one in the U.S. and the other in France, and is preparing a third.*

We regret the past. We should all have done better than we did. We made so many, many mistakes. Even when we made our coup against Diem in '63, I don't say it was a mistake, but it was a mistake not to have had better coordination with the American side. The Americans didn't understand very well what to do. They wanted to make a big war. But at that time it was not a big war. It was an insurgency. We needed more aid to pacify South Vietnam and not to fight against North Vietnam. At the time—1963—the North had not yet sent its troops to the South. It was a job of pacification. But they [the Americans] didn't want to pacify. They wanted to make war.

In '65 they sent their troops. I was not in favor of U.S. combat troops in Vietnam. What we needed at the time was an aid commitment from America and its allies just like the North was getting from Russia and its allies. But unfortunately on the non-Communist side there was no bloc of nations to give us sustained aid. On the Communist side they had the same, consistent policy from beginning until the end, even until now.

Also on the American side there was not enough patience. It's like what you are doing in Central America. You always want to make a democratic country. But how can you teach democracy to a people who are not politically educated, to a people who do not understand what is freedom? It always made for confused relations with the French and Americans. The French wanted to keep their colony. Why didn't the French do what the British did with their colonies—or what the Americans did with the Philippines? You Americans came and told the Vietnamese that it was legal in the country to be against the policy of the government, that you can be in the opposition. The Communists used that to push the people to say and demand more. The Americans built a politically confused situation in South Vietnam.

———————•———————

DR. NGUYEN BUU TRUNG *is one of the most successful members of Vietnam's Class of 1975—those who fled Saigon with the departing Americans. It wasn't always so. Though he was a talented plastic surgeon, specializing in the reconstruction of war-damaged hands, when he arrived in the United States he had to spend two years as a mere physician's assistant to the Portland, Oregon, doctor who sponsored him out of Camp Pendleton, California. Then came six months at the Loma Linda Medical School to prepare for American medical exams, followed by several penurious years of residencies while his wife, Thi Bich Hang, worked to support the family. He finally landed a prestigious teaching post at Cornell Universi-*

ty's New York Hospital. In 1983, he moved back to the more hospitable California climate and a six-figure salaried post at Bellflower Hospital in Los Angeles. He and his wife and four kids live in a Spanish-style two story house in Orange County.

I grew up in Tam Vu town, ten miles south of Saigon, same town as Prime Minister [Tran Thien] Khiem. My grandfather was Khiem's teacher. My father was forestry service chief. I went to medical school at the University of Saigon, and got another degree from Paris University. I finish my medical school and residency in 1965. Then I was chief of the medical team in the 22nd Division in Camau because when you finished medical school, you had to join Army. And after one year, I moved to Bac Lieu, near Camau. My first year I had to go to combat and my friends, a lot of soldier die near me. I just talk to him and boom! Just one or two meter, a few inches from me. I see a lot of killing almost like you see in that movie *The Killing Fields**. If you stay in the province town you don't see anything. When you go to combat you see a lot of killing, a lot of killing.

I go with the colonel, chief of the battalion. I had to go with them. Otherwise, soldiers are scared. They don't want to fight if they do not see the doctor. I go in the field with the soldiers for the first six months. I know a doctor who went to combat and died but I was not work with him. I was not with him because for the first six months, they had to go with the small units and then he die for the first two months.

After Camau I still do combat but with a general. I go to Bac Lieu with the general. I did not have to work with the danger whenever the general go. I just go with the helicopter. I did not worry any more. Before I had to worry about the mine. They bring from the front to the airport. I always stay at the airport and I do some initial care and then I send to the hospital. You stop bleeding right away. If they got chest wound you put the chest tubes. If they go to the head, you put the tracheotomy tube so they can breathe. If you can save their life, they can go to the hospital. Something not emergency, I take care of it there.

We don't have time to think because we had to work. We don't have weekend. We work every day so when you go home, you're too tired, you don't have time to think anything. Like you do mechanic work, you don't know anything. They have maybe four or five doctors for one brigade. We had the same supplies as U.S. Army,

---

*An extraordinarily accurate and realistic film about a Cambodian journalist's escape from the holocaust visited on his country by the Khmer Rouge regime that had toppled its pro-Western government.

so very good. Better than many hospitals here because we had everything new—new instruments, new medicine. It's very good supplies.

After a year I go again to training, and then I go to Danang military hospital. I was orthopedic surgeon, but usually we do everything. In regular day I was orthopedic surgeon, but when I was on call, I am general surgeon, neurosurgeon, thoracic surgeon. We do everything, because you cannot call anybody to help you. Everyone was very tired so you do everything. Usually work more than ten hours a day.

Then I come back to Cong Hoa Hospital in Saigon, near Tan Son Nhut Airport, with three thousand beds, a big hospital. I train for two years under an American plastic surgeon in Saigon, and then I became chief of hand surgery at Cong Hoa. I had a hundred patients always ready for me to do the operation, so I knew all the most famous hand surgeons in the world, they come to visit me. I was learning by them. Then I became the chief and I wrote some paper same way they do.

In Saigon we used to living in the wartime so freely, so nobody worry. Nothing happened with our daily life, everything normal. Nothing affect me and my family. We don't know much from Vietnam TV and radio, because they try to hide the news. Just like in Soviet now. If you read from outside, *Newsweek* or something, you know. The Vietnamese newspaper, the TV, you don't know anything. They tried to hide everything.

Even at the Tet I still use my car to go to work from my home to the hospital. We don't get scared. These things happen often so nobody care. At the Tet we are not ready to fight because really we take a month off for the Tet, so nobody is ready. But we don't think we lost the war at that time. I was at Cong Hoa hospital and I was hear a lot of noise. Usually we have a lot of firecracker, so we don't think anything happened. But a few hours later, I heard the news on the TV and radio. They come right in front of the gate at Cong Hoa, shooting in front of the gate. But I was in combat so this thing is nothing.

In '73 we were optimistic the war would end up. Activity was reduced for a few months. I think capitalists need South Vietnam to counterbalance Communists. I do not think Communists can enter Saigon. They are no stronger than the South. I was optimistic. I resigned as chief of hand surgery a few months before the end. I opened an office for private practice in plastic and hand surgery on the first floor of my home.

I was elected chairman of the city council in Gia Dinh province, with two million people just beyond the Saigon city limits. I not really interested in national politics, just provincial. Gia Dinh offices were one mile from Saigon city hall. So I was the friend of generals and province chiefs. Nobody told us anything bad about anything to do with Gia Dinh. We thought maybe there going to be some neutralist solution. We will have election, and Communists will just leave Saigon alone.

Even at the end, a few hours before I left Vietnam, we don't think we lost the South. Even Thieu resigned, we don't think anything happen because we usually saw this thing happen. So a president resigned, a prime minister resigned, nothing happens with our life. Nothing changed. Just normal for us.

———•———

NGUYEN VAN HAO's physique belies his remarkable background. He is very tall and well-muscled for a Vietnamese, and his tastes run to windsurfing and tennis. But Hao is in fact an economist of international repute. He alternated in the sixties and seventies between working abroad—two years with the Food and Agriculture Organization in Rome, and four years at Harvard University—and serving as a minister in the Thieu regime. In 1974, Thieu made him Vietnam's economic czar. He stayed on as a consultant to the Communists after the fall of Saigon—treated well, quite possibly, because he had successfully maneuvered in the closing days of the war to prevent the Americans from shipping South Vietnam's gold reserves to the United States. Hao left Vietnam and applied for entry to the U.S. in 1982. His application was denied because of his association with the Communist successor government, though his wife and sons lived in the United States. He now works in Africa for the United Nations.

The tale of America in South Vietnam is you were lacking the will to do a proper job. To me it's a political problem which has a general international impact. Communist and capitalism. It's not a regional problem. It's not a Vietnamese problem. It's a superpowers problem. Balance. It's East and West. But they forget about the issue—a human fallacy. You never appreciate what you have. You just begin to value the things which you lost. You have a good wife, you never appreciate it. You see always other wife is better than yours. And once you lost it, you say oh my goodness, my wife finish. Because every day you don't appreciate she serve you. We have a country, we have a good system, but nobody care. Once we lost it we say "Oh, what the hell. Before it's so fantastic compared what we have now. Why we haven't defend ourself before? If we know we lose out like this, maybe we fight until last man."

One thing in Communist strategy you have to admire. They have the best system to train people when to take opportunity. They always look for opportunity. Study opportunity. Analyze, is it the right time to take opportunity? The opportunity at that time because the U.S. with the Watergate, Nixon down, Ford is not elected, and they are sure if they do something here, Ford is a President not elected to have the power to take action. Opportunity. Take chance. It's why they are ready to go in South Vietnam and sure they have no reaction from the Americans.

During all the time of war the people in Hanoi launch a business as a professional full-time job, nothing to do except making war. South Vietnam politicians are not professional. Is why the tragedy. Amateur, amateur.

Diem, for four or five years, from 1956 to '60, he did a very good job. He knew how to organize the functions of the state. And Diem was respected at that time. In the North they have Ho Chi Minh and at least here we have a man called Diem. Good family. Good background and a lot of position. In just four or five years he did a very good job. In a way the Vietcong become threatened. The Vietnam history you should separate between 1956 and 1960. The good year is 1958. Peaceful, prosperous, and at least a lot of people think they have one nation.

But the army become a force after Thieu and Ky come to power. Because in '65, the concept at that time we have nothing to do except to make war. The Americans think the best way to run the war is with the army people, the military people. It's why in that time nobody think about a civilian government. And then the war drag on and it's impossible to persuade the people it's better to run this war by a civilian government. And Thieu and Ky once they taste power, it's like everybody taste power, it's become for you like opium. You like it. You love it. It's very understandable.

After from 1960, young Vietnamese have been sent to U.S. a lot to be trained over there. And in 1965 a lot of people in Europe that time never go back. Stay there, especially good technician. That not my case. After I have been working for United Nations, FAO in Rome, I work there two years, government asked me to come back, I say yes immediately. I never refuse to go back to my country. I think the country needs the young people and technical people, I just go back.

And at that time there is one wave of technician come back to Vietnam, especially people have been trained by U.S. scholarship. And we come there and especially the middle echelon of the administration run by young people. But in 1965 we still very young, not enough experience in order to go up to the policymakers' decisions. It take five six years. Eventually I think in '65 it's still a good year, and if Vietnam have a chance maybe five years in order to get right people in right place in a professional way, could be a big chance for Vietnam. A new generation come to power. You know my generation in '65 we just around forty. Not young but not old enough to do a good job.

Now from the time Paris Agreement, we know that time the military stronger so we must press to economic competition. Even in Thieu regime at that time is the hour of the technician. And we have enough experience how to run the country in a professional way. It's why we come to power without any backing. With ten years experience we are ready to change the guard. If I hadn't believed in the survival of Vietnam, I would never have joined the Thieu government. After the Paris Agreement signed by fourteen countries, a guarantee by you westerners, in military aspect will be sure two, South Vietnam and North Vietnam.

That's reason why Thieu asked me to join the government. Because that time I was maybe the only man not heavily involved in corruption, scandal, and others. And before I decide to join the government, we discuss between Thieu and myself almost forty days before we came to agreement and with conditions I did join the government. I did this because I have before some problem with Thieu in 1970, and from 1970 to 1974, when he asked me to join his government, he never say hello to me. I knew him very well before, and he loved me before. That's why I get to Harvard that time. This time Thieu was with me, really with me. After I took the job, I get very close. For me, the power is not an end in itself, just a tool, because my principle, my philosophy, you cannot do nothing for your country if you do not have the power.

———————•———————

For all the rumors that he brought millions with him out of Vietnam, former Prime Minister, Vice-President, and Air Force Commander NGUYEN CAO KY *did not appear to thrive financially in exile. Ky filed for bankruptcy in 1984, blaming his business reverses on high interest rates. His major asset was a handsome, airy, two-story home in Huntington Beach, California, its living room adorned with photo enlargements of a flight of three ancient T-28 prop-driven fighter-bombers and of himself in a group of flight-suited Vietnamese pilots. Ky, who has recently invested in a fishing enterprise in Louisiana, seems nearly as trim as in the days when he held the world stage.*

I said at the time there was not winning policy, from the beginning. I first told President Johnson and Dean Rusk, and all of them— McNamara—I said, if the U.S. plan is to build massive military forces in Vietnam, a half million, Air Force, Navy, Army, then you have to use it in a more conventional way to stop aggression. The best defensive is offensive. Many times I said in public: "We have to go North."

During the Guam conference in 1967 I proposed to them an invasion plan to the North, using only Vietnamese troops. Also, I said, if they accept that plan I will resign as premier and volunteer to head that invasion. I said, if *you* cannot fight them, at least the presence of two or three South Vietnamese divisions in the North will keep the North Vietnamese troops home. Otherwise they would have a free hand to send all their reserves south. It's very logical. It's elementary strategy. Now they recognize that they were wrong.

I also told Johnson that, knowing American thinking, I don't think Americans can sustain a war for ten or fifteen years, especially in a country far away like Vietnam. So that's the two reason I recommended *quick* action and *offensive* action, instead of always defensive. Maybe they are just too afraid of the Chinese intervention. They remember Korea. They believed it was the right policy, that in the long run we can stop aggression and build a strong South Vietnamese democracy.

At the end there were no alternatives for Americans. They had to pull out. You don't have the patience—and it is wrong from the beginning. They had to find some way to pull out. But the sad thing to the Vietnamese was that Watergate came right after that. When the Communists began their final offensive, there was no government in America. America was the one who signed and guaranteed the treaty in Paris, and the Communists, very clever, benefit to the maximum when you have trouble here in America. There was nothing the government could do, and the Communists knew it. If Mr. Nixon were still a strong President, the government of the United States will take some strong measures against the violations of the Communists.

CHAPTER SIX

The Slippery Slope

To insiders and outsiders alike, U.S. policy in Vietnam seemed from the start to be on a slippery slope. Good intentions notwithstanding, American actions always seemed to leave the effort further from the goal than ever. The vignettes that follow are not a recital in detail, but a sampler of the way things went wrong over a period of years.

To restore popular government in Saigon and settle a roiling crisis between the Buddhist majority and the Catholic elite, American policymakers fomented a coup against Ngo Dinh Diem late in 1963. The generals who seized power proceeded to spend two years battling each other for control, and the communal hatreds festered on through 1966.

Lyndon Johnson tried to use the White House as a command post from which to run the war, but merely succeeded in persuading his subordinates that the best course was to say yes to his face and ignore him behind his back. He became so secretive, so paranoid about leaks, that when he decided in the spring of 1968 to leave the presidency, he withheld the news from even his closest subordinates— who might well have advised him how to get the maximum, rather than the minimum, leverage out of his supreme political sacrifice.

The attempt to turn terrorism back on the enemy through the Phoenix program no doubt destroyed much of the Communist cadre in the South, but it also helped to imbue American troops with a careless disregard for civilian lives. That attitude reached a zenith in the massacre at My Lai. There, the U.S. command was trying to blood a poorly trained brigade in what it thought was a quiet area already "pacified" by South Korean Marines. But the Koreans had salted the area with mines and booby traps, which took a fierce toll in American casualties. The absence of institutional memory left the Americans in the blind about who or what was maiming them— so they blamed their losses on the local Vietnamese. In retribution,

144

they annihilated an entire village, an act that had devastating political consequences when it was uncovered.

To pacify his riotous home front, Richard Nixon launched a program to "Vietnamize" the war and withdraw American troops. But the twin passions of civil rights and war resistance, along with the drug culture, had already arrived in the combat zone. The announcement of an impending end to the U.S. war effort, however distant, instantly corroded what was left of American morale.

Over the years, American generals—and some diplomats—argued strongly that the only way to control the war in the South was to disrupt Communist supply lines from the North by cutting the Ho Chi Minh Trail. But the United States was never able to summon the courage to make such a move where the terrain was favorable, in North Vietnam. When the military finally did get a "Go" from Richard Nixon in 1971, it was for an invasion of Laos, where it would have been difficult in the best of circumstances to support the invading troops. The only forces available, the South Vietnamese, were beaten decisively.

And in perhaps the supreme irony of the conflict, the Americans and the Saigon government actually began to succeed in controlling the guerrilla struggle in the South in the early seventies, largely by arming local villagers for self-defense. But by then, with American troops virtually out of action, Hanoi was able to shift with impunity to the large-scale conventional tactics with which it eventually brought South Vietnam to its knees.

WILLIAM SULLIVAN

In July of '64 I went out to Saigon with Max Taylor. After Kennedy was killed, Johnson struggled with it himself for a while and then he just wanted to get rid of the whole mess and he gave Max carte blanche and sent him out there as Ambassador. Max wrote his own ticket so he was not only Ambassador but head of military operations as well—Westy reported to him. Max had his own idea about the structure he wanted, and he asked me to come out with him to get that organized. I was on my way to Vientiane as Ambassador. I have some pretty vivid memories of that, some funny and some not so funny.

During the summer of '64 there had been a series of coups, and the fellow who was then in charge of government was a roly-poly general named Nguyen Khanh. There was another coup attempt on a

Sunday morning and Khanh disappeared. Late in the afternoon we discovered he was in Dalat, up in the Highlands. Well, by this time Nguyen Cao Ky was getting quite annoyed and he was buzzing planes over the city to try to suppress those who wanted to make the coup. So General Dick Stilwell and I flew up to Dalat in a little plane to get Khanh and bring him back to Saigon. We landed fairly close to dusk and went to the old Bao Dai* palace, and there he was, surrounded by a whole bunch of people including Nguyen Van Thieu. So we took Khanh into the dining room and said "Look, you've got to come back." And he said "If you broadcast a message saying that you're still supporting me, I'll do that."

So Alex Johnson, who was the chargé, because Max Taylor was out of the country, said he would broadcast the message. But while we were waiting for that to happen a Vietnamese pilot with a purple scarf came in with a lavender-scented letter, which he handed to Khanh. And Khanh read it and then he looked at Dick and me and said "Well, I'm prepared to go now." This was before the broadcast. So we went out and got in the plane. It was pitch dark by then so we had them put some lights on the runway and we took off and came back down to Tan Son Nhut in Saigon. And we were greeted warmly by everybody, including Ky, and we broke out champagne and so on. Finally I got Ky over in the corner and I said, "Did you send a pilot up with a letter to Khanh?" And he said, "Oh yes." And I said, "What was in the letter?" And he said, "The letter said that if he didn't get out of that building in fifteen minutes, I was going to bomb it." And I said, "Did you know that Dick Stilwell and I were in the building?" And he said, "Oh yes."

There were also some real nightmares. The Buddhists and the Catholics were contesting for control of the government. One day I was on my way back from a dental appointment when my car was held up by a bunch of youngsters from rival Buddhist and Catholic schools who got into a scuffle. They were probably from the ages of ten to fourteen and they were in their school uniforms. And I saw one little fellow breaking out and getting away and being pursued by others and finally surrounded on the knoll of a hill in a little park and I remember watching as these youngsters began to close on him and then suddenly realizing what they were doing. By the time I could get out of my car or other people could get out of their cars in this traffic jam, they were stabbing him and he died right there from multiple stab wounds by the other little youngsters. It was a sort of *Lord of the Flies* episode and it captured the sense of violence and the

---

*The former French puppet "emperor" of colonial Vietnam.

diminished regard for human life that was one of the corrosive effects of the war.

RICHARD HOLBROOKE

When I got to Saigon I was twenty-two and I believed everything I had been told by the United States government. I believed that the commitment was correct—freedom of choice, self-determination, save the country from Communism—and that we were doing the right thing because the U.S. government *did* the right thing. In those days you didn't question it. But after my Mekong Delta experiences, the miscounted hamlets and so on, I knew that the assessments were wrong and the reporting was perverted. I knew that the press corps' version of how things were going was correct. Men like John Paul Vann were their sources and what John Paul Vann was telling [David] Halberstam, John Paul Vann couldn't push through the chain of command to the chairman of the JCS.

When I moved to the Embassy and became a staff assistant to Lodge and Taylor, and got to see men like Westmoreland, I began to question the tactics—harassment and interdiction fire, free-fire zones. I remember a very strong argument I had once with Westmoreland and Lodge. The three of us flew up to some inspection, these two senior people and this twenty-four-year-old aide. And I look back and I was talking to a four-star general commanding half a million troops and to a proconsul. But it didn't even occur to me. I remember saying to them, "It's crazy, these planes are allowed to dump their bombs on these specified free-fire zones as they come home if they see anything moving. There are people living down there." [One of them said] "Well, they're Communist-controlled areas." I'd say, "No, this is crazy." I'd give all the standard counterinsurgency arguments. And what I believed then was that if you improved the strategy you could win the war. You could gain control of the population and to turn Mao's aphorism on its head, dry up the terrain in which the Communists operated.

But the critical phase in my thinking about Vietnam did not begin until I got back to Washington in 1966. The day I went to work our staff was called to meet with the President. I was twenty-five, just back from Vietnam, and I thought I knew more about the place than anyone else in the whole city. So we walk into the Cabinet Room, and of course Johnson talks for one straight hour.

He says to Komer, "Ah, Bob, I've been reading a report that they cut Route Four between Saigon and Can Tho." And he says "You know, in Texas if the price of pigs goes up, you get thrown out of power. You lose elections. The price of pigs is power in Texas." And then he says, "Komer, I want you to get the price of pigs down by fifty percent in twenty-four hours and get that road open."

And Komer is saying "Yes, Mr. President." And it's like Hitler at the end of World War II, moving around divisions that don't exist. Komer is being ordered to open a road which is in Communist control. We *can't* open the goddamned road. Johnson is going on and on. Then finally, after an hour of this, Johnson says, "I have another idea, Bob. You know at the end of World War II we had all these civil affairs advisers who ran occupied Germany and occupied Japan. We ought to reactivate them and get them out there to run Vietnam."

Well, I know now that Johnson said things like this all the time and all you did was say "Yes, Mr. President" and ignore him. But at the time I thought this was the President of the United States starting a policy. I suddenly had this vision of battalions of paunch-bellied, aging colonels who had run Munich in 1945 for two or three months, going to Quang Tri. This was too much for me. I'd never talked to a President before. But I said, "Mr. President?" He looks around the table like "Who's this punk?" So very, very carefully I say, "Mr. President, I've just come back from Vietnam and, you know, I'm a little worried about this. I'm not sure American advisers of that sort would be quite qualified. You know there are some limitations to what Americans can do in the civilian field in Vietnam." He takes off his glasses and he looks at me with that sad look of his and he says, "Son, your job is to get rid of those limitations." And he gets up and walks out of the room. That was my introduction to the White House.

But it was unforgettable, and for me it was an unforgettable time. Nothing in the world excited me more. I idolized McGeorge Bundy, Bob McNamara, what Teddy White called the "action intellectuals." To work among them was very exciting. And *they* didn't know what the hell was going on in Vietnam. Worse, some of them, like Walt Rostow, were deliberately misrepresenting the facts, not only to the public but to themselves and the President. There was a perversion of information that really upset and worried me.

And then at the same time, I saw for the first time what I'd missed because I'd been in Vietnam—and that was the eroding base of popular support, which to the extent it still existed was dependent on the public misunderstanding the truth. Since I knew, I felt I ended up being part of the famous credibility gap. And at that point, the objectives of the United States in Vietnam came into question in my mind for the first time.

Now, at no point in this process had I yet reached the understanding that I later got of what the North Vietnamese were about. As I now look back I recognize one thing that is neither a hawk's nor a dove's point but gets to the heart of the profound error we made in Vietnam. That is, we all were wrong to think that pacification could *ever* have won the war. The liberal interventionists' theory—a successful pacification program confined to South Vietnam with interdiction of the supply routes from the North—was a wrong strategy. The North Vietnamese would have simply sent divisions down one way or another, and kept fighting until we lost. If we had succeeded in getting rid of all the indigenous Viet Cong, as some people argue we did in the Tet offensive, all we would have done is brought in the North Vietnamese Army faster.

The deepest and most profound error—which I certainly did not understand in the sixties—was Bob McNamara's. If Vietnam was as important to the United States as Lyndon Johnson said it was, then we should have put in much more force, much faster. If it was only as important as the resources we were devoting to it—limited manpower, constraints on the use of firepower, one-year tours which meant we never kept people there long enough to do anything—then we shouldn't have been there at all. So in a funny way, I came out of the Vietnam War neither hawk nor dove but with the simplest of things: You can't ask the American public to commit its sacred lives and treasure without having an absolutely clear readiness to achieve the objective and the objective must be clear.

Now, if you apply that standard to Vietnam you come up with the answer that this was a no winner from the beginning. To win the war, you had to put in triple the number of forces. You would have had to have faced the possibility of an indefinitely open-ended invasion force in North Vietnam—an occupying force. And you would have had to contemplate use of firepower even higher than the awesome levels we reached. And even that might have done nothing but flatten a small country which was not as strategically important as we claimed it was. Therefore, on the merits, the whole Vietnam adventure was misconstrued from the very beginning.

Did Johnson believe in '68 that it really would be possible to cut a deal with the North Vietnamese?

I think not. There was an enormous confusion in the period from January 30, 1968, to March 30, 1968. Notwithstanding all the memoirs that have been written claiming that intelligence predicted the Tet offensive, the simple fact is that the Tet offensive caught the Administration unprepared. That's a fact. You can always go back later and find the intelligence that predicted [an attack], but we weren't ready for it in Washington. I was in Katzenbach's office then, and I can tell you that there was horror and pandemonium all the way to the top. Rusk and Katzenbach sent me out to Vietnam ten days later to make a personal assessment. I saw Bunker and Westmoreland, and Barry Zorthian and Phil Habib and the others and with the exception of Habib, *they* were all in a state of shock, too.

Now, in that context, there was a tremendous battle going on over what to do, centering on the famous Clifford group. I worked on [Lyndon Johnson's] March thirtieth speech as a junior drafting officer with Nick Katzenbach and Harry McPherson and Phil Habib. A tremendous debate went on over what that speech should contain. That's been very well reported. But what hasn't been analyzed is this: Those of us who were working on the speech did not know that Johnson was going to withdraw. We thought it was partially a campaign document. Therefore, when we knew that Johnson had come down in favor of a limited bombing halt north of the nineteenth parallel, we were very pleased.

But there are two critical issues. One, what were our expectations of the North Vietnamese, and, two, what would we have done if we knew Lyndon Johnson was going to withdraw? The overwhelming consensus in Washington was that Hanoi would not respond. Bill Bundy predicted a less than twenty percent chance of response. Therefore, you have to ask why it was being done. And primarily it was being done to shore up American support, not to bring Hanoi to the table. Number two, if we had known that Johnson was about to make himself a lame duck with ten months to go, I think a lot of people—certainly Nick Katzenbach and Harry McPherson—would have gone to Johnson and said, "Look, Mr. President. If you are going to end your public career tonight over this issue, stop all the bombing and see what you can get for the next ten months. Don't make a halfway gesture, which is either going to get no response or at best a limited response," which is in fact what we got.

As you may recall, on April fourth Hanoi made this very clever decision: "We will talk to you, but only about stopping the rest of the bombing." Next day Lyndon Johnson accepts. And from May seventh until October thirtieth, 1968, five days before the election, we talk to the Vietnamese only about stopping the bombing. And finally, with Humphrey and Nixon locked in a dead heat going down to the wire, we stopped it. And Lyndon Johnson loses his one chance to have attempted to negotiate, to the bitter, bitter distress of Averell Harriman, Cyrus Vance, George Ball, who wanted desperately to see Humphrey elected, and others.

Now, what did Lyndon Johnson want? I don't know but my guess is he was torn. He didn't want to be the President that presided over the defeat. He'd rather pass it on to his successor. He was even ambivalent by this time as to whether Humphrey was a fitting successor, despite his dislike of Nixon. He hurt Humphrey during the '68 campaign very much. Humphrey might have been able to win if he'd been able to distance himself, though there were a lot of other factors.

And yet there we were, in March of '68, drafting the most important presidential speech that's been given in the last generation and we didn't *know*. Not just me—I was a junior man—but even people like Harry McPherson and Clark Clifford and Dean Rusk didn't know. Johnson only hurt himself by not telling even the two or three people he could have trusted the most: "Listen gentlemen. Supposing I don't run again. Supposing this is a speech not geared to the election but to a ten-month effort to end my presidency in a way which permits my achievements in the Great Society and elsewhere to meld with Vietnam in a decent chapter in our history." Then these men might have—might have—given Lyndon Johnson a different strategy. They weren't afforded the opportunity. And Johnson, therefore, will always carry through history a tainted legacy.

———•———

BRUCE PALMER

We take an oath of office, in uniform, to uphold the Constitution and to obey the rules of civilized warfare. I don't think it's right to put a uniformed man in a position where he has to violate that deliberately. Yet we did involuntarily assign military men to things like the Phoenix operation where one had to do things one shouldn't have done. Covert things that amounted to killing suspected Viet Cong agents. Bill Colby insists it was, on balance, a relatively clean operation. But I'm sure even Bill would recognize that more than once they killed some people that were innocent.

That kind of a program to root out the Viet Cong infrastructure and neutralize it, a euphemism, basically destroy them, was probably a necessary thing. Apparently it was effective. Hanoi really feared it. It was using their tactics, I suppose. They're not inhibited as we are. I just don't care for it. The military values are, you're not supposed to do those things.

I can understand war crimes committed in the heat of battle. I have a diary of my grandfather, who fought on the Union side in the Civil War, and got involved in a battle where they captured a farm building, and some Irish troops from Wisconsin and Illinois slaughtered the Confederates, some of whom were wounded and trying to surrender. He tried to stop them and was almost killed himself. But that was the heat of battle, their blood was up, their buddy was killed and so on. So pretty bad things happen in wartime.

In Vietnam it was very, very difficult to know who the enemy was. And this was related to that problem of hostile villages, where old men, women, and children were all your enemy and if they had a chance to kill you, they would. Yet I still don't find it in my mind or in my heart to forgive American troops for killing people like that, particularly if they were helpless as occurred in My Lai. American soldiers don't go around killing unarmed, helpless people, even though they're your deadly enemy.

I can understand it. They were fed up. They had taken a lot of casualties in that area from an unseen enemy—booby traps and mines and things. I can understand that their frustrations were very high. But I can't forgive them, nonetheless. There were American officers and soldiers there who tried to stop that thing, and almost got killed themselves. I still believe that that was an aberration. There were other war crimes, but they were individuals or possibly two or three men. This was a whole unit, deliberately organized.

The Americal* was pretty isolated up there in Chu Lai, and it had been thrown together out of the 11th Brigade and some other units. The 11th had been formed up and was training in Hawaii, but it wasn't ready yet. And there was a ceiling imposed on the theater that was to go into effect at the end of December of '67. So General Johnson [Chief of Staff of the Army] asked Westmoreland whether we should send this brigade over there or not, because it hadn't completed its training schedule. Westmoreland didn't want it, but the pressure was on. "Here you got this brigade. We hate to see you lose it when you could use it." So Westmoreland was pressured into accepting it.

That was the first mistake and the second one was, we put them in what we thought was a quiet sector, where the ROK† Marines had been. The ROKs had been moved north to work with the U.S. Marines—and they had left behind in their sector all kinds of unmarked mines and booby traps. So unknowingly, we put this brigade in what we thought was a nice place to get used to the looks of the country and the people—and right away they started taking casualties from mines and booby traps left behind by the Koreans. They didn't know whose they were, and so they got off to a very bad start.

So the mines around My Lai that the Americans thought were being

---

*The division of which the My Lai killers were a part.
†Republic of Korea—the South Korean Marines.

laid by unfriendly villagers had actually been left behind by the Koreans?

Well, that still doesn't excuse it. But there was something about the command also. They apparently inculcated in this brigade the idea that the Vietnamese people were bad, worthless—just a bunch of gooks. They had contempt for them and anything went. This is all hindsight, which I learned later. But I'd have to blame the original commander of that brigade who brought them in there. And he was never touched by this thing, because he went home before it occurred. And Colonel Henderson, who had been his deputy, took all the heat. He was very foolish about it. He tried to accept the blame hoping that people would forget about it, but it just wasn't going to go away.

BOBBY MULLER

What's odd, and you may consider this remarkable, is that I never ever had one political discussion in Vietnam. Never. I saw a lot of things that didn't compute, but when I joined the Marines I didn't tolerate protest. I knew where I was going, so why listen to something that was simply going to make it harder for me to do what I knew I had to do? As far as I was concerned whether the war was right or wrong didn't matter. What mattered was that we had decided we were going to fight and once you made that decision to commit the troops, okay, we've got an obligation to do what's got to be done. They're bad, I'm good by definition, by the color of the fucking uniform and I don't need to get beyond that. I didn't get into why are the blacks going their way and the whites going that way.

Remember this was '68–'69 and it was a transition time in the war. When I hit my unit, things were still tight. We had unit integrity— guys would stay together on a base as fire teams or squads. About a month before I got dinged—seven months or so after I'd gotten in country—I went on an R and R from the ARVN, and I went back to our base, at Dong Ha to see my unit, the 2/3 Marines. They had an officer hooch and you had armed guards all night around the hooch. I asked why and they said, "Look at the hooch." And the hooch was peppered with shrapnel holes because it'd been fragged a couple of times. I don't know if anybody got hurt. I don't know if it was a warning and nobody was there. All I know is that it was peppered with shrapnel and we had armed guards. And I thought "Holy shit." When I'd arrived in country none of that stuff was going down. But by this time there was a clear breakdown along racial lines.

Blacks stayed with the blacks, the whites with the whites and you didn't have two black guys pass each other without going through a very heavy ritualistic salute. There was a real degeneration.

My platoon sergeant, Edwards, he and I got to be pretty good friends. We were sitting at a base one night. I had taken over another platoon, and his platoon commander was with a bunch of guys that were flying a Confederate flag over their bunker. And he said, "You know, I don't understand that. Why is he with those guys and why are they flying a Confederate flag? Don't they understand what that means to me and to the rest of the guys?" I didn't have an answer, but blacks were denigrated—they were portrayed as cowards. That was the rap—that the civil rights movement had gone hand in hand with the antiwar movement.

When Martin Luther King was assassinated you had riots and outrage that reached a fever pitch out there as well as here. And a lot of black guys felt they were going over to be cannon fodder. At one time twenty-three percent of combat deaths were blacks.

———◆———

BRUCE PALMER

What caused the decline in American troop morale?
I think it was because the troops realized we were pulling out, and no one wanted to be the last one killed. That happens in any war when you see the end in sight. It happened in the Pacific in World War II, after the German surrender in Europe. The question was no longer if, but when VJ Day would come, and you could see a similar letdown among the troops. But remember too that in Vietnam we had one-year tours and units were constantly changing complexion because of rotations. The average rifle company would change over one hundred percent in eight or nine months, and the replacements were coming from the States, where dissent had reached a peak in '68 or '69.

Remember also that back home the permissive society sort of burst upon us. I had a boy in Jeb Stuart High School in Falls Church in 1968, and in one year that school went from a very conservative institution with a dress code and a behavior code that everybody followed to a complete shambles. And this was northern Virginia, a conservative part of the country. Two years later it was even worse. The drug culture. Racial disharmony. I was in Vietnam at the time of Martin Luther King's assassination. We had no clue over there just how bad it was. Then I came back to Washington and suddenly discovered My God, they've had a war in Detroit, and Baltimore and Washington.

And I remember my son coming home and what they were being told in school in terms of values and ethics was that anything you felt comfortable with was perfectly all right. You did your thing regardless of the consequences or what it might do to somebody else. It was the Me Generation. I think our morale problems over there stemmed from that as well.

WILLIAM COLBY

The South Vietnamese won in '72 and lost in '75, and the difference was American support and American bombing. The American people had just dismissed the war as being footless, and largely over the Tet attack with a . . . "Somehow we're doing the wrong thing there. We have a half-million soldiers over there and we don't seem to be able to not only fight the enemy but find him." Looking back, why did that happen? It was because President Johnson came in, saw an imminent defeat as a result of the overthrow of Diem and the revolving door sets of government that followed him, and felt he had no other answer but to send the troops.

Hanoi considered the overthrow of Diem incomprehensible, and consequently they were very cautious about exploiting it. They really weren't prepared to move to the next stage. Their plan was based on organization, mobilization, and offensive. And they were caught with not really having completed the organizational phase. They didn't know what the hell to do. So they floundered around and then started to see that they were making progress in the countryside, so it was time to move: "Let's go, boys. Let's end the war." Their books tell you this. Their estimate and our estimate was that the war would be over by about the end of '65. Their motive was to give the coup de grâce. So Johnson sent the troops and that led eventually to the repudiation by the American people.

But at each stage, nobody took a rather wide look as to the strategy of the problem. Eventually, we put together a program, Bob Komer did, which pretty well eliminated the guerrillas. And I don't mean the Phoenix, I mean the pacification as a whole. It was better, it was more efficient and all the rest of it, but the other side had the strategy and the initiative. And in a battle, the key is the initiative, and we really never had the initiative to fight his war. We were always wanting to fight our war. Usually war is for soldiers. This one wasn't.

For a long time it was for villagers. So we totally got frustrated when our soldiers didn't seem to be able to close with the war.

You're familiar with the military theory that we were afraid to do the necessary to cut off supplies to the South? I see you shaking your head . . .

I shake my head over the cutting off of the supplies. The supplies were sufficiently marginal for a good part of the time that there was no way you could cut it off. You had a comparative trickle of supplies. We equated our forces with theirs, but they didn't need all that much. If they lost a hundred guns and got one in, that was all they needed. They could move in, make their visitations to the villages in the night, disappear, and they didn't need many supplies for that. A few rockets here and there, sure that was useful to them, but marginal.

And if in the end they had to use very large forces, it was because they lost the people's war and that's my point. We finally got ourselves cranked around to a strategy of building strength rather than striking the enemy. The key is build your strength and make a solid base. If you're always out chasing and striking the enemy and thinking therefore the war is won, you're doing exactly what his strategy says you should do. When we finally got around to the business of organizing the villages and having elections and building up the territorial forces and self-defense forces, we started to win. When I went back out in '68, I was resolved that one thing I would produce would be a self-defense force. And it took quite a lot of argument because a lot of people were afraid of the idea.

I remember arguing with Vice-President Huong one time. He insisted that A. it will lead to a lot of internecine fights, and B. the guns will go to the Communists. I said, "If the guns are going to go to the Communists, you don't have much of a cause anyway. You do have a cause, though, and your people will fight the Communists if they can. If three men walk into a village with pistols and nobody else is armed, they can dominate the village, give the speeches, shoot the mayor, do whatever they want. But if ten of those villagers have antiquated old guns and an ability to call in some reinforcements, the three can't get in. It's as simple as that."

I was responsible for handing out half a million weapons, not to soldiers and not to policemen but to villagers. Now, we just didn't throw them off the backs of trucks; we'd give them to the village authorities and then they would arrange for the local kids to stand guard, one night a week or two nights a week. They would parade up in front of the girls and be dramatic. They weren't great fighters. But the way you win a guerrilla war is you don't shoot the guerrillas, you recruit them. And by 1971, I could go down the canals in the

Delta in the middle of the night. I drove out in the country around Hue, with the province chief, the British Ambassador, and me in one jeep and one other jeep equally unarmed. And we drove all around the place, said "Where do you want to go, right or left or where?" And again these were people standing guard exactly where divisions had been fighting three years before. I mean, the hell with the numbers. I don't know about the numbers either but by God, I did it.

But the curious and interesting thing, see, is that the Communists started out talking about the people's war, and when eventually, we beat them, they then shifted to straight military. We actually defeated the military attack in '72. But then the politics of disgust here that came out of the earlier experience were so intense that we rejected even the minimal support that would have been necessary to hold it.

———————◆———————

BRUCE PALMER

One of the monumental goofs of CIA, until we went into Cambodia in 1970 and got positive proof of it, was that they never accepted that the main Communist supply route was by sea, through Sihanoukville [in Cambodia]. The CIA stonewalled for years and said, it ain't so. When we got into Cambodia, it turned out that it was even worse than MACV had thought. All of the Delta, all of III Corps, most of II Corps and even parts of I Corps were being supplied by that route. And one of the great unfortunate ironies of the war is that when we went into Cambodia, it boomeranged on us. It forced Hanoi to rely on the Ho Chi Minh Trail for resupply. They turned it into an all-weather road system that could handle tanks and self-propelled artillery.

But I think Bill [Colby] misses the basic point though. The *troops* didn't go by sea. They came down the trail and, God, at the January '73 cease-fire, the estimate was, as I recall, a hundred and fifty thousand NVA troops and that's a lot of combat forces. They had moved most of their strategic reserve, which had been built up by seven divisions, into South Vietnam, and they modernized them and turned them into powerful mechanized forces. All that came down the trail. And why did they do it? They had to if they were going to deal with South Vietnamese forces of the size that we had equipped.

South Vietnam needed more time, and the real tragedy was that if we had concentrated more of the time we had on building the South Vietnamese forces rather than trying to win it ourselves, we might have done better in the long run. I think it could have been done. We misjudged just how tough it was. We were dealing with a mandarin society and many of the officers didn't believe in rolling up their sleeves and getting their hands dirty. We were finally getting peasants promoted as noncoms and then officers. God but that took a lot of doing. It went against the South Vietnamese grain completely. It's hindsight, but in Korea we were able to develop from scratch a decent army. The difference was, the Japanese had occupied Korea for forty years, and they would not let Koreans assume any leadership. So the Koreans were all in the same boat, and we didn't have this class-consciousness question.

The outcome shouldn't have surprised anybody. I was surprised at the suddenness of it. I thought they'd last a little longer, but at the final run, I couldn't see how they were going to survive. Again, in hindsight I blame ourselves. We had not thought the problem through. Once we realized that we were going home, it should have dawned on us that when you pull out eleven divisions and two hundred B-52s, enormous tactical air support, most of the U.S. Navy, virtually all the helicopters the U.S. Army owned, to expect the ARVN to do the same job was just whistling "Dixie." And then for Kissinger to have negotiated a cease-fire that allowed the North Vietnamese to remain in place and announce to the world we had "peace with honor" was baloney.

———————◆———————

WILLIAM SULLIVAN

A lot of military people argue that if we had gone into Laos, we could have cut the Trail, isolated the battlefield in South Vietnam, and won the war.

They eventually did in 1971. They didn't take their own but they took good, crack Vietnamese troops into Laos to cut the Trail in Lam Son 719, and they got their tail beat off. Now, frankly, I supported within the Administration the move into Cambodia and the Parrot's Beak because it seemed to me to be a piece of cake. We could get in there on flat land with our vehicles, with air and artillery cover, and clean up those camps that had been building up on the borders and come on back with very little lost, which is what happened.

When they came along with Lam Son 719, [Air Force Gen.] Johnny Vogt briefed the President on it when Alex Johnson and I were out of town. When we came back, Henry Kissinger called us and said, "Here's this JCS thing that they've come up with. It's Westmoreland's plan. What do you think about it?'' And Alex and I said, ''We want to get the same briefing the President got.'' We went over and got the briefing. It was on a map with no terrain features, and I said, ''Johnny, did you use that map to brief the President?'' And he said, ''Yeah.'' And I said, ''Now, that's dishonest. You didn't show him that the cordillera runs north and south and the Vietnamese can bring divisions of troops in there very rapidly [along the valleys] and you're going to have your people going *over* these hills.'' ''Oh, but all our people are going to be inserted by air.'' And I said, ''Yeah, they're going to get their tails beat off. How are they going to get out?'' So we opposed it, but by that time the President had already agreed, and it went ahead.

So they tried their thing. Now, their contention is, ''Oh hell, if we'd used the 82nd Airborne and our other hotshots up there, that wouldn't have happened to us.'' Well, it would have. That's awful jungle. I've been down on the Ho Chi Minh Trail and this is not the kind of place where our people could have fought any better than the Vietnamese elites that we put in there. No, I don't think they could have operated with El Paso or Left Hook or anything else.

A Canadian Army infantry major who headed a regional team of Canadian ICCS personnel in Vietnam after the '73 Accords, JOHN HASEK *was selected by sheer chance—"spewed out of a computer," as he puts it. He now teaches at York University in Canada and is working on a film about Vietnam meant to illustrate why military establishments have to be more open with the press in order to avoid having their political base eroded.*

There were about two hundred and eighty Canadians and roughly equal numbers of Indonesians, and Poles and Hungarians. We were called the CHIP nations: Canada, Hungary, Indonesia, Poland. The previous commission had been tripartite, and had ground to a complete stop. They figured with two on each side it might work better. We weren't going in there as Boy Scouts. We really thought we were going to do the same sort of a job we had done in Cyprus—be impartial and referee, and that people would listen to us. It took a little while to adjust to the fact that the Poles and the Hungarians went in with absolutely no thought of impartiality. And, of course, they were much more carefully selected for the job than we were.

We were on the aircraft bound for Saigon the day the cease-fire was signed. We really had no idea what to expect except we thought it was a cover up to save face for the Americans who were leaving because South Vietnam was in imminent danger of collapse. The map we were briefed on could have been straight out of *Time* or *Newsweek*—it was of the leopard-spot type and it seemed that a large part of Vietnam was one massive spot. I was the senior operations officer for Region Four, an area from the coast to the Cambodian border south of Pleiku. My headquarters was in a town called Phan Thiet. And from my quick impression of the briefing map, it appeared that in Region Four only Phan Thiet was a non-pink area.

When we landed, Tan Son Nhut had just been under rocket attack, and one of the overweight young American airmen was there and he was terrified. He said, "I've been here for eighteen months. This is the first time that this has ever happened." As we landed in Phan Thiet, we could see a Communist attack going on near the airfield and on the way into town, a couple of mortar shells landed on each side of the road. And we said to ourselves, "Aha! The Communists are getting ready to take this last bit of non-pink off the map."

But after that nothing happened and we started slowly feeling our way around. We lived in an old ramshackle hotel that had been used as an American quarters. After the military left there were still State Department people, a few lonely CIA guys that used to come and drink with us, the CORDS* people, and above all PA and E, Pacific Architects and Engineers, who had provided all the heavy logistics and third-line support to the American Army. They ran the messes, they maintained our transport. And that was another thing the Americans gave us. I had a whole compound full of jeeps—one for every day of the week.

Personally, having served in Africa and in Cyprus, I'd always believed that you eat what the natives eat, you do as the local people do. And I liked rice and *nuoc mam*.† Phan Thiet is where they make the number one *nuoc mam* in Vietnam. I liked going to the local little places. Sometimes I was quite surprised at what I had ordered. I used to have a breakfast of rice and hot soup at a restaurant just down the road from our quarters which was run by an old fellow who was a great Communist sympathizer. And again, that was the incredible thing about South Vietnam. This place was a popular haunt of the secret police. When they were going off work in the morning we'd sit there and this guy and I would argue the relative merits of Communism and America and these detectives would be listening and sometimes joining in.

---

*Combined Operations for Revolutionary Development Support—The joint military-civilian rural pacification program.
†Fermented fish sauce.

One of the other guys that always used to eat there in the mornings was a French Army deserter whose name was Robert. He'd stayed behind after '54 and married a Vietnamese girl. He was completely yellow and wizened and looked just like a Vietnamese. He was a guard at the CORDS compound and he and this restaurant owner were great friends. And they were the two focal points of the argument because Robert hated the Communists.

Gradually, the South Vietnamese were telling us [of the occasional military incidents] "Hey, that's nothing." But the Americans weren't very communicative and it was only later on that I began to realize that it really *was* nothing. I'd say to the South Vietnamese, "Where can I go?" and they'd say, "Song Zu," and I'd say, "Is that area under your control?" and they'd say, "We wouldn't send you there if we couldn't guarantee you safe conduct." So I'd drive out there and sure enough the area would have South Vietnamese flags up and would be under South Vietnamese control. And so I'd ask the South Vietnamese officers, "What do you own in this region?" and they'd say, "We own everything, every occupied hamlet, every piece of arable land. We don't lay claim to the jungle, but we could own any of that at any time if we wanted it."

So we asked the Provisional Revolutionary Government members of the Joint Military Commission, "What do you own?" And they'd say, "We own everything." And we'd say, "Hold on, comrade. If you own everything, why are you in this compound with barbed wire around it being guarded by South Vietnamese troops?" They'd sort of stay quiet then—we'd have another cup of tea and another one of their foul cigarettes.

Finally I started putting out my own patrols and after a while I realized that if the South Vietnamese said, yes, you could go somewhere, you could go. A little later on, after the Americans had gone, the province chief, who was a South Vietnamese colonel, said, "You like hunting?" And as part of the macho image I had to say, "Yeah, yeah." I don't actually. But he said, "Good, I'll pick you up at four o'clock this afternoon. We're going to go hunting—at night in the jungle." We drive out to one of his fire bases and we had dinner and after dark we got into two jeeps, and there was a guy with a big searchlight.

They lifted the barrier, and we drove out onto the jungle trails and the soldier, shined the light along the bush line until he picked up the red eyeballs of a civet cat which they called foxes or a little antelope which they called deer and you'd blast the hell out of this thing. It was jacking was what it was. We used M-14s, the predecessor to the M-16, but they had fixed the sear so that it only fired single shots because that was more sporting. You know how sporting it was to shine this light. But on the floor of the jeep we had M16s and other stuff in case the little red eyes we picked out belonged to something else, I guess. It was kind of spooky driving through jungle that supposedly belonged to the VC at night, happily shining these lights, shooting small game. But we did this most of the night, came back, had a few drinks and I said to the colonel, "Can we do this again tomorrow night?" And he said, "We can, but not in this area." But this was of course his way of demonstrating to what extent he had control.

Later on I had access to both sides to a certain extent and the South Vietnamese, you know, when they said they had a battalion somewhere, they had a battalion there. Or there'd be places in villages where the Communists would be trying to get food and they'd be shut out by the local ruffs and puffs*. They were just the farmers with a weapon, but they were okay to man those defensive perimeters. The whole war was in fact going well for the South Vietnamese.

They were different from the sort of army that I was accustomed to. One couldn't get quite used to the fact that if an infantry officer wanted fire support during a counterattack, he'd have to more or less send a certified check back to the battery commander. They'd been fighting for a long, long, time and they weren't a terribly aggressive army. There'd be a Communist attack and they'd counterattack and have the thing in the bag and just at the last moment, they'd call time out and go back and have a cup of tea and call it a day. And being in the gung ho Western school of military thought, I thought, "Jesus what a slack-ass lot. Why don't they go and finish them off?" But, of course, when you're doing it for twenty years, that's not how you do it.

The sort of incidents we ran into were not so much military as they were intended to destroy the fabric of South Vietnamese society. There was a small Catholic community near Phan Rang, where President Thieu had come from, and on Easter Sunday the priest was having a picnic in the grounds of the church. Somebody smuggled in a bomb and it killed a few children and hurt a huge number. It was a mess and it was nasty and it seemed to serve no purpose whatever except pure terror.

I talked to one fellow who had been captured and he started telling me about the Arrow Action teams. This was something that we hadn't been briefed about, and it was strange because it was something that we should have known. I talked to this fellow for several hours. He was a North Vietnamese and I said, "Okay, what rank have

---

*Regional Forces and Popular Forces (RFs and PFs, hence ruffs and puffs), the village and provincial militias.

you got." He said, "I'm not a soldier. I'm a policeman." And I said, "Well, what sort of policeman?" I was expecting that he was some sort of secret political gumshoe and he said, "My specialty is traffic." "Traffic?" And he said, "I am the head of the traffic department for the Phan Thiet police force." I said, "Wait a minute, I live in Phan Thiet and there's a South Vietnamese police force. You're sitting out in the boonies with the guerrillas." And he said, "That's what I do out there." He had been conscripted from the police in Hanoi and he'd been in the jungle now for several years, waiting to take over the traffic department of Phan Thiet.

Another time my contact on the Joint Military Commission said there was a grenade thrown in a hamlet not far from Phan Thiet and there were a couple of people killed and "We've caught the person who did it. Would you like to come and talk to him?" So I went out with my own interpreter and I talked to this boy for a long time. He was from the village and his mother was a widow and she had three kids. The father had been a soldier in the South Vietnamese army and had been killed. They had a hard time making ends meet and the boy had to take the buffalo down to the river every day to water and he felt that he was being made to work too hard and that his sisters weren't helping enough. A typical teenager with a grudge. He was met there by the Arrow Action team—the duplicate government for the village, sitting out there in the boonies, ready to take over.

And they said, "You know, if you stay you'll be given a hard time by your mother and you'll be put in the South Vietnamese Army and killed just like your father. You should come and join us." He sat out there and learned how to throw a grenade and how to fire a weapon and that sort of stuff and then eventually the leader gave him two grenades and told him to kill the hamlet chief. He went back there and he was hiding behind a wall and he panicked when he saw some people and threw one of his grenades, dropped the other one, and ran. It was just getting dark and he fell in the bush somewhere and went to sleep. The next morning, he woke up when two of the village farmers passed by going out into the field. They were talking about how terrible it was that there were people killed and who could have done this thing, and all of sudden he thought that maybe he had killed his mother, so he rushed back to the hamlet chief and gave himself up. And when I got to interview him, all of a sudden I realized how the whole process really worked at the very lowest level. So those aren't very dramatic events but they were the ones that left the greatest impressions on me.

His squat, heavily muscled frame, bull neck, and raspy voice give off an aura of raw physical power—the kind that usually comes from years of roughnecking in the oil fields or driving an eighteen-wheel rig. RICHARD ARMITAGE *does lift weights, but he is in fact a man of keen intellect with a thoughtful approach to foreign policy. He was Assistant Secretary of Defense for International Security Affairs—the head of what is sometimes called the Pentagon's "Little State Department"—in the spring of 1986. As such he was one of the two or three key Reagan administration policymakers on Southeast Asia. He was a principal architect of the U.S. policy that led to the fall of Ferdinand Marcos in the Philippines. He went to Hanoi several times in the Reagan years, mainly to negotiate on the POW-MIA problem. But on his later trips Armitage, who speaks Vietnamese, began in informal conversations to lay the basis for an eventual normalization of relations.*

I first went out there on a ship as a young naval officer in 1967 and served on the gun-lines. Later I volunteered as an adviser. I didn't want to be part of a U.S. unit. I didn't think U.S. units, per se, had to be there. I went to what was supposed to be a six-week language school in San Diego as part of preparing to be an adviser, but after four weeks the fellow I was going to relieve was shot in the buttocks, and he came out a little early. I didn't finish my schooling, but my appetite had been whetted and living with a hundred and fifty or so Vietnamese and their families was a great impetus to learning Vietnamese.

On my first ground tour I was an ambush team advisor. I went out in April 1969 and stayed there for a year. I went back short of a year later as the senior advisor to a twenty-boat PBR* division at Tay Ninh on the Cambodian border. Returned to San Diego, for a short time and then returned for a third tour at Coast Group 21 which was in II Corps, just south of Bong Son. And then I went home at the withdrawal of American troops, got out of the Navy and returned to Saigon in the Defense Attaché Office.

I quit the Navy for two reasons. One, my naval career was going nowhere. I was a Naval Academy graduate and I had spent a lot of my career in Vietnam. I had only one tour on a ship. One tour in Vietnam as a combat advisor was certainly something that you should try to get. Three tours was something that put me too far behind my

---

*Patrol Boat, Riverine—high-powered, flat-bottomed craft used to patrol the canals and waterways in the Mekong Delta.

contemporaries. But also, I was very frustrated. Here this was a war. This is where a military officer should serve and I was frustrated that we were pulling out of it before we were ready. I thought we should be able to be able to stay and advise and we should make this thing work.

And I have to say that I was also appalled by the discussions in Paris. What was being negotiated was the removal of all troops. I thought this was bizarre—the setting up of zones where the Communists had control, and the naive acceptance by some people that the Communists would obey the same rules we did. Setting up ICCS commissions to observe the cease-fire violations when you couldn't get the Communist members of the ICCS to go out was absurd. You could have bodies strewn about a schoolyard, you couldn't get a report out of the Polish members of the ICCS.

I could see that the war was not over, and the only way to keep fighting it was to become a civilian and join another branch of the government that was still involved. That was what I did. As a civilian I got to travel the length and breadth; up to then I had been on the rivers and in the rice paddies. That was my war, a nice war—all small units. When I got up into II Corps, I saw that they did it in a bigger way. We ran up against main force North Vietnamese companies and battalions. The first time I saw enemy tanks, whoa, really frightened me. More frightened of hearing them than of seeing them. I was in Bong Son, and in those mountains, at night they'd run those engines, it would scare me to death.

I remember driving down the road from Bong Son to Qui Nhon one day and they were fighting on both sides, and I just couldn't believe it. It was like being in a movie but not being there. We were flying down the road and here were the NVA on one side and ARVN on the other, fighting right across the road. I can't remember the town but they fought there all the time. You'd go to Qui Nhon and things were fine.

After the Easter offensive in '72, I had thought we could do this. That was just about as tough as it gets and there weren't that many U.S. there then still. The airpower was what did it. I realized that if the U.S. were willing to make a limited use of airpower, we could win this thing. The Christmas bombing. The Twelve Days of Christmas was when we had the North Vietnamese. After the seventh or eighth day, no MiGs, none. The [North] Vietnamese were on the verge of surrendering. They were pulling their troops back that had crossed into South Vietnam to protect in North Vietnam against general uprising. And then we called the bombing off. The pressure got too much on Mr. Kissinger and Mr. Nixon.

For the last two years, when I was the Naval and Marine operations adviser, I traveled to each and every province, each and every naval facility, seeing what was happening with our aid and seeing how they were doing. I went once to visit a base called Nam Canh, way down in the Delta and it was nasty. Yuck. I mean, it was mud up to the waist and mosquitos—an awful place. Well, there was a village in there called Dang Yoi and under the agreement, this was a Communist village because at a certain time on a certain day they had the flags up. It was a click or two away from the river and every time Vietnamese Navy boats went down the river, they'd get hit. What you wanted to do was take out the village. But if you weighed on a scale the relative advantages, it wasn't worth it. The agreement was a joke. But they felt that the pressures that would have been brought to bear—they would have killed women and children—were not worth taking it out. I mean, we find ourselves a very moral people and this would have been an outrage. The United States would have been outraged that we had violated the cease-fire agreements.

One afternoon in 1974 I happened to be at a Vietnamese base along the Cambodian border. Some fairly large number of Cambodians had come across the border. The Vietnamese would not let them on the base for security reasons, but they were huddled close to the perimeter. Some vendors were out selling ice cream and sweets. And suddenly from across the border a barrage of rockets was fired at us. And one rocket landed in the absolute middle of these Cambodians. When the shelling lifted, we went out from the base to see what we could do. There were scores killed—my memory is forty-seven or forty-nine—and well over a hundred wounded. And I thought to myself, first of all, what a terrible tragedy and secondly, I was so frustrated that here we were being hit from Cambodia by Vietnamese and their targets in this case were Cambodians and that could not be understood or appreciated or even viewed with any sort of equilibrium by the American public. And I think that one episode was the most frustrating moment of my experience in Vietnam.

I went through stages in the years I was there. In my first year everything was new and different and I was fascinated by the culture and the history of conflict which Vietnam had had. The second tour I got a little frustrated with the pace of the war as it was being prosecuted by the Vietnamese and with a lot of the corruption that I saw. In my third tour I finally evened out a little bit. I realized that in Vietnam, just like in the United States, there are good and bad people, good and bad aspects of the culture and of the history, and you should take things as they are from a pragmatic viewpoint.

I ended up feeling that some Vietnamese tried quite hard and gave the ultimate sacrifice and others spent their time trying to get rich. I had, in that time, some commanding officers on the Vietnamese side who were trying to be as professional as possible, and others who wanted to sell the limited quantities of gasoline we had, or who were more inclined to figure ways to get back to Saigon than they were to prosecute the war. So it wasn't a case of saying the Vietnamese did or didn't try hard enough; some did and some didn't. The fact is that South Vietnam and the United States lost their will together.

The Vietnamese lost their will, I guess, by having been engaged in struggle for so long that it was something that they accepted more than should have been the case. In the United States we lost our will because we became divided as a country. Our leadership couldn't explain competently to the public why we had an interest in Vietnam. We took the easy way out, trusting to rely on promises about zones of control for the Communists and things like that, and we split.

CHAPTER SEVEN

Getting a Bad Press

AMONG the targets of those who would alter the history of Vietnam, the press is a particular favorite. Journalists are blamed for having undercut the war effort by creating an image in the United States that was at odds with the reality on the ground. That was never so, as former Defense Secretary James Schlesinger, Jr., observes at the end of this chapter. In fact dispatches from the war zone reflected mostly what the reporters themselves saw, or heard from soldiers and officials. They may have emphasized what was going wrong, but it was an emphasis supplied by their sources. The press did not manufacture events, and its details came from the participants—often key figures who believed U.S. policy was in error, and who pushed their views by making public bad news the policymakers refused to heed in private.

The argument that the press was somehow responsible for losing the war had its origins in an early quarrel between journalists and the U.S. Embassy. The Embassy resented the fact that the handful of young reporters in Saigon in the early sixties refused to swallow the official line, which was that the government of Ngo Dinh Diem was making steady progress against the Viet Cong. In fact, says Charles Mohr, who was one of those reporters, American military advisers in the field were telling them that the Vietnamese Army was being beaten by the guerrillas, and that U.S. aid and advice weren't making much difference.

The quarrel escalated in mid-1963, when the struggle between Buddhist clerics and Diem's Catholic-dominated government suddenly made Vietnam a page-one story. Ambassador Frederick Nolting, backed by Gen. Paul Harkins, the U.S. military commander, and CIA Station Chief William Colby, strongly supported Diem. However the war might be going, these officials and their backers in Washington saw him as the foundation-stone of South Vietnam's political stability. The journalists, based on their field reporting, believed the opposite—that the policies of Diem and his brother, Ngo Dinh Nhu, were causing the war effort to founder in the countryside. They also thought that Diem, Nhu, and Nhu's wife were mentally unbalanced—and that the Buddhist uprising was proof positive that the Embassy appraisal of their ability to maintain political equilibrium was wrong.

As the disagreement between the Embassy and the reporters sharpened, editorials, columns, and articles appeared at home, complaining that the Saigon newsmen were young and inexperienced, and subtly questioning their loyalty and patriotism. These were wounding charges, and they overlooked the fact that the Buddhists themselves had devised the medium—ritual self-immolation on streetcorners in downtown Saigon—for the message that they resented the dominance of a Catholic minority of ten percent. It was the overtone of religious persecution, compounded by Madame Nhu's public likening of the suicides to "barbecues," and the sheer shock value of seeing monks burn themselves to death on television, that gave the story its keening editorial punch.

One of the complaining articles led Mohr to resign from *Time* magazine. He returned later as *The New York Times* bureau chief. Others among the young reporters on the scene—David Halberstam, then of *The New York Times*, Neil Sheehan of UPI, and Malcolm Browne of the AP—left Saigon in the months following the coup.* They were replaced, in many cases, by older men who had covered Korea or even World War II, and who arrived with no particular predisposition against the U.S. government position. Nolting, Harkins, and Colby also left, and for a time relations between the Embassy and the press settled down.

But something had begun to happen that shaped journalism not only in the war zone but in the United States ever afterward. That was the creation of a climate of skepticism about the government's word, and the establishment of an arm's-length relationship between officials and the press. Coming out of World War II and the Cold War, many journalists had felt themselves part of the establishment. They tended to believe official pronouncements, to report them at face value, and to help keep secrets whose disclosure might damage the country. That changed in Vietnam because the U.S. Mission's judgment on Diem was so out of line, and the "facts" it offered from the field were often so demonstrably in error, that the old trust had

---

*Halberstam and Browne won Pulitzer Prizes for coverage of the events leading to the coup, and Sheehan later won one for the Pentagon Papers. All three went on to become journalists of the first rank.

to be abandoned. In a sense, the scales were forced to fall from journalistic eyes.

As the U.S. role in the war expanded, so did the size of the Saigon press corps. Eventually there were more than five hundred reporters, photographers, television correspondents, cameramen, and others accredited to the Military Assistance Command, Vietnam (MACV). Many of the newer correspondents were young and spent time in the field, where it was as visible as ever that for all the dying, the U.S. was making no real headway toward victory. Their reports once again generated distrust and hostility from the Embassy.

Journalists produced a host of stories and pictures that contradicted the official vision of reality. Morley Safer of CBS showed a Marine unit torching a village with Zippo lighters. Jonathan Schell depicted in *The New Yorker* the destruction of a village to pacify it. Peter Arnett of the AP found U.S. forces using nonlethal gas to drive the VC out of their tunnels. Harrison Salisbury's trip to Hanoi in late 1966 produced evidence that U.S. bombing had failed to dent the North's war effort. Other reporters wrote about the endemic corruption in South Vietnam, about the military's propensity to use the war as a testing ground for new weapons, and about the flaws in American strategy and tactics.

The reporting was at times so hostile that Lyndon Johnson personally pressured some news executives to send out people who would write upbeat accounts of the war. It gave the U.S. government particular heartburn in the autumn of 1967, when Johnson needed an image of progress to support a request for an income surtax to pay for the war. Gen. William C. Westmoreland, the U.S. military commander, even journeyed home to assure Congress that the war was being won. Three months later, the Tet Offensive demonstrated that the press's pessimism was well founded.

But then an extraordinary dispute developed, in which official and other critics charged that the offensive had been misinterpreted. They dwelt on the fact that enemy forces had taken far worse casualties than the government, and proclaimed that Tet was therefore a great victory. Later, that argument grew into a broad assertion that the United States had been misled into thinking Vietnam was in flames, which created a political reality at home much bleaker than the one in the field. Though it was seldom put so baldly, the import of this argument was that a biased press unfairly magnified the disaster in a way that undercut Lyndon Johnson and sapped American will.

What this argument ignored, of course, is that the Communists, not the journalists, had conducted a nationwide surprise attack that spoke volumes about the U.S. position in Vietnam, and it was Lyndon Johnson, not the press, who decided to retire from office. The crit-

ics' attempt to separate out combat from the rest of the equation so
as to claim a "victory" simply showed that they had not read or did
not understand Clausewitz's first and most important maxim:
"War is an act of violence intended to compel our opponent to fulfill
our will."

The war's outcome did not rest on whether Communist forces were
defeated in a given battle or campaign; indeed, by American reckoning they were defeated in *every* campaign. What mattered was
that over time they managed to undermine American will in a way
that caused a superior force to retire from the field of combat, leaving the way open to Hanoi's domination. Tet marked the beginning
of that process not because of the way journalists wrote the story,
but because of the shock it administered to the American political
system. To claim that Tet was really an American victory masked
by biased journalism is, as Walter Cronkite puts it, "an excessive
rewrite of history."

———————•———————

Having arrived in Southeast Asia for Time *well before Vietnam
became a front-page story,* CHARLES MOHR *had the luxury of being
able to travel without deadline pressure and to make up his mind
about the incipient war independently. What he unearthed got him
into in a famous imbroglio with his editors a year later. He quit,
and afterward returned as* The New York Times *bureau chief. Mohr
covers national security affairs for the* Times *in Washington.*

I first went to Saigon in May of '62 to do a crash cover on Paul
Harkins. I had just gotten to Hong Kong from India, and what I
wanted to do was get measured for some suits and do a lot of reading-
in, but Otto Fuerbringer* liked crash covers and it all had to be done
in five days. [Ambassador John Kenneth] Galbraith had tried to talk
to me about Vietnam while I was still in India. Tried, anyway. I
didn't even know what he was talking about mostly, but he had made
a big effort to talk Kennedy out of it—"Don't get your toe in this
shit." In those days all I had was a half-assed, vague idea that something was going on in Vietnam.

When I got to Saigon I saw Harkins and his chief of staff, a Marine
brigadier. The Ambassador at that time, Nolting, was already in a
very testy mood. I saw somebody in the political section and actually, just a few other people—an AID person and so forth. I didn't
get a chance to see Diem or Nhu. I had brought along a former Sai-

—————————————————————

*Then *Time*'s assistant managing editor; later its managing editor.

gon stringer, Jerry Rose, from Hong Kong, and the current stringer, Mert Perry, got me a corner suite in the Caravelle and we just put down a typewriter and cranked out a file. I took note of some things they were trying to tell me, the main pessimism themes and a lot about the [Ngo Dinh] family and the rest of it was just an interview story—General Harkins says such and such.

But that stimulated my interest. I began to see it was going to be a major story, and I started going in fairly often. That summer, [David] Halberstam replaced Homer Bigart and opened a *New York Times* bureau for the first time. In '62 and '63, two kind of weird things stuck out. One was certain people in the press started grousing and bitching about the coverage. The Washington *Star* wrote editorial after editorial about the youth, shortcomings, and lack of maturity and understanding of the press corps, and [columnist Joseph] Alsop repeated a variation of the theme. The other was that they [editors] were not sending people out there to cover it.

You had very small wire service setups and Halberstam was the only resident newspaper reporter. There were no satellites in those days, so the networks had to ship film and they covered it entirely on an in-and-out basis. There were some strong stringers but very few. Mert Perry had left UPI to string for *Time* and I was an in-and-out guy. So what you had was essentially a very small resident press corps, like six guys. Really, I don't think American journalism did the right thing.

The good aspect of it was that editors didn't want a story every day and that permitted us to get out in the countryside quite a bit. In '62 the main action was the Delta and you could nip down quite easily. My Tho was only forty miles away and the roads were secure enough. You could get down to see John Vann* and you could get over to Fred Ladd's† division and so forth. So the controversy over the coverage really came from the fact that these guys were getting out and finding out what kind of questions to ask. And they were coming under the influence of Vann, who was telling them how to look at the war.

I covered my first combat early that summer, right outside Saigon, with a Vietnamese battalion. There were American advisers by then, but MACV wouldn't do anything for you—you had to fight your way into everything. Anyway, we tramped around and they captured several prisoners. One of them was shot in the chest and had a sucking wound and they wouldn't give him any medical attention.

---

*Then a military adviser, later a USAID official, who was intensely critical of the way the U.S. effort was handled, and became a prime source for a number of reporters. Vann was killed in a plane crash near Kontum during the 1972 offensive.

†Ladd was another adviser, who later ran the U.S. military aid program in Cambodia.

He finally died—and the Vietnamese castrated him. We were in a house and the women were all cowering around and they brought in his balls and said, "Do you want to eat these?"

The senior advisor got very angry. He had been angry earlier, because they were slamming people around with rifle butts and they did a little bit of water torture, too. He had tried to tell them we had found out in Korea that you get a lot more out of prisoners if you treat them well, and to cut this shit out. I remember that the testicles being cut off and the torturing of prisoners I didn't regard as a big terrible moral issue, but I didn't like it much either. Anyway, I told Perry, "I don't think this is going to make a story," but I filed it—this was an operation. This is what's been going on around here—and I didn't even get a response.

The same [no-response] thing happened on a number of operations in the Delta. Then this guy Ivan Slavich came along, an Army aviator, a major, who had invented the armed helicopter. The Air Force was determined to fight tooth and nail against armed helicopters. And what Slavich brought in were just Hueys with machine guns and rocket pods hung on them. They had been put together in Okinawa, but it had to be refined because half the time it didn't work too well. The Air Force had them blocked from Vietnam for a while, but the Army finally got them in-country. The Air Force had this reputation for great public relations, but Slavich just killed them—and the way he did it was he got friendly with this little small press corps, realizing that if they did a lot of noncosmic stories on armed helicopters it would help. And, besides, he was one of the guys, like Vann, who liked reporters.

Anyway, the armed helicopters were such a success that [after a time] he divided them up into four platoons and at least one platoon was going on every operation. And it became a big convenience in covering combat, because they were out at Tan Son Nhut and they'd leave at dawn and go in and marry up [with the infantry] on the ground. So you could see a hell of a lot and sometimes you'd get back the same night to Saigon and then have some drinks with Ivan and his guys. Ivan became a pretty good source on what was going on around the country.

Since they were flying all around the place, Ivan kept finding Viet Cong, and he'd come back to the commanders saying "Geez, they're right over here." And the Vietnamese would say "No, no, no, no, Major, they're not over there." "But I saw them." "No, intelligence says they're over here." And what he was finding out was one of the biggest problems and one of the main themes of that whole period—the Vietnamese lack of aggressiveness. I also saw a lot of Diem and his family because of the *Time* relationship. I had, in not quite a year and a half, maybe six interviews with Diem, about the same number with Nhu and for the cover story on Madame Nhu, eight hours of talking at several interviews. I watched her for everything she was saying. Diem's character was weird and his brother was very much the same. The interviews were all much longer than a reporter wanted. You'd run out of cigarettes and have to smoke his, and he smoked these little beady cigarettes that would give you lung cancer instantly, and you had to wear a suit and he didn't like air conditioning.

The Buddhists had been kind of plugging along, but I didn't pay too much attention and when the [uprising] actually began in Hue with somebody throwing a hand grenade, I was back in Hong Kong. Halberstam and another correspondent came over on R and R and I rented a junk and took them out for a day, and they were telling me about it. And I said "This is going to cause him a lot of trouble and the funny thing is, to get out of it all he'd have to do is just apologize or say he's sorry, but he'll never do that and it will turn into a worse thing." And Halberstam has always said how prescient Mohr was about this.

Did the image of this Catholic autocrat repressing a Buddhist majority touch something in the American psyche about religious persecution?

I think it touched a big chord in the United States for the intellectuals and policy types [but not necessarily the religious persecution chord]. We're so shell-shocked and beat up now with Khomeini and Beirut and so forth, but there was really no parallel up until then of the fanaticism of a guy burning himself to death. When Mal Browne got the picture of the first monk, I don't believe there was any motion-picture film. But a total of eight or nine burned themselves to death that summer and fall, and the Buddhists got to the stage where they made damn sure that there was film at eleven.

I have a feeling there's a kind of broader, deeper thing there. But I think a lot of the time reporters were baffled by reaction in the United States. It was never our job to figure out what American public opinion was going to be. I really think it was the idea of immolation and the opaque impenetrability of the whole thing. What is all this? Who are the Buddhists? What are they mad at? Burning yourself to death was so alien that I think that was much more important in the States.

And as far as Diem is concerned, I think it was much more the fact that you couldn't work with the son of a bitch. It began to occur to practically everybody except Nolting that whatever needed to be done you weren't going to get anything out of Diem. Diem was like a dog with his bone.

What set off the fight with Time?

I used to say, and still say, the best solution to Vietnam was to win. But I was being influenced by American advisors like Vann and, I suppose, by other reporters and what they were learning and also by Agency people. One of the big sources of realism and truth in Saigon was CIA, which was saying this wasn't the way to do it. That began kind of a subtle conflict with New York and in the fall of '62, I came home on leave and Otto took me to that rooftop restaurant in the Time-Life Building for a two-man lunch to talk about it. So I said, "Well, I'll tell you that the war isn't going very well and the biggest problem is the family. I don't think it's ever going to go well with them, and on top of everything else, they're really anti-American. They're stuck with us but they don't like us or our values. They think democracy in the American sense is the craziest thing they ever heard of and they're not going to have any of that horseshit. They don't stand for anything we stand for."

He didn't even get mad. He just got amused and he gave me this patronizing goddamn lecture about "We don't have to have people like us. It's just important that they respect us," and "Essentially Diem is an instrument of American foreign policy." I don't blame him for this because I was suffering under the same wrong premises too. But the point is I wanted to report accurately and I wanted to look good. If you think for one minute that I wouldn't have loved to be exclusively reporting a victory and make everybody else look like horses' asses two years later, of course I would have done it. What I didn't want to do was be Pollyannish and say everything's going to be all right when it more and more became clear that it wasn't.

Essentially the American line then was the exact opposite of the Maine fishing guides. They always say "You should have been here last week when the fish were biting." In Vietnam it was "You ought to be here next week." You had, after a while, people like Harkins and even Nolting taking the line that "Right, the stuff you just came in here to tell me—they won't chase the enemy and they don't want casualties and they're corrupt and the strategic hamlet program is all a fraud—Yes, Mr. Mohr, not only is that so, but we went in there last week and we talked to the President [Diem] again and said, 'We've got to get those commanders out there and get them fighting,' and he's going to do it now. What you're saying is more or less true but it's all going to be all right."

In any case my files became more and more pessimistic. I was kind of a young star at *Time* and they felt they had to deal with this. And so the worst thing that can happen in journalism, a kind of bargaining, took place. It was all informal and unstated, but it was one week

"We'll let Mohr have this," and then the next week they'd have second thoughts. So one week you'd have a gloomy, pessimistic story and another week you'd have a purely argumentative—the Buddhists are not men of God—kind of piece.

And that finally led to the real problem, which was over the Madame Nhu cover story after she'd made the barbecue remark [describing the monks' fiery suicides as "barbecues"]. I could see an opportunity there because she was important in a negative sense. And she cooperated. She just talked, talked, talked, and Nhu also was quite good. He had long narrative stories that sort of involved her—and everything was a lie. And it was useful because that was the whole point of the cover story—that this was the most neurotic family I ever ran into.

I mean Diem himself was incredibly neurotic but his brother and sister-in-law were priceless. I asked her why her morality included no more divorces, whereas everybody [in the upper classes] had concubines, and she said, "I know, I understand that there are these mad, impetuous people who are seized with a kind of passion and feel that they have to do something about it. I have never felt those feelings myself, you see."

In any case I got this stream of hero-grams, one of which said this is the best single cover ever filed to *Time*. But when I saw the magazine, two things struck me: Because of the space problem it wasn't as good as the material in pure entertainment value, although essentially it said the family's nuts and they are doing tremendous damage. And then the last few paragraphs said "Yeah, but on the other hand there is no alternative to Ngo Dinh Diem, and they aren't so bad." There had been an incident when Nhu's secret police physically attacked the reporters and [Peter] Arnett [of the Associated Press] got hurt pretty badly, and they described it in a footnote as a scuffle involving the anti-Diem reporters.

Well, I wrote a Dear Otto letter and said this is just dreadful and someday the editors of *Time* are going to regret what you're doing. And I added that another thing I wanted to know is why the prescient editors of *Time* keep referring to reporters as anti-Diem. It was an intemperate letter and it caused an explosion. I know now that Fuerbringer would have fired me, but he couldn't, so it developed that I could be on the payroll but he wasn't putting my stuff in the magazine anymore.

I went back to Saigon in September and found things worse than ever and I wrote a file saying "The war in Vietnam is being lost. Period. Paragraph." The Pagodas had been raided and they threw the monks out the windows and people were just in despair, including some who for a long time had stuck to the "It's all going to work out" routine. And nothing got in the magazine. Instead we had the famous press story saying that the reporters in Saigon were biased. It had no names; it said "the press" in Vietnam, so it obviously included me, and it wasn't a story in any sense; it was just an essay. And there was also a story contradicting the gloomy reporting from myself and Perry, and I was much more upset about the main story than I was about the press story. The night the magazine got to Saigon we all went out and drank, Halberstam and Keyes Beech* and a number of people, and they all started trying to talk me out of quitting. I didn't have any intention of quitting, except that the more they tried talking me out of it the better it sounded. And finally, I decided to go back to Hong Kong and talk to my wife, who said, "You don't have to work for these people. Of course, you should quit." And that's the way it ended up.

———————◆———————

BARRY ZORTHIAN *arrived in Saigon from New Delhi in February 1964 to manage American propaganda operations directed at the Vietnamese. As the American role grew, however, he became effectively the czar of U.S. press relations in Saigon. Among other things, he freed access to U.S. officials for reporters, and established an informal daily briefing that eventually became the celebrated "Five O'clock Follies," a daily piece of guerrilla theater between reporters and spokesmen. Zorthian is currently an adviser to the Embassy of Oman in Washington.*

You once said you'd advised LBJ that he might get better press on Vietnam if he put pressure on the editors back home. Did he?
This came in a meeting at the White House. Whenever LBJ would see me, immediately he'd connect with the media and sort of explode. "Goddamn media, why can't you handle it better," and "Who's that son of a bitch?" and all the rest of the bull. There were a number of occasions where he sort of just unloaded and that was it. But on one occasion, at least, the discussion involved Leonard Marks, John Chancellor, Frank Stanton, myself, and the President, in that little side office he used to have. This was in '65, shortly after the fighting started, and Morley Safer had just done his spot about the Marines burning the huts, and that had received a great deal of negative attention.
Leonard was there as director of USIA and John was there as the

---

*Then of the Chicago *Daily News*, a highly respected older correspondent who had been in Asia for many years.

new director of the Voice of America. Frank Stanton [then the head of CBS News] was just sort of an adviser to the President. The President engaged in more or less a monologue, and I remember him zeroing in on Stanton, saying specifically that there was a good deal of questionable background on Safer and telling Stanton that he'd better get that newsroom straightened out or he, LBJ, was going to blow the whistle. I asked Walter Cronkite early enough to where his memory would still be fresh, whether Stanton put any pressure on them. And I'm happy to say—I'm sure Walter would have told me—that as far as he could remember, Stanton just took the beating himself.

But that theme of talking to the editors, I certainly kept endorsing for the four years I was there. Correspondents do respond to where you get played: whether you make the front page or [get printed opposite] the truss ads or whether you make the nightly news. And either directly or implicitly, editors influenced their coverage. And the effort to bring a better twist, a better balance, a more positive story, should be focused as much on the editors as the reporters. And I'm not sure we ever did enough with editors back here—down to the headline writers and copy editors, or the producers on TV shows.

The reason I ask is in '65 or '66, when I was with UPI, I was told that LBJ had personally pressured the president of UPI to send people to Saigon who would write upbeat stories about the war.

I have no doubt what you're saying, but there was one other factor: The U.S. Advisory Commission on Information came along and in addition to Stanton the members included a UPI fellow, Frank Bartholomew* and an AP guy, Frank Starzell. The commission normally was far removed from this kind of thing, but under LBJ it became involved. On paper their job was to look into complaints about USIA, but I'm sure the charter from LBJ was come back and report to him. And LBJ expected answers to what he saw as a very real problem: the nature of the coverage. There is no doubt LBJ and a lot of people around him, and some in Saigon as far as that went, thought the coverage was out of bounds: hypercritical, negative, destructive, all that jazz. There were endless hours of discussions on what to do about it.

In June of '64 I was appointed czar, so-called, of information in Saigon. I took the approach that probably the only way to achieve a balance was to be completely available. If our story was complicated but basically positive, the only way to get it out was to have it wide open. And in that framework we put out a hell of a lot of infor-

---

*Then the retired chairman of the company.

mation, made people at the mission level very accessible and encouraged correspondents to go anywhere they wanted.

Now it happened to be a very down period. Vietnam was having revolving-door governments. And then we came in with U.S. troops. The media and the Embassy were probably closer than any other time. It didn't start to go sour again until Harrison Salisbury's visit to Hanoi in late '66. That was a signpost. There had been generally promilitary coverage, and suddenly Salisbury said, in effect, the emperor has no clothes. The bombing in the North has not been pristine and you're not having much effect up there. And all that had been put out sort of lost credibility. There was a feeling "Hell, we've been getting all this good news and, Christ, none of it's accurate." And then came the realization, as the level of deaths went up, that this was not going to be a Sunday picnic. So things started to go sour and the military situation didn't move and skepticism about the war grew. But still, as far as public impact, the great devastation didn't come until Tet. That was the ultimate collapse.

The Salisbury trip and Tet are like two or three other episodes that provided big news triggers. The first one was clearly the issue of religious persecution.

And it came all together in that burning monk. And a second one was corruption, and a third one was "Goddamnit, you guys lied to us." The "lied to us" syndrome was a very tough one. I, personally, did not experience one incident where the facts spelled out one thing and I was told "Forget it. Say something else." There were certainly some instances where we held back some information or didn't know as much as we should have. But very often the mission believed what it was saying and its information justified that. What was happening was the information was being seen through the reverse side of a looking glass. Some province advisors inevitably oriented themselves to the positive, and as [their information] goes up to the Corps and to Saigon, the positive kept building up.

This is in the very nature of things. You don't ask the province advisor to report his failures, you ask him about his successes. And he puts pressure on himself: "I want to show I'm doing a good job." That's one reason I left. I used to try to visit every province every year, and I went through my fifth briefing down in Long An,* and you say, "Goddamnit, I've been hearing about that area being cleared five years in a row and every year it's cleared again. And that advisor isn't lying to me consciously; he believes there's progress, [but] he doesn't see the other side." And finally you say, "I've had my time out here."

---

*A province near the point at which the Mekong River crosses the Cambodian border.

Take combat figures. At the end of the day, a company commander totes up his actions: He looks over the field and says, "That artillery was shelling like hell. We must have killed twenty of them." And he writes down twenty, or he says, "Eighteen, I'm going to say, twenty looks funny." The battalion commander gets the reports and puts them together and moves them up. Finally it gets to MACV and they're very precise figures. And what's MACV to do? Say, "No, no, those are soft figures?" The only thing that we can do is pass that out. So the briefer gets up at the Follies and says, "We have one hundred and fifteen killed and we killed three thousand two hundred and twenty-one of the enemy." But the system isn't set up for accurate reporting to correspondents. It's an operations system, not an information system.

Where did body counts start? People like Halberstam would go down on a Vietnamese operation. There'd be a battle and the commander would say, "Christ, I must have killed two thousand guys today." They didn't have the faintest idea whether they did or not, but that's the report he would send up, and headquarters would probably add a little bit to it. And meanwhile, Halberstam had come back to Saigon and he'd hear this and he'd say, "How do you know that?" "Well, this is what our report said." "Yeah, but did you see those goddamn bodies?" "No, we didn't." So finally orders went down, "Go out and count the bodies." Well, any guy in his senses knows you don't go out and count bodies on a battlefield. We put out advisory after advisory saying, "The so-called body count is not a body count, it's a battlefield estimation and don't take it literally." But we never got away from it. And that kind of problem never came up in World War II or Korea or if it did, it never got the attention that did.

Those were front-line wars. It was like a football game almost. You moved forward or you moved back and at the end of the day, you said "We've covered this much territory." In Vietnam, the scenes of some of the most major battles were abandoned. Ia Drang,* a very bloody fight. A week later nobody was there. And who the hell knows what we gained in that.

That's why the Pentagon put so much emphasis on statistical yardsticks. They needed something to get their teeth into, so you'd get all these indices, how many incidents, how many hamlet chiefs sleep at home, how many roadblocks and so on. We were looking for quantitative measurements on a war that was qualitative. Many a day in the mission council I'd say, "Look, this sounds fine but the press

---

*Scene of the first big set-piece battle between U.S. Army and North Vietnamese troops.

won't buy it. Where are the facts to back it up? How can I prove it? You're just talking judgment."

This would happen very often on weapons or techniques we would use. Agent Orange—"Why do we have to spray that area?" "Well, the VC are all over it." "How do we prove it? How many VC are in there? Where are their operations?" You can multiply that many, many times. The use of tear gas was another trigger. Peter Arnett finds tear gas, but when he writes it, it comes out "nonlethal gas," and who the hell knows what "nonlethal gas" is. But these are the words. We had an enormous flap and fell flat on our face.

Why wasn't there censorship?

Censorship would have been damn near impossible to enforce. In World War II, correspondents were under the military's control. They were in uniform. They had simulated ranks. They were dependent on the military for housing, logistics, accommodations, travel, communications. None of that existed in Vietnam. We had French correspondents in Vietnam who weren't even accredited to MACV. The wire services had their own communications. You could rent a car or fly Air Vietnam. There were no controls.

Anyway, there has never been in any recent war acceptance or an effort to impose censorship on political developments, strategy, morale, nature of the enemy, nature of our forces, all the broader questions that get away from the battlefield, that people criticize the press for in Vietnam. I think if you ever tried to impose that, you're into, in practical terms, a thicket out of which you can't get.

So we went for ground rules, and by '68 it had gotten to about fifteen of them, covering troop movements, starting time for operations, weapons capability, readiness of troops, takeoffs of combat aircraft, all of which correspondents accepted. And despite all the grumbling by the military, there was an absolute minimum of complaining that the press was jeopardizing tactical operations. The complaining was about something you could never get the American public to accept for censorship, and that was the civilian political side and the strategy of it.

We went through several groups of correspondents, and the numbers were always increasing. When I got there, there must have been maybe twenty regulars and even those weren't all residents. By the time of Tet we had six hundred accredited. Now that included spear carriers, cameramen, non-journalists. Out of those six hundred, half had to be involved in television. The network approach was bring in teams. You know, the U.S. government used to be criticized for one-year tours. The TV networks, not the bureau chiefs, the producers, but the correspondents were on virtually six-month tours.

But one of the things that the press would never do in Vietnam was organize. They said, "That's not our responsibility," and we had no way to determine who was a legitimate correspondent. So any joker who walked in with a letter from an editor in the middle of Montana, saying "Johnny Jones is our man and if he writes something and I like it, I'll run it," would get accredited. Well, a lot of them didn't give a damn whether they wrote anything or not. That accreditation got them into the PX and transportation and so on. So you had all kinds of adventurers out there. Come out and see the war, have some excitement.

And the visitors came by the droves. The three-days wonders, the one-week wonders. One time I did a very rough ball park estimate and I figured in my four years there were at least two thousand correspondents accredited. They ranged from Mary McCarthy who came out to do stories for the *New York Review of Books* to European correspondents CIA was underwriting. We even had some Yugoslav Communist correspondents come out. The Washington *Post* sent Moshe Dayan as a correspondent at one point. And every so often you'd get the Oriana Fallacis of the world.

One of Oriana's trips, I ended up in a book. She claims she thought I was going to make a pass at her. Though she's a pretty brave girl, she really wasn't for going out to see the action first hand. She had come in with a reputation of being very critical and the only way I ever figured out to handle those was open the door and say, "Come see it. We'll go with you." But she didn't seem too damn interested in probing at things and I kept getting the feeling her mind was made up and all she wanted was the local color to lend a little authenticity.

And in her book she took off on me. That's all right. I got a kick out of it. She said I invited her up to my bedroom. Well, after Tet when people were throwing grenades over the walls, rather than eat on the ground floor I had a veranda off my bedroom and when it was a small group, I'd lunch up there. So she said I invited her up to the bedroom and took her through and sat her down to a very intimate one-on-one lunch and rolled my eyes at her and she thought she was made a pass at. And she says I said, "Tell me, Oriana, are you a Communist?"—as my first romantic opener.

Another thing, I don't say it critically, but a lot of this younger press, with all the criticism they were making later about the GIs smoking pot and so on, well sometimes the press thinks the guys on the government side are nincompoops or blind. They used to have Saturday afternoon pot parties, but that sort of thing never surfaced. There were no mea culpa stories about the amount of pot that was being smoked in Vietnam by the younger media. And whatever else. I guess there was opium available in various forms. You used to fly up and see the poppy fields in Laos, if you remember.

Was television as influential in turning off the public as we are often led to believe?

There are academics who have studied this and say no. If your predisposition was pro the war, TV made you more so and the reverse as well. But it certainly had an effect on the people who counted in terms of my paycheck. LBJ or Congress or whatever, assumed it affected the guy in Des Moines, so Washington would react violently to a TV spot. TV is a headline service; it hardly lends itself to subtleties and nuances. What the hell are you going to show in a war where turf is not the benchmark? Rice growing on TV? Hearts and minds being seized? You show action. And this is where I would criticize New York editors. It was "Go out and get me combat footage. NBC had better battles tonight than you do. Get off your ass out of Saigon." I think there were conscientious journalists out there. But they were under the gun. Inevitably you cover the wrong kind of story and you don't get on the nightly news. When you do it the second time and you don't get on, the third time, you cover a different type of story.

It was Tet that drove LBJ out, and Tet was really only five or six days of serious fighting—except for the twenty-eight days of Hue. Did the TV coverage of Hue prolong Tet longer than it really lasted?

Yes, it did in my judgment continue an impression here of intense conflict that didn't exist. And to that extent, it distorted the picture, put it out of focus. Now, having said that, I would ask you, and the question sort of answers my judgment, whether the front page of *The Washington Post* the day after Tet showing a devastated Embassy with dead lying on the lawn, the starkness of those pictures, whether their impact in this case on official Washington, wasn't as great because they were such a complete reversal of everything that had happened in the earlier two or three months? *Life* [magazine] was then still publishing and there's a very well-known *Life* cover of an armored personnel carrier covered with dead Marine bodies, must have been fifteen bodies, in all kinds of grotesque forms. Did that have more impact than TV? I don't know. It certainly got one hell of a lot of reaction, so I'm not sure you can blame all that on TV.

It was a hothouse. It was intense and very close quarters, if you will, with the media. You see, you say bitterness. I'm not sure I'd use that word for the time I was there. Certainly criticism, certainly at times frustration, "Goddamnit, why did they run that story?" I don't think it got bitter again until the end of '68 or even '69 when the military itself changed with the whole drug period and the incipient mutiny period and all the rest of those horrible years of '69, '70, '71.

He is balding now, and gray around the fringes, but his mind and his pictures are as young as ever. In Vietnam between 1965 and 1968, EDDIE ADAMS won a Pulitzer and a host of other prizes for his spectacular images of the war. His most famous photo of that era showed National Police Chief Gen. Nguyen Ngoc Loan putting a bullet through the head of a Viet Cong on a Saigon street at the height of the Tet offensive. Adams now lives in New York and works as a photographer for various publications.

My first year there was 1965. I was really scared. I thought I was going to die. So I asked to come back to the States after about a year. I was here about one month. I walked around, I looked at everybody, and I didn't like anyone. I thought, "Nobody really cares about these guys who are getting killed." I saw a veteran on crutches almost get run over by a cab. I talked to people about the war, and they didn't give a shit. The only people that cared were wives, girlfriends, parents. So I volunteered to go back. I felt more comfortable there. But again I thought I was going to get blown away, and I asked to come back home. I never wanted to ever see the war again. I had my fill of it. But I was asked a year later. They needed some help there, so I said all right. It was '68 when I went back. I didn't want to go back that time.

I've often wondered how anyone had the guts to take the pictures that came out of that war.

It's all in your head. You're a correspondent, not a soldier. You don't have to be there, so you build this shield. I was frightened every time I went out, but I didn't think about it. You've got to wipe your mind of anything else. You didn't know if you were going to get killed the next day. So we would go out at night and get blasted, do everything you shouldn't do, and then go back into another battle. There were two types of correspondents—the hard core and the guys who covered everything out of Saigon, "the big picture." I was in a small group of the hard core. And I think all these people saw more combat and more war than any soldier. But in the middle of battle, when the medevacs came in, you could jump aboard. You didn't have to stay—although most of the time, you did. This helps.

As the war progressed, nobody really cared, so photographers would go out and drive themselves harder to try to get on the front page. I don't think any of these people had a death wish. Two of my closest friends were killed there, Kyoichi Sawada*, a Japanese photog-

---

*For UPI, who also won a Pulitzer and may other prizes, and died in an ambush in Cambodia.

rapher, and a guy named Henri Huet.* When Henri died, I ended up in bed for three days. I just couldn't handle it. Then you had people like Sean Flynn, the son of Errol Flynn. He thought he was his father, and Vietnam was a movie. He was very handsome. He used to go into a battle, and when everyone was huddling around, he was the only one standing up taking pictures. Well, he disappeared. He rode toward North Vietnam.† That was the last we ever heard of him. If you're going to do stupid things. . . .

One thing we used to laugh about: We used to go out in teams, so that if one of us got blown away, the other could cover it. A bit sick. That was also a way of survival—joking about everything. There used to be a standard joke amongst the correspondents. If you go out in battle and there's no fighting, there really isn't much of a story. So we had this saying, "If we're lucky, we'll be ambushed today."

There have been two instances when I could have had great photographs but I absolutely refused to push the button. One was in Vietnam. We were in a battle with the Marines around Chu Lai. The Marines were taking about fifty percent casualties. We were on a hill being pounded by rockets. I was scared to death. I was lying on the ground. I put my head sideways to give a couple more inches for bullets or shrapnel to pass over. About three feet from me was a Marine about eighteen years old—blond hair, blue eyes, with fear on his face like I've never seen before in my life. It was just like a frozen image, with big, glassy eyes. I slid the camera in front of my face. I tried to push the button. I couldn't do it. There are certain moments that you just don't disturb. Yet I knew at that time it would have been a *Life* cover, it would have been on page one of every newspaper around the world. I've never seen that again, before or since.

The inevitable question, I'm afraid. The famous photo . . .

All right. I expected it. The Associated Press and NBC offices were in the same building. We were very close. There was a battle taking place at the An Quang pagoda in Cholon, a Chinese section of Saigon. Someone from NBC found out and asked if we wanted to come. There was nothing else going on, so I said, "Why not?" I took several photographs of police and people moving and shooting, but there didn't seem to be that much going on, so we decided to go back to the office.

---

*Who worked at various times for both UPI and AP, and also won a large number of prizes.

†Flynn and Dana Stone, another photographer, set off on a motorbike from Phnom Penh during the early stages of the Cambodian war, saying they intended to try to make contact with North Vietnamese troops camped across the border from South Vietnam. They disappeared.

We were walking down the street when we saw the South Vietnamese police walking with this guy. We started following him because it was a prisoner, and like any photographer, you stay with a prisoner until he's out of sight. They stopped on the corner, and I was thinking, "This is boring." Just then Loan walked in out of nowhere and I saw him load his pistol. And I thought he was going to threaten the prisoner, which they always do. As soon as he raised his pistol, I raised my camera. Well, later on the U.S. military studied the picture and it turned out the moment he pulled the trigger, I pushed the shutter of my camera. It was all an accident. I just took it because I thought he was going to threaten him.

After Loan shot him, he walked over to us and said, "They killed many of my men and many of your people," and he walked away. The prisoner was later identified as a Viet Cong lieutenant, which I'll tell you a little more about later. What happened when the lieutenant fell to the ground, I'd never seen someone shot in the head like that. This is ugly. Blood started out of his head like a water fountain. I didn't photograph it. I just walked away. When I got to the AP office, I dropped off the film and said, "I think I got a picture of some guy shooting some guy. I'm going to get some lunch." That may sound callous, but it was a war.

A few days later over the AP wires, a lot of messages came in from New York, saying "Who is this guy? Give us a story on him." I volunteered to do a story. The guys in the office said "Stay away from the guy. He'll blow you away after what happened." But for the next two weeks I went to the police headquarters to see him. He wouldn't see me. One day the door opened, and this colonel let me in to see the general, who was then a colonel. So the first thing I said to him was "I'd like to do a story on you." I never mentioned the photograph. He got up from his chair, came to the other side of his desk, put his head right next to mine, looked right in my eyes, and said, "I know the Vietnamese who took that photograph." Then he went back and sat in his chair. He said he "knew the Vietnamese." What that meant was that he wasn't going to blame me for taking the picture. I was just doing my job, as he was doing his. Then he started talking. He said after the picture came out, the first thing that happened was that his wife gave him hell for not confiscating the film. He said, "She thinks that's all I have to worry about— photographers."

I went to see him a while ago. He has a coffee shop now in Virginia. He sells pizza. There's a big urn where they make good coffee. The general's watching me as I come in. The first thing I said to him was "General, you haven't changed a bit." And he said to me, "You've gotten very, very old." The bad thing is, the State Department tried to deport him a few years ago. His attorney called me and wanted to know if I would testify in his behalf. I said, "By all means." In the meantime, I got hold of Peter Arnett and said, "Let's get a story out on how they're trying to screw him up." It stopped the whole thing, and he's still in the States.

Anyway, when I did this story for *Parade* on my return to Vietnam, I got a lot of letters. One came from a former Air Force colonel. It turns out that the Viet Cong lieutenant who was killed in the picture had murdered a police major—one of General Loan's best friends—his whole family, wife, kids, the same guy. So these are things we don't know at the time. Everyone condemns Loan for shooting this guy. But I tell everyone: "If you were General Loan and there was a war going on, and your people were getting killed, how do you know *you* wouldn't shoot him, too?" Cold-blooded execution? Bullshit. He was doing what he was there for—to win the war. I just happened to be there. How many times did this happen that we *didn't* see?

There were things a hell of a lot worse that happened in Vietnam. We had pictures that we never released. There were pictures of Americans holding heads of Viet Cong they'd chopped off. I talked to one soldier who said "Oh, you should have been here a little while ago. I cut me a heart out of one of them Viet Cong. I just buried it." Very gruesome, but this is a war. People are dying, your friends are getting blown away. In the next two minutes *you* could be dead. Everything is fair in love and war. There aren't any rules. It's just war.

———◆———

As a young second lieutenant, PETER BRAESTRUP *led a Marine rifle platoon on the front lines in Korea. He was a combat correspondent in Vietnam for* The New York Times *and later for the* Washington Post. *He is the author of* Big Story, *a critique of press coverage focusing on the Tet offensive, and editor of* Vietnam as History: Ten Years After the Paris Peace Accords. *He leads a quieter life now, as editor of the* Wilson Quarterly, *a scholarly journal published by the Woodrow Wilson Institute in Washington.*

I first went out in May 1966. There had been a certain amount of terrorism in Saigon the previous year, and there was a curfew. The day I got in I ran into Bernie Kalb who told me about this truckload of Vietnamese civilians who by some gross mistake predawn had been shot up by the MPs, who thought they were coming to do them in. And then that night there was a birthday party for a fellow named

Kaplan who was the deputy PAO.* It was done in somebody's house. Orchestra, Vietnamese, American college girls, State Department guys, journalists, CORDS guys. It was the damndest thing I'd ever seen in my life. I couldn't believe there was a war on.

Next day I went up to Danang and down to visit my old Marine battalion in Chu Lai. When I got back to Danang, there was kind of a mini civil war going on between the Buddhists and the central authorities. We went out to the pagoda, and when we got back to the press camp, there was a young guy from Reuters there, dictating a story, "Tension mounted in this war-divided city," and I looked at him and I retched. When he got through dictating he said, "What's the matter with that lead," and I said, "God, cliche city." And he said, "That's the old Berlin lead," you know, "Tension mounted in this divided city . . ."

This was the first war for a lot of these guys, so a lot of them loaded up with gear. You could go out with the South Vietnamese airborne and jump a few times and you would get ARVN airborne wings. A lot of guys got right out there with the troops, particularly the wire service photographers. After David Greenway and I were shot down in a helicopter during Tet, I carried a little Belgian pistol. I mean it wouldn't have hurt anybody if I had managed to hit them with it. But psychologically, you were freeloading if you were with an infantry outfit and you didn't have a weapon. What good were you if you were attacked by the bad guys? So I had that little peashooter sitting in my pocket.

One of the things [those experiences] underline about the way we worked is the very narrow, day-to-day sense of things. There weren't many great minds out there. A lot of the wire service guys were "Bang! Go get it"; that was their thing. Short takes. A few people, like Charlie Mohr, had enough experience and could draw back and think about it. But a lot of guys temperamentally aren't that way.

The inherent contradictions in the whole policy, we did not understand. We knew there was something wrong on the surface. It reminded me in retrospect of investigating the New York City slumlords. I got them indicted and I was nominated for a Pulitzer, but the fundamental problem was not the slumlords; it was rent control, and I never understood that when I was writing about it. That's true of journalists all the time—very few of them by temperament get at the fundamentals.

We're snatch-and-grabbit guys. The dogs have to bark for us to know what's going on. Then if we don't believe what we hear, we fish around for a critique. We're getting "both sides" of the story. When

---

*Public Affairs Officer.

we're getting hosed down by the Administration on something, we're very sensitive to what looks like the contrary argument. But there may be more than one contrary argument, and there may be something that isn't being said at all that's fundamental. We missed that in Vietnam, often.

In '65–'66–'67, Lyndon Johnson kept everybody thinking that what he wanted was peace rather than victory, and that it was possible to have a compromise. And as his memoirs show, he was flimflamming everybody. He did that by setting the terms of the debate. He did not want Vietnam to become a bigger war, and he did not want it to take precedence over the Great Society. If he had asked the Hill for the money and the men to fight the war, Wilbur Mills* would've cut him off at the knees on the Great Society. So he was caught, but what he did was to make us think of Vietnam as an island, so there would be no wider war. It squelched the Joint Chiefs and Westmoreland, who knew you couldn't win the war except by cutting the Trail. Since the Joint Chiefs were muzzled, the debate inside the administration, which was essentially a three way debate, came out in the press as a two way debate between the doves and Johnson. And only rarely was the military strategy analyzed in terms of whether ultimately our inhibitions would kill us.

You can fault Westmoreland for this, too—that he didn't resign in protest against being asked to get troops killed in a war of attrition. You couldn't cross the borders. You had to sit in South Vietnam and kill them as they came in, and that was unending, unending. It just depended on how long North Vietnam was willing to do that— and they were willing to do it forever. So he was stuck with an impossible situation, and either he or the Joint Chiefs should have resigned in protest. But we weren't any smarter. We assumed Westy was getting everything he asked for, and that he liked the strategy. So we tended to blame Westmoreland not for going along with the strategy that was imposed upon him, *but for the strategy itself*. Well it was Westy's fault for going along with it, but the strategy was laid down by Lyndon and McNamara.

When Tet came along, Lyndon Johnson got in his bunker. There was no national TV address saying "This is what we've done and this is what's going to happen." He was very defensive. He'd been told there was going to be a major enemy effort by the CIA, by Westmoreland, by everybody. He'd warned the Australian cabinet back at Christmastime, when he was traveling around the world, that there was going to be a kamikaze attack. But he hardly mentioned Vietnam in his State of the Union address. I think Johnson was going

*Then chairman of the House Ways and Means Committee.

through something mental. I think he was trying desperately to play for time, hoping something good would happen. Then Tet comes along and he doesn't *react* to it. He could have done anything at that moment and he probably would have zoomed in popularity. Everything Nixon did in '72 he could have done—mine Haiphong, send in the B-52s. Look strong. That's what we want in a president, whether we like him or not. Nobody liked Nixon, but he had cojones. Lyndon Johnson was like the squad leader caught in an ambush who gets down and doesn't say anything when the shit's hitting the fan and everybody's looking at him for something to do.

The real clamor on the Hill didn't start for about a week. Everybody was waiting for the President to take charge, but he didn't do anything and then everybody was on him. When the government is incoherent, the press is twice as incoherent. In a crisis the President at least has to set out a story line to work with. But there was no story line here, and the press *kills* a President when he does that, by going to the people who *are* saying something. Well they went to the Hill. And all these guys who were critical of the policy came out of the closet. And the longer the President stayed in the closet the more his critics got the spotlight. The debate suddenly became a cacophony. Everybody was quoting William Butler Yeats, "The center cannot hold." What they were really saying was "The President hasn't taken charge." In retrospect it's just like Carter during the Iranian hostage crisis. He started saying "I'm spending all my time in the Rose Garden thinking about this." Poor Carter couldn't do anything about it, and he let *himself* become a hostage. So did Johnson at Tet.

The fact that Tet was a setback for the other side, you can't blame the press for not knowing right then. *Nobody* knew it then. But since there was no leadership, they magnified the damage and prolonged the image of a great disaster.

In your view, why did we get the Tet story so wrong?

We wanted to call the score, so we did. We were reflecting the political reality back here, and confusing it with the military reality. Tet came after a great propaganda campaign. Johnson was hoist by his own petard, and newsmen love that. Johnson had set himself up. He was trying to buy time and buy support for the war. And for the first time in American history, a field commander, Westmoreland, had allowed himself to be snookered into becoming a political spokesman. It was his vanity. He loved being on TV and he came home twice at Johnson's behest to speak, and it tainted him not only in the eyes of the press but in the eyes of a lot of military men. Westmoreland had in effect taken the king's shilling and become a propagandist—a soldier for the administration.

Did you ever hear of the Administration putting on pressure back here to get reporters sent to Saigon who favored the war?

It would have made everybody happier, but it just doesn't work. Wes Gallagher [then the AP general manager] used to grumble over some of the stuff that Arnett would write. Arnett was a New Zealander, didn't like the Yanks. But he did some good stories. Arnett complained later about censorship during the 1970 Cambodia invasion when he reported looting by American troops and it was taken out of the story.

See one of the interesting things is what rouses indignation. Looting when it's done by people in Watts is a "political protest," although it may just be looting. But we tend to get excited about looting in war. We tend to get excited about corruption. You read the reporting out of Phnom Penh or Saigon and we're always talking about corruption or black marketeering. We were applying our yardstick to other people. "The corrupt Lon Nol regime." "Bombing." "War." Nothing could be worse than what was going on. What they forgot about, particularly in Phnom Penh, was that something *could* be worse—genocide.

And that was our big hole. We discounted, because we never really understood the other side, what would happen in South Vietnam. There were a lot of little massacres and assassinations, but we tended to believe that it was selective terrorism. That was within the rules of the game and corruption was not. To us the "corrupt Thieu-Ky regime" was no better than the guys who'd take over. It was a moral equivalence kind of thing. If anybody had said a million boat people, no one would ever have believed it.

———•———

DON OBERDORFER *was one of only a handful of reporters who were able to cover Vietnam from both the war zone and Washington. He made half a dozen trips to Indochina between 1966 and 1975, and in between covered foreign policy in Washington, first for the Knight-Ridder chain and later for the* Washington Post. *In the late sixties he published a striking book about the turning point of the war, titled simply* Tet. *He is now the diplomatic correspondent of the* Washington Post.

The thing that probably makes my experience different from most is that I went in and out over a long period of years, and secondly, I was covering Vietnam both in Washington and in Saigon, and that gave me a sense of the disconnection between the rhetoric here and the reality there. There were a lot of things being argued forcefully here that seemed almost irrelevant there—such as whether the National Liberation Front was independent, and could an accommodation be made with the NLF where they would break away from the North. And it was just not pertinent to the real world.

I guess really the best example I can think of is one I participated in. They used to have briefings Thursday and Friday afternoons by Rusk and McNamara for twenty or thirty foreign-policy reporters in Washington. When I first started covering the war in '65, I went to a briefing McNamara gave in the Secretary of Defense's Dining Room in the Pentagon. He had a big chart, and two lines on it. One line was tonnages of bombs dropped on North Vietnam and this was going up, and the other line was tonnages of supplies going from North Vietnam to South Vietnam and this was going down, and he said, "When these two line cross over, we have begun to win the war."

Bernard Fall* was a neighbor of mine. One day I told Bernie what McNamara had said—that when the two lines crossed we were going to win in Vietnam. We were standing on the front steps of his house and he said, "That poor man. He's going to end up like Forrestal, jumping out of a window somewhere." He said, "That may have something to do with the Ford Motor Company but it has absolutely nothing to do with Vietnam," and, of course, he was right. He was dismayed because he realized that McNamara believed this. Fall got from Pham Van Dong the one quote that to me tells the whole story of the Vietnam War in two sentences: "Americans do not like long, inconclusive wars—and this is going to be a long, inconclusive war. Thus we are sure to win in the end."

When I was in Vietnam I spent a lot of time in the field but not really the same field that most American reporters spent time in. I spent some time with American troops to get the smell of it and the feel of it, but I spent much more time in the countryside, trying to get a picture of Vietnamese reality at the grass-roots level. It's not only that I didn't think that I would be a qualified critic of military tactics but that it did not seem to me that was, in the end, going to be decisive. I did not believe that the war of attrition could succeed in itself. I thought if the war was going to be successful, the United States was going to have to foster something in Vietnam that could be left as a sustaining force and that what happened in the countryside was more instructive about the potentiality of success than was the combat action.

---

*A French-born journalist who had written about his own country's defeat in Indochina in *Hell In a Very Small Place, Street Without Joy, The Two Vietnams,* and other books. He was killed by a land mine in South Vietnam in 1968.

So I concentrated much more on stories that other reporters did not have the luxury, perhaps, to do. I established certain villages in Vietnam where I went repeatedly, so I had some kind of bench-mark. I selected them on the basis of being reasonably accessible, and having some person who could help me understand. So I had one village in the Mekong Delta near My Tho which had been stud-ied by the Rand Corporation, and another in Binh Dinh, which was clearly an important province. And then I had some people that I knew in Hue.

I was often scared. I didn't like a lot of shooting. I was on patrol once and there was shooting and a couple of people got killed. I was once, I guess, wounded. I was with the chief of Binh Duong province on election day in '66 when we were ambushed in a fairly tough area. We had a kind of informal pool arrangement [for that election] among the American press. Instead of everybody going the same place, we split up. I took Binh Duong and went up with another reporter. The province chief said, "I'll take you with me. I'm going to go to the polls." He was driving the jeep. There was only one road in, and on his way down he saw somebody standing beside the road he didn't like, and he was nervous. We didn't spend a lot of time there and on the way back, he really put it right to the floorboard. There was one of those three-wheeled Lambrettas in front of us on the road and as we came up to it he gunned the engine. And just after we passed it an explosion went off. Somebody had been sitting along the road waiting for him to come back and deto-nated this mine. But he was going too fast and the guy wasn't quick enough on the trigger. It detonated right behind us. Some pellets penetrated the carburetor and other things in the jeep but it kept on going. I got a few fragments in my feet, minor. Then some automat-ic weapons fire opened up, but we were long gone. That's the clos-est call I ever had in Vietnam, but I wasn't that scared because there wasn't time.

Was the press biased in Vietnam?

Not in the simple use of the word. The coverage of Vietnam was a complicated subject, most of which is conveniently forgotten by one side or the other in the debate. For the American press, Vietnam was a learning experience—much as it was for the rest of the coun-try and the government. We knew very little at the beginning, but as the war progressed people in the press, along with people in the government who were our sources after all, began to get this very hazy, fuzzy situation into focus. And this picture was not the same picture that was being portrayed in the official reports. We know now, because of the Pentagon Papers, people's memoirs, and other things that the picture portrayed in the official reports was not the one that was believed by many of the policymakers.

One of the things that happened was that the consensus within the government broke down and suddenly instead of having one monolithic viewpoint presented to the press, you had conflicting viewpoints and therefore conflicting sets of sources. And if you look at the stories, it's quite clear that many of the things in Vietnam that were taken as press enterprise [came] from military or civilian officials who knew what was going on and communicated it by the back channels to the press. And they did it because they objected to the policy or objected to the deception about the policy, and also because some of them saw the press as the way to advance ideas which had been rejected from the top of the American government.

Your book and Braestrup's book are often cited as evidence that the press did the country a disservice in Vietnam: That Tet really was a great military victory, but our reporting created a political reality in the United States that was the reverse of the reality on the battlefield.

All the evidence is that the Communist losses were extremely high. But the political losses in the United States were equally high. I said in the book that the first question asked of a chronicler of Tet is who won? And the answer is nobody; the North Vietnamese and the Viet Cong lost a battle; the United States government lost something even more important, the confidence of its people. And in the end the losses in the United States were more important.

Now, how could it be that a battle lost by the Communists created a loss of confidence in the United States? I do not think the answer is misreporting. Tet was the shock that it was because of a chain of events which had begun months before. The Tet offensive seemed to many people to prove that there was no way that the war was about to be won, that the end of the tunnel was in sight.

One reason it had a tremendous impact was little understood at the time, and that is television. The Pacific satellite had gone up a few months before and this was the first time it was possible to have, on the same day, pictures and sounds of dramatic events. The impact of these pictures and sounds and the symbolic nature of them—attacking the American Embassy, the very headquarters of the United States in Vietnam—was very powerful. You could make a case that the attack on the Embassy, which involved [just one] squad of troops was, in a way, the most important battle of the war for American viewers. Now, was this due to misreporting? I don't think so. The fact is no matter what is said now, for the first twenty-four or thirty-six hours of the Tet offensive, American commanders did not know how this was going to come out.

Didn't the fact that Tet was mounted with the complicity of tens of thousands of ordinary Vietnamese also leave us feeling there was no way we could ever sort out our friends from our enemies?

I think there's no question but what there was a shocking truth inherent in the fact that they were able to simultaneously mount attacks in every substantial city and town, a nationwide surprise attack. And that said something about the capability of the Communist forces to move easily through the population and do things without getting caught. Again, go back to Pham Van Dong's comment about Americans not liking long and inconclusive wars. American patience was nearing the end of its tether in January of 1968. In my opinion, the two really decisive moments in Vietnam were Tet and one that preceded it by a few months, which in a way made the Tet offensive what it came to be in terms of American opinion.

That event—the minute when the beginning of the end for Vietnam came—was on August third, 1967. President Johnson stood before a blackboard full of budget numbers in the Roosevelt Room of the White House and asked for a ten percent income tax surcharge to pay for the war. The political disaffection from Vietnam snowballed from that moment. People were willing to go along with the war, but they were not willing to pay for it. And that led Johnson, in order to keep the public and the political establishment from simply running away from the whole thing in the fall of '67, to [generate] all sorts of optimistic reports: "We're about to win. Just wait a little while longer. Your patience will be rewarded." And at that point the Tet offensive absolutely shattered the waning patience and confidence of the American public.

———————◆———————

WALTER CRONKITE, *the* CBS Evening News *anchorman throughout the war years, traveled to Vietnam during the Tet offensive, and on his return stepped out of his impartial observer's role to broadcast a one-of-a-kind commentary that helped persuade Lyndon Johnson to give up on the war. Though retired, Cronkite still does occasional commentaries and documentaries for CBS. In 1985, when he sat for this interview, he had just returned from a visit to Vietnam.*

In 1968 you went to South Vietnam during Tet and you came back and said in a commentary that it seemed Vietnam would end in a bloody stalemate. Was that trip a watershed for you?

I had resisted doing commentary on the *Evening News* even when it had been suggested to me. I was concerned about whether it's possible as a professional journalist to wear two hats. But when Tet came along, the public was already divided and confused. We had been told that the war was practically over, that there was light at the end of the tunnel, that we had won the hearts and minds, that the Viet Cong was decreasing in strength and popular support, and then suddenly it can conduct a military operation of the scale and the intensity that it did in Tet. Well, everybody was throwing up their hands saying "God, what in the world is happening out there?" And we decided that we had pretty good credibility of having been as impartial as it's possible to be, and maybe it's time to go out there and just do some pieces on what it looks like and try to give some guidance.

My personal approach had been impartial because I found it hard to make up my own mind. In the early stages I thought we should be involved in trying to preserve a territory where democracy might be permitted to flourish in Southeast Asia. I began to get opposed when the military commitment was made. I didn't think we ought to have our troops there. And then I got more and more concerned as more and more troops [went out]. My particular concern was that the Administration did not tell us the truth about the nature or size of the commitment that was going to be required. And I think that's where the Administration lost the support of the American people—in trying to pretend it was something we could do with our left hand, without asking the people at home to share the heavy responsibility. At any rate, I went out there and what I saw led me to the conclusions that I made. And I gather that Johnson saw the broadcast and said despondently, "Well, if we've lost Cronkite, we've lost Middle America."

I didn't expect it to be that effective. It should have shocked the President only if he didn't know the full scale of the thing himself. I think he may have been as surprised by Tet as everybody else was, and while the military was putting up a brave front—"Oh, boy, we sucked them right into our trap and we've given them a great, magnificent military blow from which they'll never recover"—it was an optimism that, my God, you couldn't see on the ground out there. The Viet Cong was right in the city of Saigon. That was what kind of turned so many of us at that point into saying, "Come on, now. This is the end. Stop it."

Recently the Vietnamese have acknowledged that in fact Tet set back their war effort. Did the U.S. press cover both sides of the story?

You know, that admission I haven't found to be that strong, and it certainly wasn't when I talked to them last week. That's not what they say at all. They say, "We took a serious blow, but we anticipated taking a serious blow, for we did exactly what we expected.

We expected to deliver a severe psychological blow and perhaps drive the Americans out of the war.'' It's clear they didn't get the uprisings they expected, no doubt about that. But there's no doubt also that they inflicted one hell of a blow psychologically and they cost an awful lot of South Vietnamese troops as well as ours. That the American forces claim they won a victory in Tet is an excessive rewrite of history.

———————•———————

There is a certain working-man's quality to him; a short, powerful frame, blunt mechanics' fingers, a thinning lid of curly hair gone to steel, quiet, plain-spoken in a deep, East Tennessee drawl, painfully, searingly honest. LEON DANIEL *grew up in Knoxville, the son of a railroad man, enlisted in the Marines at nineteen, spent a year on the front lines in America's forgotten war, Korea, and went to college on the GI Bill. He covered the civil rights movement for eight years, the U.S. intervention in the Dominican Republic in 1965, and then went to Vietnam. He spent most of the next decade in Asia, in and out of Vietnam, and then returned to become UPI's national correspondent, working out of Washington.*

When I asked to go to Vietnam I didn't have any political view on the war. I guess I was a cheerleader when I first got there. I was a grunt reporter and I thought the grunts were admirable young men. I was writing stories about the bravery of American GIs and I did it in good conscience because they *were* brave and they did behave well under combat conditions. I was trying to be the poor man's Ernie Pyle. And so if anything I was biased not so much toward the war as toward the people I was covering.

There was a kid I ran across, a tunnel rat. He was from Tennessee. I don't remember his name, but I remember talking to him before he went into the tunnel and he had, as I think I wrote, the same hill country accent I have. He was from somewhere up in East Tennessee. And then about an hour later he went down into this well that had tunneling in the walls. And after throwing all kinds of charges into that well and pumping gas into it, evidently there was still a live VC or two in there, and this kid was executed. He was gut shot as he was lowered down the side of the well. As I recall it was a single shot and we all heard it. Some of the things I saw in that war were just so starkly brutal.

I was often frightened. We all were. I was in a helicopter that took some rounds once, but nothing happened and we landed okay. A few times I went into what we used to call hot LZs, where you were taking fire when you landed. I was absolutely petrified then. And once Sawada and I were with a Marine unit and we had dug about a twelve-inch hole to sleep in. That would have been in '66 or '67 up around Gio Linh, just below the DMZ. A young lieutenant of Marines had dug in right next to us, about three feet away, and he was blown away that night by a mortar and we weren't touched. But I wasn't frightened when that happened. We didn't know until next morning when we saw pieces of him on us.

I was probably in the group of people who came to be disillusioned with the war early on. After my first thirteen-month tour there I couldn't say unequivocally that it was unwinnable. But I did feel that the search-and-destroy missions were not working. It was obvious to me that the body counts were not accurate. On the few occasions when I came in out of the field and attended the Five O'clock Follies, like many others I felt that the briefings were far more upbeat than the facts warranted. And they used these crazy euphemisms in those days like "meeting engagement" for a firefight where our side might have gotten the shit kicked out of us. And I think it was that type of management of the news that mitigated *for* changing your mind if you were a newsman. You resented this condescension.

Did you ever have any sense there was any particular political direction from your editors?

I've been asked that question before and I would be very hard-pressed to come up with an example of that. I may have been conscious that some of the people I worked for supported the war, but it never influenced anything I wrote.

I do recall one conversation in New York right before I left, with I believe Fran Leary, the managing editor, and he says, "Go out there and write about the pacification program. We don't have anything about the pacification program." And I took from his remark that he believed it was working and that we were undercovering it. Well I kept that in the back of my mind. I concentrated on the horseshit and gunsmoke stories. But once I got in a place where they were removing a whole village to somewhere else as part of the pacification program. This struck me as idiocy. You can't defend the village, so you move all the villagers to someplace you *can* defend. I wrote a pretty tough story about that, and I don't recall anybody objecting to it.

During the Cambodian invasion of 1970 where Peter Arnett and I covered the destruction of a village called Snuol, I saw a pretty clear example [of politics affecting a story]. Peter I consider probably the best reporter for an American newspaper or news agency throughout the long war. Peter and I were with an armored cavalry unit, and we got to the edge of Snuol, and there was a little small-arms fire. The lieutenant colonel ordered his troops to fire [back], and I remember flat trajectory shells from a tank, I guess a ninety-millimeter gun, going straight into that village for a half hour or an hour. When resistance had stopped completely, we walked through and found maybe a half dozen dead, some of them were children, right in the center of the town. And we saw some of the kind of fighting holes the Viet Cong dig, but they had gone.

But [we also saw] the young American kids, the grunts, ripping off soft drinks and one motorcycle was strapped on a tank, and some things like that. I had never seen American soldiers looting before. Arnett and I got a ride back on a CIA plane from somewhere, and we discussed the story and I was almost certain that we would both write the same lead, which was that American troops had virtually destroyed a village after taking some fire from it, and then the troops did some looting after the fighting was over. And that's precisely the lead I wrote. And I do recall when I wrote the story back in Saigon, a couple of people I worked for said something like "Are you sure? Because if you're gonna charge looting you better damn sure be correct." And I said "Yes I'm sure," and the story moved promptly.

And I later heard that Arnett's story did not move and there were objections from very high in the AP to it. I never discussed this with Peter, so his version might be different. But I am reasonably sure it didn't move the way he wrote it. And the story I wrote was run in the *Washington Post* on the editorial page, with a little note over it saying something like "We don't know precisely what happened but we think this is a statement on how the war is going."

There are a number of stories that people cite as unfair, and one of them is Arnett's piece in which tear gas came out as "nonlethal gas," leaving a different impression than if it had just said tear gas.

That's a bad rap. Nonlethal gas is not pejorative. Perhaps you could use a better term. But that stuff they were using was more than tear gas. It was much tougher. It was a CS* agent that you wouldn't use on rioters. I wouldn't say that tear gas would be much of a problem. Tear gas is so much less lethal than everything else they were using in that war. But that stuff made you vomit. It immobilized you, it was tough stuff. It was a humane tactic, but it wasn't because we were so humane; it was because we wanted prisoners so we could extract information from them. It was as simple as that.

What finally turned you off the war?

I can't look back and see any single incident. For me I think it was a gradual thing and a feeling that it was just such a terrible waste.

---

*CS is a two-letter code for a nonpersistent riot gas, 0-chlorobenzylidene nalononitrile.

And that came pretty early, toward the end of my first tour. I used to listen to Armed Forces Radio out in the field, and I'd hear President Johnson saying, "Our purpose in Vietnam is to defeat the success of aggression." You'd hear that over and over and over, all day. It was a spot they played. And if you're covering search-and-destroy operations, you get mixed up about who the aggressor *is*. Here you're covering the armed might of the United States, helicopters, massive armaments, and it becomes less clear that these old guys running around the jungle are the aggressors.

I also came to have an abiding respect for the VC and the North Vietnamese. You'd see those bodies stacked up and you'd see prisoners who stayed in the jungle after they were jaundice-yellow, and guys with a little bag of rice, and the incredible hardships they went through. You couldn't help but admire their courage. We were still the good guys, but on the other hand you became very sympathetic to the young kids on the other side.

In the latter stages of the war I would see helicopter units where young grunts would carry business cards saying "Professional Killer" and things like that, and that turned me off. Some of these kids had only been there for a few months, and I couldn't understand why this almost calculated brutality was infused into these guys' slop chutes while they were drinking their beer. But on the other hand they were risking their lives every day and so you didn't want to write bad things about them because they were just like I was when I was nineteen years old in Korea.

At the time of the Laotian invasion it seemed to me that morale had deteriorated significantly. You had senior NCOs evacuating themselves for alcoholism—lifers, not just grunts. There was large-scale dope use. The talk of fragging was rampant. I never could pin down any fragging incident hard enough to write about it, but it was going on. And there were cases of mutiny, units that refused to go forward. In the end I came to believe that the war was destroying the U.S. Army.

———◆———

JAMES R. SCHLESINGER, JR., *has served both Republican and Democratic Presidents in senior national security positions. He was Secretary of Defense when Saigon fell. He is now a counselor of the Georgetown Center for Strategic and International Studies in Washington.*

There still is a whole lot of residual bitterness toward the press, isn't there?

There is a great deal. I think there's a natural antagonism between the military and the press, but it has been reinforced by the military's experiences as they saw them at the time and as they now reinterpret them in the light of this war. For a large number of people in the military establishment, the reason for the outcome was not that our political and military strategy was deficient or that our allies were weak; it was the damned press that was undermining us. That is the way they view it today. I don't think it was the way they viewed it at the time. They were irritated frequently, but they had not embroidered this theory that the basic cause for the undermining of our position was the press.

I went a couple of years ago to the Carabao dinner*—not this year, but last year—and I was really amazed at the emotions that developed when they began to make nasty comments about the press. I thought the press did not behave itself well in that period, but it seems to me rather nonsensical to try and blame the national performance in Vietnam on the press. The press was reflecting to a large extent some larger, substantive problems. They certainly were reflecting the deficiencies of our strategy, tactics, and operations in Vietnam. Because what most of these young lieutenant colonels of today don't know is that the people who were telling the press all of those things that were going on were officers like them out there in the field.

In their thinking it's only the exception, the malcontent, that's going to leak to the press. They don't know that back then there were lots of people who disagreed with strategy and tactics, and many of them, perhaps a majority, were prepared to leak. I remember talking to one U.S. senator who'd just been elected and who got dragged along out there sometime in '66 or '67 for the briefings. And he got through with his formal briefing, and one of the generals called him aside and said "Don't take that briefing too seriously. This thing is not going well. Just two miles up that road Vietnam civilians are paying taxes to the VC." This may have been embroidered, but the fact of the matter is that those observations, those very same judgments were coming from the military.

---

*The Carabao dinner, or Great Carabao Wallow, as it is properly called, is an annual get-together of the military establishment in Washington to commemorate the U.S. Army's fight to pacify guerrillas in the Philippines after the Spanish-American War. A carabao is a Filipino water buffalo.

CHAPTER EIGHT

Secret Wars

S ECRET warfare—the idea of moving covertly against targets that can't be reached by conventional means—has an obvious logic to it. Nothing could be better suited to the military principles of surprise, concentration of force and striking where the enemy is weak. But it is also fair to say that what can be achieved with clandestine forces against a determined enemy is not always worth the cost and risk involved.

Over the years, American secret wars have seldom met their objectives, and there has been a tendency to cope with failure either by making them bigger or by pursuing desperate schemes to try to multiply the leverage of inadequate forces. On both accounts, many of the secret wars have become political embarrassments. In that sense, secret warfare contradicts another dictum from the pen of Clausewitz—that "War is a mere continuation of politics by other means." In Vietnam secrecy was often used to conceal large-scale warfare not from the enemy but from Americans who might have opposed it.

The current style of secret warfare is about a half-century old. It dates to Franklin D. Roosevelt's decision in the thirties to help China fight the invading Japanese. His instrument was a "volunteer" air force called the Flying Tigers, led by then-Col. Claire Chennault. The operation had to be conducted under cover until Pearl Harbor, because official U.S. participation would have been an act of war against Japan, and would have generated a tempest at home, where isolationism was still ascendant.

One of the more fascinating and perhaps less-known sidelights of this is that the core of the Flying Tigers group stayed in China after World War II to fly air support for Chiang Kai-shek as he fought the Communists. When the mainland fell in 1949, the group evacuated with Chiang's Kuomintang to Taiwan, where it became Air Asia, and set up a subsidiary firm that later became the CIA airline in Southeast Asia, Air America.*

During World War II, American secret operations focused on supporting the antifascist resistance in Europe and Asia. Much of the responsibility went to the Office of Strategic Services, which in 1947 became the nucleus of the CIA. The postwar intelligence establishment thus was born with an instinct, a predilection, and the institutional arrangements for covert operations. That was reinforced when it participated in helping the Greek government to snuff out Soviet-backed guerrillas in the late forties.

In the fifties, the locus of conflict shifted to Asia. During Korea, American intelligence operatives tried unsuccessfully to enlist the Viet Minh to harass southern China, according to William Corson. After the 1954 settlement of the French Indochina War, they busily sabotaged facilities in Hanoi before the Viet Minh arrived, and helped arrange the U.S. evacuation of hundreds of thousands of Catholic refugees to South Vietnam.

In 1958, when Hanoi began moving cadres through Laos into South Vietnam to renew the "revolution," the secret warriors once again sprang into action. Their first move was to recruit Meo tribesmen in Laos to ambush the infiltration trails down the Annamite mountains. Support came by way of Air America supply drops from Thailand. North Vietnam struck back with an offensive under the banner of the Pathet Lao Communists that threatened to overrun the country and destabilize Thailand, which lay just across the Mekong River. The Kennedy administration sent Army Special Forces in "White Star" teams to support the regular Laotian Army and to strengthen supplies and advice to the Meo. Hanoi persuaded the Soviet Union to start a munitions airlift, and Communist forces overran several major positions. Kennedy moved Marines to forward positions in Thailand, and the situation seemed headed toward a full-blown U.S.-Soviet confrontation. Finally in 1962, both sides agreed to back away, and the Geneva Accords made Laos theoretically "neutral."

But while that kept Communist forces away from the Mekong and the Thai border, it also ratified North Vietnam's control of the infiltration corridor—which had been its starting objective. The United States continued its "secret" war against the trail for eleven years, using hundreds of CIA operatives, Air America and other aviation companies to train, arm, advise and supply a not-so-secret army led by a Laotian general of Meo extraction named Vang Pao. The

---

*Air Asia also had a second subsidiary, Civil Air Transport, which operated for a time as Nationalist China's commercial airline, and it operated a major aircraft maintenance and renovation base in Taiwan, which serviced the planes of other semiofficial carriers, such as Southern Air Transport.

reason for the secrecy, according to both former Ambassador William Sullivan and former CIA director William Colby, was to avoid the appearance of violating the 1962 accords. But there was also strong political pressure in the United States not to expand the ground war across South Vietnam's borders.

To the Communists the secret war was a mere thorn in the side. North Vietnamese troops kept the Meo well away from what was by then called the Ho Chi Minh Trail. Eventually the U.S. had to wage a "secret" bombing campaign both to support the Meo and to try—unsuccessfully—to interdict Communist movement. Meantime Hanoi persuaded Cambodian ruler Prince Norodom Sihanouk to allow the genuinely secret use of Sihanoukville port to supply its troops in the far south. In 1970, when Sihanouk was ousted by Gen. Lon Nol, who was friendly to the United States, North Vietnam quickly seized the Bolovens plateau in southern Laos, which it needed to protect an expanded trail network. Simultaneously, it unleashed the Khmer Rouge to keep Lon Nol's troops out of the Cambodian border areas, which had for years been the Communists' secure rear area—a sanctuary from American and South Vietnamese military pursuit.

The lack of success in Laos caused the U.S. to set up a second semisecret front on the South Vietnamese side of the frontier. In the early sixties it recruited Montagnard tribesmen to harass and interdict the trail where it entered South Vietnam. The U.S. actually signed an agreement to guarantee the Montagnards' tribal lands in exchange for their help. Unfortunately, the South Vietnamese regarded the Montagnards as inferiors (the Vietnamese word for the tribespeople was *kha*, or "slave") and did not honor the compact. Ngo Dinh Nhu insisted on moving the Montagnards into strategic hamlets, provoking a revolt in 1963. The rebellion was eventually settled, but as Corson and Bruce Palmer observe, the Montagnards never again fought with enthusiasm.

Beginning in 1965, American Special Forces set up dozens of base camps on the border, using Montagnards and Chinese "Nungs" of mysterious origin* in Civilian Indigenous Defense Groups. The camps were supposed to give early warning of major cross-border movements, and to covertly monitor and harass supply lines and base areas across the boundary. But their locations were well known, and they were usually circumnavigated by the Communists. When they were really in the way, the camps were brought under siege.

---

*There were uncheckable stories in Southeast Asia at the time that the "Nungs" were actually recruited from the ranks of Nationalist Chinese (Kuomintang) armies that fled into the Indochina peninsula aafter the fall of China and set up opium-trading warlord empires in the mountains of Thailand, Burma, and Laos.

The harassing missions were risky, and they did no visible good. The Army finally concluded they cost more than they were worth.

A U.S. headquarters in Nha Trang, called the Studies and Observations Group, was responsible in the early years for so-called 34-A commando operations into North Vietnam, almost all of which ended badly. One such action provoked the PT-boat attack that began the Tonkin Gulf incident. Other CIA operations, such as Phoenix, which aimed to eliminate local Viet Cong, and a black pajama program to put cadres into contested hamlets, had mixed results. Eventually some CIA operatives were caught up in the intelligence scandals of the mid-seventies, when it was revealed that they had, among other things, "terminated with extreme prejudice" suspected double agents by booting them out of helicopters.

One of the most dubious aspects of the secret wars was the fact that to keep Laotian, Thai, and Vietnamese officials on board, the U.S. often had to ignore their hip-deep involvement in the opium and heroin trade. There were even allegations—never proved—that American planes and pilots sometimes were used to move drugs. Though most of the narcotics moved into the international traffic in the early war years, a booming trade developed with the U.S. military in Vietnam and Thailand in the late sixties.

Another problem with these operations was the sheer military cost. Although Colby and Sullivan claim that the Laotian operation was done on the cheap, the United States lost hundreds of planes in Laos "protecting" the Vang Pao forces. And as Palmer points out, the border camps, each of which required a fairly substantial airstrip, were expensive to build and maintain, drained off high-quality troops from other units, and frequently had to be rescued from siege. A third problem was that the operations quickly got too large to stay secret. Americans in Vietnam displayed a peculiar inability to keep quiet about sensitive intelligence matters. Many of them showed up in print, creating political embarrassment at a time when political support for the war was already difficult to sustain. A fourth, as Jeff Stein's tale shows, was that the American secret warriors were often manipulated by the Vietnamese for their own ends.

But the underlying flaw with all of them was that secrecy made possible many actions that, on reflection, the United States ought not to have undertaken at all. Whenever the secret soldiers made real trouble, the enemy trumped them with superior force, to which there was generally no response—displaying for all to see that what they were up to was closer to gamesmanship than it was to serious warfare.

WILLIAM CORSON

I first went to Vietnam in February of 1950. There was a mission, and very few people are aware of this, to evaluate the Bao Dai* armed forces of the Associated States of Indochina—the army that later became ARVN. It was to assess their ability to operate in conjunction with the French and to be able to stand alone, because of the increasing Communist-inspired insurrection. The French were badgering Truman for military assistance, and you have to realize that before the Korean War, military aid wasn't the growth industry that it became later.

Vietnam was a far-off place about which we knew very little. The man who led the mission was a Marine general hand-picked by Harry Truman. His name was Graves B. Erskine. He was lacking in all kinds of couth, but he was one of the most highly decorated Marines, and he was the director of OSO, the Office of Special Operations.

The people that came along, including the general, could speak a little Chinese or *parlez français* or maybe a little Malay. The only Vietnamese speaker around at the time was a young [Navy] lieutenant junior grade by the name of John McAllister who's now a banker out in California. He had a Ph.D. and had written his dissertation on early Vietnamese history, but he was only the assistant naval attaché, so he didn't get listened to much.

Anyhow the Erskine team fanned out to take a look, and at the end there wasn't a kind word said about anybody in the Associated States Army. Erskine himself said, and this is hilarious, because the fellow involved was Nguyen Van Thieu, "I ran into this corporal who couldn't count *socks*." So the report basically says "Harry don't be a fool. It's throwing good money after bad and it won't make a bit of difference. The Associated States Army couldn't pour piss out of a boot, and the French Legionnaires aren't gonna go out there and die for no good reason. To turn that into a fighting force we would have to resurrect Joe Stilwell† and even then it ain't worth it. It's a nice-looking country, but what the hell is in it for us? Nothing."

But it was overtaken by events. And the event in question was the Korean War. In 1951 I got sent back down there. We wanted to get

---

*Bao Dai was the French puppet "emperor" of the postwar Associated States of Indochina.
†Gen. Joseph Stilwell, who reorganized the Nationalist Chinese army after it had been beaten by the Japanese, and was the principal liaison with Chiang Kai-shek until the end of World War II.

the Viet Minh to put some pressure on the Chinese down in Yunnan so they wouldn't send any more Chinamen to Korea, and I was asked to do the negotiating. We thought money would talk, but the price wasn't right.

I met them out probably about forty or fifty kilometers northwest of Hanoi. I'm not going to tell you how I got there. That's a method and I don't talk about methods. But there was an area the French weren't going into out there, and they had a camp. And they were very taken when I talked with them, and I talked with Giap and I met the old man [Ho Chi Minh], but I was handed off to the people who were going to do the deal. Pham Van Dong and that kind of people.

It was pretty straightforward, because we had had some contacts with these people. This was cowboy-and-Indian days in the Far East, a crazy period in the history of American espionage. The objective was simple enough. They were still building their force for their move against the French. We made them a straight money offer, twenty million dollars in gold, take it or leave it. We wanted them to mount a series of raids along those classical invasion routes that lead into Yunnan, merely as an "Are more coming and who is it?" deception operation. The Chinese would wonder is it the French using the Associated Army or what?

But it didn't work out. I don't know whether there was somebody else in the bidding. And actually it didn't make any difference in the long run because the Chinese could not have deployed any additional troops to Korea anyway. The supplies from the Soviet Union were not enough to support any more.

After Korea I was down in Malaya for a while, and then back to Vietnam in '54. After that ended I was operating basically out of Tokyo and Yokosuka and spending some time down in Indonesia, and then I went up in the hills in Laos in '58–'59 to help run the Meo tribes. After the 1954 accords, the North Vietnamese started sending cadre along what later became the Ho Chi Minh Trail. And we tried to use the Meo tribesmen to stop them. It was a good war. The clowns and idiots were not around yet. The Meo would go out on an ambush and they had the patience of a saint. They could lie there in the bush for hours. And seriously, if a guy took four rounds of ammunition and didn't hit three people he lost face. And one of the things that they thought was sort of fun was not to kill them all, but to wound the biggest guy because then they'd have to carry him. You didn't want to wipe them out. You wanted to bleed them. The idea was to use surprise, hit predetermined targets with one or two rounds and be gone. The Vietnamese would get confused and start firing back into the weeds.

But then things heated up and the White Star* teams came in. They
were gonna do it the Army way—"We're gonna have single-issue
logistics: Everybody's gonna be carrying an M-2 carbine." Well,
you might as well have told them to wear an enamel American flag.
In the earlier days we had people with Nambus [a Japanese rifle],
Enfields, Springfields, blowguns, fuckin' crossbows. Once you give
everybody an M-2 carbine you are making him advertise "Me
Amellican Plick." When the White Stars got there I embraced the
first ones and said "Good-bye. Boy am I glad to get the fuck out of
here . . ."

*The Special Forces tried to set up a similar operation in Vietnam
using the Montagnards, and wound up making mistakes that may
in their way have been even worse, Corson continued.*

. . . Kennedy gave them their [green] berets and sent them in there
to do something they weren't prepared to do. You see their primary mission is as stay-behinds. And it's a big mistake to think that
because some guys know how to blow up a bridge, they also are
experts in how to protect one. People who are offensively oriented
have trouble thinking defense.

*Bruce Palmer makes the point that most of those hill camps were
Beau Geste forts, and therefore sitting ducks. The point of not operating out of visible bases in a guerrilla war is so simple it boggles
the mind they didn't understand it.*

Well the Special Farces (yes, Farces) camps were advertised as fire
bases. Now in addition to having some close-in defense, they were
supposed to be able to call on air and artillery from way back to
maintain their tactical integrity. But any position can be taken if
you are patient enough to watch its patterns [of operation] and find
its vulnerabilities. Now what was their function? Was it to become
literally an ensconced forward observation post? Or was it their mission to find and seek out and track the enemy? Or was it to go out
and kill the little red bastards?

They felt they were going to expand the notion of using the Hill
people and be out there killing red bastards. The idea was to exploit
the capability of indigenous resistance. But see you gotta do it in an
appropriate style with indigenous forces. And this is why it failed:
In '62 and '63 we had made agreements with them that they were
going to have their tribal land. The Montagnards are nomadic people. They're not farmers. They might grow a little opium, but they
don't stick in one place. But they are also a sovereign nation operating in the middle of Annam, a tribe with their own kings and their
own succession and their own history.

---

*U.S. Army Special Forces.

The Montagnards were noble people. They had a straightness of character and their beliefs were simple: the good guy and the bad guy. It was "You tell me that's a bad guy and you pay me and I'll kill him." They were the ultimate mercenaries and shit, we had them. They were with us. And then we made this stupid promise. We signed this goddamn treaty. We thought we were back in the period of Ulysses Grant, signing treaties with the goddamn Indians.

And then this other decision takes place and doesn't take account of that commitment. And that was Nhu's decision to force them into strategic hamlets, which caused the Montagnards to feel we'd crapped all over them. That's like taking a Geronimo or an Apache Indian and putting them in a reservation. They just about died. And so right after some of us have signed with them, others of us are saying that it's a military necessity to put them in strategic hamlets. And if you so much as said "Wait a minute. Let's weigh the necessity in terms of the effect it would have on these people," you were considered Asiatic. You had been out there too long. The response was "They'll do what they're told. We're looking after their best interest." Some of our people were wondering "What are they upset about? Geez, we're giving them food and all the betel nut they can chew and why are they so ungrateful?" So we put the poor bastards in the strategic hamlets.

And this is why I was sent back there in '65. In the summer of '65 the border firebases had just been conceived and the feeling was "We're gonna do more of it and we've gotta get more people there." So they wanted to reestablish the bonds that existed before these people were herded into the strategic hamlets. The strategic hamlet thing had been abandoned and these people had returned to their tribal areas, but they were still unhappy with us.

At the time I was on the faculty of the Naval Academy and I received a phone call. I was directed to present my body and spirit at a location in Washington by direction of the "appropriate authorities." It was "School's out colonel and the man wants you to go and do this because of what else we're planning to do and we need to know how much we can count on these fellows." And I said "Well okay, I go where I'm told." So they suggested I put in for a sixty-day personal leave, and "make your way to Vietnam."

So I flew out to Saigon, went up to Pleiku and took a chopper out to a 'Yard* village about thirty clicks [kilometers] west where a contact had been set up. I call it a village, but it was really just a camp. The 'Yards were still moving around in the summer of '65, and a village was wherever they put up their poles for the season. It's in a

---

*When speaking, Americans often shortened Montagnard to "Yard."

clearing, and the campfires are going, and I've always said Vietnam is hard to understand unless you can explain the smells. You may forget everything else, but if you get a whiff of *eau d'essence de l'Indochine*, you're transported in time. You hit the same fuckin' campfires, same cookin', same burning undergrowth and same decomposing hay, and it raps you right between the antlers.

I began my evangelism there, and the first thing I realized was that "Boy, you are trying to sell the wrong thing to these guys this time." I saw some old friends. This was sort of the return of the native son so they were willing to talk to me. And I took a few weeks and pretty well worked my way up the mountains from tribe to tribe and came out on a black helicopter to Danang. And by the time I got down from the hilltops, what I'd found out was that they'll play for dough but you can't turn the clock back. They were willing to come on our side, but the strategic hamlet thing had left them still asking, "Are you really with us?" I remember sitting around one fire and here's the shaman teaching the history of the tribe so the children can memorize it, with all the begats and the begats and the begats. And what he was teaching was how the deceitful Americans had lied to them. We had made a big mistake. We spoke with forked fucking tongue, and they knew it. And if you look back at what happened to many of these bases, the hill people fought, but only up to a point, and then they bailed out. This is what I reported—that they're not gonna die for us because they believe we sold them out.

———————————•———————————

COL. JONATHAN WAGHELSTEIN *spent two tours in Vietnam, first with the Special Forces and later with a U.S. Army line regiment. In the early eighties, he was sent to El Salvador to manage the retraining of the army to cope with Communist insurgents. He is now Commander of the 7th Special Forces Group at Ft. Bragg, North Carolina.*

I never was satisfied that the necessity for reform was ever really taken seriously by the Saigon government. I worked with the Montagnards my first tour, so we were kind of isolated and did not have a lot of the problems that were facing other parts of the country. I found there were some advantages, in that things the government could do, even on a very low scale, really had an impact. We had a Vietnamese counterpart officer who was much in tune with the Montagnards' aspirations and as a result we had a really good working relationship with the tribes, and never had any real problems with local VC.

My mission was to train civilian indigenous defense groups, the

CIDG [pronounced "sidge"], which are the Montagnards. We worked the border trying to cut the flow of supplies and troops into the South, and were fairly successful, at least during my tour. As long as it was at a fairly low level, we could deal with it, but then when the NVA regulars started pouring in it became more than we could handle. And then, of course, the Marines later went up to take over the camp at Khe Sanh.

Having been a student of the French experience, I remember the line from Bernard Fall in his book, *Street Without Joy*, something to the effect that "I hope that somewhere in that Valhalla where warriors gather we'll reserve a small place under our canopy of tall trees for the sacrificed tribesmen and their comrades of their French Composite Commando troops." The French pledged their honor to the Montagnards and even after Geneva, many Frenchmen refused to pull out, refused to abandon these people. And I had this terrible feeling that the Montagnards were going to come up on the short end of the stick again and as it turned out I was right.

The Vietnamese, when they finally took over, one of the first targets was to get rid of the "savages," as they called them. So the purging and destruction of the Montagnard tribes was high on their priority list. There is no love lost between the lowland Vietnamese, either North or South, and the Montagnard tribes. To me, that was one of the tragedies. A lot of them were driven out or collectivized. The political baggage the Communists brought with them just added to the problem. So, those little people got the shaft again.

BRUCE PALMER

Why did you oppose the Army's secret operations in Vietnam?
The CIA started it, as I recall, and then the decision was made to turn it over to the Army Special Forces. In the beginning the idea was to develop a counterguerrilla force not only to get intelligence but to be able to disrupt enemy attacks. The Special Forces took it over before any Army ground troops as such got in there. They were coming in from the First Special Forces Group on Okinawa, and taking repeated six month tours. Some of them had six or seven tours from Okinawa.

Whether it was CIA or the Special Forces I'm not sure, but someone started the concept of building bases, clearing out fields of fire and wiring them in [surrounding them with barbed wire]. And remember these people had their families out there. It was something else, God. This was the unreal thing. Mostly they looked like an old fort up on top of a hill. Cleared off all the vegetation, they'd dug in gun emplacements and had little connected trench systems, and the families lived right on the position. In behind the perimeter would be the huts, and it was weird. There was nothing secret about it. Everybody for miles around got to know where they were and who they were—the precise coordinates. And it was static. You set up the base, now you had to defend the darn thing.

They were widely scattered and they weren't mutually supporting at all. They were just little islands and they soaked up a lot of resources because you had not only U.S. Special Forces, but Vietnamese Special Forces. These were generally elite people, so the camps wasted good men in exposed positions. We also were spending a lot of money and effort to build these darn things and maintain them. They all wanted a C-130-capable airstrip, which took more resources and manpower. And when you visited one you came back wondering what in the hell are we doing this for? It seemed to me they were constantly getting into trouble and we'd often have to declare a Tac-E, a Tactical Emergency, and bring in other forces or air power to bail them out. We had some overrun, as you recall. I don't fault our men and the people. God, they were brave and they fought well, but to what purpose? It was never clear to me.

We were supposed to get the benefit of whatever they learned, but I just couldn't see anything productive. The main mission was reconnaissance, trying to get some intelligence. But many times it was reported to me, and as far as I could find out it was true, that because of the constraints, the average CIDG crowd would go out a few clicks from camp, sit down, spend some time and then come back and make a report. Some of them were Montagnard tribesmen, but most of the CIDGs were Chinese Nung mercenaries. I don't know the origin of the Nungs, but I wouldn't be surprised if some of them were recruited from the Kuomintang.* They weren't patrolling in any depth, because they were scared to death of the Vietcong or NVA. So they weren't accomplishing much and yet they were a very attractive target for the enemy.

I guess you could argue that they were like an outpost line and they gave you some warning, but I don't think they did. They were too remote from where the U.S. and ARVN Forces were garrisoned, or even their own fire support bases. From where I was, in III Corps, I couldn't see that they were much good even as advance warning. They either were just like magnets that attracted the Viet Cong as something to attack, or the Communists would just go on by them.

---

*The Nationalist Chinese armies referred to in a previous footnote.

Time and again people would come down through War Zone C or the corridor of the Saigon River and hit you unexpectedly. You never got any warning from the CIDG camps that I can recall. I could not see any useful purpose. I wasn't quite that blunt in my book.

Weren't some of those camps being run out of SOG* and tapped for cross-border missions into Laos and Cambodia?

They were, but again it was just telegraphing the punch—giving away all secrecy. The enemy knew exactly where they were. SOG did the unconventional stuff against North Vietnam. This is partly what got us into trouble on the Gulf of Tonkin thing in August of '64 when they had these DeSoto patrols as they called them, where we were putting people ashore by boat or infiltrating by parachute. As I recall, all those things failed without exception. They either starved to death or were immediately identified and picked up and executed. Later SOG also ran the cross-border operations into Laos and Cambodia, but that was not done with the CIDGs. For that SOG had what they called the Delta Force. And those were Special Forces tailored for cross-border operations. I was sort of unhappy about some of those too, because again they used up very scarce resources and often had a lot of people shot and lost some valuable helicopters without much to show for it.

The purpose of it as far as I could see was purely harassment, and it wasn't enough to hurt them much. Again, I wondered whether the cost was worth the benefit. It was MACV, in frustration because they couldn't go in force across the border, that set this up. It was a case of doing the best they could and saying "Well, half a loaf is better than none. We'll go in and try to disrupt them."

I didn't much like the secret bombing of Cambodia, either. If you're going to bomb, I don't think a military man should be put in that position of having to lie about a perfectly legitimate operation, which the enemy knew all about. The whole world knew. After I retired, I worked at the CIA for about six years and one of the really funny stories is that these analysts right after the bombing began would keep coming into their bosses and saying "Hey, boss. This is on the other side of the border. Here are these enormous bomb craters. What the hell's going on?" Obviously, they were not just bomb craters, they were B-52 craters, because the B-52's made this nice long target box. And their boss would say "Go away! What bomb craters are you talking about?" Well, it leaked fairly quickly and it had to leak.

---

*The "Studies and Observations Group," headquartered in Nha Trang.

JEFF STEIN *enlisted in the Army in 1967 to get an assignment to intelligence school. Though he came from a conservative New England background, Vietnam helped to radicalize him. As a civilian, he has specialized in uncovering intelligence coverups. He is now in the process of starting a new magazine,* Fathers, *in Washington.*

The brother of a friend of mine was in the New York field office of Army counterintelligence. He hadn't worn a uniform since he was in basic training. He lived in an apartment and did mostly background checks. It sounded like my kind of Army. But he says "No, no, no. Don't do that. There's a much more interesting program called area studies. They send you to language school and you get to be a political officer in an Embassy and stuff like that." I said "That sounds terrific."

So I went to see the recruiter and pushed the buttons. Right after basic training I went to the military intelligence school at Fort Holabird in Baltimore. We learned traditional case officer techniques and it was great fun, although it was done in a Three Stooges kind of way. We raced around the parks and the department stores, learning how to plant little microfilm boxes and retrieve them. One time they sent us down to Dundalk, which is an industrial suburb, in the middle of the day when everyone is at work. Imagine thirty guys with short haircuts in drip-dry, tan Dacron suits and Army shoes on deserted street corners in Dundalk, passing envelopes to each other "secretly." And the first thing everyone thought of as soon as they finished was "Where's the nearest bar?" Of course we had been given strict instructions not to even let on that we know each other. So I found a bar and I walk in, and there are twenty-eight guys standing there in tan suits and army shoes, drinking beer and not talking to each other. And then you learned lock-picking and all the traditional, unchanging tradecraft of the profession—invisible writing and so on. All this stuff was fascinating.

At the end we got to fill out dream sheets which said where you wanted to be assigned, and one of my choices was Vietnam because I knew I was going to go there anyway, and I knew also this was the major event of my generation and I wanted to participate in it. So I spent a year studying Vietnamese six hours a day. I was still in language school during the Tet offensive, and the fellow that had sat next to me in intelligence school, who was by then operating under Army cover as an infantry lieutenant but was actually running agents, was found out and brutally murdered, tortured. It really ly shook us up because we considered ourselves sort of above the war. We were case officers. We weren't going into combat. When that happened we said "Shit, this is serious."

I went over in October of '68, and in December I went up to Danang and took over an existing net of agents. One of the agents had just recruited a turnaround North Vietnamese captain who headed a rocket squad, so he had been getting really timely intelligence on rocket attacks. This stuff went through all these secure dead drops and eventually got couriered to me. I would meet my courier when I'd see a load sign on a wall. There were five locations, walls and lampposts, that I would check every day. And essentially my agent would go take a piss and make a chalk mark while he was doing it and that would tell me that he had reports. I would go meet the courier, who was his son. The son sold ice cream on the beach, and he would hand me a cone and the reports would be wrapped around it. I'd translate them and get them out to the combat units and you could see the whole city going on alert.

But it's part of the story that my predecessor had set up the net without much checking about who these people really were. He had recruited this agent out of the American construction company RMK-BRJ.* This guy was a middle-class Vietnamese and he had previous intelligence experience with the French. He spoke French, Chinese, and a little English, and nobody had ever really thought a lot about why he spoke Chinese.

So part of my job was not only to run the net but to find out who the hell these guys were. And one thing we did was to polygraph people. This guy was regularly polygraphed and he always bounced on one question. They'd ask "Are you loyal to the government of Nguyen Van Thieu," and the ink would go all over the paper. But they'd say "Are you a Communist" and nothing would happen. And no one could figure this out. Now a case officer is trained that when you are suspicious about someone you really start digging because you don't want a penetration on your hands. It happened that one other thing I did was to read the Vietnamese newspapers, and one day I ferreted out that this guy was a member of a nationalist political party, the VNQDD [Viet Nam Quoc Dan Dang]. I did some research on it, and found out it was an ultrarightist offshoot of Chiang Kai-shek's Kuomintang. In fact Kuomintang and Quoc Dan Dang were the same in Chinese characters.

And meantime this guy had begun to bring in a lot of political intelligence, which was going to the Operation Phoenix people, and all the people he named were An Quang Buddhists. And I remember reading back through his reports, sifting through a lot of CIA reports, Air Force reports, the Vietnamese newspapers, and going back over my interviews with my predecessor. And all of a sudden the proverbial light bulb came on. Holy Shit. This guy is using us to wipe out his enemies on the left.

I could not say for certain they were being murdered, but you did not give names to Phoenix to invite them to a party. Phoenix was a combined military-CIA program whose operational units were often run by a Special Forces type with a Vietnamese counterpart. They were called "PRUs"—Provincial Reconnaissance Units, and their job was to eliminate the Viet Cong infrastructure, which basically meant wiping them out.

Anyway, my very strong suspicion was that this guy was using us to get rid of his political opponents. So I went to my superiors and told them and made a pretty good case. What I wanted to do was break up the net, phase out this agent, recruit another guy, and split away that part of the net with the North Vietnamese rocket officer.

And you know what? They wouldn't give me permission to do any of this, and one of the reasons was that my commanding officer was manipulating the assessment of the agent's reports to make them look better than they really were. My commander, who was a former West Point Russian-language instructor, had never worked as an intelligence officer. Intelligence work, at least when I was in the Army, was not a fast track to advancement. You got ahead by being out in the field leading troops in battle and killing Commies. So what you had in intelligence was a procession of time-serving amateurs who were just rotating through and had not the slightest idea of your problems and needs.

So not only could I not fire this VNQDD man, but my commanding officer was making him look better on paper than he really was, and not even saying anything about my suspicions. Why? Because to make my agent look better made my commanding officer look better. And at that point I realized that the whole intelligence-reporting system was rotten.

Of course this was not the only problem we had. My cover in Danang was that I was a civilian working on refugee resettlement. So I go to this party at the consulate and I'm talking to this American, and he said "What do you do?" I said "Well I'm an Army civilian and I work on the 108th Refugee Relief Team," and he said "Oh, you're a spook." I almost had a heart attack. I'm taking this all very seriously, right?

The team lived in a three- or four-bedroom villa with a wall around it in a side street of Danang. So I come home and I say "Geez, this is terrible. This has gotta change." And they said "Oh, don't worry. Special Forces captured a map six months ago with an X on our house, and it said *dak viet*—special intelligence house." I said Holy shit. I was really freaked.

So it was agreed with my team chief that since they were all going to be leaving anyway, I should get a more insulated working cover. There was an office in Danang hiring Vietnamese for the Navy and the Marines, everything from cooks and bottle washers to Kit Carson scouts. In intelligence the most successful cover is when you recruit somebody and they never know quite who you work for but they agree to it anyway. So we told the head of this office my job was being eliminated but I wanted to stay in Vietnam because I was having marital problems and needed the money. Since I was Vietnamese-speaking I could be of help to them, and the Army would take care of the paperwork. So the guy, with a raised eyebrow, says "Sure, I'm a patriotic American." I guess he assumed we were CIA. So I began to work as a civilian personnel officer with no salary and no backup in their files, no paper trail on me at all.

Even then I had problems with cover. One guy used to come up to me at the Navy Officers' Club and talk to me. This guy is in uniform and he's known as an intelligence type and he's not even supposed to *know* me. He used to violate cover all the time. One time he even brought a South Vietnamese intelligence colonel to our house for dinner. We were ready to jump out the back windows. We were unilateral—not only didn't we work with the Vietnamese, the government was one of our targets. That happens everyplace—on the theory that a government may turn hostile, we want to have our own sources in their security service.

One of the other things I found out was that our agent nets didn't work the way they were supposed to, either. Theoretically the cell leaders were in the district capitals and their subagents were woodcutters and farmers—people who could spot Communist movements. Well in fact all these cell leaders lived right in Danang, and what we had was a paper army of agents. And actually some of them worked for several agencies and were cycling stuff back and forth. You get a great confirmation rate when you do that. You would be able to say "Well my guys say that too." Well, this was an Army operation—military music.

When you left, how did you turn your operation over to the next guy?

With best wishes. My replacement was a captain who had had not much intelligence experience. So I told him what the situation was. I got a letter from him about six months later and he recounted how Dinky—we called our agent Dinky; his last name was Dau, so we called him Dinky Dau, which you may remember in Vietnamese means crazy. It's really *dien cai dau*, which means "electricity in the head," but Americans pronounced it Dinky Dau. So he wrote me that Dinky was still throwing darts at the An Quang Buddhists, and how he had fought the good fight to get rid of this guy and it was a fucked up situation, and he was just counting the days to get home.

All kidding aside, I tried hard to be conscientious, do my job and save American lives. On one level it's comic. I guess what makes good comedy is tragedy. I guess the way we rationalized being part of the war machine was to say somehow we were saving American lives by providing timely intelligence. But the whole thing was falling apart by the time I left.

———◆———

BARRY ZORTHIAN

Did you make a deliberate effort to open up the CIA to the press corps while you were there?
The Agency in Vietnam was much more operational than it probably should be and certainly than it had been earlier. My earlier experience with the Agency had been sort of casual and almost distant. You knew they were there and occasionally brushed against the station chief but you didn't do a hell of lot with the individuals. In Vietnam they were very much in the mix of things. They were operational in some of the fields I was involved in, like psychological operations. They were dealing with the USIA staff in areas like those black pajama troops, and eventually they got into the Phoenix thing, the assassination program that Colby ran.

Early in the game I had somewhat of a down trip with them. One of my people brought me one day a document from the captured materials showing that the VC were facing corruption in their ranks. I got that and I was frankly trying to establish myself with Malcolm Browne who was still then AP there and had been a real critic of the war. I wanted to show Malcolm that my intentions were good and forthright and I fed him this thing, and he recognized it for what it was, which I had not. The sons of bitches had planted it and were kidding me. Malcolm worked me over on that thing and told, in print, how I tried to plant a story with him. And I blasted him publicly for that and then discovered I was very much wrong and promised myself I'd never get burned like that again.

In any event we did work together. They were one of the elements in JUSPAO [the Joint U.S. Public Affairs Office]. They assigned officers to us like AID and the military and State. In fact, Doug Ramsey, who was captured, was an Agency guy filling a JUSPAO role. I would go through their interrogation reports and find items I wanted and ask to use them on a background basis. Secondly, they were ready to respond to briefings and they had a credibility no one else had. They were having their own battles with the military and they had a different viewpoint, and there were correspondents who liked that. And I must say the Agency was more right than wrong in measuring the capabilities and the lasting power of the North Vietnamese.

They also, incidentally, provided for JUSPAO a very major asset, which was a black bag of money so that our province reps had unaccountable piaster currency that they could use here and there to get things done. If you'd had to go through the normal bureaucracy of getting it out of Uncle Sam it would have been impossible. They supported the Vung Tau black pajama teams, for example. The concept was to meet the VC on their own terms—to put friendlies in black pajamas out at the village level, providing military support and assistance to hamlets, and civic action as well. The concept was good but it got caught between the ARVN and our own overwhelming presence.

In the sense that the word "secret" was one of the triggers that set us off, were the black operations worth the price?

Which black operations? There were so many of them, starting with Marops on the water to the cross-boarder LRRP teams to the CIDG business and the Laos business and the Phoenix and so on. But most of the press respected and maintained that secrecy. Any knowledgeable correspondent in Vietnam in '64–'65 knew about black operations. They knew at least the broad outlines of Marops [operations by sea against North Vietnam], they knew things like the incipient Phoenix. And they didn't write about it. They knew about SOG but they didn't write very much about cross-border operations. They didn't write about LRRP teams. We talked about it and they wouldn't write. It was part of, to quote Dean Rusk, their being on the team. Now, eventually visitors broke that story. I remember Dick Dudman came out and wrote a story about those cross border teams, and Dick happened to be a pretty good friend and I said to Dick one day, "For Christ's sake, Dick, those are classified operations. Why are you writing about it?" He said, "Listen, my newspaper thinks that this is a wrong war and this thing is pretty widely known and there's no reason we shouldn't write about it and I damn well am going to write about it."

But there's no doubt in broader terms that the media was going through a transitional period between being part of the establishment and gradually getting into a stage of saying "The hell with it. If we see it, we're going to print it, regardless of what classification." And a lot of the difficulties came out of that change as well as the change of Uncle Sam and how it approached its own citizens.

———————◆———————

WILLIAM COLBY

There wasn't much secret war about Vietnam. People talk about the Phoenix program. We deliberately made Phoenix an open program—started it with a parade with the Prime Minister and put up posters about it saying "These guys are wanted; this guy is the one who blew up the bus on the road, if you find him tell us. And Mr. Jones, if you see this and you turn yourself in, you will be given full amnesty." These were public programs. The other side was not just shadowy Communist units out there, but individuals who were the proselytizer, the tax collector, the logistics guy for the district or the province. That was what Phoenix was really all about. Sure, you had shooting back and forth, but the real concept was to understand the nature of the Communist structure. Then you can do something about it. Laos was secret, but that was a diplomatic action because Kennedy and Khrushchev had agreed that Laos was no place for us to have a faceoff. So the Soviets stopped flying their airlift and we stopped ours and took out all our Special Forces teams in '62. Only one country of the fifteen that signed the treaty didn't pay any attention to it and that was North Vietnam. And when the Hmong [Meo tribes] began to get kicked around, the question was whether they would get away with it or we would help them out. So Kennedy said "CIA, go ahead and help them out but let's keep the military out so we don't have any issue with the Soviets." Everybody knew the battle was going on, but the Soviets kept their embassy in Vientiane the entire time. And in total contrast to the Bay of Pigs decision, here there was a reason for keeping CIA in the thing. The CIA put about three hundred people into the Lao war. We were prohibited from engaging in combat. We lost about four or five in air crashes and things but the enemy force was about seven thousand in '62 and it grew to about seventy thousand by '73, and the battle lines were about where they were when it started. I think that's a hell of a record. It was done without talk.

———————◆———————

WILLIAM SULLIVAN

When I got to Laos in late '64 we had had some photographic missions over the Plain des Jarres, a couple of which had gotten nicked;

the first plane was shot down shortly after I got there. We had complied with the Geneva Accords in '62, and pulled everyone out. But we had started to put a few things back in, mostly communication teams which were American-trained but not Americans and operated out of Udorn [Thailand]. We wanted a network among the Meo to keep tab on what the Vietnamese were doing. They *didn't* pull out and they kept forcing.

We didn't have any U.S. encadrement [of the secret army]. We had a little Thai encadrement but our operations were definitely noncombat. We were doing communications, logistics, and—except for some air support—our people did not get into combat situations. And the air operations were against the 316th North Vietnamese Division which kept coming back and forth depending on the rainy season. Of course, there were other operations in the Ho Chi Minh Trail area, which were bombing operations.

The communications cadre were remnants of what had been organized before the '62 accords [to support the White Star teams], and Vang Pao* had an association with them. But actual combat units that depended on U.S. logistics and U.S. pay and so forth started I think in 1965. And through the time I was there, our tactic was never frontal combat. We were strictly engaged in a guerrilla operation. We would use helicopters to infiltrate them, but otherwise the standard tactic was to cede ground in the dry season, and to get behind the Vietnamese as they started their regular rainy season pullout, catch 'em in a narrow place, and beat the hell out of them.

We didn't go beyond that because Kennedy was convinced, and Johnson after him, that we could somehow reach an accommodation in Vietnam. They thought, shades of Nicaragua, that Vietnam was a place where we could bring to bear military pressure that would force these people to negotiate. Laos was different. Laos was up in the middle of a jungle. The LOC [line of communications] ran all the way from Bangkok on a flimsy road and rail structure. You were very close to the Chinese and Vietnamese borders. It was a hell of place to get bogged down in a war. Vietnam, on the other hand, had a great, long coastline. We could come in there with ships and planes. We could do all the things we were best disposed to do except, of course, in the final analysis we chose to accept the fight on their terms, in the jungles.

A second consideration was our conclusion that the Geneva Agreements were as good as we were going to get anyway, so let's not disrupt them. Even if the other side is violating them, it's in a way that you can't prove. You couldn't get the goddamned Indians [on

---

*The Meo tribesman general who commanded the CIA's secret army in north-central Laos.

the International Control Commission] to go in and say they saw
Vietnamese because they wouldn't go close enough. And whatever
the Canadians said, they were the third man on this team and nobody
paid any attention to them. So rather than go for a showdown we
decided to do it in a subliminal way: a way that was reversible; a
way that the U.S. military wasn't in there with a whole big packet
of stuff; a way that could be economical and in which our people
did not actually get physically engaged but had people who were
willing to fight.

The Meo were proven fighters; all we had to do was give them logistics and communications and air support and money and a little
tactical guidance. We never had more than about two hundred
paramilitary types, Americans, in country at any one time. It was a
very economical way to fight a holding action. It was to preclude
them from getting out into the area of the Mekong because then not
only would they become a menace to Thailand but they'd also have
another logistics route—Highway Thirteen that went down the
Mekong River south of Savannakhet. That would have added a new
dimension to the Trail.

Anyway, Laos was never intended to be the area that produced the
results. Vietnam was where we were supposed to drive these guys
back into the territory that had been granted them by the 1954
accords. Now, you know the great optimism of our military: They
were going to wrap up Vietnam in eighteen months or less. So Laos
was not ever foreseen to be anything that would last on for ten or
eleven years. And clearly once you got beyond a certain point you
began to get enormous attrition to the poor Meo, with the final result
being that [when] it was all over, there was nothing to stand in the
way of the North Vietnamese taking over Laos lock, stock, and barrel. And I suppose had anyone foreseen that it was going to last ten
years, they wouldn't have done it.

I always used to contend that there was absolutely nothing secret
about Laos. There really wasn't. You could never get an American
official to confirm it, and you guys used to come in and try all different ways from Sunday to get me to say it. You knew that I knew
that you knew what the hell was going on. Had I said it, that would
have changed the political dimension of it. But to say that it was
secret was tautological. It was not secret at all. I would be out there
at an event with the Soviet Ambassador and you could see a KC-135
tanker up there fueling four aircraft and he would say, "Beell what
is that?" And I'd say, "Boris, I don't see a thing. I have the same
problem there that you have in the jungles where you can't see the
Vietnamese." So there was a lot of euphemism and evasion but had

we ever attempted to keep it secret we would have gone out of our heads.

Some people think we paid a hidden price for the war in Laos because the tribes and the Army were hip deep in opium and eventually heroin, which found its way to our troops in Vietnam.

We were aware of all the stories. We could never actually put a finger on General Ouane Rattikoun.* We had narcotics agents in the country, the predecessor of what became the DEA, who were able to spot the places where raw opium was reduced to morphine base on its way to becoming heroin. And we were aware of all those stories of trafficking from the Golden Triangle in Burma through Ban Houei Sai.† We attempted to put pressure on Ouane through showing him photographs and saying we want these things cleaned up, and they would disappear. Of course, they were primitive huts and I guess the stuff inside would probably be moved somewhere else. But the stories of heavy trafficking in Air America planes, we policed against that pretty carefully. I was never able to get a convincing account of any American who was actually involved in that.

Now, Lao involvement, I'm sure, was significant. I don't think Vang Pao was involved. They did have opium up in the hills. They used opium as a medication. The hospital we had up there, when these patients came in who had been using opium all their lives, let them continue using it. But the big traffic as far as I could get reports, was still basically controlled by Chinese with all sorts of connections who primarily had used Corsican pilots and Corsican couriers. The French were aware of it too, but the ability to come to grips with it was pretty minimal unless you put agents on the ground up in the hills. At that stage, we didn't have that sort of mandate. We had agents who would take photographs, but they were not in the business of attempting to intercept caravans and blow things up.

In '65–'66 there was no specific movement of it towards our troops in Vietnam. It was moving out into the international trade by way of Bangkok and a lot of it was going to Amsterdam. We had rumors of the movement toward our troops in Vietnam in '68 or so, but I guess the big movements must have started about '69. Now, how much of that heroin came out of Laos, I don't know. I have always assumed there was a certain amount of North Vietnamese complicity. Much better to get your enemy sodden on heroin than to meet him in battle.

---

*Commander-in-Chief of the Lao Armed Forces.

†A town near the junction of the Thai, Lao, and Burmese borders that became an eastern terminus for the mule caravans operated by former Kuomintang warlords that brought much of the opium harvest out of the Golden Triangle. It was also the site of a substantial CIA base.

CHAPTER NINE

Captives

> Honor is to serve without vanity, and
> unto the last consequence.
> —ARTHUR KOESTLER, Darkness at Noon

AMID the passions and hatreds of war the cry of dishonor becomes a ritual incantation. In most conflicts it is directed at the enemy; in the civil battle that Vietnam became for Americans and Vietnamese alike, it was often turned inward. Those who fought the war became brutes and fiends to those who fought against it. The opponents in turn became cowards and traitors—supporters of an alien and enemy cause. And yet nowhere more than in the tales of those who became captives because of Vietnam is it clear that all fought with honor by the lights that gave them guidance.

We tend to think of the prisoners of Vietnam in a single category—those hundreds of men, mostly pilots but a few plain soldiers, who spent their prime years in the dank cells or barren encampments of Hanoi. But there were many others taken prisoner as well, and of these, too, we have tried to take a sampling: those who live to this day in prisons without bars, not knowing the fates of loved ones still officially "missing in action"; those who, as a matter of principle, went to jail in America rather than serve in a war they detested; and those who fell prey to the gulags of the "new" Vietnam after the shooting had stopped. What is evident in all their stories is that they served without vanity, and unto the last consequence.

———◆———

JAMES STOCKDALE

I was flying flak suppression on a strike against the Thanh Hoa Bridge, and we had to abort because of bad weather and go on to a secondary mission. I was just tooling around with my wingman. I didn't want to waste the bombs, so I wheeled in to drop them on a railroad siding where a bunch of freight trains were parked. I'd been there the day before and there were no appreciable guns around and I whistled in at treetop level to drop 'em with those snake-eye fins that would slow 'em down enough to keep me out of the flying debris. And then believe it or not, I could hear this great big gun hammering away even over the cockpit noise and I looked out to my right and looked right down into four barrels that were just spewing fire. I had nothing but red lights and the plane went out of control and I had to get out of it.

I landed in, of all places, the main street of a village. I'd been in the chute maybe less than a minute, and people were shooting on me during that minute with rifles and stuff. The town big boys gang-tackled me in the street just as I was unbuckling my parachute. And I think I would have expired there under the pummeling, but I heard a police whistle, and that was the arrival of some local constable in a pith helmet. I was sitting in the middle of the street, and they started cutting off my clothes and they said, "Take your boots off." I looked down and oh my God, my leg was bent the wrong way. They had broken it while they were beating me, and I had also done some damage to my shoulder and my back in the ejection because the airplane was going so fast I had been flailing in the air.

Three days later I was in Hoa Lo Prison. It's a nineteenth-century French prison in downtown Hanoi, and it's the headquarters of the prison system for the whole country. That's the Hanoi Hilton. They made an incision in an attempt to get my leg under me, but it still doesn't bend. I lay on a table for several weeks in isolation before I got into a place where other Americans were. Solitary was the typical situation for the first weeks or months after you were captured, but as more prisoners came in they had the problem of space. You hated to see a lot of guys get shot down, but it made your chances of getting a cell-mate greater.

After I could get around, they put me side by side for a while with the other senior officer in the system, and that was [Robinson] Risner from the Air Force. He taught me the tap code and we got a burst of arrangements made. Then we were called in on Christmas Eve, one at a time, to see the man we called The Cat—the commissar of the prison system—and we were each told that we must cooperate with him to stop this war and to use our influence to bring the other prisoners around. Ha ha. So we knew the clock was ticking. We both came to bad ends soon thereafter and were arrested for minor misdemeanors. And that was just a trip-wire system that allowed them to take us into an isolated part of the prison and to torture us.

Risner was some months later isolated. I knew him to be isolated, and so that left me as the senior officer present, and that condition existed throughout all the years that torture was going on—until sometime in 1970.

Being the senior officer cost me, because we had to get a communications system going and to really build a civilization. I mean we didn't go at it that methodically, but that's what happened when we started tapping on these walls. We had our own law, our own traditions, our consensus, and that's what saved us I think. This took place over a period of time. And the highest crime you could commit there was to "incite the other criminals to oppose the camp authority"—that was their word for leadership—and since that was what I did, I spent four years in solitary confinement. There was a big purge in the summer of '67 in the section of Hoa Lo we called Las Vegas, and they found out I was behind the unified resistance.

What was the nature of the resistance?

For example, we would not bow in public. We had to bow the rest of the time. Whenever your door opened you bowed. The man that opened it was usually a boot soldier, a farm kid, an enlisted man of the lowest rank, but you bowed to the waist. If you went out and you were walking across the campus so to speak, every time you saw a Vietnamese you stopped and bowed down ninety degrees.

Stay off the air, that was another one. We would make them torture us before we would ever talk into a tape recorder or a microphone. We would admit no crimes was a third. And we would accept no parole. That came out as "Don't kiss them good-bye." So the acronym for my first set of orders started out B-A-C-K: "Do not Bow in public. Stay off the Air. Admit no Crimes. Do not Kiss them good-bye." And then for a general slogan, I thought our mode of operation should be typified by "Unity over Self." So "BACK-US" was our first slogan in the winter of '66–'67.

They found that out in that purge of '67. A new guy came in, a sweet guy and one of my good friends now, and we didn't know that he hadn't been through the initial torture. I had insisted that whenever my orders were put out my name be given, and they gave him all of it. And the next night he's in the ropes and he's screaming for mercy and they say, "Why won't you do this?" And he said, "My commanding officer forbids it." That got their attention. "Aha! You've got a commanding officer?"

And anything they know you know, they can get with rope torture. It was a very methodical process. There were two guards that we knew as torture guards and in my experience only they administered this. One was a big farm kid, strong as an ox, we called him Big Ugh. And the other was an enigmatic person that we called

Pigeye, for his expressionless eyes, and he was older and he was balding. He was a real hatchet man. He was not the least bit emotionally involved, but he was the best at it.

First of all you are accused of violating the rules, and you're given an opportunity to atone for your crime by performing an act they think is appropriate—like as not to write the Secretary of State and tell him to get out of the war. When you say no, then enters Big Ugh and Pigeye. They will box you around enough to let you see stars. Now this part is not brutal. They don't break your nose. It's just the shock effect to get you down and get the ropes on you.

They bind your arms with manila rope in such a way as to draw your shoulders together, and give them a purchase. I've never seen it from the back, but when they pulled it was irreversible, so that your blood circulation stopped. And about that time, you'd see Pigeyes' automobile-tire shoes* whizzing by out of the corner of your eye as he kicked them off to get up on your back to pull vertically and at the same time push your head down between your legs with his heel.

Now this takes twenty or thirty minutes but you can shut it off any time by yelling "I submit." That means you're willing to make that atonement. So it's not like the movies, where you're brutalized. You can't kill yourself. People say, "I will die before I give up," but you can't get hold of yourself from that position. And when you get up, your hands are useless. We almost had a calibration table—the number of minutes your arms have been robbed of blood supply is proportional to the number of weeks before you can tie the drawstring on your pajamas. A lot of people suffered nerve damage that still persists—numbness in the hands and so forth.

This feeling of helplessness to avoid giving in made you feel guilty until you realized that no man was capable of avoiding it. Even then, a few Americans could not shake off the shame borne of those barracks-wall posters back home which, in total contradiction of the meaning intended by the author of the code of conduct, showed the POW successfully sealing his lips except for name, rank, serial number, and date of birth, no matter what. There are some horror stories. One prisoner who, after talking some, suddenly became obsessed with returning to those "big four" items, invoked the rage of a hot-blooded Cuban interrogator who put him in those ropes, which even good men managed to handle only thirty minutes, and left him there overnight. He was heard to scream until about three A.M. and then fell silent. Next morning, when the Cuban and Vietnamese came, they were stunned. The prisoner looked seventy years old.

---

*Ho Chi Minh sandals—thong shoes cut from used tires.

His hair had turned white overnight. He had snapped his wire and became an insane old man. He no longer talked. He would not eat, and died in prison.

So anyway, they got my name and then a purge started—first of all in torture sessions to get data about my organization, and then they set a trap and got me.

How do you mean, they set a trap?

I should have known better. They put me in a little cell in a place called The Mint, where you could sit on the bunk and touch both walls with your arms outstretched. My old pal Sam Johnson was right next door. I could hear him cough and wheeze and bump his elbow on the wall. But this was right in the northeast corner of Hoa Lo, and up above us was a machine-gun platform with a watch guy who was not normally concerned with prisoner discipline. He was a green-tab guard, like a Marine sentry. One morning Sam did what he did every morning—he tapped on the wall "shave and a haircut," which we used for the call-up. And so we could tap quietly, we listened through our drinking cups, big porcelain mugs, to focus the sound. It's just dawn breaking and I put it up and started to tap on the wall, and "Yeeow!" I heard this guy up on the wall and of course that was the trap. I mean he was up there prepared to see me answer the good morning call. He could look down into my cell, and I never thought of that. I couldn't even turn around in the leg irons and look up there. And they needed that because even though they had obtained confessions of my rules from other prisoners, it was unethical for them to close in until they found me in an overt violation—caught me "red-handed."

It was the imposition of guilt. Fear and guilt are the driving forces. I've talked about torture, I've talked about solitary, but when you really want a person to let go of the past and start going for the present and to spew out anything-to-get-home type information you've got to have him in a depressed state. And you find out after a while that the real pincers that break people's hearts and wills are fear and guilt. From the moment you enter a political prison, you are told and forced to act as though you are subhuman—a dreg of society. And there's every effort made—they're not smooth psychologists—to remind you daily that they're looking at you: You're not to look at the sky. That's enough to give you a left hook to the jaw. You're to bow down. You have no rights. You have no name. You have no nationality. You are a criminal. You are a worm. There's nothing you can do to atone for yourself except to try.

I've read a lot of books about political prisons since I returned. They are one institution where they have had a string of very good, literate inmates. Political prisons date back to antiquity. Cervantes, the

Spanish writer, was a political prisoner in Algiers, and Dostoevsky and Solzhenitsyn and Koestler all tried to break down the essence of the particular predicament. A political prison is a place where you have commissars with deadlines to meet and their inmates are not there to be safeguarded or kept off the street or punished. They're there to be used and they have to have public confessions of guilt because they have to discredit the inmates' causes.

Now you can make people do things by torture and you can make them do things by isolation, but if you want real, authentic, heartfelt confessions, you have to have something a little bit more. You have to somehow penetrate their inner conscience. And the mechanism is fear and guilt. You have to impose the feeling of guilt on them if you want to start getting them out of the shell and start pouring out their guts with material that's favorable to you.

And you soon realize that you are pounced upon in a political prison after something has happened that might give them the moral advantage—like violating a rule. They may find out from third parties, as they did in my case, that I am running an underground organization that is devastating their program because I have unified resistance on certain hold points where we all take torture. But they would never come to me on that kind of evidence. They would only come when I had experienced the agony of realizing that I had transgressed some particular rule and they caught me in the act.

There's something psychological about it. They're not deep thinkers, but they know that if they can possibly manage to find you in a compromising position, "Hah! I've got you." It makes you feel guilty and you're tempted to do anything to prevent them from telling anybody else. When you live in such a situation where you're constantly being baited and tempted to do something that will allow them to pounce on you with this moral advantage, you realize the power that gives them. As I sat in my cell and I waited to go to interrogation, I didn't build up my physical strength or grit my teeth or flex my muscles. I had to think about the way my eyes would focus on the interrogator. How I would show no fear. How I would evidence no guilt. How he could ask me questions about things that he could logically have found out about, like tapping to this person or leaving that note, and I had to figure out a way to project myself in a way that would defuse his attack on my inner self via the route of guilt. And of course the big whammy I had to be ready for was his closing in on the Tonkin Gulf.

That's a long-winded way of saying that in this bath of extortion you come to the conclusion that the only way to get yourself out of there with any self-respect is to live an absolutely pure life. You know when you transgress what you're giving away. You're giving away the look in your eyes. You're giving away your conviction. If I knew that we had done something of which we ought to be ashamed, that was exactly what they wanted.

And I would have known [after] I was in prison never to do anything like what the government had me do before I got there. I would have realized that we were committing the very sort of act that would give them all of this emotional self-righteous energy.

So when they dragged me out and took me into the interrogation room, I *wanted* to tell my story. I said, "Okay, enough of this crap. BACK-US, I know that you know it." I knew they had interrogated and tortured a lot of guys and they had even made some of them make movies about my organization. So I said to this young interrogator, "Don't bother me about tapping on that goddamn wall. Let's get onto this thing. I want to get into this. I'm ready to take it. You give me the worst you can hand out, 'cause I've done this." Finally they had a trial, with guards with bayonets fixed behind me. I was brought before this officer I'd never seen before. And he said, "I've never been here before but I've heard a lot about you and it's all bad." He spoke English.

To make a long story short, I wouldn't answer some questions so here came Pigeye and Big Ugh and they knocked me down and got me in the ropes. And Pigeye knew I had a broken left knee and he decided to bend that instead of the other one and he broke the damn thing again right there in front of all these people. And the meeting sort of disintegrated after that, and I couldn't get up off the floor for a month. This was October of 1967, and outside my room they had loudspeakers that were booming all the time. Well, they were warming up for the fiftieth anniversary of the October revolution, and they were playing Russian music. And I remember thinking what a time to be lying there, trying to get myself together again while they celebrated the Russian Revolution.

Later I was in a little place attached to their Ministry of Defense, which we called Alcatraz, where they took the leaders of my organization. There were eleven of us and we were in leg irons for nearly two years. We had another riot there, and I was even expelled from Alcatraz as the ringleader, to a place where they thought I could never communicate from, because it was outside the wall. But a good cooperative friend and I devised a way to work over that wall at certain times of the day, and I got back into the command business.

Then they caught me with a note and I figured that was about it, because the '67 purge had resulted in the deaths of one or maybe two of my friends, and I was running out of gas. It seemed like the earth always caved in on us after a few months. That was really a way of life, to build and be torn down and build and be torn down, but I didn't realize it at the time. So I was taken in for torture again, and I decided to pull out all the stops. In the middle of the night I went to the window—the only window in Hanoi that was accessible to a prisoner happened to be in this torture room—and I broke it and took the shards and tried to kill myself. But they revived me—and then they called off the dogs.

By this time it's late '69, and the thing started to change. It's hard to determine what caused it. Ho Chi Minh had died the week before. My wife, at the very time I was cutting myself to shreds, was having a standoff with the North Vietnamese in Paris, and she was the leader of the families in the League.* They suddenly decided they couldn't afford to have me killed, and things got better.

What did you use for a tap code?

It was the quadratic alphabet. You throw out the letter K and use C instead, and you have a five-by-five matrix with ABCDE across the top. So A is one-one, B is one-two, F is two-one and so forth. And this is an interesting story because some of those who went home early knew the tap code and told the government to please tell all the pilots to learn this because it was useful, and it would save a lot of blood, sweat, and tears trying to pass it to new shoot-downs. And when we finally came back, we wanted to know why in the hell these new guys never had it. Well it turned out that the government had put a top-secret classification on it [*laughs uproariously*].

You're kidding. It's in Darkness at Noon.

Not only there. I ran it back to a Greek historian of the second century BC by the name of Polybius. He was a cryptographic fan, and he had it, only instead of dropping out K he dropped out J and let L be the same letter. That's the only way it's changed in twenty-two hundred years, but it was top-secret to the government bureaucracy.

Why didn't people use Morse?

It is an order of magnitude more difficult to use two different sounds, and this thing had so much flexibility. That is to say, a tap like I'm tapping on the phone [taps] could be a unit, but it could also be a big toe under a door pulsating in rhythm. In fact we had many variations of it. We even had a vocal tap code with coughs where you could get a few letters out. But we figured that even the dumbest guards would understand that, so although one was one cough and two was two coughs, three was a throat clear (hmmh-mmh), four was a hawk (chuui), and five was a spit (ptui). So anyway it had a lot of flexibility. And you had to be able to tap in the most minutely quiet way because to be caught was a trip-wire. And it sounds silly but for being caught tapping on the wall you could be tied up and

---

*The National League of Families of Prisoners of War and Missing in Action.

brutalized and put on public display. You see it gave them license, the guilt, and it gave them moral justification not because you had violated the little dinky rule so much as because you had demonstrated ingratitude for their "humane and lenient treatment."

They really had a big emotional content in everything. I thought at first it was cynical, but it wasn't. And it ties in too to that idea of what happened in the Tonkin Gulf—the belief in moral leverage. You see they *knew* in '67 that I had an elaborate set of instructions out there that had infiltrated the whole system. They once told me that "You have set our camp back two years!" But they would not move in to the pinch until they had found me actually tapping. They had set a trap and they had to catch me in the act. Somehow this all had to do with moral leverage and it had to do with showing to the guards that the country operated on an ethical basis.

When I was at Las Vegas we had good peepholes but we couldn't ever acknowledge seeing anything because they'd come and find our hole and plug it up. We were all in leg-irons but they still had a man patrolling out front, and I could roll off my bunk and get down there under the door and see him. There wasn't much else to do. And the guards one season were all scribbling on little pads of paper. They would stop and get out this paper and pencil and write. And I was going into interrogation and the officer who was there to quiz me saw me see a man fooling with this paper. So when I got in I said, "Listen, I'd like to ask you, I see all your soldiers seem to be involved in some kind of writing exercise."

"Oh," he said. "I'm glad you asked. That is part of my winter enlisted man's training program. I have asked each guard to write an essay describing how their duties bolster the national war effort and how they fit into the overall national scheme of things." I mean he wanted the guy to sit down and describe how standing his watch was for the benefit of Ho Chi Minh. Now that sounds silly and yet it's the epitome of leadership. If you can get every soldier to think that he is a part of the national purpose why then you've got it knocked. So that was kind of an eye-opener.

Well it was not all bad, I mean it was bad but it was kind of a high caliber of life. The years with my gang in Alcatraz were the happiest. People were considerate and the friendship, the comradeship, seeped through the walls in ways that are hard to describe. The eleven of us got up to dump our buckets in the morning, and you got an old stiff broom to wash it out. And you had an open water vessel that you dipped out of, and everybody'd scrape out a few letters with his broom as he did it. One day they tapped to me on the wall and said "Today, stand by for a chain message." It happened to be the third anniversary of my shoot-down, and I listened with intense raptness as the brooms tapped out "Here's to CAG for three great years. We love you. We're with you to the end." And that was a funny thing for a bunch of forty-year-old pilots to tap about. You see I was the carrier air group commander, and it was abbreviated to CAG. I still hold that. Most guys they see me now, sixty-two years old, soon to be sixty-three, they say "Hello CAG." Well CAG is usually a virile forty-year old aviator, but I'm still CAG.

Did the North Vietnamese try to give you political indoctrination?

Not much. One time they asked me to describe the American public's attitude toward war, so I talked about the Korean War and I said the American public was disaffected by the Korean War until the word got back that American prisoners were being brainwashed. And this struck anger into American hearts, and mobilized the nation. I don't think that alone did it, but brainwashing was something that worried them. They thought that was a stigma, and so some of the few compliant prisoners were overheard to be warned not to make it so bad, because "People will think you've been brainwashed."

They weren't trying to make Communists out of us. They were trying to put us into the category of the radical antiwar element. But the best they could do was to have a small colony at an outlying camp that was civil enough to listen to Ramsey Clark and Jane Fonda without being belligerent. The camp was set up late in the game, when they had learned more about the American psyche. They had a couple of real dropouts, a Marine lieutenant colonel named Edison Miller, and a Navy commander, Eugene Wilbur, and they built this whole thing around them.

Miller, so the story goes, came into camp as a strident opportunist. He's a handsome dude. I never talked to him but I saw him over a fence. He looked like Cary Grant. He had a great career going in the Marine Corps, but those that were the first to see him in Hanoi [said] he walked into the room and he told those young officers "Don't look to me. I don't want to hear any talk about codes of conduct. That's not worth the paper it's written on." [He said he knew] from Korean War stories that none of these so-called punitive articles have any teeth at all. "So forget that and forget me, and if I want to go talk to the Communists that's my business." And that was the way he talked. I think he wanted to go home early. They had what we called "the fink release program," this amnesty program, but some of my friends say that by the time his turn came he had had such violent anti-American propaganda on the radio they were afraid to let him out for fear of this brainwashing charge.

Even after the torture stopped, they'd keep new shoot-downs in solitary for a month and scare the hell out of them. Then they took half of them and put them out with Miller and Wilbur, and the other half in the regular cell blocks. What Miller and Wilbur did that irks me doesn't so much have to do with their broadcasts to troops in the South, which were discreditable, but that they would get these fuzzy-cheeked ensigns and JGs* and advise them to make anti-government tapes. And some made them. Their resistance was down. And the tapes were broadcast through the cellblocks downtown, and the rest of the prisoners came to hate the names that were associated with these voices. And in a sense Wilbur and Miller destroyed the reputations of a lot of fine young men. It's indelible. That's what I really hold against them.

———————◆———————

Though his hair is white and thin, SEN. JOHN MCCAIN, *an Arizona Republican, comes across as a young man in his prime. A former Navy pilot, shot down over North Vietnam and held as a POW for five and a half years, he was a prize captive for the North Vietnamese. His father was Adm. John McCain, who commanded the U.S. Seventh Fleet and later became the Commander in Chief, Pacific (CINCPAC). McCain ran for the Senate seat vacated by Barry Goldwater, and won the election in November of 1986.*

There are two things I remember. One is the years of solitary confinement and loneliness, and the other is the last period, when we were still in prison, of camaraderie when I was moved into a cell with forty-five or fifty others for the first time—a camaraderie that had been established over the years when we were all just tapping out messages to each other. Brotherly love is the only way you can describe it.

Probably the single incident I remember more than anything else was Christmas of 1971. A group of us had wanted to hold church services and the Vietnamese had refused, and we had had a demonstration. The Vietnamese took about thirty-five or forty of us away to a punishment camp. The food was terrible and all my guys got sick—dysentery, hepatitis, and that kind of thing. Anyway, they brought us back into Hanoi in time for Christmas. I was the room chaplain, and two days before the holiday the Vietnamese allowed us a copy of the Bible. So I read the Christmas story in segments from four books of the New Testament, and we accompanied it with carols. And when we got to the birth of Christ, we sang "Silent Night," and the faces of those guys, almost without exception, were

---

*Lieutenants Junior Grade—the Navy equivalent of an Army first lieutenant

in tears. But they weren't tears of homesickness, they were of pleasure that we had been allowed to celebrate together.

The other Christmas I remember with vivid clarity was 1969. At that time I had lived alone for a very long time. I'd been shot down in October of 1967, so it was almost two and a half years. It was in the Hanoi Hilton, which was the old French prison in Hanoi, a real prison with stone walls and cells and bars. It was cold in Hanoi that winter. You know most people think of Vietnam being in the tropics, but in Hanoi it can really get cold, especially in a building like that. After the bombing stopped in November of 1968, we had all thought we'd be out in a matter of months. There was a loudspeaker in every room, and that Christmas Day they played a lot of songs. But one of them was a record of Dinah Shore singing "I'll Be Home For Christmas." And at that instant I knew, and I later found out everybody else knew, it would be a long time before we went home. You see the last line of the song says, "I'll be home for Christmas—but only in my dreams."

———◆———

COL. GEORGE SHINE *(USAF, ret.) and his wife, Helen, are captives in a very special sense of the word. They sacrificed for Vietnam as much as any American family. All three of their sons fought, and only one returned alive. The youngest, Jonathan, a West Point first lieutenant, was killed in combat in October 1970, a month after he arrived in Vietnam. He was twenty-three. The oldest, Anthony, a pilot, served two tours in Indochina and disappeared with his plane on the second—officially listed as Missing In Action. The middle son, Alexander (Sandy), also went to Vietnam twice, in 1967–68, and in 1970–71. He was badly wounded and offered a medical discharge, but chose to stay in the Army. By 1985 he had reached the rank of colonel. The Shines' daughter, Sally, also served in Vietnam, with the Red Cross. She later became an Army nurse. Col. George Shine traveled to Vietnam in 1973 and 1974 to plead for action on MIAs and POWs. He serves on the board of directors of the National League of Families.*

GEORGE: I supported the war in this respect: When our government decides to put armed forces some place, I'm for their getting the job done. This war was run by politicians rather than the military, so the military couldn't get the job done. There were too many restrictions on what they could and could not do. Tony, for example, had to fly the exact same route more or less every morning. Well, that's pretty nutty. If I were the enemy I'd just set up the antiaircraft and go after them. It'd be simple. There were an awful lot of what he called "be no's"—there will be no this, there will be no that. For example, they couldn't bomb a hospital or anything like that.

HELEN: The worst was, there will be no bombing of MiGs and other enemy aircraft on the ground. I don't think that we should ever again go into a war we don't plan to win.

GEORGE: It's so different from my experience in World War II. You didn't have to ask Washington if you wanted to knock the Germans off between St. Malo and the Rhine. You just went zooming ahead. The biggest problem there was trying to get the British to go along. But if you have all your children in the war, you pretty much support it. They were also military, and when they received orders to go and participate, they did. And so therefore I supported their action in the war. Whether the war was right or wrong and how it was managed, I don't necessarily support that.

Tony had done a hundred missions and was back on his second tour with a "different and better aircraft," as he put it. He could hardly wait to get back. He expressed it very well. He said, "If you want to get any peace with these people, you turn them on their back, put your knee on their chest, a knife at their throat—and then you can talk to them. And if we don't do this, you can color all of Southeast Asia red."

He went down through the clouds. He wasn't shot down. It was so cloudy he couldn't see the target, so down he went. We know not what happened to him after that, but there was never any radio contact, no flames, no smoke.

HELEN: The target was weathered in. They said they would conduct a search for seventy-two hours, but they couldn't see anything 'cause the weather was so bad.

GEORGE: They did all the testing with [electronic] equipment to try and locate where the plane might have been. But if he had been shot afterwards, he could have gone anywhere. When I was in Laos, they showed me his target. It was Route Seven out of China to the Ho Chi Minh Trail, so if he went down he could have gone into North Vietnam, China.

HELEN: Tony always preferred to fly alone. There was just one other plane up with him, his wingman's. His wingman hung around as long as he could, but then he had to go back because he ran out of fuel. They did go back and search for a couple of days. For the first several months, I was convinced that Tony had ejected and was making his way through the jungle, and that he would appear. I really was convinced.

GEORGE: I dreamed it. The same way Helen described. He was a great big guy, six feet two. Good athlete, a football player. I dreamed he had busted out, was fighting his way through the jungle, and he would eventually get to sea, and then he'd swim out and get some Navy type to pick him up. Many a night I dreamed that. I figured that if we didn't hear yesterday, maybe today, maybe tomorrow. I just figured he could do it. That's the kind of hope we had. We'd still like to get some word that he's . . . he's been killed and his remains are coming back.

HELEN: The day the prisoners were coming home, every time the phone rang, I jumped. I think it was 11:30 that night when we finally got a call saying that Tony was not on the list. That was a hard day. But it was still exciting watching those prisoners when they landed at Clark.

I'm an optimist by nature, but when Jon went, I felt different. I kept telling myself that it was probably because he was our baby, our youngest, and I'd had enough of wars. My father went to World War I, and George was in World War II. But I did feel a lot differently when Jon went. And therefore I cannot say I was surprised. One of my initial reactions when we were told he had been killed was "Thank God he's not missing."

When Tony came back from Thailand after his first tour of duty, we knew he was due within a month or so, but we didn't know when. And his wife and two children happened to be at our summer home. I was in swimming with his six-year-old son, and George walked down to the rocks where we were swimming. He had a camera with him, but I didn't think anything of that because he frequently had a camera with him. And then in a few minutes, George said "Look who's coming." Down the path from the house came Tony with his wife. He had come clear from Thailand and surprised us in upper New York State. After all the excitement had died down half an hour or so later, I asked his little boy, Anthony, "How did you feel when you saw your dad?" He said, "First I wasn't sure it was really him. And then I quickly closed my eyes and thanked God he wasn't killed." He was just six years old. When my father came back from World War I, my brother and I decided that if there was another war, we would take folding chairs and watch. Even in World War II we didn't know what was going on. But this generation, with war, they know everything. I wouldn't have thought that a six-year-old child would be so concerned.

Then two years later, of course, Tony was declared missing. I know Jon is with the Lord and he's fine, but with Tony, you don't know. And it's worse. A lot of times I've felt real despair, but then on the other hand I suddenly realize that although we don't know where Tony is, the Lord does, and that's what keeps you going. It's terrible for the young wives. As our daughter-in-law says, she's neither wife nor widow. Bonnie has not remarried, but she said to me once, "Even if I do remarry, I'll never be sure." She's right. We'll never be sure. It's hard on parents but it's harder on wives.

To me it's like living on a seesaw. We know nothing about Tony. Then when you hear Hanoi is going to release five bodies, you get your hopes up. Mostly, I think we'll just never know. His youngest son asked me some years back, "Do you think my daddy's dead?" And I said, "Yes, Shannon, he probably is." And then I asked, "Do you remember him at all?" And Shannon said, "I just remember him throwing me up in the air, and I landed on the bed and I laughed." And I thought at the time, if you can only have one memory of your father, it couldn't be a better one.

GEORGE: Tony was a big man and he liked combat.

HELEN: You shouldn't say that. It sounds as if he loved war.

GEORGE: I'm explaining. He was a tackle on the football team, and beating the other guy up was good fun.

HELEN: So many people seem to think that if you're in the military, you like war—without realizing that in the military you stand to lose the most by it, too. I don't know anybody in the military who likes war. It's just your job and somebody has to do it. I would hate for anyone to think that Tony loved war.

GEORGE: I didn't say that. I said combat. He loved football.

HELEN: They thought it was a job worth doing. Tony believed in freedom for all people everywhere, so that's what he was willing to die for. I know we all felt the same way. The fact that all those boat people went through all those miseries to get out of the place was proof that the job was worth doing, had we completed it. When Tony went over the first time, Sandy was already over there and two brothers didn't have to go at the same time. So Tony's wife said—joking, of course, because she knew her husband—that she was going to write to the Pentagon [for a deferral]. Tony said, "Okay, You do that and I go to Reno."

There's more interest in the MIA situation now than there used to be. In the first few years after Tony was declared missing, there was nothing. Nothing. Nobody cared. I remember saying to my neighbor one day, "I cannot understand why people don't even care." And he said, "All anybody wants to do is forget the war." But in recent years we've had the Memorial in Washington. People are looking at Vietnam from a farther perspective. There isn't the anger and emotion that there was. The first few years we couldn't get into any magazine, or if we were in *The New York Times* with something we thought was important, it was on page forty-nine. My daughter and I marched around outside the White House and the U.N. It didn't do any good.

GEORGE: Then the Administrations we have had . . . Kissinger signed the Paris Peace Agreements in 1973. That was about all that was accomplished by Nixon's organization. Ford and Carter did very little. It was only when Reagan got in that we got any real action. It was frustrating and irritating that for years we got nothing from the government but a lot of "Don't you worry. We'll take care of it." When Reagan came in he gave it high priority. You've probably heard that they used to have three or four people in the Defense Intelligence Agency working on the missing in action. Now I think they have over sixty. And the American Legion, and some of those within the Vietnam Veterans of America are now ardently supporting our cause, which is great. We have very good support now. In '77 it was like a vacuum. You couldn't talk to anybody, even our own government.

HELEN: I remember thinking I should go to Laos and ask permission to go in the jungle and look for him. I figured either they would give me permission or else they would refuse permission, I would go anyway, and they would shoot me. Then at least we would get some publicity. But then I thought the publicity would probably be of the stupid mother sort: "Look what some stupid mother did. Now we've got another MIA." You get so frustrated. Nobody cares. I wrote a number of letters to *The New York Times*. After one of them, I received a reply from some man in Brooklyn. He said that if our son cared to go around bombing innocent women and children, he had gotten his just desserts. And if that's the way we had raised him, then we had gotten ours, too.

The day after Nixon ordered the [Haiphong] harbor mined again, I was at a prayer group, a Bible study group in our church. This woman walked in and said, "Oh, I just pray for those North Vietnamese." And I looked at her and I said, "Did it ever occur to you to pray for the South Vietnamese?" It hadn't. I believe that you should pray for your enemies. But from her point of view, we were the bad guys, so she was praying for the good guys.

GEORGE: Uninformed, she was.

HELEN: I don't know, George. She was informed from her own point of view. With the hostile letters, you read them, tear them up, and put them out of your mind. We've also had some good letters in recent years. I just got a letter from a pilot who flies for United. It turns out Tony was his instructor when he got his wings, so he wrote a letter (from which she reads):

"I often think of Tony and the impact he had on my life. I'm sure most students have a hero worship for their instructors in flight school, but in my case I had six more instructors after Tony, so my opinion is more objective than the average student's. Tony was the finest instructor and pilot I ever flew with. By example, he taught me not to accept mediocrity, and that with hard work and self-discipline, anything can be accomplished. Those lessons not only resulted in an excellent flying course, but also proved helpful in my civilian life. It was a rare privilege to know Tony, and my thoughts and prayers have often been with him and his family over the past years, which I know have been difficult.''

After the government declared him dead, we did have a memorial service. Our other son, Alexander, spoke beautifully. A couple of hymns, Bible reading. I just thought for the children's sake this thing shouldn't go drifting off into nothing. There should be some kind of a cutoff point. I think I was in the minority, but everyone cooperated with me.

GEORGE: A lot of people had the idea we were declaring him dead, which we weren't. There is still the possibility he might return alive. We're ever hopeful we'll find some accounting. As Helen said, we believe there are some alive. I do. I think the government intelligence people do. They cannot say "Yes, we do." But they have no reason to say they aren't. So we believe that we could find out something tomorrow. You can't help but watch the news just hoping, hoping. We're ever at it, day in and day out. It's never off our minds.

———————◆———————

Retired Marine LT. COL. EDISON WAINWRIGHT MILLER came home with the rest of the POWs in 1973, after five years and four months in captivity. But beginning in 1970 Miller had made statements against the war—and he had often been trotted out by Hanoi for the benefit of visitors, including Jane Fonda and Ramsey Clark at Christmas, 1970. On the day Miller retired after twenty-four years of Marine flying, with a 60 percent disability for hearing loss and a broken back, Navy Secretary John Warner placed in his file a searing letter of censure for alleged collaboration with the enemy. Warner acted without a formal hearing, and at a time when a number of ex-POWs were demanding that Miller be court-martialed. Miller, now a lawyer in Southern California, spent years trying to get the letter expunged. Though a Navy hearing board ruled in his favor, and so did a federal district judge in Washington, an appellate panel overturned the lower court and sent the matter back to the Navy Department for further consideration in the fall of 1986.

I came home and I would have been happy to put Vietnam behind me, but I've never been able to. I have had to relive every minute of prison. It has had an effect on me. I'm tired. When will it end? Probably never. The day they close the lid on my coffin, maybe, and there'll be press for a day or two after that: "Ex-POW Edison Miller, Controversial."

Being a POW was a very boring and frustrating experience. If they could have crammed it into two or three months, I think I could have learned all the lessons in that time. But five years and four months . . . There were maybe a few minutes of stark terror, but boredom and frustration most of the time.

Part of the problem was my personality. When people complained and bellyached, I'd point out we were professional soldiers, most of us career-oriented, well-educated, officers, pilots. And I used to say "What are you bitching about? Live by the sword, die by the sword. Take the good with the bad." If someone was picking specks [lice] out of his beard I'd say "Pretend they're caraway seeds." My advice was to forget it and get out of there in one piece.

The first time they strung me from the rafters, I laughed and thought "They're putting me in traction." It was the best my broken back had felt in a week. Instead of feeling sorry for myself when I got the crap kicked out of me, I'd say "Come on, Ed. You've taken worse beatings in a good football game." That's what got me through the experience. A shrink once asked me how I handled solitary. If you like yourself, it's all right. I got so I could project movies on my cell wall—an entire Western, for example. I tested whether I was losing my mind. Could I turn the movie off? Click! I could. It's people who can project those images that are healthy.

Probably my worst moment was the depression when there was a complete break between me and the [rest of the] POWs. They were not going to accept any belief that I might have had. You can yell and scream at Communism and Ho Chi Minh if you want to, but if you want to be brave, do it when there's some risk involved. By 1971 it was easy to be brave because the guards weren't leaning on you. By 1973 we were a Boy Scout camp more than a POW camp. The food—rice and pumpkin stew—still wasn't very good, but no one was beating you in the head, either.

My Mother's Day message of '70, they still make a big deal about. I wrote a letter to my mother which a lot of people misinterpreted. They [the North Vietnamese] asked me to put it on tape. The thrust was, we haven't given a lot of thought to what we're doing here and where we're going. The war was nothing we were going to be very proud of as a nation or as individuals. I think history has shown that to be correct.

They really singled me out. There were accusations I revealed methods of communications. I don't know how many other people were accused of that. Someday I'll write a book. Another prisoner wrote a letter calling the war in Vietnam illegal and immoral soon after capture, a very gushing letter praising the North Vietnamese for their humanity and kindness. He's now a general. Why don't people get all that? Robinson Risner, one of my accusers, who came off as a big hero, must have met every delegation that came down the pike.

———————•———————

Her hair is short now, and flecked with gray. In concert she sings a song about an older woman having an affair with a younger man. She does aerobics to Bruce Springsteen and even takes voice lessons. But JOAN BAEZ, *whose long, straight hair and resonant, untrained voice made her an icon of a generation in rebellion, still mixes politics with song. And though she has come to grips with the unpleasant realities of postwar Vietnam, she remains a stalwart pacifist in an age of apathy. After an a cappella hymn she says: "Eat your heart out Jerry Falwell." Billy Joel's "Goodnight Saigon," she tells her audiences, is not about heroes. During a 1985 stopover in Chicago, she recounted the memories of her visit to the POWs in Hanoi during the Christmas bombing of 1972, and some of her feelings about the war.*

While we were there we went and visited the POWs. They were like big, innocent kids. We talked a little bit. I mean I'm sure it was a very unpleasant situation for them and they couldn't really say anything and we also knew it—just chitchat. There's one big guy standing there with a piece of shrapnel about a foot long in his hand. He said, "This stuff came flying through the window last night." And they didn't have any bomb shelters. That outraged Telford Taylor* more than anything else, that the Americans didn't have bomb shelters.

And the POW said "What's happening?" I said "Well. . . ."—I was trying to be funny—I said "These big planes go overhead, they're called B-52s, and they drop these bombs." And he said "But Kissinger said 'Peace is at hand.' " And I just started to cry. He didn't understand anything. He didn't understand what he had done dropping those bombs on the people. He didn't understand what was happening to him—that he was diving under the bed and the stuff was flying through the window and Kissinger told him everything was

---

*A prominent physicist who also made the trip.

going to be okay. I said "Kissinger lied. I don't know what else to tell you." Then I sang him "Dixie."

I think I've blocked out a lot of that trip. Coming to terms with one's mortality is a kind of a scary business. Occasionally I wake up at night sitting up in bed in a sweat and I realize that a plane has just gone overhead. I mean those things are down there. But I consider that a very rare gift— that as an American I was able to experience something like that and live through it. So I had two things. I had some idea of what it was like to live in that kind of situation, and I could share something with the people who lived that way all their lives—running in and out of bomb shelters and wondering if you'd be the next one to be blown up.

I met a man sitting next to us at Yvette's [a restaurant in Chicago] and we got chatting and he was a pilot out of Guam. He was there for the Tet offensive and came directly home after it. He said he has three children—they're twenty, eighteen and seventeen—and they don't know anything about Vietnam, and he won't tell them. I said, "Did you block it out instantly?" He said, "Instantly. I never think about it. I never tell my kids about it." It was all [about] things that we're not proud to say about ourselves.

But I don't think it'll stay that way. I mean you know how long it took before they said "Holocaust" and before they showed the film *The Holocaust* in Germany. That was the introduction to the Holocaust for a lot of German children. In a lot of ways it is similar, 'cause of the shame issue. Shame is a funny thing. Shame causes political prisoners to not talk about the past. You can learn a lot from them, but they don't want to talk about it. Who wants to talk about sitting naked in a room full of men who are smoking and about to rape you? You don't want to: It's humiliating. And I think shame has just clammed up that era. And where we open it up again, just for history purposes, it might be a long time before we can be straight about that, especially during this pendulum time when everything's supposed to be terrific.

———————•———————

DAVID HARRIS *went to prison for refusing the draft during the war. His book on the experience,* I Shoulda Been Home Yesterday, *was published in 1976. He has become an author of nonfiction books, and lives with his second wife*, novelist Lacey Fosburgh, in Marin County, outside San Francisco.*

---

*Harris was married for a time to Singer Baez.

One of the things that characterizes Vietnam for me is that only one group of people were asked to pay any price. The rest of the country didn't even pay for it on their tax bill. It was all charged off on the national debt so they wouldn't be forced to build any kind of political consensus. The only sacrifices were from the people with the least representation. So as a young person there was a sense of "This is our question. It isn't their question. The guys who are giving these great speeches about the Commies don't have to go do this." And there was also a sense that if you were going to be a real human being, you couldn't ignore it. People were dying every day for no good reason, so the question you had to answer personally was whether you were going to be part of that or not. There was no way to be a neutral. If you submitted to the law you were part of it. So that issue worked on me to the point where I returned my draft card.

In the spring of '66, when the Selective Service was giving student deferment tests on campus, I couldn't bring myself to go because I felt if America fights, everybody fights. Because you don't have the background or money to go to Stanford doesn't mean that you're supposed to be exempt. In the summer I remember very vividly the sense of liberation typing up this letter to the draft board. And I put my draft card in it, walked down to the mailbox, and walked back about ten feet off the ground. I never felt more whole and liberated in my life. And that way, Vietnam forced me to take the abstractions of being a good citizen and make some concrete sense out of them. It wasn't civic anymore. This was down and dirty.

I feel that I grew enormously from making that choice and standing behind it. On the other hand I wish I'd never been forced to make it. We should never have been in a war in Vietnam. When you think about the level of destruction we created for a policy that no American government seemed able to articulate [you felt] "Good Christ, what are we doing here?" I had a sense of incredible outrage. I felt "This isn't right; this is my country and it's doing something enormously ugly and un-democratic and this is a violation of my birthright." If I hadn't, I wouldn't have had the momentum to do what I did.

People say "Well, you must have been for the Communists." It's not a question of having been for the Communists. I was pretty American. When I was drafted my attitude was "Why doesn't Lyndon Johnson go stuff it. It's as much my country as it is his. I'm not doing what I'm doing because I'm against my country. I'm doing what I'm doing because I'm *for* my country. This is my service." You're supposed to serve your country. Well, I did. If the law said you were going to be party to that, then I wanted to be on record as

an outlaw, and if the price was two years of prison, let's go for it.
From the day I sent my draft card back I assumed I was going to
jail. The only question was when and how long.

So my first step was to say I'm not going to shield myself. I felt
everybody who was in the same situation shouldn't be shielded. I
was one of a handful of student body presidents in the United States
who advocated eliminating the student deferment. Fuck it. Students
shouldn't have any right to hide. If you weren't going to make the
sacrifice to stop it, then you ought to make the sacrifice to make it
go. When people are being killed nobody has a right to sign their
separate peace. So I was the Peace Movement version of gung ho.
You have to remember the kind of time it was. The world hadn't
divided itself into grays yet. There was a lot of black and white, and
we lived a sort of simple high school civics belief that you had these
obligations, if you were a citizen, that you had to live up to.

I remember my outrage at the people who sat in Washington, D.C.,
and didn't pay any price at all but sent everybody else out to do it.
Those people, some part of me has yet to forgive. They got off cheap
and they made everybody else pay. Lyndon Johnson, Robert McNamara, Dean Rusk. Henry Kissinger, Richard Nixon. All their assembled surrogates, the high-powered thinkers, big movers and shakers
who had all the good reasons that people were supposed to get their
legs blown off in rice paddies, but never came close to the rice paddies themselves.

When I trooped out of the warden's office and saw John Mitchell's
picture on the wall, I used to mutter under my breath. Being in jail
wasn't terribly enjoyable. I was there for twenty months and then
sixteen months on parole. I'd just as soon have been someplace else
and I didn't think I belonged there that way. I didn't feel bitterness
per se, but certainly I was angry a lot. I'd look at the evening news
and just get furious at what they were doing. It still infuriates me. I
hear Reagan mouth all this garbage about the war and what a noble
cause it was and I get furious. If it's such a goddamn noble cause,
sucker, why weren't you there?

Those sons of bitches I will not shed any tears for, ever. They to
me are the villains of the piece and not the guys that went and did
what they forced them to do. Those guys I commiserate with. And
I always had a good relationship with veterans. I may be the only
draft resister to ever serve on the board of the Veterans' Administration. Those guys I could identify with, particularly after I'd been
to prison. We'd both been through the institutional situation. There
were no bullets in prison, nor were there any weekend leaves. Both
of us paid prices. I'm basically at ease with that. We paid our prices
in different ways. But that's different to me than these guys who

dealt far from the reality and with no sense of honor or obligation, and who lied all the way down the goddamn line. Not one of them told the truth until it was too late.

———————•———————

A onetime student antiwar activist, opponent and political prisoner of the Thieu regime, Doan Van Toai *stayed in Saigon after the fall— only to be jailed by the Communists. Eventually he bribed his way out of the country and arrived in the United States, where he has distinguished himself as a writer on Vietnam with a bitter anti-Communist cant. His first book,* The Vietnamese Gulag, *was published in Europe; a second, on how the North imposed Communism on the South, was written while he held a fellowship at the Fletcher School of Law and Diplomacy in Medford, Massachusetts. He helped Truong Nhu Tang, a former senior official of the Provisional Revolutionary Government, who appears elsewhere in this book, to prepare* A Vietcong Memoir, *which was published in 1985. He published a third book,* Portrait of the Enemy, *based on interviews with many former Viet Cong, in the fall of 1986. Toai is a visiting scholar at the Institute of East Asian Studies at Berkeley.*

I was raised in Vinh Long province. My father was a teacher. In the sixties, I was one of the Saigon student leaders against the war, and I was arrested many times by the Thieu government. I traveled abroad in 1970 and 1971 and spent one year in the United States, lecturing and speaking to the antiwar movement. Since 1971, when I left the student movement, I was one of the editors of the opposition magazine *Tu Quyet*—"Self-Determination." It was banned by the government. After that I did no more antigovernment activities, but I kept contact with some friends in the jungle with the Viet Cong who were students with me. I went to work as a manager for the Nam Do, or South Metropolitan Bank, a private bank.

When Saigon was falling, I decided to stay. I ignored all sorts of rumors. I thought finally we would enjoy peace there. I did not like to live in exile. I said if men like me left the country, who can stay? I contact some friends who joined with Viet Cong before. They were with me during the student movement in the 1960's and '70s. At that time a lot of VC agents came to Saigon to prepare. Days I worked at my profession. Evening, night, weekend, I contacted these Viet Cong and think about future. We were not optimistic among ourselves. We were very confused. But all of us agree that finally we accept any hard condition to live in peace and hope somehow for policy of national reconciliation, so we stay.

First day of takeover I met many of Viet Cong who were my friends. Some of them display disillusion about regime. They asked why I did not escape. I thought they test me. Finally I find out they said the truth. They told me about their suffering life in the jungle with North cadres who were very dogmatic. So they urged me to flee. And the more I met with the higher cadres who said the truth, the more I became disillusioned with the regime.

But soon some of my friends contact me. They said there are not many Southern revolutionaries, and if we do not get up to work with them, we will lose all control; the Northerners will come and take over. I said I can help, with my experience and my talent. Because my career is financial they ask me to work with the Finance Committee, to research and plan for the Provisional Revolutionary Government.

They introduced me to Vuong Ky, the [new] finance minister. Vuong Ky sounded good. He convinced me Southerners had program, at least for a period of time, that was not Communist at all. I found no Communist tone in his conversation. He was very patriotic and nationalistic, a revolutionary of the Front. Finance committee Southerners were very moderate. One month later they were replaced by North cadres.

I drew up a plan to confiscate property of corrupt generals and businessmen and work with poor people—war victims, including uncorrupt government workers, good people. My proposal was to nationalize property of bad people, build up industry, use workers and victims, veterans even of ARVN. I argue these people are only exploited victims of regime. All criminals run away, left behind only their victims. Low officials and veterans were angry with bosses who left them behind. They were ready to work for government if government have clemency and real reconciliation policy. Le Duc Tho had emphasized this many times in Paris press conference. But everything Communists said was quite different from everything they were doing.

Some people in PRG accept proposal, but new cadres from North disagree. They said [my plan] is reformist, capitalist way, not the socialist way. They asked me to draw a proposal to confiscate all property of people in South, even people not involved with the former regime. I fought with them. The quarrel was the end of May. I was in jail on June twenty-second without charges.

I was watching a band concert in the theater, former Senate upper house. I was invited VIP guest in first rows. It was very calm arrest. An officer took me upstairs and said he would take me to headquarters. He was friendly. I went to former police headquarters, where I was arrested many times. He said he received an order to arrest me. I asked why, what evidence. He said he didn't know. I was put in isolation cell like a tiger cage with no window. It was same cell, Number Five I was in prison under Thieu. I was two months there. No question, no charge. [Later] I was transferred to a collective cell with one hundred people, well-known intellectual, writer, politician, every remnant of Saigon, some student and opposition leaders. They left me there six months. They asked me to write my biography from age six, and question me on it. Every time I asked about my crime, they say, "*You* have to know. *You* have to say." I was transferred to jail in Gia Dinh province for eighteen months. Then I was released. They suspect me as CIA, traitor. They have no evidence, so they release me. I got out in 1978 after twenty-eight months in jail. My mother died when I was in jail in 1977. Communists did not let her in hospital. My family was considered reactionary.

Under Thieu they torture, but I was not scared. I was optimistic they keep you alive, because outside I knew the opposition movement was struggling for me, the lawyer take care for me, and Amnesty International, Red Cross, foreign reporters. But under Communists, even my wife at home did not know where I was. No lawyer, no opposition, no Red Cross. And when I step out of that prison there is big sign in front of jail: NOTHING IS MORE PRECIOUS THAN INDEPENDENCE AND LIBERTY.

CHAPTER TEN

The Resistance

> There has never been a protracted war
> from which a country has benefited . . .
> What is essential in war is victory, not
> prolonged operations.
> —SUN TZU,
> *The Art of War*

THOUGH it sometimes seems otherwise, American tradition grows as much from dissent, defiance of authority, and religious opposition to violence as from bare-knuckled frontier brutality. The American government has had to cope with pacifism and resistance in time of conflict at least since the draft riots of the Civil War. But never before Vietnam had a campaign of civil disobedience so undermined a full-fledged war effort. Never had thousands of young men chosen to flee abroad rather than to serve when called. Never had it seemed that rebellion might engulf the country. Looking back on the time, one is left wondering what made the difference. Nearly as many had been killed fifteen years earlier in an enterprise of equal futility—Korea—without provoking the slightest sign of domestic revolt.

Perhaps Vietnam is too much blamed for the tumult of the sixties. As former Ambassador William Sullivan observes elsewhere in this book, and as some of the interviews in this chapter seem to show, the war was no more than a catalyst for changes that were bound to come anyway. Civil rights, women's liberation, the youth and sexual revolutions were already on the national agenda. Indeed, the time they spent as civil rights workers organizing blacks and defying white authority in the South gave young liberals like Sam Brown and David Harris both a personal taste of injustice and the experience they needed to lead a national protest movement. In a sense, the war merely happened into their path.

Clearly the draft, with its assertion of a government right to demand the sacrifice of young lives in a cause that it could not explain, was the yeast that made the movement rise. Certainly violence from the right by way of assassinations, bombings, murders, open police brutality, and the intervention of troops, contributed mightily to a feeling that the time for restraint had passed. And so demonstrators did unspeakable things—splashed blood on buildings and draft registration files, flew Viet Cong flags, threw excrement on the coffins of war casualties, trashed windows and buildings, invited arrest, battled police in the streets—and eventually tried to bring the war home by resorting to guns and bombs of their own.

But there was a worse mistake yet, made by one Administration and perpetuated by a second, and that was to allow the conflict to drag on without visible end. Time was what the opponents of the war needed most—time to get the Charles Litekys to think, time to percolate their views out into the mainstream political establishment. Brown and others in the movement may have perceived themselves as no more than a band of underpaid, socially conscious youngsters whose powers were greatly exaggerated by paranoia in the Nixon White House. But given enough time, the passion and the domestic turmoil they stirred took its toll within the political system as well as on the street. Of that there could be no better evidence than Graham Martin's feeling in the closing days of the war that his main task as Ambassador to Saigon was to do battle before an increasingly hostile Congress, to sustain a dwindling flow of aid.

————————◆————————

SAM BROWN *organized the Vietnam Moratorium in 1969, and later had a fling at politics in Colorado. Now married and the father of three children, he is the general partner of Centennial Partners, Ltd., a company that specializes in the development of affordable housing.*

For me at least, the civil rights movement was the life-changing experience. It gave me the sense that America not only wasn't perfect, but had these huge internal contradictions that suddenly made you begin to look abroad and say: "Wait a minute. If we could do that at home, what are we capable of where no one can see it?" Vietnam was the place where that became most evident. It wasn't the only place. At the time, you didn't have to look back very far. The intervention in the Dominican Republic in 1964, or Guatemala in '54, or '65 when some people thought the [U.S. was involved in the] fall of Ben Bella in Algeria or the assassination of Nkrumah in Ghana in '64. And if you were of a conspiratorial mind, it wouldn't be hard to see the ugly side to American interventionism almost anyplace. But Vietnam was the place where it was both most evident and most closely felt at home, because people were dying in substantial numbers.

I got active in the antiwar movement starting in 1964–65 through some of those early marches. The first time I went to a march was a moment of exhilaration without fear, a sense of being untouchable. It was Thanksgiving of '64. It was on the sidewalk in front of the White House, everything very carefully marshaled, a fairly small group of people walking in an oval, incredibly well-mannered and disciplined—in a way a reflection of the civil rights movement. There was a sense that you lose moral authority if you get out of line, and that maintaining moral authority was important. That to me was probably the nicest moment of the next seven years. Things deteriorated substantially later on.

It was a hell of a party, though I don't personally mean in the sense of drinking and carousing. One of the things that's overlooked about that period is that for people who were privileged with good educations, it was a terrific time. The economy was booming. You could get a job. Consequently, you could take your time. There was a kind of freedom and a great sense that the future was unlimited. It was after all [an extension of] the Kennedy era and we felt anything was possible. Justice is just around the corner, was a part of it. And it was the sense of tremendous opportunity and hopefulness early on in the sixties, that made the war all the more devastating.

There were, even during the war, a large number of GIs who indicated their support for the movement. I always regarded the GIs as victims. They were caught in their own expectations, which were not that different than my expectations when I left high school. I had been the outstanding ROTC cadet three years in a row in high school. I was king of the hill. But we'd get little things—contributions with Vietnam postmarks on them. On occasion someone in the military who was fed up would come in for help or just show up late at night and want to sit down and talk about what they'd seen and what they'd done and how they felt about it. Then Vietnam Veterans Against the War began to grow, and that was different because the people I knew in it largely had been officers in Vietnam. And that became an important symbol. There was a sense we all shared of a terrible loss—of innocence or youth or lives or friends. We were people whose friends were killed or had spent time in jail or out of the country. It was a sense of "This isn't the way it was supposed to be."

In '66–67 I got involved with some of the electoral efforts to end the war, which came to be the McCarthy campaign in '67–68. After that I went to the Kennedy School at Harvard and there I taught a seminar on contemporary American politics, which turned into the Vietnam Moratorium in '69. The Moratorium was really started as an attempt to be more expansive—a kind of outreach to middle Americans around the country rather than just in Washington and New York. Its full name was the Vietnam Moratorium Committee.

There was a shifting mix of alliances at 1029 Vermont Avenue [a downtown Washington building that was a resistance headquarters]. By the spring of 1970 we had offices in L.A. and San Francisco and Denver and Chicago and New York and Boston and Atlanta and Dallas and we were spending about ninety percent of our time raising money. And at that point we did about the smartest thing in institutional terms that I've ever been involved in—though I'm not sure it was a smart thing in terms of the war itself. We all got together and said "This is just silly. We're not doing much of anything to end the war. What we're doing now is supporting a large bureaucracy." So we had a party one Sunday at the office, flew a bunch of people in, and officially killed the beast.

The reason I say it may have been institutionally smart is that there are a lot of well-intended institutions around that become insular and self-sustaining and don't really do much of anything. But in contemporary political terms the reason it may have been wrong is because some people said the Nixon White House felt free to substantially expand the war, and the bombing particularly, within days of that. They felt that an institution that was significant opposition was now no longer there. For those of us who were involved at the time, "the significant opposition" consisted of a bunch of mid-to-late twenties, well-intended, "Let's go out and change the world" people. If the White House spy network had been better than it apparently was, they would have been less concerned. It was pretty much a hand-to-mouth operation. There was never enough money to fix the mimeograph machine. The appearance to the outside was the Sunday *New York Times* full-page ads, and the marches and that sort of stuff. But it was really just a bunch of people being paid fifty bucks a week and barely keeping alive.

There came a sort of strange time. In November of 1969 we had this huge demonstration. I don't know how big—I never believed my [crowd] numbers and I never believed the police's, and either did any of the newspapers—but half a million, three-quarters of a million people. And everything had been very peaceful and quiet.

There had been some singing and a good deal of sloganeering and shouting and craziness, but it was a pretty nice day. It was bitterly cold. And then at the end of the day a few people went over and attacked the Justice Department. And the result was that instead of being seen in Council Bluffs, Iowa, where I grew up, as a day on which all those people got together and sang and marched and petitioned their government, the evening news was dominated by obscenities and slogan-shouting and Vietcong flags.

By 1970, the mood had become one of real anger and bitterness. That sense of wanting to perfect America had been lost and had turned into something ugly and destructive. By then, also, a lot of the effort ended. Unfortunately the end of the draft probably had a substantial impact on the antiwar movement. At the time, I would have liked to believe that the opposition to the war was all out of principle and little out of self-interest. And at certain levels that was true, among the most active resisters. But if you look back at it, the end of the draft had a dramatic impact on the opposition to the war. A lot of the high-minded idealists turned out, at least in part, to be interested in self-protection.

Getting out [of the movement] had to do with two things: First, sort of dropping back to write. I had had some reflections on the antiwar movement which I had published and were not terribly well received by some of my colleagues. I felt pretty strongly that we had blown the opportunities to reach out to middle America—that partly for reasons of style, people couldn't identify with the movement. Some of the actions which were undertaken out of high principle had the consequence of driving people away. There was a lot of argument about whether American society had to go through a radical transformation in order to end the war or whether the war was aberrational or a third argument which is the one I could identify with: that there was a great deal that needed to be changed, but in the meantime people were dying in Vietnam and we had to put aside some other issues while we got at that one. I don't mean to suggest that we needed to put aside fundamental civil rights, but there was a great deal of . . . if you didn't identify with Puerto Rican Independence then you couldn't speak at an antiwar rally. Well, I thought that was an insular, narrow, elitist view of what American society was about and how it was going to change.

DAVID HARRIS

A lot of my memories of the period are memories of coming of age if you will. I learned how to take risks, how to keep my own counsel, how to pay prices. The war was on one hand the most political of issues and on the other hand a deeply moral personal issue. Business as usual was impossible because there was this overriding question hanging over your head. Vietnam created for me a personal moral challenge to respond to.

The war was an extraordinarily obvious violation of everything that I had been led to expect from the country I was a part of. I grew up in the family of a World War II veteran, watching "Victory at Sea" on television and the message was quite clear that Americans fought for freedom, justice, and the rights of people everywhere to choose their own destiny. I even once wanted to go to West Point. But when my generation's war showed up it turned out to be a propping up of petty dictators so they could keep a good portion of their population in servitude.

As soon as I learned about it I thought it was fucked up. I didn't go from a position of thinking it was good to thinking it was bad. I went from not knowing it existed, to finding out and being appalled. That was in 1964. I was at Stanford and I had been a civil rights worker in Mississippi and I guess when I returned to campus, Vietnam had just started to rise and the first marches had been held in Berkeley. The teach-ins were just beginning.

I joined up. Mississippi was for me personally a necessary precursor. It opened my eyes to the possibility that a lot of dishonorable and undemocratic things went on inside the United States and it made it easier to believe that such things could happen outside the United States. So I was prepared to look at the issue with something other than blind obedience to what the President thought ought to happen. And the more I understood about it the worse it seemed.

So for me the issue was how do you respond to this? And the feeling was "Here we are, college students at one of the best universities in the country, being tossed abstractions in the classrooms, and all of a sudden here was a situation that demanded you take some of that stuff and live it. We were studying existentialism and all of a sudden an existential situation was on our doorstep, and it was not "How do you stop the Germans?" but "What do you do if you *are* the Germans?" Hannah Arendt had just written her book about Eichmann and we had discussed the responsibility of an individual in the face of immoral acts by the state. And suddenly there it was—we had to make that kind of decision. I believe those kinds of decisions are good for people, but that we had to make them was a disaster for the country.

That was a time, I think, that forced every potential soldier into a real dilemma of selfhood. Who am I? Am I the kind of person who does that, or am I not? I felt personally, having made a decision [to go to prison for resisting the draft] and carried it through, that I got a lot more closure if you will on the Vietnam experience than most of my contemporaries who didn't go to Vietnam or to prison. Most people didn't face up to the personal issue and I think that creates dilemmas that live on until today.

We didn't end the war because we thought it was a bad thing. We ended the war because it had become untenable in terms of domestic politics and military strategy. And because we ended it in that way we have yet to face up to what we did and what it means. Instead what is left is a bunch of galvanic responses. Whenever you ask the public whether they want to send Marines off to some other part of the world to do the same thing all over again, their hands sweat. As a consequence the government can't do it the way they used to be able to. But that doesn't translate into some clear redirection of our foreign policy. All it is, is a stumbling block to the executive branch's desire to use military force.

Has the government learned that lesson?

I'm not impressed that the people who have composed the governments since the war had any understanding of it. Certainly the Ford administration didn't have any understanding of it, or the Carter administration, which committed us to fighting the Russians ten thousand miles away in their own backyard in order to keep our electric forks operating.* And Reagan seems to have understood absolutely nothing from it. Ronald Reagan is the guy who ordered the National Guard to shoot people in the streets of Berkeley. He seems to have basically the same approach these days as he did then. Grenada is a classic example of the kind of lunatic machoism that pervaded the Vietnamese War—that somehow Americans have to be prepared at the drop of a hat to show they have hair on their scrotum.

And that's not the way you fight wars. That's what led us into Vietnam, this whole syndrome that somehow war is John Wayne in *Sands of Iwo Jima*. Thousands of young men went to Southeast Asia trying to be John Wayne and the lucky ones came home sorry they ever went. The unlucky ones never came home. I think we were the victims of our whole male stereotype. In 1965 on the campus of Stanford if you weren't John Wayne then you were either a Soviet spy or a homosexual. And part of the task that was thrown on us was to show that you could be indeed manly and not devoted to killing people for no good reason.

---

*A reference to the decision to support the Afghan guerrillas, partly on grounds that the Soviet occupation of Afghanistan in 1979 brought Russian troops and planes perilously close to Western energy sources in the Persian Gulf.

It's a different culture now. That's changed. Kids that are of draft age today have lots of options. I did a story about Brent Sassway, who was the first guy to be indicted under this new draft law and I said, "To assume this position, did you have to get over your John Wayne thing first?" He said, "What's a John Wayne thing?" And I said "It's changed." The United States was a much more unitary culture then. There were very strict and reasonably clear role models that you were allowed to play and outside of that there was nothing. And part of what went on in the process of opposing the war was reevaluating those role models and creating ones that were more comfortable to our consciences, not to mention made better sense.

And in terms of transformation on that cultural level it's been enormous. It's no longer enough for a President to say this is what's supposed to happen. Today if you didn't experience Vietnam, you find it hard to believe that it was ever possible. In those days it was considered sufficient reason to send half a million Americans into combat that the President wanted them there. That doesn't happen anymore and it's great. That couldn't be better for us as a country. The assumption has changed now to "If the government wants something then they'd better convince us," which is a much saner way to operate. The Reagan administration has lamented what they have described as a Vietnam mentality and the limitation it places on foreign policy, but there are a lot of young Americans and even more young Angolans or you name it, who are alive today because of that. If not for Vietnam, we would have led with troops.

———————•———————

JOAN BAEZ

I came into the movement early. In fact, I remember that when Kennedy was killed, I was going for one time in my entire life, to take part in this gala do. Within twenty-four hours there was a telegram saying "The do is still on." And then I was really torn and I'm always so rigid, I always say no to everything, so I thought okay, I'll do this and see how I feel. I went and was very blunt. I spoke about young people and that we had to be listened to and I sang "Blowin' in the Wind." I tried to be a tiny bit diplomatic, which for me in those days was very difficult. That same night his aides were after me to head up Young Democrats for Johnson. I said "No, no way." And then shortly after that I got a letter requesting the same thing and I remember writing back that as soon as he withdrew all the advisers from Vietnam and stopped contemplating sending troops in, I might consider supporting him. I was pretty clear on how I felt. I got sort of astounding writeups because it did take them by surprise. I was very open and uncommercial. And I sang "Times They Are a-Changin'." That speaks directly: "Senators, Congressmen, please heed the call. Don't stand in the doorway, don't block up the hall."

Well, it was funny. I was there on the very first marches and we were all beatniks, Commies, and hippies and weirdos and whatever. And then during the period when it sort of cleaned up its own act we were joined by nuns and priests and housewives. But I never had any doubts that what I was doing was correct. I've made mistakes. I've done some things, looking back, that I might not have done. But basically I feel as though I was on the right track.

If I had had illusions when I entered the movement, I'd have been more disillusioned later on. So many people entered their political phase by way of the war in Vietnam, and somehow thought their activities were going to change humankind. After eighty thousand years of this kind of behavior you better put your ego in very careful perspective as to what you're going to be able to do. Let's face it. The human race seems to love war. The trick is finding something that's more exciting to woo people away from it. I think Gandhi did that and I think King did that. He made it thrilling for people to be involved.

BONNIE BERTRAM *is a student at the University of California, Berkeley, majoring in English literature.*

Do you remember the war at all? You were very young . . .

I remember drawing peace signs because they looked neat, but of course I didn't know what they meant. When I was first learning to read, I recall being happy that I could read a sticker on my cousin's suitcase that said "War is not healthy for children or other living things." I thought that flowers didn't like war. See, I think that is exactly where the peace movement went wrong. It became a cutesy arts and crafts thing. It wasn't, damn it, it was serious. My friend's mom was selling feather and leather peace-sign key chains that she still keeps around the house as her generous contribution to protesting the Vietnam War. I really get mad at that because that is trivializing a very good cause. To me, key chains are not a political statement, they are an attempt at being cool or chic.

My older brother had a bad back and I remember that my parents were very relieved that he would not have to go to the war. He did not participate at all. He just went through college without thinking about it except in the most personal terms. My sister was only interested in the social aspects of the peace movement. I resent my sister for not taking more of a stand. When I ask her about that time, she remembers it in a very lighthearted way—as if nothing violent was going on. She was very noncommittal about the whole thing and I doubt that she even knew what was happening.

I guess it was good that the media made people aware that so many students felt so strongly about the issue. But, I think there is a vicious cycle because the media attention made it all seem romantic and trivial. As for the protesters themselves, I'm sure that many were very sincere but I have met a lot of people who joined in the peace marches because it was the thing to do at the time. I would have marched if I had been old enough, since so many other students would be marching beside me. I don't think that would happen today. Nobody really knows or cares about what is going on.

I still like listening to some of the music of that era because people like Neil Young really express intensity, vulnerability, and a kind of eerie frustration which I can still identify with. Listening to the Grateful Dead leaves me feeling sad and helpless. I don't feel any sweet nostalgia for that time. One, I was so young. Two, I don't think it was a very good period. Maybe students were more unified that they are today, but where did the unification get them?

———————•———————

Sandy-haired, square-jawed, and stolid, LARRY MARTIN, *who grew up in San Diego and fled the United States in 1969 to avoid the draft, is a social worker and occasional concert promoter in Vancouver, British Columbia.*

I didn't believe in killing. I came from no organized religious background, but my mother is so opposed to killing she's been a vegetarian since she was fifteen. My father died when I was seven, so I was raised in a pretty pacifist home. I didn't have toy guns or anything. When I was about sixteen, somebody came home in a box, a very early casualty. He was a friend of the neighbors. You're fifteen, you see all the guys who are eighteen going off, it's a lot of pressure to spend your teenage years under.

I decided I didn't want to go to Vietnam while I was still in high school in San Diego, I kept getting drafted, and I kept appealing my classification as a C.O. and physically unfit from the residual effects of polio. I was called four times and each time I refused induction. In 1968 Selective Service said they were turning over my records to the FBI. In early '69 the FBI came to the music store where I was working in La Jolla to arrest me. They gave me a few days. In the four years I was fighting the draft, all the time I was planning to go to jail. By chance, I'd read a pamphlet on how bad jail life was for C.O.'s., so I decided on Canada. I got in touch with the Quakers and Unitarians, and they helped me get on the Underground Railroad.

I was twenty-three when I reached Canada in April 1969. I knew nobody here. I didn't know what to expect, but I felt like I had a real heavy burden off my shoulders. I had been planning for a jail situation. The pressure made my life pretty intense down there. I'm just sorry I didn't come to Canada earlier.

I ran a hostel for deserters and draft dodgers from 1969 to 1975. I stayed after the Ford clemency and the Carter pardon. Like most people, I was pretty much established here in Canada. I had a three-year-old daughter. When you came to Canada, you never expected to go home. There was never a pardon or amnesty from any of the other wars. You didn't plan your life day to day for an amnesty. People entrenched themselves in Canada.

There has never *been* an amnesty. Ford had "earned reentry." You had to do up to two years of alternative service. It was a farce. The military paid your way down and processed guys through. To placate the right wing, they had alternative service but nobody was prosecuted for not doing it, so few did. Carter had a blanket pardon for draft evaders, and "case-by-case review" for deserters. Now any Army deserter from the Vietnam era can get out in one day. But two thousand are still wanted, including some who went to Sweden.

I have some negative feelings about the States, having to go through all that for something you believe in. When you grow up in a country saluting the flag every day and you have to leave the country for something you believe, you lose a lot of your nationalism. I don't think I was ever wrong in my opposition. I feel okay about not having gone to Vietnam. The rite of passage in our case was coming to Canada, a strange country.

To me it was strictly a class thing. Draft dodgers came to Canada from middle-class backgrounds. They had information about dodging the draft. Just because of my background, being lucky enough to be born into a situation where I had the information to get up here, some guy from a poor family went in my place and got his head blown off. I feel bad about that, but I'm not tormented by it. It's a common feeling. I've counseled probably twelve thousand war objectors. The majority of people had those feelings, a kind of guilt.

Deserters were [different. They were] often disowned by their families. Many of them had never been away from home. They always had a rougher time in Canada. Generally the draft dodgers were people from college who had some work experience. The deserters were mainly from conservative, lower-middle-class backgrounds. Of course there's also been some guys who deserted after two tours of Vietnam who probably don't have that kind of guilt feeling.

People always say, "Well, what if somebody was attacking your daughter?" That's really difficult. I think I'd defend my person, my self, but there was actually one time when I didn't. I was accosted by two guys in an attempted robbery in a shopping center parking lot five years ago. I said, "I'm not going to fight you." One of them hit and kicked me a couple of times. I finally broke away. I refused to fight back. Or, "Would you fight for Canada?" A lot of people are selective C.O.'s. There are war objectors who would fight for Canada. But I don't believe in any war. It's the only defensible stance.

———————◆———————

Though he was born and raised in Milwaukee, LARRY KIEWIT, *who went AWOL from the Army and defected to Canada rather than go to Vietnam, now speaks in the measured accents of western Canada. A self-employed house painter, he lives in Surrey, British Columbia.*

I was in training at Fort Rucker, Alabama, to be a helicopter door gunner. I hadn't yet been ordered to go to Vietnam, but it just didn't seem to make much sense to fight for democracy for people, probably the great majority of whom do not know what the word means. It didn't matter to them who would be in power, they'd still be going to the field every day. Communists or capitalists don't make much difference to them. I went AWOL in 1968 and got to Canada in the fall.

I have no second thoughts. It was something that was happening at that time. America is a fantastic place, a great place to live. But occasionally, the people, they make a mistake. I have no feelings that in missing Vietnam I missed out on my generation's rite of passage. One reason is that when I first came here I associated mainly with Americans who were here for the same reason. Now I don't. I think a lot of the guys went home again.

I don't have any bitterness. Over the years things more or less have worked out OK. As far as being away from my family, there are a lot of people who do this through being transferred in business. It did force a big change, but it by no means turned out to be disastrous. I'm pretty much established here now. I became a Canadian citizen in 1975. I own a home, I'm married to a Canadian, I have my own house-painting and decorating business. When Canadians do find out my background, they don't care. Many of them say they would have done the same thing themself.

There were several times I got home to Milwaukee between 1969 and 1981 without incident. Then, in the fall of 1981, I was pulled over at the border. An hour later I was in jail in handcuffs in Bellingham, Washington. There was some type of amnesty which Jimmy Carter had started, and I could get my name cleared. I felt that accepting an amnesty was sort of an admission that I'd committed a crime. I didn't feel I had. I was in the Fort Lewis stockade for two weeks and then spent four weeks at Fort Ord. I was completely cleared and got my discharge papers. It was an expensive pain. My wife came down to be with me. The hotel bills were huge.

If it hadn't been for Vietnam, I would most likely be living and working in the American Midwest. It's a nice place to live. I'd much rather see my family more often—I see them at least once a year, either my going there or they coming here. Other than that there's really not much I miss about the States. If it wasn't for cablevision I'd probably miss American football.

———◆———

CHARLES LITEKY

It was the creative act of Father Daniel Berrigan in pouring his blood on the draft files that first motivated me to question the war. I respected him. I had never met him, but my brother had. And when somebody you respect does something outside of your value system it makes you take another look. That's what happened to me. I was in Vietnam when he did that. The next Sunday I went to a day of recollection in Saigon with priests from all over that area—they'd come in and have a meal together and pray. These were American chaplains, and it was our way of getting some community. I was sitting next to a Jesuit and he started talking about Berrigan and he says, "I hope they hang the son of a bitch." I said, "What are you talking about?" The guy says, "He's broken the law of the land." Now this is a Jesuit priest and by and large they're pretty smart people and I just couldn't get over that. So he's broken the law. Is the law of our land sacrosanct? And I began to think more about what was going on.

After my second tour ended I went to Fort Bragg, North Carolina. I had already received the Congressional Medal of Honor and, having been the only chaplain in Vietnam to receive it alive—there were two or three others who got it posthumously—I was invited to do a lot of speaking. I was struggling with what we were doing over there and all the opposition—Berrigan, Jane Fonda going to Hanoi. My head was going round and round but I still hung on defending our position with the traditional Catholic, "Just War" theory.

While I was still at Bragg I was invited to give a talk at Manhattan College in New York, a Catholic college. They had a class on peace and they wanted me to come and give the military position and talk about being a chaplain. I went and I wore my uniform. By that time I was a major. And I was the only one there supporting the war. And these kids started asking me a lot of the same questions I'm asking people in Washington now about Central America—the morality of it all. And I kept coming back to the "Just War" theory. A couple of them got pretty angry but we did have a dialogue. And when I got home the professor wrote me a letter. He thanked me for coming and then said, "I don't think you're going to solve your own dilemma until you rise above the assumptions of your subculture." At the time I hadn't enough sociology to even know what he was talking about.

But I started thinking about it. I was born in America, into a military family and a military church, so I really hadn't questioned things. But I started to do some reading and I realized I had just assumed so many things that had been taught me by the church and the country and the government. It was from my reading that I understood we never had to go in there in the first place. That we, the great democrats, were the ones that torpedoed the elections in 1956 because eighty percent of the people would have voted for Ho Chi Minh. I hadn't known about Ho Chi Minh asking the United States for help after the Second World War, or that we picked up where the French left off and tried to prop up Diem, who represented ten percent of the population, or that there was a subterfuge to get the Catholics out of the North and down to the South—that they were told they were going to be martyred so we could transport them from the North to the South with the U.S. Navy. And finally I said [of the government position], "Do I really believe these things? is this really so?" And I ended up leaving the Army and leaving the priesthood.

I didn't want to stay in the military because the military mind, I found, was not very open. They're very provincial and circumscribed in their thinking. Of course I was struggling also with my vocation to the priesthood every bit as much as I was struggling with the Vietnam War, and it was very difficult for me to finally leave. That's one of the reasons Vietnam was so late in hitting me: It was a far greater decision for me to leave the priesthood than to leave the service. It took me three times before I was finally able to do it.

———————•———————

CASPAR WEINBERGER *served Richard Nixon and Gerald Ford as Director of the Office of Management and Budget, and later as Secretary of Health, Education and Welfare. It was his knife that took the "peace dividend" out of the Pentagon's hide as American troops left the war zone. That was an act he rectified with a vengeance after he returned to Washington in 1981 as Ronald Reagan's Secretary of Defense. He seems headed toward a record tenure in the Pentagon in length of service as well as outlays. Yet curiously, his perception of the Vietnam experience has made him far more cautious about the use of military power than any other senior aide to Ronald Reagan—a feeling illuminated by his running public debate with Secretary of State George Shultz.*

I suppose the most vivid memory I have of Vietnam was the reception of the troops coming back to San Francisco and the really terrible way they were received, with pickets and boos and all of that, because of the unpopularity of the war. The thing that struck me was the basic unfairness of taking that out on people who had participated in it, suffered very greatly, and had done a very good job and had not been supported sufficiently to win.

This carried over even to the reception of the very young infants and children who were brought from the nurseries and the hospitals in the days just before the end of the Vietnam War for safer-keeping, so to speak, in the United States. And the demonstrations against these infants were because they were Vietnamese and they were a visible reminder of the war.

I was in the government then, in HEW, but I came home from time to time to San Francisco, and I came home once for the specific purpose of looking over the facilities that were being made ready at the Presidio [an Army headquarters] not as a military thing but to receive these refugees, these orphans, these children of the war that had been brought from camps that were getting into the war zone at that time.

This was a couple of months before it ended, and at the Presidio they were taking old buildings, warehouses, and doing various sanitary precautions and then putting in cots and sheets and blankets and getting volunteers from the community to help. I looked over the facilities and found them extremely good. And there was a bunch of pickets outside, booing and jeering as these little children were carried in.

It was a pretty vivid recollection. I don't know if that happened in other parts of the country. It was a terrible period in our history when we had that kind of demonstration against people who had nothing whatever to do with the war except to suffer. And it was an indication of what length people would go to demonstrate their anger against that kind of war. Utterly illogical, terribly unfair, and yet there it was.

———————•———————

GEORGE S. PATTON III

I was so busy in Vietnam that I had not been affected by the dissidents in the United States. But as soon as I returned, I was hit in the face by it. When I arrived in the United States at Travis Air Force Base in April of 1969, I went into the ticket office to arrange air travel to the East Coast, where my family was awaiting me. While I was in there, my sergeant major came in and said there was a disturbance out in the yard. I asked what it was and he said there were some dissidents out there throwing mud and human waste on the three coffins that had been with us on the aircraft. They contained three men who had been killed in action, and their coffins were draped with the American flag. You should print that. I was absolutely shocked, as you can imagine.

———————•———————

GRAHAM MARTIN

I spent half my time in the July of '73 to April thirtieth of '75 period back here working either in the Administration or up on the [Capitol] Hill. That's where the battle was, on the Hill. The Administration request for fiscal '75 [aid to Vietnam] was for a billion six. It was cut before it went in to a billion one. The authorization was passed for a billion one by the Congress. Then they went back for the appropriation. Now, your peace movement comes in, and amendment on the floor cut it by [another] three hundred million. It went on to the Senate and they just didn't bother about it. Kissinger was engaged in the Middle East or something—anyway the State Department and the Pentagon weren't successful in getting it back in.

In State they were worn out, I guess, in fighting this damn peace movement. It was getting pretty violent and vicious. They could see what was happening to me because I was speaking out, and so the people in the Bureau of Far Eastern Affairs were just scared to death of it. They just didn't ever bother to answer any of it. So when you're a congressman and you get all these well meaning people coming in from your district, and nothing [from the Administration] which gives you either a counterpressure in the national interest or a reason to explain to your people when you go against what your constituents want, you vote the other way. It's not all that important to you as an individual.

How much of the antiwar movement at that point do you think was orchestrated from Hanoi or the Soviet Union?

I've always hesitated to ascribe motives. I told you earlier about my intelligence background. I was never really away from it, ever. I have many friends in the French services, the Italian services, the British services. The CIA, far better than you think, really did not fool around with Americans abroad. So I finally got the French, who do watch this kind of thing, to begin to give me things about Cora Weiss, the Rockefeller church, Coffin's church, [Fred] Branfman [of the Indochina Resources Center in Washington], all these people coming to Paris for meetings. They would tell me who was there, who the North Vietnamese were, and basically things that were decided, the kinds of things these people would go back and push. *But, but.* These people would argue that what they were doing was patriotic. This was all legal, you see. These Americans thought Vietnam *ought* to win.

———————————•———————————

RICHARD HOLBROOKE

Let me make a point which to me is central to the political legacy of Indochina, and it is a point that galls me above all others. I spent three and a half years in Vietnam and I spent another three and a half years working on the war when I was in Washington, not counting when I was assistant secretary of state. Seven years of my life. I got shot at. I believed in the process at first. I saw it wouldn't work. I have no quarrel with America's objective out there. It was a valid objective.

But the latter-day hawks, who win the Tet offensive every time they go to a seminar in the 1980s, by and large are people who weren't there and have no right to criticize those of us who spent years fighting that war and trying to make it work. It's easy to be a hawk in the 1980s and win the war at a dinner party or in a lecture. George Will with his pompous and arrogant attacks on people who he thinks didn't stand up for America—where was he when a lot of us got shot at? And where were Dick Perle and Richard Burt and Pat Buchanan and David Stockman and Norman Podhoretz—or Rambo Sylvester Stallone, for that matter? Stallone was teaching English at a school for the children of the rich in Geneva, Switzerland. Stockman was hiding out in Pat Moynihan's garage at Harvard as a divinity student.* Yet they have made it appear that the war was lost by the people who were in fact the ones who had the courage to say "There's something *wrong* here. It isn't working."

These are the guys who go around saying "If only we would've been tough we could have held on, and you guys wimped out"; that the press and the Congress lost us the war. This is the Nixon argument. And it's utter nonsense. The press didn't lose the war for us. Congress didn't lose the war for us. The war was lost because the strategy was wrong. The military lost the war; the political leadership of this country lost the war; Lyndon Johnson, I regret to say since I served in his White House, and Richard Nixon and Henry Kissinger are the men who cost us this thing. Not the Cooper-Church Amendment, not David Halberstam and Walter Cronkite, and not the antiwar demonstrators.

Now one of the things that makes this so difficult is that some of the opponents of the war did inexcusable things. They burned American flags. They waved Communist flags. They saw in the Viet Cong and the North Vietnamese attributes of nobility and decency and revolutionary fervor which were not there; in fact we were dealing with a brutal, ruthless enemy. And they demeaned the United States. Raising the Viet Cong flag over the Peace Corps headquarters was an obscene act. And Jane Fonda's behavior in Hanoi was inexcusable. And the accusation that people like McNamara and Rusk were war criminals was grotesquely unfair. But the distastefulness of some of the antiwar demonstrations does not change the fact that that war was not lost, as Nixon always likes to write, in the halls of Congress and on the pages of *The New York Times*; it was lost in the rice paddies of Indochina.

---

*Buchanan was writing editorials in St. Louis, and later campaigning and working for Richard Nixon; Perle was an aide to Sen. Henry Jackson Podhoretz, much too old to have served, was editing *Commentary* magazine.

CHAPTER ELEVEN

Watergate and Vietnam

IF the South Vietnamese felt abandoned when their time of reckoning finally arrived in the spring of 1975, the emotion was justifiable. The final offensive was one of only two occasions in the Vietnam War when the kind of power the United States liked best—massive air strikes that could inflict maximum damage at minimum cost in American lives—might have been used to good military effect. As in 1972, when a conventional offensive across the DMZ had in fact been rolled back by air power, once again the enemy was out in the open, concentrated in large conventional formations and making heavy use of armor and artillery. But this time no jets flew and no bombs fell. Vietnam had led to Watergate, which poisoned the American political bloodstream. The giant was prone on the world stage, paralyzed by the domestic consequences of a distant war. In a sense, the politics of Vietnam had come full circle.

The thread of events that led the war effort to self-destruct is sinuous, but not impossible to untangle. By the time Richard Nixon took office in 1969, domestic opposition to the war had left the United States no real alternative but to cut casualties by withdrawing its forces. Like Lyndon Johnson, however, Nixon had no intention of being the first President to lose a war. Nixon and his national security adviser, Henry Kissinger, therefore, devised a three-pronged strategy: As American troops went home, the Vietnamese would be retrained and rearmed to take their places. As the Vietnamese became more capable, the U.S. would begin a serious effort to negotiate an armistice in Paris. To protect South Vietnam while this process was going forward—and to maintain a credible threat of renewed intervention against Communist transgressions—Nixon and Kissinger secretly escalated American bombing. U.S. planes renewed limited air attacks against southern North Vietnam under the guise of "protective reaction" against antiaircraft sites that fired on American reconnaissance missions. Air operations against the Ho Chi Minh Trail were beefed up—and the Air Force also launched a secret campaign by B-52 bombers against Hanoi's military base camps across the border in Cambodia.

It was that decision—to make peace in public and more war in private—which began the unraveling of Richard Nixon. Like the other clandestine wars, the bombing campaign was to be kept secret not from the Communists, who could hardly help knowing about it since they were the targets, but from the American public, where any open escalation was judged likely to create a new firestorm of protest. But as with most military developments in Vietnam, the secret of the Cambodian bombing proved highly perishable. Less than four months after Nixon's inauguration, Pentagon correspondent William Beecher gave an account of it on page one of *The New York Times*. That leak, following on several others, put Nixon and Kissinger in high dudgeon. Through FBI Director J. Edgar Hoover they ordered a major program of wiretaps aimed at several of Kissinger's aides on the NSC, among them Morton Halperin, and at a number of journalists as well. The aim was merely to uncover the source of the leaks, which the program failed to do. But a far more important effect was to establish at the highest level a tolerance of unethical acts in the name of national security.

That came home to roost a year later, when the *Times* began publishing a series of articles based on the Pentagon Papers, a twelve-volume official history of the war written from (and reproducing many) top-secret documents. The history had been constructed, beginning in the summer of 1967 on the orders of Robert McNamara, who had soured on the war and begun preparing to leave the government. Three years later reporter Neil Sheehan, who had been a member of the much-criticized press corps in Saigon during the Diem days seven years earlier, was given a copy of the history by a Rand Corporation analyst named Daniel Ellsberg, who had worked on it and who had also been a longtime associate and sometime employee of Kissinger. Although the history contained very little that was still truly secret, it was bound to strengthen the increasingly violent opposition to the war. Ellsberg's involvement compounded the problem, because his connection with Kissinger had given him access to many other Administration secrets about Vietnam.

All that sent Nixon and Kissinger into a panic. Nixon ordered creation of the so-called Plumbers Unit, whose task was to plug the leak by finding material that could be used to defame Ellsberg. He also gave orders to another aide, Charles Colson, to retrieve from the Brookings Institution, a liberal Washington think tank, the only existing copy of a Johnson-era paper on the bombing of North

Vietnam—"surreptitiously," if necessary. Colson and his subordinates hatched a scheme to divert attention while they did their dirty
work by fire-bombing Brookings. The plot was never executed, but
it summed up the total disdain for law and order that by then infect-
ed the White House.

The Plumbers Unit included E. Howard Hunt, Gordon Liddy, Egil
Krogh, and a Kissinger aide named David Young who had played a
minor role in the wiretap affair. Hunt, a former CIA agent, Liddy,
and several Cubans who had CIA links dating back to the Bay of
Pigs, went to Los Angeles and broke into the office of Ellsberg's
psychiatrist. They planned to go on to his residence before they were
ordered to stop. A year later Hunt, Liddy, and several of the same
Cubans were caught in the burglary of the Democratic National Committee offices at the Watergate office building. They had been trying
to gather evidence that might be used to undercut the Democrats
during the impending presidential campaign. Realizing that White
House complicity in the earlier burglary in Los Angeles might be
exposed, Nixon and his aides began plotting the coverup for which
the House Judiciary Committee eventually voted articles of impeachment.

It was the fall of Nixon that brought the story circling back to its
origin. The President's ability to continue supporting the Saigon government had already been severely weakened by congressional imposition of an absolute ban on American bombing in Indochina, and
by the War Powers Act, which limited to sixty days any combat
commitment of troops overseas without congressional approval. Now
the legislators also slashed military aid to South Vietnam. Reading
the signals, Hanoi decided the time had come to launch a probing
attack that would test the American reaction. When none came, the
final offensive began.

———————◆———————

MORTON HALPERIN

I first met Kissinger in 1960. We were together at Harvard and were
colleagues at the Center for International Affairs, where we both
had our offices. We were both in the Government Department and
we taught a course together for four years, called "National Security Policy," a graduate seminar. I went to the Pentagon in '66. I
expected to spend my life teaching and I thought I should get to
Washington for a year or two just to see what the process was like.
But I was still in touch with Kissinger—we tried to persuade him to
be a consultant on the Pentagon Papers, and in fact I spoke at

Kissinger's last class at Harvard. And it was when I went up to do that, that we talked about my going to work for him [in the NSC].

As far as I could tell, Kissinger and Nixon wanted to stay in Vietnam indefinitely and recognized that they had to cut back the degree of U.S. involvement, which meant the number of Americans and the level of the fighting, in order to get public support for a permanent U.S. involvement. And that they set about by slowly taking the troops out, and slowly trying to negotiate a way to maintain enough of a presence in Vietnam to keep the government in power, but not so much as to engender continuing political controversy in the United States. That's the line they were trying to take.

But weren't they also escalating the war?

The escalation was part of it. To persuade the North Vietnamese not to step up their involvement as we withdrew ours, they had to persuade them that the response would be the destruction of North Vietnam. And so the process of escalation was designed to make credible the fact that so long as the President was withdrawing American forces and reducing American casualties, he could get away with other forms of escalation. They succeeded to some extent in keeping the initial escalation secret in order not to accelerate the pressure in the United States for withdrawal.

And I think that if not for Watergate, the policy would have worked. I don't think the North Vietnamese would have given up, but I think they would not have invaded. They would have proceeded much more slowly. It would have been a much longer, much more complicated process that would have gone beyond Nixon's second term. Because I think they would have tested and Nixon would have resumed the bombing, and I think he would have gotten away with it.

The threat, which I think they meant to carry out, was of massive bombing, even the destruction of North Vietnam. They had threatened and were planning to do what we did in North Korea and which used to be done, which is you bomb civilian targets for the purpose of destroying civilian targets. And I think faced with that the North would have held back and said we'll let this one go by and we'll do it three years from now.

Didn't the uproar over the leak of the Cambodian bombing precipitate formation of the Plumbers Unit?

That's a compression of events. The Cambodian bombing led to the wiretap program, and to an atmosphere of tracking down leaks in various illegal ways. But the Plumbers were not created until the [leak of the] Pentagon Papers. We now know that [the story about the bombing] produced a lot of phone conversations between Hoover and Kissinger. But as far as I could see it was a short uproar and nothing happened. Nobody else picked up the story and it went away. Three or four years later the Senate held hearings in which it was announced that we had bombed Cambodia and everybody treated it like a great secret.

But there had been previous leaks they had been concerned with as well, and when this one occurred, it was the limit. You know all Presidents go through periods in which they are very concerned about leaks. The Reagan White House is in one of them right now. And I think wiretapping seemed natural to Nixon. I think that it was Nixon who ordered the program, saying we better do something about this, and Kissinger responded by picking the people to wiretap.

Kissinger I think was protecting himself by showing that he was willing to wiretap his own staff. But it didn't make any sense because many more people in the Pentagon knew about the [Cambodian] bombing than people on the NSC staff. And of the people that Kissinger picked to be wiretapped in that initial stage, most didn't know about the bombing at all. I knew something about it, but not a lot. There was a lot of information in the article [in which the leak was published] which I didn't know and which Kissinger knew I didn't know. And two other people that Kissinger wiretapped in the first stage, Daniel Davidson and Hal Sonnenfeldt, did not know about it at all.

That's why I think he was protecting himself. The three of us were the three people who had served in the Democratic Administration, who were believed to be Democrats—although I was a Republican— and who people were suspicious of because they were thought to be soft in some way; soft on the war in particular or soft in general. And those were also the three people he had known from other relationships. And he knew people were suspicious of us, and I think it is not a coincidence that those are the three people he picked to be wiretapped.

I had supervised the production of the Pentagon Papers while I was working for John McNaughton, who was McNamara's Assistant Secretary for International Security Affairs. McNamara sent his military assistant to see McNaughton to say that he wanted what he called an encyclopedic study of the war done and he wanted it done in six weeks and he left it to McNaughton to figure out how to do it. McNaughton asked me to do a memo to McNamara laying down how to do it. I proposed in the memo that I devote full time to the study but McNamara wanted me available for other things. And at that point Les Gelb was working for me on the Policy Planning Staff in ISA,* so he took on the project.

We recruited people to work on them from every place that we could.

*International Security Affairs, The Pentagon's "Little State Department."

We tried to persuade a colonel named Haig, who I had never met before, to spend the summer working on them, unsuccessfully as it turned out. One of the places we went was to organizations where we had contracts to do research and suggested that they provide a couple of people, and Rand produced a few people including Dan Ellsberg to work on the study. I had known Ellsberg before. I became a consultant to the Rand Corporation in 1960, and I went out there fairly often. I skimmed through some of them, but I actually didn't have time to read the Pentagon Papers until 1970, when I went out to Rand for the summer and read the set that was out there. That was the set that Ellsberg had.

When you did finally read them did you recognize then that there was a potential for a lot of damage?

Well I don't think there was. I think the Pentagon Papers had some important insights in them, but nothing overwhelmingly startling. The reason they got all that attention was that the government went after them. If the government had just let *The New York Times* publish them, they would have come out and gone away. I hate to use a Watergate phrase, but there's no smoking gun. The closest to it is the clear indication in '65 that the Vietnamese vigorously opposed the introduction of American troops, and the so-called request for them from the Vietnamese government was made up.

Given that, why do you think there was this reaction in the Administration?

Everything we know suggests that it was Kissinger screaming and yelling because he knew—as nobody else did—that it was Ellsberg [who leaked them], that he had brought Ellsberg in as a consultant to him, that Ellsberg had had access to defense materials—and he suspected what turned out to be true, that Ellsberg had at least one Nixon administration document, the so-called NSSM-1* response. And I think he was determined to get out front and show that he was as angry about this as anybody else, before people discovered that it was Dan Ellsberg who had done it, and that Dan Ellsberg had a link to him.

---◆---

RICHARD HOLBROOKE

My involvement in the Pentagon Papers started in early '67, when I was working for Komer at the White House. Les Gelb came to see me. Gelb had recently gone to the Pentagon and he and I had been

---

*National Security Study Memorandum, a document produced by the National Security Council staff, in this case a document laying out the Nixon administration's strategy in Vietnam.

friends. I believe I was the first person he talked to. He'd never been to Vietnam—never been there to this day. The world's greatest Vietnam expert who doesn't know what it looks like. And he said, "I got this peculiar request from McNamara to collect all this information. We've been given this list of a hundred questions. This is to do a full study. We're going to have full access." And he showed me the questions. We looked at them, we divided them into groups, we started to talk about names for a task force.

When Komer went back to Vietnam in the summer of '67, he asked me to return with him, but I really didn't want to go right back. I'd kind of had it with Vietnam, and Les asked if I would work on this. So I began to commute to the Pentagon and was part of the team which included a lot of very talented people and some not so talented people. Pete Dawkins worked with us briefly, Bill Kaufmann of MIT, and, of course, a brilliant fellow from Rand named Dan Ellsberg.

I had known Ellsberg since Saigon. I had a discussion with him once in which I said, "Dan, instead of being a gadfly you should take some line responsibility." He said, "No, no. That's not the way I work. I like to be a special assistant to people who have authority. I want to influence them that way." You've got to remember who Dan Ellsberg was, because he's become such a controversial person. He was one of the most highly regarded game theorists in the United States. He was a close colleague of Henry Kissinger's, something Kissinger now denies. Ellsberg was part of that intellectual group which included Tom Schelling and other people of the Cambridge group, who were most highly regarded intellectually. They all knew that in brain power he was their match. But there was some judgmental quality that was missing.

We sat in the back room behind McNamara's office in room 3E8O, using all the files available in the Pentagon. Ben Reed, who was executive secretary of the State Department, authorized us access to everything at State, including his files and Bill Bundy's files. We restructured the questions into coherent issues and we assigned them out and we did these reports. I remember vividly McNamara telling us that our involvement would be a secret forever and that the papers would go only to a handful of people under the tightest controls. My project wasn't one of the sexier volumes. I wrote "The Pacification Effort, '64–'67," and I learned probably more about how policy works there than anywhere else because I was looking from the top down at the same things I had lived out from the bottom up.

Afterward I went back to State, worked for Katzenbach, was assigned to the Paris talks, and in 1970, went to Morocco as Peace Corps director. One day, I was driving down the street in my Jeep

Wagoneer, picked up the *Herald Tribune* at a corner tobacco shop in Rabat, saw this story, and knew immediately what it was. I turned to the Peace Corps volunteers who were with me and I said, "This is an amazing thing, something I worked on." And I said to myself, "How did it get in the newspapers? Dan Ellsberg!" Two or three months earlier I had been in the States and I had gone to see Katzenbach, and said to him, "Nick, those things we worked on are a time bomb and Bob McNamara is the man who looked worst in them. Does he understand this?" And Nick said to me, he said, "Dear Bob, he just can't bring himself to read them." I said, "You better think about these papers. Something's going to happen. I hear rumors that they're more widely circulated than people said they would be."

I understand that Ellsberg personally peddled them to a number of people [before giving them to *The New York Times*]. He went to Fulbright, he went to other people. Ellsberg had even been to Morocco a few months earlier and we had a very weird conversation which at the time I couldn't understand. He said, "Don't you think something should be done about the war?" And I said, "Well, what are you talking about?" [He said] "I don't know," and then he mentioned the study and said, "Don't you think something should be done with the study?" I said, "No, I certainly don't." I forgot all about it.

Then this explosion happened and the State Department security people came out to Morocco to interview me about that trip. They knew he'd been there and I remember them saying that they were operating on the theory that Ellsberg might have dropped in on his way to Algeria, where he was making contact with leftists of one sort or another. Well, this was the Nixon era and unknown to any of us, this same incident was going to lead to Watergate through the break-in of Ellsberg's psychiatrist's office. So there was this extraordinary moment in our history, where Vietnam in its last horrible phase is a spark which leads to the creation of the Plumbers and to the downfall of Nixon. And it all came together in this weird set of accidents.

Well, there is a wonderful circularity about this because it is then Watergate and the limits that it imposes on presidential power that makes it impossible for the United States to respond in '75 when the North Vietnamese finally come rolling down the pike with eleven divisions.

That's right. If you read Nixon's long early explanation [of Watergate] you will see the linkage clearly: That Ellsberg triggered his myths, which were the [Alger] Hiss myths; that in his mind this justified the extra-legal actions; and that those extra-legal actions then extended into other areas. I to this day find it really mind-boggling that

Dan Ellsberg, who was an unguided missile—a man of enormous analytical skill but very little judgment—could have found himself accidentally as the triggering mechanism for events which would link Vietnam and Watergate in one continuous 1961-to-1975 story. You see it clearly, I see it clearly. Very few people understand it because it involves a study of casualities, but there's no question about it. This is not some abstract theory about the Italian Renaissance. This really is what happened.

———————•———————

JOHN LINDSAY covered Congress and politics for Newsweek *for more than twenty years and earned a reputation as a keenly perceptive and extremely well-connected reporter. His circle of acquaintances included the Kennedys and Richard Nixon. He was intimately involved in the magazine's coverage of Watergate. He is now semi-retired, but does occasional special articles for the magazine.*

Nobody had any insight at all in the beginning that the Watergate burglary had grown out of the paranoias of the Vietnam war. Only later did we begin to see that. If we had to bet on paranoias at that time, we would have bet that it grew out of paranoias that Richard Nixon carried as part of his political baggage from the beginning of his career. But I think it's very, very clear that those circles of paranoia met at one particular moment in 1970 and carried through the summer of 1971, and I think the genesis of Watergate was there.

If I had to put my finger on it, I'd say that the personal breaking point for Richard Nixon came in San Jose during the 1970 [congressional] campaign. The antiwar demonstrations were beginning to pick up. He was taunted and in response to the taunt he jumped up on the hood of a car and gave them the V for Victory sign. At this point he suddenly realized that something strange was happening: that a President of the United States—he believed for the first time ever—was actually being pelted physically with stones, vegetables, grapefruits, anything that was at hand. He went on to San Clemente that night and he brooded about this very much and he said, by God that "this pack of thugs and hoodlums" as he called them two days later in Phoenix, would not imprison the President of the United States in the White House.

From that point forward, his animus and his paranoias were triggered beyond what they normally were; he came unbuttoned. Following that you had that enormous concatenation of happenings in February, March, April, June, and July of 1971, starting with the invasion of Laos by the ARVN. It was a failure, and pressures began to build up politically in the States. Lieutenant Calley's conviction* came out in March, with a big folderol, very emotional on both sides.

In May, two hundred thousand demonstrators came to Washington. I was in the White House. They had transit company buses that circled the White House like it's the Little Big Horn, and any person, I think, under the circumstances would be inclined to believe that there's somebody out there trying to get them. And given Nixon's emotional and psychological apparatus, his response was he knew bloody well who it was, and it was the leftist, eastern establishment. These people were running around trying to force the President into imprisonment in the White House, and here he was, imprisoned by O. Roy Chalk's† buses. And then, on top of this came in June, the big one, the one that broke the back, and that's the Pentagon Papers.

It's been said many times since, that Richard Nixon did not realize that he had a political decision to make here. Mel Laird, who was secretary of defense, told them they could probably declassify ninety-five percent of it. But Nixon concentrated on the five—and also on the figure and the persona, Ellsberg himself. Ellsberg had been with the Rand Corporation; Ellsberg had worked for Henry Kissinger. Kissinger was berserk at this point, pointing out to Nixon that Ellsberg was a real loose cannon; that he had all kinds of military information, plus our fallback position—various scenarios on how we would or would not deal with the war in Vietnam or with the whole Southeast Asia problem. To make matters worse, at this point J. Edgar Hoover had decided after forty years of black bag jobs that the FBI wasn't going to do it anymore. And that drove Nixon up the wall. And Nixon also found out—it was leaked to him—that Ellsberg's father-in-law, a fellow by the name of Marx, was a good personal friend of Hoover. That fed the paranoia that there's a conspiracy going on.

Then John Mitchell came clanking in at one point in June to whisper to Nixon that before *The New York Times* published the Pentagon Papers, a copy of it had been presented to the Soviet Embassy in Washington. From Nixon's standpoint, coming from his own attorney general, he was perfectly willing to believe it. And a month later, in the midst of the furor over the Pentagon Papers court case, Nixon was reminded by somebody that in 1969 they had sought to get the full report on Lyndon Johnson's decision to halt bombing during the 1968 campaign. Nixon wanted it for political reasons, and

---

*Calley's unit, on his orders, carried out the My Lai massacre.
†Owner of the D.C. Transit Company.

he had found out back in 1969–1970, that he couldn't get it because the Brookings Institution had the copies.

And when he was reminded of it, he went berserk. This left-wing think tank has a copy of Lyndon Johnson's decision on bombing and the President of the United States couldn't get it? He went up the wall. And that was the genesis of the effort to fire-bomb Brookings. This was all testified to at the time in the Watergate hearings, but in his memoirs, Nixon pointed out that he was going to get this paper, he didn't care how—and even if it had to be done, and he uses a marvelous word, "surreptitiously."

He spoke to [White House aide Charles] Colson about this. Colson denies they were going to fire-bomb Brookings but there were enough persons involved who got the orders that they were going to get this even if it requires fire-bombing, that you could see how this thing began to develop. In addition to which, they were within a month of Kissinger's secret visit to Peking. The North Vietnamese were meeting with us in Paris at that time and it looked as though the talks were making some progress until the Pentagon Papers hit. Nixon still to this day attributes the slow-down of the negotiations to the fact the North Vietnamese were saying "Maybe this will weaken their resolve, weaken their support, and we can get a better deal."

So in July of 1971, within perhaps days of all this, John Ehrlichman was told to set up a private group that would deal with leaks and that was Egil Krogh, Howard Hunt, [Gordon] Liddy, and one other fellow, David Young, who had worked in Kissinger's office. Within a few weeks of that, on Labor Day, they were in Dr. Fielding's* office. Now, the earlier wiretaps could have been justified. Nixon to this day says there were fewer wiretaps done in his administration then were done under Bobby Kennedy. But there's no justification for the Ellsberg break-in. And that is what led to the recklessness, the attitude of anything in the name of national security. Nixon saw all this as a threat to his conduct of the war.

The emotional quality of this was terribly important. Nixon was going around the White House saying he wanted X done and he didn't care how it was done; he wanted Y done and he didn't care how it was done. This was in connection with the Brookings Institution papers and finding out who the hell Ellsberg was. It was "We have got to find out and we have got to stop this man." From Nixon's viewpoint this was utterly justifiable and in his memoirs, which very few people have read, unfortunately, he's laid it out from his standpoint very, very clearly: The ability to govern was being undermined

---

*Ellsberg's psychiatrist.

by Ellsberg and his friends. He had to go to the mat on a matter of principle.

Some wise man once said that you need only one real good reason to do anything. During this period he was marshaling five or six a day to get it done, and the instructions to the Plumbers Unit were very, very clear: Nixon was told personally there was a way to get at Ellsberg that would be far, far superior to the psychological profile material the CIA had been asked to present, and that was to break into the office of Ellsberg's psychiatrist, Dr. Fielding. Nixon wanted Ellsberg destroyed and he was going to go to any length to do it.

Now, the Plumbers had already planned to go from Fielding's office to Fielding's apartment and a call was made to Ehrlichman that they'd already made their sally into the office and Ehrlichman's response was that this was insane. "Get that crowd out of there." And Nixon and Haldeman in their memoirs both point out that in 1976, Haldeman was visiting Nixon in San Clemente and Nixon said there were a few things he wanted to clear up. And what he really wanted to find out was what his own involvement was in turning the Plumbers loose on Ellsberg and Fielding's office.

And Haldeman interpreted this to mean that "For God's sake, this fellow was asking me to tell him whether he ordered the Fielding break-in." Ehrlichman's response to that was very interesting. He was in jail at the time and it was communicated to him by Haldeman. And he suddenly realized that Nixon was acknowledging much deeper involvement in the preplanning of that Fielding break-in than had come out. And Ehrlichman said, "I had not signed off on it even though they say I did. I did not, but I knew somebody had to and I testified on Capitol Hill as far as I knew Nixon didn't. So now I, who am sitting in jail because of that break-in, realize the fellow that ordered it was sitting out at San Clemente."

All of which leads up to the frame of mind which I think developed there. Once the Fielding break-in took place, the felony had been committed and they were all very, very culpable. From that point on it seemed that all the brakes were off. It wasn't just a matter of being incautious. They lost all insight into what they were doing. Throughout the Watergate investigation, whenever anyone touched on this subject, Nixon would tell them to stay away from it. Henry Peterson got onto it at one point at the Justice Department and Nixon blew up at him. He said, "You stay the hell out of that! That's national security."

And all this was done to find evidence that Ellsberg was a "Commie-queer," but it produced zip. The evidence wasn't there.

Exactly, but the deed had been done. Nixon later said many times that as far as he was concerned the Plumbers Unit was disbanded at that point. But *Nixon* wasn't disbanded at that point; he was running around screaming and demanding that something be done about this, that and the other thing. And after the Fielding break-in there was no psychological resistance to anything Nixon had in his mind. In fact, Nixon says in his memoirs the one good thing about Chuck Colson was if you let him know what needed to be done, you could walk out the door knowing it was going to be done. And John Ehrlichman conceded, "I didn't sign off on it, but what could I do after that? I didn't call the Beverly Hills police. I didn't do all the things that should have been done." This was a crime. It was done and it became part of the mentality of the Administration.

The other part directly connected with Vietnam is Kissinger's role. This has not been plumbed anywhere near as fruitfully as it might be and I think when the Nixon papers come out and the future tapes come out, you're going to have a much broader picture of Kissinger's role. Nixon felt that this was a coup to have this brilliant genius there helping him. And it's one thing to have a Chuck Colson come in saying "We've got to get these bastards," or to have John Ehrlichman coming and arching his eyebrows several times a second saying in a waspish kind of way that these people are getting away with murder. But it was quite another to have this distinguished member of the Eastern Establishment, an academician, a person who was able to do what Nixon could never do which was to calm the press, coming in every day saying "Mr. President, this is a terrible thing that is happening to us. We've got to stop this now in its tracks or we will destroy our country, destroy our administration, our place in history . . ."

Kissinger was on Nixon mercilessly during the spring, summer, and fall of 1971 to do something. "We've got to do something." It was materially above the level of what a Colson could influence him to do. Kissinger's constant complaints: "I'm going to Helsinki and this is undercutting the SALT talks"; "I'm going to Paris, this is undercutting our negotiations"; "I'm on my way to a secret meeting with China and they may look upon us as a paper tiger"; this kind of thing fed Nixon's macho to the point where almost anything that happened could be justified on the grounds of national security.

And it was pretty clear that since Nixon was interested in getting these things done, it became a matter of "We've got a problem. The CIA won't do it and J. Edgar Hoover's senile and he's got all these hangups and he's not going to help us. Therefore we're going to have to do it ourselves." And they easily came to the conclusion, without even thinking seriously about it, that it was all right to go on from what could be justified under some circumstances—the

Fielding break-in as an emergency involving national security—to the use of the Plumbers in politics. It was part and parcel of a kind of intolerant frame of mind these people had worked themselves into. It wasn't okay, but Nixon still thinks it was today.

To this day, I look back on it and try and put myself in Nixon's mentality. Here was a war that we had moved into under Kennedy, and then Lyndon Johnson carries us into the quagmire, and finally here's Nixon, hunkered down in the goddamn White House surrounded by Roy Chalk's buses and he's saying, in effect, "I am going to have to pay politically for what these bastards did." And Johnson had already paid politically but that's not what Nixon had in mind. But it goes back again to the mentality that led them into it. And as they sat there on June twenty-third* and made this sudden realization that Howard Hunt and Liddy must have been in Fielding's office, from that point forward, it was impossible to escape. They had to build a fortress. And it's amazing looking back on it, that ninety percent of the felonies of Watergate were committed in order to protect the Administration from having to disclose other felonies that had nothing at all to do with the DNC break in.

———————•———————

THOMAS POLGAR

Nixon was elected in 1968 partly on his promise that he had a secret plan to end the war. In fact, under Nixon, while the number of U.S. ground force personnel in Vietnam was diminished, the war was expanding into Cambodia, into Laos, and it was continuing. So they got pushed into a process of negotiations with the North Vietnamese where we got under great time pressure to deliver something before the next election, so nobody could say, "Hey, Nixon you didn't deliver." Nixon didn't know that McGovern is going to be as weak a candidate as he turned out to be, and he was completely obsessed with the need to get himself reelected, which led him to Watergate and pushed him into these negotiations with the North Vietnamese. We were not negotiating as hard as the North Vietnamese were, because Nixon's desire and Kissinger's desire to end the war was overwhelming.

In my opinion, the situation became ugly with Watergate. In 1973 Nixon says Peace with Honor. Everything is fine and it was a livable situation as long as Hanoi had the fear that if they act in bad

———————————————————————

*The date of the tape-recorded Oval Office conversation that provided the "smoking gun" evidence of Nixon's direct participation in the Watergate coverup, and led to his resignation.

faith, something terrible is going to happen to them. Now, you could argue that Watergate itself was at least in part a result of the psychology that was let loose here in the United States. You know, we had the riots in 1967, in '68. Nixon thought that he was sort of living in an embattled fortress in Washington with his own psychological insecurity and his feelings of inferiority. I don't want to get too deeply into the realm of psychology because that's not my field, but it seems to me that some of the things that Nixon was doing can be explained by the sense of threat that he acquired as part of the domestic protest against Vietnam. I think there was a sort of a symbiotic connection there.

And just so, I think a lot of the congressmen that voted against Vietnam were trying to punish Nixon. They couldn't punish him directly so they were taking it out on projects Nixon was in favor of. And there was no Vietnamese voting bloc in the United States. So if you didn't vote aid for Vietnam, there would be no domestic fallout for that, whereas if you don't vote aid for Israel, that has a domestic fallout.

And the consequences of Watergate ate away at the authority of Nixon's government. And this great animosity developed between the Nixon White House, including Kissinger, on one hand, and Congress on the other, and Congress started to whack away at the President's power. Nixon was beginning to lose credibility but still he had sufficient credibility that as long as he was in office, the North Vietnamese did not do anything decisively bad.

I was on home leave when Nixon resigned, in Cocoa, Florida, with the wife and kiddies. I watched the whole Watergate on television, and I'm growing very apprehensive because I see Nixon leaving and Mr. Ford coming in and Mr. Ford was not very vocal on the subject of Vietnam. And I said to myself, "They are going to read this in Hanoi. This is going to give them a few ideas." I got back to Vietnam in September and it was about the middle of October that we got word of the COSVN Resolution for 1975.

After Nixon's resignation the Politburo in Hanoi held a meeting and they decided "Fellows, the situation has changed. Let's reconsider our position." And then they passed a new resolution, which came into our hands just about the same day that the commander of the Communist forces in South Vietnam got it into his hands. It said that '75 is going to be the year of the great offensive, the decisive battle—and in '76 we are going to finish the job. And when I read the first account of that, I thought "This has a very familiar ring." So I asked my staff to go through the reports and sure enough we found a COSVN Resolution in 1971 which used very similar language, and that was the authorizing document for the 1972 offensive. And my people all said this means that there is going to be another general offensive. It's to me a very, very frightening document. So then we write a situation appraisal. Washington is sufficiently impressed so that they send out an interagency group with the participation of the Pentagon, the State Department, and CIA, and this group concludes that yes, it is likely there is going to be an offensive in 1975.

But by this time Schlesinger is Secretary of Defense and Schlesinger doesn't believe it. Why? Well, people don't like bad news and given the political situation in the United States, the financial pressures on the Administration, and the mood in Congress, Schlesinger, I think, instinctively feels that if there's going to be an offensive, then I Schlesinger, now have got to put my political future on the line and really go to bat. And I don't think he wanted to do that. And on the other hand you have Kissinger as Secretary of State. The year before he has accepted the Nobel Prize for having brought peace to Vietnam. How can he now say peace is not even not there, but it's going to be worse?

So the North Vietnamese have said to themselves, "Maybe we can try something. But let's not do anything too drastic because we still cannot be quite sure." So what they did is they mounted an attack in December and early January against a province capital called Phuoc Long. This Phuoc Long was about as unimportant in an intrinsic sense as you could imagine. But it had a symbolic importance. When the North Vietnamese took a South Vietnamese province capital and the United States did not react, that was the signal to enable them to decide that yes, we are going to go with a general offensive in 1975.

Look at the situation in the United States at that point. Nixon is out. For the first time in the history of the United States we have a President who was not elected by the people. The important leaders of the Republican party like Mitchell are facing trial on criminal charges, along with Ehrlichman and Haldeman, John Dean. The country is still reeling from the results of the Arab oil embargo in 1973, with the gas lines and so forth. The Republicans suffer a tremendous congressional defeat in the fall of 1974, so the authority of the government is very seriously undermined. Congress with an overwhelming majority has passed the bombing ban and cut into the warmaking powers of the President. And I, frankly, don't think that President Ford had the courage or the conviction to go back to Congress and say, "Now fellas, what we told you last year about peace with honor and all that, didn't quite work out. So now we've got to go back in."

Ford at least could have made some very strong noises threatening the North Vietnamese, and he could have used his channel to Brezhnev and said, "Look, we are talking about detente but we can't have detente if this goes on." But the trouble is that by January of 1975, Ford was thinking of running the next year for President. He wanted to establish himself as a man of peace. He needed to go to China. He needed to go to Vladivostok and meet with Brezhnev—and Vietnam was small potatoes. It all goes back to the loss of authority with the departure of Nixon. There was a famous German politician, Prince Bismarck, who once said that if you have authority you don't have to use force. The United States, having lost its authority, was in the position that it could only prevent by using force. But the internal political conditions would not have permitted.

———◆———

WILLIAM COLBY

Was there a circular process in which Vietnam created the conditions that led to Watergate, and Watergate then collapsed our position in Vietnam?

There are no single origins of things in foreign affairs, but certainly Vietnam was a major influence—the unpopularity of the war on not so much the death-and-destruction front as the futility front. To the ordinary American, the whole Vietnam thing seemed to be going nowhere. And the dismay over the war and the crowd control and problems like that and the tendency to see conspiracies and all of that, sure that had something to do with Watergate and that jackass Howard Hunt.

Now, Nixon had given Thieu a straight-out pledge that "If the North Vietnamese do not comply we will react with full force." Of course, a letter by a President has no significance at all in terms of whether you can actually act, and there are two reasons that that pledge could not be fulfilled.

One was that Congress didn't appropriate the money and the logistics went down to the extent that the Communists say that Thieu had to fight a poor man's war. If you train a foreign army to use American weapons and American tactics and then deprive them of American logistics, it just can't work. And this became obvious in that first attack at Phuoc Binh [the capital of Phuoc Long province]. Thieu did not respond, and that was the signal that the Communists felt, "Oh, wait a minute, this looks pretty promising." Now, their writings tell you, their plot was to attack in early '75 on a two-year war, culminating at the time of the American elections. But of course, if you have a chance then exploit and go ahead. The importance of the two-year war aspect is that Thieu looked at his stocks and said

"They're going to have to carry me through because the Americans have really cut back so much they're not about to give me any more." Therefore, he was being parsimonious about supplies, thinking his main attack was going to be in '76. But the message to the troops was "The Americans have left us without the necessary support."

The other aspect, that Watergate more directly had to do with, was the use of the air. And here you had the War Powers Act and the general disinclination to allow a President to use the forces. In '72, Nixon could just direct the Air Force to fly missions and get at the enemy. And it's really too bad in a way because the North Vietnamese [in 1975] were natural targets for exactly our air at that stage—both the carriers and the B52s. Using air against guerrillas is baloney. Using air against massed armor on the other side would have made a lot of sense.

So that one had something to do with Watergate, the whole War Powers Act, and the disinclination to let Presidents take that kind of action. It certainly was a factor. I wouldn't say *the* factor, but the disinclination to get involved [again] in Vietnam was enormous.

CHAPTER TWELVE

A Failure of Will

THE Army of South Vietnam collapsed in the spring of 1975 as though struck by a bolt from the heavens. From the assault on Phuoc Long province along the Cambodian border to the fall of Saigon, Hanoi's final offensive took only four months. The real disintegration, however, occupied an even shorter space of time. It began early in March when Hanoi's troops occupied the Highlands city of Ban Me Thuot, and ended just fifty-five days later, when a North Vietnamese tank smashed through the palace gate in Saigon. In seven weeks and six days, a regular military establishment of six hundred thousand, supported by a half-million full-time militia, had torn itself to shreds in a headlong rush for the exits.

Some Vietnamese officers and not a few conservative American politicians have tried to blame the catastrophe on the fact that the U.S. Congress had sharply reduced military aid. But the facts do not support the case. No unit was overrun for lack of weapons or ammunition. At the moment the offensive began, South Vietnam owned two thousand tanks and armored vehicles, fifteen hundred artillery pieces, well over four hundred warplanes, and more than seven hundred helicopters. Yet for all the combat power it possessed, the regime of Nguyen Van Thieu failed to mount a single major battle in its own defense.

The Saigon government knew as early as the previous autumn that Hanoi had decided to launch a major offensive in 1975. If it had any doubts, they should have been dispelled when Phuoc Long was overrun in January. Intelligence from spies, defectors and captured documents soon showed that a major thrust would be aimed at Ban Me Thuot in March. Yet Thieu and his generals sat on their hands. Never mind reinforcing the threatened town, they did not even bother to send up reconnaissance planes.*

After Ban Me Thuot, Thieu behaved less like a general or a wartime president than like a child whose hurt feelings had put him into a deep funk. Depressed at the decline in aid and the manifest lack of American will to reenter the war, he convened his senior military aides at Cam Ranh Bay for a muzzy discussion of a plan to consolidate his forces by withdrawing from the Highlands and the northern reaches of the country. The plan, which had been dreamed up by a retired Australian officer who was Thieu's unofficial military adviser, had never been thoroughly studied. After the discussion, Thieu left the room without issuing clear orders. His Saigon generals thought he had done nothing, but the Highlands commander, Gen. Pham Van Phu, believed he had been told to pull back, and he did—with himself in the lead and his troops left to fend for themselves. With that began a military rout so breathtaking that for a time even North Vietnam distrusted the evidence of its eyes. Hanoi repeatedly warned its commanders in the South that they might be walking into a trap.

Phu ordered his two divisions to evacuate immediately down a little-used dirt track without even preparing the way, never mind taking care to destroy what had to be left behind. As they made for the coast, the divisions were ambushed and destroyed in Phu Bon province, along with virtually all of their armor. Behind them, Hanoi's troops captured not only massive supply dumps but a substantial piece of the Air Force, left sitting on Pleiku airfield.

Within days, a similar collapse began to the north. Thieu's priority after the Highlands disaster seemed less to defend the country than to defend himself. He ordered the Airborne Division south to Saigon to guard against a coup, and then issued a series of contradictory instructions on whether and how the remaining troops should defend Hue. As a result the two divisions below the DMZ self-destructed—the Marines on the road to Danang and the First Division in a disorderly effort to escape by way of the only remaining seaport at Thuan An. The pandemonium soon spread to the Second and Third Divisions, closer to Danang.

As in 1972, the entire population of Hue fled south by road—and this time, with the Army in collapse, the people of Danang also panicked. Riotous crowds massed at the airfield, and managed to put a

---

*When, in the wake of Ban Me Thout, the U.S. wanted to know what was happening in the Highlands, CIA Station chief Thomas Polgar had to jury-rig a camera on an Air America Beechcraft—and the pictures he brought to the south Vietnamese high command were a great surprise. This failure, too, was not for lack of capability: The U.S. had given South Vietnam's Air Force (VNAF) sixty reconnaissance planes.

halt to aerial evacuations with a clawing rush to board the last plane that landed there, a World Airways rescue flight whose pilot feared even to stop taxiing.

For the handful of Americans remaining in the north there was nothing left but to organize as best they could a harrowing evacuation of civilians by sea on barges and eventually freighters. Meantime their superiors in Saigon and Washington seemed transfixed and unable to cope with events. Ambassador Martin, who had gone to Washington in late February to make a final appeal to Congress for aid, did not bother to return until the day before the fall of Danang. Even then, he refused to acknowledge the crisis. Though perceptive Americans had begun to liken Saigon to the decadent prewar Berlin portrayed by playwright Bertholt Brecht, no shots had been fired and all seemed normal on the surface. So long lunch hours continued, and such irrelevancies as overtime pay or Vietnamese economic concessions to American investors occupied the time of the Mission Council. Pessimism in reporting to Washington was suppressed, and great care was taken to avoid any public signs of worry. When Polgar began getting signals from his Hungarian contacts on the ICCS* that Hanoi might be willing to grant a face-saving accommodation, Martin treated both the message and the messenger with disdain.

An American survey mission headed by Gen. Fred Weyand, who had been the last American commander in Vietnam, flew home in early April to recommend an extra $650 million in aid. Gerald Ford kept Weyand cooling his heels in Palm Springs, California, while he played a round of golf, and then took his own sweet time to send the request on to Congress. William Colby, by then the CIA director, insisted that Saigon could still salvage a "southern redoubt" around the capital and in the Mekong Delta. Wiser counsel came from Defense Secretary Schlesinger, who said bluntly that the war was lost and that there was no way to reverse the congressional prohibitions on further U.S. intervention, and from Ford's political advisers, who urged that he avoid committing his own prestige to a war whose loss would be blamed on his predecessors.

What happened to the South Vietnamese and the Americans is written off by many military commentators as "a failure of will," a phrase applied to armies and societies that suffer a loss of resolve before they have lost the power to fight. That description may be technically correct, but given the behavior at the very center, particularly in Saigon, it somehow seems almost too charitable for the circumstance.

----

*The International Commission for Control and Supervision, established under the Paris Accords.

THOMAS POLGAR

You can mark Phuoc Long as the beginning of the end. During the battle the South Vietnamese did not give a very good account of themselves. The town could only be supplied by air and the North Vietnamese quickly shot down two C-130 transports. At that time the South Vietnamese had maybe thirty of these transports. And the Air Force—and President Thieu himself—may have said, "Here is an insignificant place and we have just lost ten percent of our transport. We are just not going to resupply."

So the South Vietnamese were beginning to fight a poor man's war, and by the way that phrase, "fight a poor man's war," occurs in the memoirs of General Van Tien Dung, the North Vietnamese commander. And this has affected morale and combat spirit. After it happened, the Ambassador and I both played the same tune—that the loss is not militarily significant but it is psychologically significant and if we do not react, the North Vietnamese are going to gain encouragement. Obviously no U.S. military involvement could be possible because of the War Powers Act and the bombing ban that Congress had imposed. But we thought that resupply, or a very firm statement out of Washington that Hanoi is going to be punished might have been called for. But that didn't happen.

In February we had a bunch of congressmen come out there, but a lot of them thought we were trumpeting up this threat to put pressure on for more funds. By my count, we must have had eighteen congressmen and two senators in Saigon. The time of the Embassy was completely taken up with preparing for these people, briefing them, talking with them and running errands for them, and it really was a circus. Some of them were very gung ho; others were opposed and some were on the fence. For example, Leo Ryan, the fellow that got killed in Guyana, came out opposed and said he changed his mind. Pete McCloskey was blowing hot and cold; one night he was over at my house until four in the morning debating.

And Bella Abzug was there. Oh yeah, oh yeah. She arrived late for a meeting, kept the whole senior staff of the Embassy waiting. I introduce myself and Bella says, "Oh yeah, I've been warned about you." And she was really insulting. She came with a list of people who were in jail that she wanted to talk with. She wanted to see the people who would be most difficult to get to. I went to work and when we have everything arranged she says, "I'm not interested, I don't have to see them." She was only interested as long as maybe

we would say, "You can't see them," so she could go home and
shoot her mouth off saying she was prevented.

But the Ambassador felt keenly that the future of South Vietnam
was with Congress. He was desperate because he sensed that the
Ford administration was not pleading the cause and he thought that
were he to go there, he could help. So he arranged to go back with
the Congressmen on their airplane and on the twenty-seventh of February, Ambassador Martin left South Vietnam. Now we were already
in that phase of Vietnam where anything that could go wrong, went
wrong, and while Martin was in Washington he had to have surgery
on his jaw, as a result of which he did not get back to Vietnam until
a month later.

One thing to remember about this entire period is that they did not
have a very experienced deputy chief of mission. Martin selected
his DCM from among the consuls general in Vietnam, and he picked
a guy who was experienced with military matters and spoke good
French, but was not particularly assertive. And Thieu as a matter
of protocol would not deal with the deputy chief of mission. So for
a whole month, during this difficult period, no American has seen
Thieu and the Embassy drifted without any real leadership.

[By early March the South Vietnamese] were reporting the enemy's
preparation for a major offensive against Ban Me Thuot. We had
this information also, but here we run into something in Washington which deserves mentioning because the problem is still with us.
The Defense Department is so technically oriented that if intelligence is not confirmed by technical means, they tend not to credit
it. The North Vietnamese kept radio silence during this period so
our communications intelligence was not picking up the information. We had spies, we had defectors, we had captured documents,
but the Defense Department says "If it's not confirmed by communications intelligence, don't even tell us about it."

The North Vietnamese attacked Ban Me Thuot on the tenth of March
with elements from four different divisions, and the South Vietnamese had one regiment of the 23rd Division there. Saigon tries a
counterattack by bringing down the other two regiments of the 23rd
from Pleiku, but the roads are blocked. Now, Ban Me Thuot was a
nothing town, but it was the administrative center of the Montagnard region. We had a permanent presence there and seven or eight
people got captured.

By next day it was clear that things are going very badly, and in
less than a week the situation was unraveling at a dramatic speed.
Ban Me Thuot [demonstrated] some problems that became much
worse with the lack of mobility. Vietnam on a map is like a very
long sausage. The population was along the coast so when you got

into these high plateau jungle areas the Army could not afford to have any concentration of forces. When the Americans were there and the enemy attacked some point like Khe Sanh, we had plenty of air mobility to bring forces quickly. But the South Vietnamese didn't have that. If the roads were cut, the troops couldn't move. Another problem was that the dependents were always with the troops, so when you told a regiment to move, that involved wives, children, fathers, mothers, and widowed sisters and it was always a terrible mess.

Now, after Ban Me Thuot the Vietnamese decided to evacuate the Highlands. Thieu will insist that he never ordered that. But it had become clear to the South Vietnamese long before this that they will somehow have to reduce their commitments to meet their resources. And there was an Australian general named Ted Sarong who fell in love with an American lady in the Defense Attaché's Office, took his retirement, and set himself up in the commercial tugboat business in Saigon. Sarong had a confidential consultant relationship with the government* and he had worked out a plan which called for giving up some of the Highlands and of Military Region One in the north. This was never adopted; it was in the category of people saying, "You really got to do something, one day, about the highway congestion." Prime Minister [Tran Thien] Khiem had told me about this, and I knew Sarong quite well.

So Thieu and his generals meet in Cam Ranh Bay against this background. And Thieu's habit was to go on terrific long rambles, talk for an hour or two hours or three hours and at the end say "You all agree with this?" And they would say "Yeah." This meeting, which now looms so momentous, was attended by Khiem, Vien,† General [Dang Van] Quang, the president's military advisor, and General [Pham Van] Phu, the commanding general in the Highlands, and at the time it appeared to be of very little significance. I saw General Quang the next day and I said, "What happened?" He said, "We discussed the situation and it doesn't look good and we'll have to do something pretty radical." Vien says he didn't think Thieu had ordered the evacuation, but General Phu thought Thieu had ordered it, and Phu put it into effect.

But even if Phu's understanding was correct, the way he went about it was terrible. He never initiated any planning, staff work, reconnaissance, or coordination with the Air Force. The Air Force didn't even know that there *was* an evacuation, so many of the planes were

---

*With Thieu himself, according to Martin.
†General Cao Van Vien, the Chief of the Joint General Staff.

captured undamaged. The average house buyer who makes a move goes through a rational process of thinking out how he is going to move. But Phu just said "Let's go"—and he was the first one to go. No word was given to destroy supplies. No attempt was made to move things forward such as fuel for the trucks and the tanks. And in the meantime the highway is cut and Phu tries to move his forces on a dirt road really not fit for jeeps, let alone heavy equipment. And as they are driving through Phu Bon [province], they are intercepted by an NVA armored column.

By Sunday, it was clear that things were bad, but in Saigon, nobody had a true picture. On Monday we jury-rigged an Air America Beechcraft with an aerial camera and they brought back the first documentation of what a disaster they suffered. We could count in the area of Phu Bon all the burnt trucks and tanks and artillery pieces. We knew what they started with, so it was fairly easy to figure out that they had practically nothing left. The evacuation cost the South Vietnamese two entire infantry divisions and most of their [the divisions'] armor. Even more important they lost their cohesive command authority, and never recovered.

And then I reported to Washington. We were still hoping the Congress would do something and that the President would go to the Soviets and say, "Fellows, unless hostilities cease by such and such an hour, I'm going to send the B-52s back against Hanoi." But nothing happened. Washington came back that we should have a worldwide propaganda effort in favor of South Vietnam.

The Vietnam that Martin came back to on the twenty-seventh of March bore no resemblance to the Vietnam that he left on the twenty-seventh of February. [Because of his surgery] he is away from classified traffic, maybe even from the newspapers and the radio. And he comes back with a mental image of the situation as it existed when he left on the twenty-seventh of February. And this one-month gap, in my opinion, he never caught up with intellectually or emotionally.

You come back to Saigon and one of the great paradoxes is that Saigon was astonishingly normal. Not a shot had been fired, everything was functioning. The restaurants were going, the schools were going. The Embassy club was operating normally. You could still get fantastic meals for relatively little money. Excellent French wines. The international airlines were flying in and out. Nha Trang is about to fall and one of my people walks into the South Vietnamese military headquarters [there] and it's absolutely skeleton staffing and he says, "What the hell is going on?" And the guy says, "Nothing is going on. Don't you know this is Easter Sunday?" And twenty miles away they are fighting for their lives. Crazy.

And after Martin came back, we had also another problem, and this was that he continued to run the Embassy as he has always run the Embassy. For his last month in Vietnam he was not only talking and taking measures as if there would be a lot more time, but he insisted on a working tempo which was totally unsuited to the situation. For example, in Vietnam, as in most tropical countries, people have a nice lunch and a siesta and the American Embassy has a two-hour lunch period. I kept arguing that this is overtaken by events, let's forget about two-hour lunch periods and start to cope with the emergency. But the administrative counselor say no. "If people are working ten hours a day I have to pay overtime and my budget is shot to hell."

We also had the Mission Council meetings around an oval table, and it was the invariable pattern that the DCM speaks first and then the senior military representative and all around in order. Well, I was getting always hot information and I kept saying, "With all due respect, shouldn't you listen to me first to see what the situation is, in light of which perhaps some of your remarks would not be relevant?" Like we would spend half an hour talking about what kinds of terms the South Vietnamese government should offer to the Hyatt Hotel that's going to be built in Saigon, while MR-I is collapsing.

I sent Martin written memoranda, with the concurrence of the military people, that we should change. But the system never got changed. We had a wonderful relationship until he came back. But then he simply doesn't want to hear the fact that the end is at hand; that he loses his Embassy. Martin was an unreconstructed cold warrior, and he wouldn't believe what was happening.

GRAHAM MARTIN

Why did you decide to go back to Washington with the congressional delegation that visited Saigon after Phuoc Long?

We weren't getting anywhere at all [with Congress] and things were slipping. If it didn't go well, you were no worse off than you were before. And you might, you just might get them caught in some reality. I would say about sixty percent of them we convinced. You're never going to convince Bella Abzug, for God's sake. I was in Washington before they came out, and I went back to resume trying to [reinstate the cuts in the aid request] and to explain what the actual situation was. People like Hubert Humphrey and others would listen to you with some sort of sense. Others wouldn't.

Phuoc Long didn't amount to a hill of beans except that psychologically Thieu had never been willing to permit any provincial capital to be taken. That was a signal to the North Vietnamese, in retrospect, that the Americans certainly weren't coming. God knows, they should have understood that already. If we had chosen in late '73, when evidence of massive infiltration began to take place, to have used a few B-52s strikes to have said, "We told you you couldn't do this," they might have had something to fear. By God, we should have done what we said we would do, and I am convinced that if we had done so that place today would be viable and operating on its own.

With Watergate, everything had stopped. Nobody in Washington was considering anything. North Vietnam, Saigon, Hanoi, where are they? Supplies got so low that if you were a South Vietnamese battery commander and you were fired on you could shoot two shells back and not any more until you got permission. When Tran Van Lam came to Washington in January of '75—he had been foreign minister, and was then president of the Senate—he tried to see [Senate Majority Leader] Mike Mansfield and Mike wouldn't even see him. This was right after this big clambake out at the National Presbyterian Church with George McGovern presiding for two days and everybody brought in from all over the country descending on Congress. When Tran came back to Saigon he told Thieu "You're not only not going to get any restoration from these cuts, but you're not going to get any more aid at all." I had been telling Thieu quite candidly what the hell the problems were, but they were living in the euphoria of Nixon's promises. I kept saying "Nixon is not here, and other laws had been passed. And while I'm sure that the people will try to get as much aid as they can, you have got to be able to handle these things on your own."

NGUYEN VAN HAO

When President Thieu ordered to withdraw after Ban Me Thuot, I'm not surprised. I expected it. I think it was the right direction. Before he decide to pull out Zone II we have a very hot session in the cabinet meeting. We have argument between myself and Chief of Staff, General Cao Van Vien. Chief of Staff come to cabinet for money to raise one hundred thousand of new soldiers. At that time we have more than one million, but he want more soldiers to cover entire country. I say "For me to raise new taxes to pay extra hundred thousand people could be a problem. If you as Chief of Staff can guarantee the impact of the new hundred thousand people, we decide to discuss, because for me cost is important. But your Army strategy is now like a piece of rubber. You have one piece, you want to cover all the country, you extend the rubber. And if I was the Viet Cong, I concentrate my forces like the point of the needle. And I puncture you and you explode because you expand so much. And now with hundred thousand more you think strategy change?"

He say "We raise this hundred thousand people more but I am not sure what is the result. Maybe it's the same." I say "In this case I have to vote against you." He became angry. I say "My feeling we have to buy time. I think we should change our strategy. I would concentrate my forces to defend only what is the key to South Vietnam." And I think after this discussion President Thieu gave the order to pull out from Pleiku.

I have to say we didn't see yet the dramatic consequences. The enemy just use a few regiment to attack and create panic, and it's a mess. But we have a meeting before with General Ngo Quang Truong* and he said "I can guarantee Danang can be defended a minimum of six months." And Danang fell just a matter of weeks after that. Vietnam have been defeated because drained away our will to fight. The morale of the soldiers is quite different from the morale of the high officers. When the officer is not there, how the soldier can fight? When General Truong flee from Danang, how the colonels, commanders, majors can fight? "Oh why general has leave? Maybe something is wrong." They have to take care of themselves. And so exactly they have take care of themselves. We are not defeated in the sense of defeated.

———◆———

THOMAS POLGAR

We had in the north the best fighting elements of the Vietnamese Army, the Marine Division, the Airborne Division, the First Division, the Second Division, and the Third Division. This was twenty-five percent of the Vietnamese army in quantity but more than twenty-five percent in quality. When things started to unravel in the Highlands, Thieu decided to move the Airborne out of the north to constitute the strategic reserve for Saigon. And I think he also had in mind that "If I had some trouble in terms of riots, uprisings, I'd better have a good mobile strike force here."

However justified he may have been, when he took out the Airborne Division, this completely unraveled the defenses of General

---

*Commander of Military Region I, the five northern provinces.

Truong. Now, his northernmost division were the Marines, and they were allegedly pretty good. But then Thieu decided that Hue is not to be defended, that the defense line should be around Danang. So Truong moves his units out of Hue and they're carrying all their equipment, their tanks, their artillery as well as their wives and their kids. This is not a very big distance, perhaps fifty miles, and they're about midway in their march when Thieu changes his mind and says "You must defend Hue after all."

Now moving a division is a complicated thing and there's only one road. To turn this thing around resulted in a fantastic confusion plus again, I remind you, you have the women there yelling "We don't want to go back to Hue." And the soldiers are torn: "This is what my officer says and this is what my wife says and obviously the Communists are going to come from the North so maybe I'm better off going to the South." But he turns them around and takes them back up north again and then the orders are changed again to turn back after all. And in this series of contradictory orders they just couldn't extricate themselves.

Just the physical act of turning around the big artillery pieces on a narrow highway is impossible. They slip off into the mud. They can't move and dark comes on and the tank commander wants to get through and he says "Shove that son of a bitch off the road." So without the Communists firing a shot, the Marine Division has managed to lose all its heavy equipment. And once you are down the slippery slope, you keep on slipping.

———◆———

Do Duc Cuong

After Ban Me Thuot, situation in Hue, Quang Tri, Danang very normal for about two weeks. I was driving Jeep at night, no problem, but difficult to reach my boss and other high-ranking officers. I don't know where they go. I am told they are away at meetings, there is something going on in headquarters. After Ban Me Thuot we knew General Truong must go to Saigon for special meetings.

I expected heavy defense around Quang Tri. One meeting I suggested evacuation of Quang Tri people. General Nguyen Van Diem, commander of our [First] Division, agreed. We started to move the people, but first serious fighting happen not around Quang Tri but in Hue. First Division is spread out in defense, spread thin, in mountains to west of Hue. Marine Corps on coast on Highway 1, Airborne just to west on other side of Highway 1. Our three divisions to Communists' five.

Around March 18 or 19 heavy fighting very close to our headquarters at Phu Loc.* General Diem gave green light for Hue [civilians'] evacuation next day or day after. I flew on helicopter. On highway, unbelievable! People could not move because so crowded. Using any equipment. Many have bamboo sticks. Carry child in one hand, property in other. People moving twenty-four hours, day or night. No vehicle, nothing. They just *run* ninety-eight kilometers to Danang. But also people not scared. It was the second time for them. In 1972 they had done it. They had strong hopes they would come back with victory, so they don't worry about home stuff. No one thinking about we lose Hue forever.

Three days of fighting, Hue not captured. March 20 or 21 I go around empty city. I saw just some dogs and chickens and ducks, doors open, like a ghost town. Very lonely. I feel like I stay on moon. At five o'clock that evening was a special meeting at First Division headquarters. General Diem is sitting at table with head in hand, saying nothing. It was a short meeting, twenty minutes. General [Lam Quan] Thi [Truong's deputy] spoke, not Diem. The order—withdraw from headquarters [Phu Loc] to city. At end of meeting Diem stand up, eyes red, he cry. In Hue First Division occupied the university. Front-line Corps headquarters were in Imperial Palace. Two battalions of Airborne, two battalions of Marine Corps were close north of Hue. One seaport was open, Thuan An. Next morning we are in university building. General Diem in tearful speech say "All my fellows who born in here, grew up in here, dig a hole. Will be buried your body here." I go around city with jeep, try become the headquarters' eyes. It was funny, no fighting at all.

Around end of twenty-first I go back to university. It is no control at all. Most of people tried to go to Thuan An seaport to get out. Nobody at temporary headquarters. I still have my twenty fellows. I tell them find dynamite to blow up communications equipment. We sleep at university. Next morning, I tell fellows, "You be on your way to Danang, any way you can get there." Five stayed with me. They tell me "If you are dead, we will die, too." Six of us find our way to seaport Thuan An. Most incredible situation there. Terrible! Lot of cut-off soldiers without commanders, or broken-up units, triggers cocked, trust nobody. And thousands of them like this in small area, artillery firing around, Communists moving forward. No Navy ship. No boat. Front of them the sea. Back of them the enemy. Thousands of young men running around, and no one obeys orders, no commander at all. Next morning two of my five men killed. We run away south. With my three men I find a bamboo raft and go

---

*About twenty-five miles south of Hue on the highway to Danang.

on sea with wood stick paddles, and one Navy LCT stopped to pick us up.

I arrive in Danang in the morning of March 27. Everything is normal. Markets, restaurants are still open, owners welcoming the customers, traffic lights still run by cops, kids on sidewalk. I feel happy. I thought I would rest and go back to the combat. I go to First Division intelligence headquarters to see my boss, Colonel Nhon. I ask him, "What we do next?" He say, "Whatever you think." Way he talk isn't normal. So sad. Sometimes he upset. Then he cry, hit table, sweep away everything on top. He said someone tried to defend Danang, but government order to withdraw in ten hours.

Danang is number two city of South Vietnam, three hundred thousand of people, crowded normally, and the people from Quang Tri, Hue, Quang Nam, Quang Tin, and Quang Ngai are there now too. But police kept control. I lunched with the colonel at a very fancy restaurant. Owner still welcomed us. I had a very wonderful lunch of chicken and pork. I remember it because is last fancy restaurant food I have. The restaurant is on corner of a very busy and beautiful main street by the riverside. We finished, paid the tip, and turned around to face the street. Kids were running the traffic lights, police were gone, it was like I was dreaming. People running around trying to leave, heading for Navy base.

My boss asked if I was carrying a weapon. Yes, I say, but only five bullets left. He told me pick up other weapon. I go look for weapon, saw M-16s on sidewalk, thrown away by fleeing soldier. I picked up two weapons and went back to restaurant. Owner, waiters are gone. The thing changed in front of my eyes—so fast! Boss said he go back to office to destroy communications. I go, too. But Special Interior Communists* already there. We go into Buddhist temple near gate. I look out, saw Major Le Cuong running out of intelligence headquarters. He captured at gate. They knew his picture though he is in civilian clothes. Communists shoot him through his right and left hand, tie him with barbed wire through wounds. And he cries so terrible! Most of Special Interior run into headquarters. From there I hear some dynamite blow up, maybe a booby trap. Street becomes crowded. Boss and I tried to get close to Major Cuong. He recognized us and begged us, "Shoot me!" I point the gun to him but I couldn't. My boss yelled, "On your way!" and shot Le. After that I lost my boss.

I tried to get to Navy base along very narrow street. I pass by Trinh Minh The bridge. On other side of river high point look over city.

---

*Shock troops whose job was to infiltrate cities and seize key installations ahead of the regular NVA.

Crowd look like millions of eggs in a pan. I try to flee away. Along river are big navy barges, no engine, but people try get on. Two dozen of them full of people, with no power. At three P.M. big LST comes in. I get up there to LST first because I am single guy. I saw a friend with his family. They couldn't get up there. He begged me for help. So I jumped into water and tried to help him. I lifted them to the ship's cargo net and they could climb up. Then the net was cut away. And the ship is crushing people heads against the dock. So terrible—a thousand of them! The LST left without me. The sailors were scared. People were caught in the closing big loading door. There is a famous picture of that. Thirty, maybe fifty people killed.

I couldn't go anywhere, so stayed overnight. Next day I left and took a small seaside road. Later I find out location they pick up families of Navy officers. An LCT takes us to sea to Panama commercial big ship. Families get on, leave me alone on small ship. I am tired and hungry, just lying there, too tired to move. I have with me one-year-old boy I picked up, I cannot let him alone. I tried to find water for him. I don't know that but he is my friend's son—a First Division battalion commander's son. His wife flee and lose son on small ship. We are one day and one night on sea with artillery coming down, sailing around. I try to go to any ship I can reach. Finally I got on a Navy repair ship.

April fourth we reach Cam Ranh. They wanted to empty ship, not land at Cam Ranh. All people are ordered to jump to water, be picked up by fishing boats. I jump into life preserver with boy. Small ship picked us up in evening. You never even see any scary movie like this! Many dead bodies, mostly children, floating in bay. And on base thousands of people coming from everywhere and no direction to go. I look around for sign of cooking food. I saw battalion commander—boy's father, now living in San Jose [California]. He recognize his boy. His wife had been crying for him. A miracle! The boy very big now, he still call me Father.

———————◆———————

PAUL VOGLE *originally went to Vietnam as a U.S. Army linguist in 1956. His ear for the language was so good that when Vietnamese spoke to him on the telephone, they often couldn't tell they were talking to a foreigner. After leaving the Army, he taught at the university in Hue. In 1963, Vogle went to work for the Saigon* Daily News. *Eventually, he became a correspondent for United Press International, and was one of a handful of journalists who stayed on after the Communist takeover, only to be expelled five weeks later. He made several trips back to Vietnam to try to extricate his wife and three children. They were released in 1982. After the fall he remained with UPI in Bangkok for a time, and is now an editor with UPI in Detroit.*

Right after Ban Me Thuot I was in Danang and I went up to Hue with Al Francis, the consul general, in a helicopter. I hired a motorbike to ride me around the city, but after a while we saw it wasn't safe. We spent a good deal of time in ditches while rockets were going over. The Vietnamese were terrified. I had lived in Hue for a long time and had very close associations there. People would come up and grab me and plead, "Get me out. Save me. If the Communists ever take over, I'm dead." And that was really much more horrifying than the rockets and stuff.

I flew back to Danang with Francis and pretty soon things started coming apart there, too. [When the exodus from Hue began] Don Oberdorfer and I decided to drive up to the Hai Van Pass just north of Danang, on the road to Hue. We got to a point about three miles from the pass and we couldn't go any farther. It was simply one mass of people coming down the highway. There was a cliff on one side and a steep drop on the other, and it was like one big block coming down on you and if it just veered you would be just, boom. Untold numbers of people and just really acting as one.

The only other thing I'd seen remotely like it was when they'd brought Our Lady of Fatima to Saigon and the rush to get near the statue was so great that my feet couldn't touch the ground. It was like that at the Hai Van—tens of thousands of people. I remember seeing one old man. He's pulling a cart with his wife, two kids, and an old woman, all their pots and pans clanking along the side, pigs and chickens and everything. He had pulled that cart all the way from five miles south of Hue, up and over that mountain pass and down to where we were—and it had two flat tires.

A month later, when the battle of Xuan Loc was going on [outside Saigon], I went out there, and I saw exactly the same thing: a mass of people coming down the highway, heading straight for me. I pulled my jeep over to the side of the road and I got out and I threw up. And I remember saying to myself "Oh boy. I'm not going through this again."

Life in Danang itself was a nightmare. The streets were overflowing, and a lot of military units had broken. People tried to stay away from the soldiers because they would stop you and hold you up for whatever you had. There were a number of people that were killed because they weren't fast enough at giving up their possessions. We watched them [the soldiers] coming in from Hue, getting off trucks and carts and boats. They didn't know anyone. They didn't have anyplace to go. They were afraid the people would turn on them, afraid the enemy might be in the city looking for them, and afraid if they turned themselves in they might be shot for deserting. They acted like hunted animals. Their skin seemed taut, and it was like there was something high-powered behind their eyes.

They'd been in their units and they were told to lay down their arms. Most of them I talked to were angry about that. I ran into guys I knew, and this scene was repeated over and over again. "We could have held out," they'd say. "We could have held out." So they felt guilty, as if they could have prevented what they themselves were doing, which they were ashamed of. But most of these guys were not from around there, and they would do anything to get where they wanted to go. That's why there were these mob scenes at the airport—thousands of people lined up behind barbed wire, trying to get on the one flight a day.

I was back in Saigon when Danang finally collapsed. I knew Ed Daley, the president of World Airways, and he told me he was going to have an evacuation flight. I got on the airplane and there was even a hostess. Daley had to have somebody to serve us booze—and a fanny to pat. Well, we landed on the main strip and went over to the taxiway. You could see mobs of people standing behind this barbed wire fence about a hundred fifty yards away. And all of a sudden the fence comes down and here come people, thousands of them, on motor bikes, jeeps, running and every one of them wants to get on that airplane. The pilot said, "Hey, we can't hang around here," So he kept the aircraft moving, and I remember him saying, "I don't know if we can do this, but it's the only way." There were rockets coming in. You could hear them.

And the people came and charged aboard, using the ramp in the back of the plane. People are grabbing onto anything, trying to get up that ramp. There's only a certain number of people that can get on one of those ramps, but these people weren't worried about scraping their arms or anything. By this time I'm at the back trying to calm people down, but it doesn't do much good. There was this one woman who got halfway up the ramp, and two soldiers grabbed her around her bottom and just threw her back down the steps and knocked a few other people out of the way, too. And they kept coming. A couple of guys formed a chain with each other to let three of their buddies get on. Then I remember this one guy was coming up the ramp and this old woman was tugging on him because she was limping and wanted him to help pull her up. He just turned around and slugged her right in the face. And she went plop right down on the tarmac. She's the last thing I saw. This old woman lying there on the ground.

———————◆———————

During his years as an AID official in Vietnam, RUSSELL MOTT *was known as Robert Lanigan, a name given him by his mother and stepfather when he was seven. Mott took his original name back in 1981 as he tried to cope with an identity crisis brought on by a severe case of Vietnam readjustment blues. Mott was a Marine Corps officer before he joined AID in 1965, and he served in Vietnam from 1968 to 1975. He left the government in 1977, was divorced from his Vietnamese second wife, worked for a time counseling Vietnam vets, and wandered restlessly around the country until he settled with his third wife in Las Cruces, New Mexico. He now works as a commercial photographer and maintains a small psychotherapy practice on the side.*

By March 1975 I was the only American left in Hoi An, the capital of Quang Nam province, which was a thirty-five-minute drive down the coast from Danang. I did not want the war to end for my own private reasons, but going home the night Ban Me Thuot fell, I wondered whether to send some of my stuff to the U.S., or at least to Saigon. In the end, I didn't. I thought South Vietnam was in better shape than it was, and I felt it might panic people I knew.

In the ten days between Ban Me Thuot and the fall of Hue, we continued to march along as usual. There were no Americans in Quang Tin, the next province south of me, so Al Francis asked me to spend the night down there, just letting the province chief know the Americans hadn't boogied. I bounced down there a few times—and discovered that several troop emplacements weren't there anymore because of pullbacks that weren't being reported to Danang.

On the twenty-third or the twenty-fourth I was playing tennis with the province chief, who was worried that he was about to lose his capital. There wasn't much advice I could give this man. He was facing the bullet. I told him I was just as frightened as he was. After dinner on the military radio in my Jeep I could hear till one or two A.M. troops reporting to Danang about the convoy mounting up and leaving Hue, abandoning the city.

When Hue fell, Quang Tin turned into a ghost town. The shops closed and the people, who were terrified, started packing. I became very frightened about all of that, wondering how long my days were going to be in Vietnam—a country I had come to adopt. Next day I drove back to Hoi An and packed up my gear, and went to Danang.

By then the writing was on the wall. The cops and soldiers were often gone. Finally Air Vietnam stopped running flights, and the airfield closed, and the panic turned real. The only hope was to go by sea. Francis asked me and Mel Chatman and a couple of CIA people to stay. His deputy, Brunson McKinley, also stayed. There were also a couple of Alaska Tug and Barge people, contract folks. We had a task force of eight or nine people.

[On the last day] we arranged for a barge to stop at the ferry landing in front of the Consulate. But by the time the barge arrived, word had gotten out and it was chaos. People were crawling up the side and finally the barge got so packed that they were falling off. Finally it was towed into mid-harbor and let loose with the people on it. I went to meet the other Americans at a beach a mile from the consulate. I spent the day on a CIA boat, taking the last of the German Hospital doctors, some Vietnamese officials, and American missionaries out to the *Pioneer Contender*, an American merchant ship that was in the harbor.

In the late afternoon we finally went out and got aboard the tug *Osceola*. By this time there were six big barges, with fishing boats tied up to them, in the harbor. People were getting out to the barges on basket boats, rowboats, sampans. People were shot trying to board the barges and thrown into the sea. The plan was to wait till shipping came in and transfer the barge people to the ships, but we didn't know when the ships were coming. The alternative would have been to hook up the barges and take them out to sea. But the weather was unpredictable, and we were afraid of high seas. The biggest barge, *Big Blue*, was flat across, with only ropes for rails, and there were between seventy-five hundred and ten thousand people on it.

We spent the next four nights and three days on the *Osceola*. A CIA radio tech set up an antenna for radio contact with Saigon, which kept screaming they wanted us out of there right away. The embassy thought an NVA patrol fleet was coming south to block the harbor. In the harbor, it was ninety-five degrees during the day, and we had no fresh water on the barges. The *Osceola* had water, but not enough to share, and we could not go back to land for fear of losing control of the tug. The city was being rocketed. There were fires and smoke. We had to keep control of the *Osceola* or no American ship would come in the harbor to load.

For three days, the *Osceola* would hook up all the barges in the daytime and drag them around for wind. The second night Chatman and I were in the back of the *Osceola*, and the barges were tied up behind. Some noise started, and we could see people in the night waving white handkerchiefs, pillowcases, hats. There was an eerie, continual cry from all the barges: People were yelling, "Nuoc!"—

Water! It went on and on for hours, like a sea of white. People had brought fans, saxophones, television sets, gold strapped to their legs, whatever they thought was negotiable—but they had not brought water.

Next day somebody got the idea of having Saigon fly us water, and we asked by radio. They decided to fill a plane with plastic canisters and drop them to us. The American pilot starts a low, slow run, dropping the canisters. The people on the barges knew it was water and there were big cheers—the Americans were coming to the rescue. One canister scored a direct hit on the *Osceola* and took out our antennas. The rest of the canisters exploded when they hit the water. They had been filled wrong—too full or not full enough.

About three or four A.M. on the last morning—Easter Sunday—a Vietnamese tramp called the *Saigon Singapore* showed up, and then a whole convoy came in and we evacuated the barges onto the steamers. There was a lot of rioting. At the end on *Big Blue* I counted seventy-five bodies, mostly women with small children, some old men. Mel and I were checking one of the last barges to see if all the people had gone. One old guy was left at the far end, alive, hugging a TV. We got him up, but we couldn't get the TV away from him. He said, "It's the only thing I have to trade for water."

———————◆———————

DOAN VAN TOAI

In February 1975 I was manager of the Nam Do bank branch in Qui Nhon. My wife, Yvonne, was with me. My boy Dinh was four. The second boy, Binh, was three years. The last, Huy, was one year old. Dinh means country, or state. Binh means Peace. He was born at the time of the Paris agreement. Huy means glory, triumph. I was not optimistic but idealistic. Because Thieu ordered his troops to leave Pleiku and Kontum through the jungle to the south, not the main route to Qui Nhon, it creates rumor that they cut Qui Nhon off at the north. So people panic. But it was not panic like Danang, Hue, or Nha Trang. The people who thought it would be dangerous when Communists came, run away—rich people, the government, middle-class and soldiers and officials. They spread over anywhere they have relatives, going south. Most poor people stayed.

The city closed—restaurants, activities. I bought a boat and evacuated the bank employees and equipment and dossiers to Saigon. [But] I had decided to stay till the last minute. I wandered around maybe ten days or two weeks. With my youthful spirit of adventure, I would like to witness last-minute historical moment of Vietnam, the last days. The city was very quiet, like a death city. I had no more friend there. My wife and children were sent to Saigon. I drove car around and watch people's reaction.

I left Qui Nhon finally when I saw one commercial plane land at the airport. It was an Air Vietnam DC-3. It was supposed to go north to Danang, but the airport was closed there so it land at Qui Nhon. It had no passengers. I saw friends from the city there. They ask, "Why don't you take this plane?" It was free. There was no panic. Not many passengers. The trip took about ninety minutes. I cried in the plane. I don't know why—maybe the landscape and the atmosphere around the city.

Saigon still see the usual activities. Nightclubs are still open, rich people still enjoy, and the people crowded in the street. There is no agony. At the bank some businessmen and rich Chinese customers offer me passport and money if I can help them get their money out faster. But I refused. I *had* a passport. My brother and his family went for the American way. It cost five million piasters. This was half the price of buying a government passport. Some Vietnamese worked for Americans who would take bribes to sell [plane] seats as members of their families.

I had many friends who worked for the South Vietnamese government. They were province administrators, province chief, colonel, major. I convinced them. I was not very optimistic but I said things would not be worse. So most of them decided to stay because they were influenced by me. I feel very sorry and guilty about that. More than me, it was *dignity* that convinced them not to leave the country and leave behind soldiers or followers. They thought the high official who decide to leave, they are cowards. What if they come to the U.S. and then want to be leader again?

Most of government workers do not believe Americans abandon the South. They say it is a trap to lure Communists in and kill them. I think even Thieu himself did not believe American abandonment until last minute. Some say he withdrew from Pleiku and Kontum to test reaction of Americans. When they did not react, he knew Americans would not save the South. He denounced Americans at end, on television. "America is brutal allies—Inhuman! Inhuman! Inhuman!" He repeat many times. He showed a Nixon letter on camera. "I can't imagine president of a superpower deceive me like that!" he said. But to Communists the speech proves them right in saying he is lackey of Americans because he collapsed without them.

The problems of whether Thieu leave or Quong Van Minh take over makes no difference to most people. Some with experience of Communist brutality—the Northerners before 1954—attempt to flee at any price. But most of Southerners, even anti-Communists, they wait and see.

———◆———

ALAN CARTER *was the last U.S. Information Agency chief in Saigon. A career foreign service officer, Carter arrived in September of 1974—just in time to watch the Vietnamese ship of state slide beneath the waves. He soon concluded that Ambassador Martin was deliberately lying about the deterioration. Carter also blamed Martin for the ineptitude of U.S. evacuation efforts. His inability, at the end, to evacuate hundreds of Vietnamese associates left Carter deeply embittered. Carter is now vice-president for international programs at The Experiment in International Living in Brattleboro, Vermont.*

Right after I got to Saigon in September of '74, I began to get this Brechtian sense about the place. It's the only word I can use. Brecht would have written about Saigon the same way he wrote about the Germany of the late twenties and thirties. It was pathetic. You could sense the decay. And when the offensive began, you could sense first fear and desperation in the government, and then a crumbling as the fear turned closer to panic. And as it went along it crumbled worse. A large contingent wanted out, so the machinery kept sputtering. And the more that left, the less the likelihood was of anything that possibly could happen to stop the offensive.

In early April, I was asked by Washington to send a memo describing the mood. This really caused Graham [Martin] great heartburn. It was a page-and-a-half summary saying that the mood clearly was going into increasing decay, and that the fear was palpable. I remember using that word. You could walk through the streets and sense it; talk to officials and sense it. I would go occasionally to a Vietnamese club where one of their famous singers performed, and you could sense that desperate quality when the dancing began—these young couples going out onto the floor and dancing, zombielike. It was going through the motions, saying "I'm dancing, see?" Or you'd go to the French Club there, the Cercle Sportif, on rare occasions and it was the same: Everybody going through the motions. What struck me was—it's like they're not aware and obviously they are. There was a striking sense of deliberate unawareness shielding them. "I'm not going to look over that wall and see what's happening."

By April, for most of us, we would go home at night from the office and there would be a line of people waiting to see us. They wanted out. And I'd wake up in the morning and there would be another half dozen. I'd get to the office and there'd be another half dozen. They'd range from government officials down to businessmen. And they were all there, asking: "Get me out of here."

My cable about the mood in Saigon had gone out a couple of days before the C-5A crashed with all those kids on it.* When the plane crashed, I was on the phone with Martin and his reaction was: "I never would have authorized the use of that particular plane. I've been around planes long enough to know something about them. But Washington didn't ask me. I'll tell you why they didn't ask me. They didn't ask me because they're getting other reports that misled them. If, for example, they hadn't felt there was palpable fear here, they might have asked me." I said, "Do you mean to tell me that I'm responsible for that plane going down?" I thought that he'd back off, but that's exactly what he said.

Graham felt that it was necessary that we support the South Vietnamese regime for three years—the decent interval. His goal number one seemed quite clearly to be to persuade Congress to give aid in large amounts. For example: A lot of reporting from the Delta when I first got there was suppressed or delayed. There were stories about the so-called military weakening of the South Vietnamese position there. If the U.S. Congress was to get word that the Delta was in jeopardy, the chances of getting [more] military and economic aid was minimal. So you controlled the information. His whole strategy was to do nothing that would jeopardize impressing Congress with the need for military aid.

And later many of the early losses up in the north had to be put in a more optimistic perspective. You just couldn't say that they were getting kicked around because Congress would then never approve more aid. He felt that he could influence policy-making through these kinds of shenanigans. Even if he understood Congress was not going to give any more aid, I think he believed the effort had to be made. But after Ban Me Thuot and the northern provinces fell there was nothing the U.S. government or Congress could have done to change the eventual outcome.

But my question is not the inevitability of it all, or even his stoicism and his control. My question is that over a long period of time he practiced a brand of deception designed to try to manipulate Congress. That's not the role of an American ambassador. He was manipulative, Machiavellian, out-and-out lying. There is something in the ethic of that, saying the end justifies the means, that bothers me.

---

*An Air Force C5-A that had flown in with military supplies in early April was loaded for the return journey with hundreds of war orphans and adult women awaiting evacuation. It crashed just outside Saigon after takeoff. Others discuss the incident more fully in the next chapter.

I've worked for a great Ambassador, Ellsworth Bunker, and never saw that. I don't think it's necessary. In this case it's a little bit like saying the general was terrific, but by the way, all the troops got wiped out.

———————◆———————

GRAHAM MARTIN

You got back on the twenty-seventh of March?
Danang has fallen. Nha Trang is just about at final evacuation. I came back with General Weyand and a whole group of people: George Carver, the deputy director of CIA, Erich Von Marbod [of the Pentagon], other senior people from AID. It was a top-level team. So, a lot of time with them, arranging for them to go up-country as far as possible to see how Vietnamese morale was, and then to meet with [the] Vietnamese economic and military staffs, the general staff and finally with Thieu.

In the meantime I was trying to keep as well informed as you could at what was going on all over the country. I am an omnivorous reader. Above all I like to get the raw reports from the field, before somebody else has made his own assessment—and by the time you get through four or five assessments you're maybe one hundred eighty degrees away from what the fellow said. I like to talk to the young officers, and get them out circulating. I depended a lot on the Marine guards at the Embassy. They were going out through the town, and the Marines sometimes made better judgments than some of the political officers on the state of morale and the way things were going. So you get all these individual little tiny vignettes and you form a big impression.

You keep listening to intelligence reports, above all the panic stuff coming from CINCPAC, how fast they were coming down on us. The intelligence business I know just about as well as any of them. But I had to be concerned not just with capabilities, but with intentions, too. And I make up my own mind about it. I had suggested to Kissinger that maybe detente ought to have a price about now, and how about going back to Moscow and saying "Let's knock it off here, briefly." He went to them. The Soviets allegedly went to the North Vietnamese and they said two weeks. That would have run about until the sixth or seventh of May.

So Weyand goes back on the fourth with his report to the President. Meets him in Palm Springs, and they get off the golf course and talk about it. Kissinger is there and they consider this about the eighth or ninth. Then they go back for consultations with the Congress, and it's not until the seventeenth that they conclude it isn't going to sail. And meantime, I've got to keep everything relatively stable for them to make up their mind and see what happens.

But what Weyand says is that if we evacuate, the lessons of Danang indicate it will require a reinforced division, supported by tactical air. Now, you bring back a reinforced division of American troops and tactical air, you are still not going to be able to move out all the people who would want to come—which would be half of South Vietnam. So you're going to end up fighting the South Vietnamese on your way out, which is the worst of all possible ways, by God, to leave. So I said "I don't want anybody. Anybody at all." So they said "We have a thousand Marines to come in." And I said "I don't want them." I asked to borrow twenty because I needed them for the perimeter guard [at the Embassy], but they wouldn't give me those. They'd give me a thousand but they wouldn't give me twenty. It turned out the Vietnamese thought we had been abandoned as much as they had been. So there was never that resentment. I don't know to this day why. If I had been a South Vietnamese I would have tried to cut some throats.

———•———

NGUYEN VAN HAO

What happened with the gold reserves?
At the time Thieu decide to move the gold to Switzerland, he say he wants to put some place secure, neutral. Because of the fighting, it's wiser now to put some over there, but maybe he can use gold to buy food, arms. I agree with that, but at that time there was rumor Thieu moved this gold for his personal use. And as vice-minister in charge of the economy, I give the interview. I say, "I can guarantee to you if we gonna have decide with the gold, it's a government decision. The President I can guarantee you never decides alone. He cannot use the gold [of] Vietnam as his personal property. I don't want to defend him, but it's unfair." First place. Second place, because the war we didn't have any planes would like to carry this because nobody like to insure it.

Then Dan Ellerman [the U.S. Embassy economic counselor] come to see me and propose we send it to U.S. I ask, "If we transfer it to U.S. what is the procedure when we want to use it?" Answer is we must have permission of U.S. government. And I don't answer. He come every day put pressure on me. "Now because of situation we have a military plane ready at Tan Son Nhut day and night." I played cool. I say "Tell me more. What is reason behind. Why you are so willing to help us move out this gold?" He say "You know it is unwise to leave this gold here, because the bomb can hit it." I say "You know, Dan, if you think Reserve Bank—is where we store the gold—can be destroy, all the population of Saigon will be destroyed before. And just give me as friend what is behind? I want to know because for me is fate of the country."

He say the safety of the gold, just. After Thieu resigned he comes to me again. And I say "If you give me only the safety reason I don't believe it. If now you think you can, talk to new president, and if President Huong* give me order [snaps fingers], I just comply." Next day he come to see me and he say "We have now the answer, because our Ambassador have been in touch with the president and he say yes." In the meantime I brief the situation to President Huong. I say "You know our gold represents something. The people believe in us. And you know I have been approached by the Minister from U.S. Embassy." I said "I advise you not accept this because if the public opinion know you just only three days the president and you move the gold out of the country, could be a disaster. Your new government is there. You are living there. Your economy is there. Why? Why the hell we have to move the gold out of Vietnam? I think from political point of view it a wrong and unwise decision." And when Ellerman talk me about this, I say "Okay good, let me take it to president." Actually I call the president, and he say he never have been approached by any Americans.

———◆———

GRAHAM MARTIN

I came to the conclusion, finally, that if there was any chance of forming a government the North Vietnamese would tolerate for a while, it wasn't going to be with Thieu. And if his generals could negotiate something to avoid an all-out battle over Saigon, why the hell should we try to stop them? Anyway the generals were getting restless. But if you have a military coup what the hell happens? Ky was out there chafing at the bit, so with General Timmes, who is a civilian adviser to the CIA, we drive out to the JCS compound. Ky wasn't expecting me. I had never met Ky the whole time I was there. We talked a lot and Ky wanted to fight it out to the end. I sort of stalled the whole thing off with "We're working with the Soviets

---

*Vice-President Tran Van Huong, who was old, sick, half-blind, and just as unacceptable to the communists, succeeded to power for about a week after Thieu fled the country.

and the Vietnamese," "This is not really the time to do this," and so on. It needed a coup led by Ky like it needed a hole in the head.

And then I went to Thieu and laid it all out on the line. He was subdued, but he was a collected, calm man. We got along easily together. And as I said in the last sentence of the cable to the President, afterward I came back and I took a bath with very strong soap. The day before, I had told Kissinger and the President that I was willing to do this if they did not have any overriding objections. I would say then and later that I had done it on my own. They came back and said okay, just try to keep a handle on the timing. Get some final asset out of this before the Soviets say, "*We* will get rid of Thieu." We *would* get rid of Thieu, but in order maybe to get something else. But you don't control that kind of timing. Once you've started it in motion you don't stop it.

The next morning Thieu called his senior people in and described the situation, both politically and militarily, and then he repeated what I had said: That I was not giving him advice—the Americans had long since forfeited any right to give advice—but I was sure that he'd keep in mind the best interest of the country. And they agreed that the best interest was for him to go. So then he made an emotional speech and resigned while holding up Kissinger's letters. We were very concerned about what he was going to say about us. What I was afraid of, he could be so damned emotional, he'd turn against the rest of us there.

———————◆———————

NGUYEN CAO KY

I don't use Monday morning football quarterbacking. You see a lot of things wrong. People are talking about corruption, the low fighting spirit, the capabilities of the military leaders. There are a lot of things. There is corruption in every country. Even today, among the Communists in Vietnam, corruption is worse than before. So I don't think corruption is the cause. I still think it's purely errors in military strategy and tactics. Some said we didn't have a democratic system with support of the people. Well, the regime in North Vietnam is worse. They had the strongest leadership, and that's what we need in wartime—leadership, a strong regime.

Thieu always ran a one-man show. Regardless we have the semblance of democracy, a Senate, a House, this and that, through Thieu's maneuvers he had control of everything. And he's the kind of man that never trusts someone else. So at the end, I can say, he didn't have not only the support of the people, but also the help and contribution of other elements in South Vietnam. Take myself. It's possible I'm not a good leader or a good politician, but all Vietnamese recognize I'm a good soldier. Yet many times, especially in the last two months, I call up Thieu and ask him, "Give me something to do. I can help. Put me on the front lines of the troops, and they will stay and fight." He was afraid I become some sort of war hero, so he kept me out until the end. How many other good people were willing to cooperate with Thieu? But he kept everything for himself until the end.

It's true that at that time, not only the Air Force, but all the armed forces, were talking about making a coup. People suggested to me that we destroy the palace. I said no. The Communists are outside Saigon. We should have a smooth transition of power or the Communists will take advantage. It is better to convince Thieu [he] should go. I told the general officers, all of us sit down and make some sort of motion to Thieu that it's time to *voluntarily* step down so we can establish national unity government.

Very funny. They all agree that if Thieu stay, we are going to lose the country. But when I asked, "Well, let's do something," they just say, "You know . . . " Some tell me frankly the Americans are against removing Thieu. That's something I really blame on America. When they finally agree for him to go, they replace him with an old man, Huong, and then Minh, a guy we all know will surrender. The impression of the majority of the Vietnamese, even today, is that America must want and plan to give it to the Communists. If not, instead of a Huong or Minh, they should give it to somebody like myself, a fighter.

Maybe one week before the end Martin come to my house and told me I would take over from Thieu. We talked about who to bring into a new government. I was told later that Martin was trying to keep me quiet, but I still believe in what Martin said. I believe he is very strong anti-Communist, that whether he like me or not, I'm the only choice, the one that can stand and fight the Communists. I remember what he said. "Give us a few days." I don't think violence or a coup can really help, so when Martin came to my house I said, "OK, fine."

———————•———————

FRANK SNEPP *the senior CIA analyst in Saigon when Vietnam fell, set down his recollections of the event in* Decent Interval, *a book that stung the Washington establishment to the quick. Though Snepp revealed no classified information, the CIA sued on grounds he had breached the secrecy provision of his employment contract. The*

Supreme Court eventually ruled in the Agency's favor; all Snepp's royalties from the book, a best-seller in the late seventies, were awarded to the government, and Snepp was barred from writing on foreign affairs without getting a CIA clearance. Snepp now teaches at Long Beach State University in California.

We got Thieu out on the night of April 25. Polgar called in "Joe Kingsley"* and me in late afternoon and told us of our "great privilege." It scared me witless. There was lots of information that Ky and others were going to try to zap him. We got cars and went out to Prime Minister Khiem's place. It was a night made for the movies—the stars were out and you could see tracers along the horizon. Kingsley and I were armed to the teeth. We had portable radios, and standing in the yard waiting, we heard messages about a firefight in Saigon. It was the soundtrack of the last days—my portable radio screeching and bleeping even when I was sleeping.

Thieu finally showed up, looking like he had just stepped out of *Gentleman's Quarterly*, and went in the house. As I waited for him and his party to come out, aides materialized in the shadows, hanging back here and there. They were four or five dark-suited men carrying large suitcases. Two came up to me. I tried asking them in French, "Can I help you with them?" They said, "No, no." Joe and I pointed them to cars and looked at each other. You could hear this tinkle of wind chimes—bing!—when the suitcases hit the trunks.

The party came out. [Retired General Charles] Timmes got in my car with Thieu. The radio was going. I turned it down so it didn't offend Thieu, who smelled of alcohol. The talk in the car was forced. Timmes mentioned he had been together with Thieu in MR-I. Thieu nodded. I looked in the mirror. Thieu looked at me with what I thought could be fear that he was going on a Diem ride. Timmes jokingly called me a "high-class chauffeur." Thieu nodded and said "Good chauffeurs are hard to come by."

It was a ten-minute ride into Tan Son Nhut. The car had tinted windows, so you couldn't see in. Our arrival on the Air America tarmac was a comedy. Polgar ran in front of the cars, which were driving with lights off. The cars screeched to a stop. Martin was standing there in all his magnificence, like an Oxford don, wearing glasses that evening, with his bodyguards standing around. Thieu reached over, shook my hand and said, "Thank you so much." I had an impulse to say, "For what? For all the boys who died here?" But I kept quiet. I did feel the old fellow had been through quite enough.

---

*A pseudonym Snepp assigned to a CIA colleague whose real identity he wanted to shield. Other names in quotation marks are also pseudonyms.

Martin said later, "We didn't say anything on the plane except 'Goodbye.' "

Thomas Polgar

I want to make clear that in my opinion Thieu's resignation on the twenty-first of April was too late. Had he resigned on the twenty-first of March, saying "I accept the blame for what happened in the Highlands," it might have been different. But he is still believing that he has the strength and the wisdom to rally the forces. Even on the American side people found it impossible to believe that this thing is going down the drain.

Since the Paris Accords we had in Saigon the ICCS. The whole thing didn't work but it brought a little bit of color to the Saigon scene [and] from an intelligence point of view, having all these Hungarian and Polish officers to whom we could talk was a very significant thing, because in Poland or in Hungary you don't talk to active-duty military officers if you are an American diplomat, let alone an American intelligence officer. Also, we had good reason to talk with anybody who in his turn talks with the North Vietnamese. Gradually a sort of relationship developed. The Poles and Hungarians could identify [with us] as Westerners. And the Hungarian Chief of Staff comes to me one day and says he has had conversations with the North Vietnamese and he got the impression that if we would do certain things, the Vietnamese Communists would be prepared to arrange a political solution—a kind of fig leaf for Communist control.

He named a couple of conditions: Thieu must resign, the government must be established composed of people the North Vietnamese considered acceptable, the United States must guarantee they would limit their role in Vietnam to that of a normal embassy, and no more U.S. military intervention. And he says "If you are prepared to do these things it is my impression that the North Vietnamese will talk with you about the modalities of how we can bring this thing to some kind of an ending that's more elegant than North Vietnamese tanks driving down the street."

I reported all this to Martin and to Washington—that the Hungarian said these were "prerequisites. If you do this then I think that maybe the Vietnamese Communists would be willing to talk with you." Martin was interested and he had several exchanges with Kissinger on the subject. But in fact the American government could not get itself organized to say in effect, "Okay, we surrender, what are the terms?" In the event, none of these things were done. Thieu resigned a couple of days after this overture, but the other things were not happening. One day the Hungarian came back to me and said, "Look, remember when I talked with you I said these things have to be done promptly. By promptly, my friends in the North don't mean a couple of weeks or a couple of months. They mean a couple of days."

But nothing happened. We were not able to deliver on these prerequisites. Because we were unwilling, we were unable. Looking back, it was a wasted opportunity. It seemed to me we had nothing to lose at that point. I think anything would have been better than taking the Embassy out from the roof and leaving thousands upon thousands of people who depended upon us.

———— ◆ ————

GRAHAM MARTIN

Now, the two Hungarians would like to get together and talk Hungarian, reminisce about Budapest. Polgar was a Hungarian refugee. It was legitimate information as far as *he* was concerned but what he had in mind certainly was not what the North Vietnamese had in mind. You listen to all of it. You never know when something might pop that you can use. But Polgar [was] sucked in by his fellow Hungarian. I didn't even know he was doing that. It was one of the few times that things kind of got away. He was passing it on to Washington, and Kissinger came back and says, "You know what's going on here?" He wanted to know what in the goddamn hell am I doing letting this go on. He was using Malcolm Browne of *The New York Times* as a conduit to the people in the North Vietnamese delegation out at Tan Son Nhut. I called him in and I told him that if I had any more trouble I'd cut off his balls and stuff one in each ear.

They were assuming that you could put in a third force, a government that would somehow be acceptable to Hanoi. There was no way in which that could be done. You could have had some kind of coalition, but not that. The first thing the North Vietnamese did was to kick all those people into the dustbin. That [third force] never existed except in the journalists' and some of our erudite intellectuals' minds. They were all sent to concentration camps. It never amounted to a damn.

It became clear during the last week that the North Vietnamese weren't going to negotiate with Huong either. Then the great pressures arose to install General Minh, Big Minh, as president. The French were pushing this. My friend Jean Marie Merillon [the French Ambassador] wanted me to go to Huong and parallel his recommendation that a government turnover would be good. And I kept asking "How about Hanoi?" And he was honest; he said he didn't really know. I said "You'd better find out."

In the last few days I counted on it, that they [the North Vietnamese] would be sensible. There were lots of things going on. We had Colonel Harry Summers go up to Hanoi on a liaison flight for the North Vietnamese contingent at Camp Davis. We took some of the North Vietnamese up and brought others back down. And I wanted Summers to sort of casually indicate when he was sitting around the airport in Hanoi that he hoped the Americans wouldn't be back up there in the next week or so, and if you interfere with us, what the hell happens to Hanoi? I was running every kind of thing. The Hungarian wanted to know what all that power was doing out in the Gulf. I said "I hope we never have to find out, old boy."

There's one more thing and it really ought not to be lost sight of, and that is who is smart enough to know what the North Vietnamese would finally decide to permit the South Vietnamese to do? They did what I thought they would do, but in many ways it was the wrong thing for them to do internationally. It would have been much more sensible to have permitted Big Minh to go on for a while, then move him out and take it over. You would have had a lot better acceptance back here. Aid, trade with Japan and Germany, and so on. So, you didn't do anything to destroy the possibility of whatever the Vietnamese could work out for themselves.

———•———

JAMES SCHLESINGER

When I became Secretary of Defense it was my obligation to maintain the flow of U.S. assistance as we withdrew. I don't like to overstate it, but it was a *moral* obligation to keep that up because we were throwing the ARVN, which had never been particularly strong, on its own resources. And I was steadily appalled at the actions that were taken on the Hill to reduce the aid package, which was the justification for the withdrawal of our own forces.

To many members of Congress, Vietnam appeared to be a lost cause and they felt we were just throwing money away. But I think there were two, more fundamental problems beyond that. One was that there had developed an abiding distrust for the objectives established by the executive branch. And the mistrust between the two branches could only be overcome temporarily and with a great deal of work. And secondly there was a tremendous momentum to the anti-war movement, which spilled over from what was perhaps the logical objective of getting our own forces out, to the general objective of having done with Vietnam altogether—including support for what was regarded, unjustly, as the "corrupt regime" of Mr. Thieu. The attempts on Capitol Hill to reduce aid became such that we were putting in one third of the resources that we had pledged ourselves to put in. There was indifference up there to the fact that we had made the pledge, and to the obligation.

Beyond all that I think that in their erroneous belief that somehow getting shut of Vietnam would be a victory for the United States, the antiwar forces in Congress did not realize the political consequences to this country of the loss of Vietnam. On the other hand, I think it's also fair to say that many of the supporters of the war in Southeast Asia exaggerated the penalties that the country would pay.

My first inkling that we had lost came when the North Vietnamese began to make maneuvers toward the end of 1974 and in January of 1975 and we did not respond. They were testing us. They did not really believe that they were getting away with what they were getting away with. But given the constraints under which we had to operate, *I* knew they were going to get away with it. Then of course came the attack in the Central Highlands and the total collapse of the ARVN divisions. At that point it was all over. I had been making menacing sounds in public whenever the subject of North Vietnam had come up—they'd just better beware, and so forth. But the congressional restraints that had been established in the summer of '73 wouldn't permit our taking effective countermeasures.

Now, many of the people who were with me were people who had served there, and they had emotional ties to the country, and they just could not—and I understand it, and I'm not criticizing them—back off and say "We did our best, but it is now hopeless." They kept seeing hope where hope did not exist. [General] Fred Weyand, for example, whom Ford had sent out to Southeast Asia, was tied to Thieu and to the Vietnamese with bonds of loyalty. He came back and reported to the President, that six hundred and fifty million bucks is needed.

Before Mr. Ford asked for additional assistance in Vietnam we had a meeting of the NSC, and I said "Mr. President, it's all over." He was kind of rankled by that, quite indignant. I got sort of the Michigan fight song. And I said "Mr. President, you should go up to the Hill tomorrow and say we have suffered a severe setback, call for blood, sweat, and tears, and a national effort to deal with the consequences, but there's no way that you can persuade anybody that Vietnam is salvageable."

Bill Colby, who had been an operator during the war and was then the director of Central Intelligence, lost all of his detachment and gave a briefing about the Southern Redoubt that was going to be established around Saigon and the Mekong Delta. But the fact was it was all over. And I just said "Mr. President, the North Vietnamese are all over the place. There's no way that you can stem this thing. The [South] Vietnamese have lost their nine best divisions up there in the north. These divisions in the south [near Saigon] are not the same quality. They're selected for political reliability rather than fighting skills. And they're outnumbered. The North Vietnamese are pulling forces in from the rest of the country."

Now, you ask what do I remember about this period. The thing that I remember most about this period was the emotional involvement of the people in the Pentagon. It was admirable, sympathetic, but not very productive, either from an overall strategic standpoint, or from the standpoint of abiding by the law that the Congress had passed, which said "Thou shalt not become involved again." And I had to have very, very stringent rules to prevent our people from walloping these "little bastards" once again, which was their inclination: Thou shalt not fire, unless fired upon. You are offshore to gather in refugees. You are not there to engage in fights to prevent the North Vietnamese from rolling in. Because all of the impulses in the Department were "These guys are coming at us. Let's bash them." And I said "Oh, no. Oh, no. We are not going to jump on that tar baby again." I gave that speech several times in the NMCC [the National Military Command Center].

Now [General] George Brown [then Chairman of the Joint Chiefs of Staff] was not atypical. George was not particularly discreet in his public discourse. He was in Djakarta on a visit and held a press conference out there. Thank God there were a lot of other things going on that day. Some journalist asked him, "Well, General, what would you do about Vietnam?" And George pointed at a map of Indochina and said, "I'd take four U.S. divisions, and land them right here at Vung Tau, and march straight up . . . " And the Ambassador heard the first ten words and said, "General Brown, you know we have another appointment," grabbed his arm, and marched him out of there. George was more indiscreet than some, but that was the general impulse. It was very painful to me as well. I can recall weeping over the collapse of Vietnam.

I think it was Easter Day. I went to church with my wife, and I found myself weeping over it, because hell, these people were going to be dragged down into this tyranny. As the [Vietnamese] ambassador said at the time, "On us there is a night descending beyond which there is no dawn." Melodramatic perhaps, but there was truth

in it. But the strategic situation was clear, and the congressional
injunction was even clearer.

———————◆———————

GEN. BRENT SCOWCROFT, *U.S. Army retired, was Gerald Ford's
national security adviser. He is now a consultant in Washington
and an adviser to the Reagan administration on defense and foreign policy issues.*

In the final days, when things started to unravel, what was really
striking was the extent to which everybody put pressure on the President to quick, pull everything out. From the executive branch, from
the Hill. He had a meeting for example with the Senate Foreign
Relations Committee, I think in early March, and to a man they
said "Get out now." And the President, Kissinger and I were almost
alone in saying "Look, we've got to hang on. We probably can't
stabilize the situation. But every day that we're there, we can get
out more of the Vietnamese who are depending on us, before they're
left to the mercies of the North."

The atmosphere in the White House was pretty grim. The biggest
problems, I think, came from the differences among the people
around Ford—the people Ford inherited from the Nixon administration, Schlesinger, Kissinger, and me, and the people he brought
with him. The people he brought with him tended to say "Vietnam
is not your war. It was Nixon's war. Don't wrap that thing around
yourself. This is not your problem." Ford never thought that way,
but that was the advice he was getting. And in one speech, a paragraph was added on the airplane that more or less said that—"Let's
put it behind us"—before it was really over. That was the most fundamental controversy. It never really surfaced, never was confronted, but it was very much in the air.

Nobody could say that the North might not overrun the place quickly and we'd lose an awful lot of Americans in addition to our South
Vietnamese friends. Meantime Graham Martin of course was saying
almost to the end that the place was resuscible. So it was a pretty
tense period. Some of the initial reaction with the withdrawal from
Ban Me Thuot was that well, maybe one could hold a truncated
South Vietnam that included the major cities and the Delta region.
But this all happened in a very short period of time so there was no
coalescing on it.

There's no question that Schlesinger was right [in telling the President "it's over"]. But our objective was to keep things going as
long as possible so we could get out those people who would be

most in jeopardy. It was a withdrawal operation, and we wanted to hold out while we extracted the people who had really thrown in their lot with us. Had we just turned around and run, had we just said good-bye, there would have been an awful lot more people who suffered than who did. And there were only three people in the Administration who felt that way, and that was Ford, Kissinger, and I. I never thought we could rescue the place. What we did was just a gesture to try to stabilize things so we could make an orderly withdrawal.

CHAPTER THIRTEEN

"The Running"

MAJOR military campaigns are not prepared in a day. Hanoi's divisions, moving farther and faster than they had expected, spent most of April mopping up bypassed ARVN units and maneuvering toward Saigon for what promised to be a climactic battle.* Fearing that the Thieu regime and its American allies might be preparing a secret counterpunch, perhaps with air power, the North Vietnamese took the time to bring forward enough forces and supplies to insure victory no matter what. That Saigon and the provinces around it did not simply go to pieces was due partly to the resulting lull in combat. But it also owed heavily to the Thieu regime's iron grip on information, its imposition of a curfew, its threat to jail ordinary Vietnamese caught trying to leave—and to the playacting skills of Graham Martin and his Embassy.

Not long after the war was over, bitter recriminations were heard over the behavior of Martin and his staff in the final month of the conflict. Critics—chief among them, former CIA-man Frank Snepp—charged that Martin's steadfast refusal to admit that the situation was irretrievably lost had left thousands of deserving Vietnamese to twist in the wind after the Communist takeover. Martin, he charged, had refused to launch an official evacuation early enough, and to warn those who had no hope of being extricated by American means to get out on their own.

It is true that though both the U.S. and South Vietnamese governments knew the war was lost, they pretended otherwise. Newspapers and broadcasters in Saigon were forced to report patently phony accounts of victories, and vast casualties inflicted on the enemy.

---

*No big battle ever took place, largely because the South had no forces left. The closest thing to it was a ten-day battle by the ARVN 18th Division to hold onto Xuan Loc, forty miles east of Saigon. Eventually, Communist forces simply bypassed the position and headed for the capital.

Martin went so far as to ask the wives of senior Embassy officials to stay in Saigon, simply to help deceive American reporters. But there were reasons. The Americans feared, as Thomas Polgar says, "a breakdown of discipline" in the capital—another panic on the order of Danang. Polgar and others even worried that South Vietnamese military men, angry at being deserted, might turn their guns on Americans. Both governments wanted time to spirit the United States's special friends out of the country—and not until the last minute did they give up hope that some face-saving coalition deal might be cooked up.

Operating mainly in secret and under cover of darkness, the Embassy and its Defense Attaché Office—the remnant of what had been MACV—bused thousands of Vietnamese out to Tan Son Nhut airfield and put them aboard otherwise empty outbound military transports to the Philippines and Guam. But the capacity of the flights was so small in terms of the numbers who wanted or needed evacuation that it was inevitable many people would be left behind. Worse, to execute the secret evacuation, the U.S. had to cut deals to take out first the families of military and police officials who controlled the routes. And the Americans who actually ran the flights often gave preference to their own friends, lovers, and families* in loading the planes. That left behind thousands whose official connections put them in real danger.

The United States might have used oceangoing freighters or even Navy ships to multiply the carrying capacity. But prevented by the War Powers Act—and by Pentagon reluctance—from bringing in troops even to protect a withdrawal, the Embassy judged it impossible to keep order on the docks. At least three freighters sailed empty in the days before the fall, and though the Embassy had secretly made a deal with the local Vietnamese commander to protect an evacuation across the beaches at Vung Tau, the Navy refused to consider sending in its own boats.

Through all this, only high-ranking Americans and Vietnamese in the military and intelligence services knew with certainty what was being done. But rumors soon filtered out, the atmosphere in Saigon became tense and poisonous, and the Vietnamese began to call it "The Running"—a mad, every-man-for-himself scramble for the exits. On the final, chaotic day, as flocks of helicopters lifted out the last Americans and those Vietnamese who could get into the Embassy, U.S. officials could do little more than tell the rest that if they got themselves to sea, the Navy would pick them up. It was

---

*It has been asserted, though never proved, that there was also a great deal of plain old-fashioned bribery.

left to a handful of Americans, operating largely on their own initiative, to mobilize water transport for their own friends and acquaintances—and to thousands of other Vietnamese to find their own downriver passage. The fact that seventy thousand of them did is mute testimony to the fact that the Vietnamese were never the helpless children so many Americans thought them to be.

THOMAS POLGAR

What happened in Saigon was very much governed in our minds by our experiences in Danang and later in Nha Trang because goddamnit the one thing we didn't want in Saigon is a breakdown of discipline. So to all the people who say, "Why didn't you start evacuation three weeks earlier?" had we done that we would have had exactly [what] we had in Danang—total panic. The only way we were able to manage in Saigon is by making all kinds of deals, saying "Okay, on this plane today, we will take out the family members of two hundred national police if you will give us your word of honor that you will stay here with us until the end and maintain order." And we made the same deal with the military and with the political police, whose chief we got out literally on the last afternoon.

When the evacuation planning began we had enough ships at sea to take on quite a number of people, but there were two big obstacles. The people could not get out and the ships could not come in. Saigon is about eighty-five miles up the river, and it was felt that if these ships come up the river and tie up at the quay in Saigon, we would have a terrible mob scene. The only way we could prevent a mob scene was to first land a division of Marines, but that was precluded by the War Powers Act. Martin says he would not accept the responsibility of the ships coming in without ground protection and Washington says "We can't give you ground protection," so we were at an impasse. And Martin felt so strongly [about it] that three big American ships sailed empty because he would not accept the risk of loading them without protection.

I think that was probably a wise decision. If the word had gotten around that "We can get on an American ship by rushing it," we had about three million people in Saigon and I think we would have had a million at the dockside. The evacuation committee at the Embassy decided that the United States simply did not have the means for a mass evacuation and what we should concentrate on is getting people out rapidly but in such a way as to not upset the applecart.

There were an awful lot of armed soldiers and policemen running around. The great risk was always that some hopped-up battalion commander fires up his troops and says "It's all the fault of the Americans. Let's kill them before they go." Maybe it would never have happened, but I can tell you that this was a very real consideration. We had Vietnamese officers who talked that way, but whether they really meant it, I don't know. We were able to evacuate a lot of people by running buses without lights during curfew through dozens of checkpoints out to the airfield. And we made a deal with every single checkpoint commander who owned the road: "Don't make any trouble and you'll be taken out, too."

***

CHARLES BENOIT

As this wave of people came south after Danang, there built up this real hysteria. It became clear that if you take care of old number one, you might have a chance; if you wait, you'll be the guy on the dock watching the last boat leave. In mid-April when I saw we were taking out the families of Vietnamese Air Force officers, it said to me, "The officers have planes; soon they'll be flying themselves out."

There was a ditty the Communists used to sing to intimidate Vietnamese from working for the Americans. The sense of it was that "You work for the Americans and we'll turn you into shoe leather." And one day in April one of my secretaries [at the Ford Foundation], said: "You know what hell is going to happen to me, don't you? They're going to make me into shoes." [By then] I was getting between thirty and fifty phone calls a day from Vietnamese friends. All they were saying was "Hi, how are you?" They were calling to see if I'd left yet. They were looking to us to tell them what was happening in their own country. And had we started bringing people out earlier, that would have made things worse. It was one of those things where if you'd started two weeks earlier, you still would have needed to have started two weeks before that.

I had always counted myself as someone who was looking for a solution that did not include a total and complete American victory, but I did not see Saigon going at that point. I had my apartment stockpiled with food and water, enough to feed twenty people for two months or so, because I was expecting a seige. I have to say, though, for having spent so many years at odds with the Embassy, that when the Ambassador started saying this was it, forget it, wrap it up, it's the last battle, it's done, I found myself [thinking], "They haven't been right before. Why should they be right now?"

Martin was righteous where I don't think righteousness was justified. He had a strong sense that there was a crusade involved and that the Communists were the only ones who broke treaties and played with a fixed deck and were dishonest. He once said, and these are not his exact words, but close, "When I came to South Vietnam, I thought there were political prisoners. I'll be honest with you, I thought there were. And I can tell you that there are none, and I have never told a lie in my life." That's the kind of person you were dealing with. How do you have a conversation with a person where your only recourse is to call him a liar?

I did not think we had a moral edge on any of those issues, and I found myself at odds with him for a year and a half. I didn't have a real solution to the problem, but for years I always said that if I could push a button that would mean all Americans would be gone by tomorrow morning, I wouldn't hesitate. But while Martin has been accused of foot-dragging on the evacuation, even though I'd wanted to push that button for years, it made sense to go slow because once you pull the plug, it's total chaos.

In 1972 I was talking to a South Vietnamese soldier. He told me: "What I hold against the Americans is that you got us to this point. There are always going to be Vietnamese fighting other Vietnamese. But we would be doing it with sticks and stones, clubs and maybe a knife or two—not with these sophisticated weapons and killing each other to this degree. So I blame you for that. And since you got us this far, if you ever let us down, if you ever turn your back on us, if you ever stop supporting us, I'll stop shooting Vietnamese and start shooting Americans." I never forgot that.

Had Martin begun an evacuation before it became obvious that it was over, it could have gotten vicious. What really kept the lid on was that the Vietnamese weren't sure what we were up to, and they were looking to us for a lead. It wasn't until that lead became clear that the chaos really started.

———◆———

GRAHAM MARTIN

[*Showing a cable*.] See if you catch a line in that first paragraph . . . "Has no appetite for the evacuation of any Vietnamese." You see this is what CINCPAC wanted to do, what the military wanted to do. They pulled beautiful little airlifts, golly and really made my job difficult by saying how wonderful it had been at Phnom Penh, where

they had lifted out, what, three hundred people? Great help. They
didn't want to get caught up in any over-the-beach thing.

The Vietnamese Marines were down in Cap St. Jacques, at Vung
Tau. I wanted two of the supply planes coming in to sit down there
to pick up their families and take them over to Clark. They were
afraid of it in CINCPAC. So I told them goddamn it, I want it. And
so we did it, took one hundred fifty people in each plane in fifteen
minutes. And from that point on the Marine general down there
belonged to me. He was going to protect the whole landing area if
we'd wanted to use that for over-the-beach evacuation.

But our military didn't want to have anything to do with anything
outside the Embassy or the Defense Attaché's Office. They wouldn't
even let us make a survey along the beach. We did it anyway, but I
couldn't in the end make them come into the beach to take people
off. I did finally tell the Vietnamese to get out into the sea. "You
find the boats and we'll pick you up." And seventy thousand of
them did.

During the last couple of weeks I was doing things that were totally
illegal and getting criticized for not doing more. We had I don't know
how many DAO civilians who would not leave without their Vietnamese wives and children—the old contract people [who] had stayed
on. If I had gotten down to that, we would have had nothing but
those people left and all the people who could have gotten people
on planes would have been gone. This was just military pressure to
get everything down to where [Admiral Noel] Gayler [the Pacific
commander] could come in and pick everybody up in one helicopter lift just like they did in Phnom Penh. Which had no relation to
reality. Kissinger would send me out these cables, and I'd tell him I
wouldn't do it. And he would go along with it. His ass was covered,
but this centered everything on me.

An awful lot of nonsense has been written about that period. One
deputy defense attaché I'm supposed to have fired because he was
getting people out quicker than I wanted them to be gotten out. This
was not so. He was Air Force and he had all this airlift coming in
from Clark, and he used it to put a lot of his own people on, going
back. I knew this, fully approved of it, couldn't care less, except
that we knew it was illegal as far as Vietnam and the Philippines
and the United States were concerned. I could not have officially
reprimanded him without putting a stop to it. So I just looked the
other way. Then we began to do more and more of this, but the
pressures got great in Washington to stop. In fact the first group
that had got to Clark Field, we were told to bring them back. Look
at this cable. This came from the part of the [State] Department deal-

ing with consular affairs. It wasn't proper, they weren't all documented, etcetera.

But it got all straightened out in the long run. I mean, you can't
just pay attention to that sort of crap. They were simply snowed
by the magnitude of the thing, and didn't know how to respond.
But I had, for four years in Europe, been responsible for coordination of all evacuation in case the Soviets wanted to come into town.
[I had studied many past examples, so] I probably knew more
about it than anybody else. The main thing is, I just wouldn't be
snowed by it.

———————◆———————

LIONEL ROSENBLATT

The thing that prompted Craig Johnstone and I to go out was an
Embassy message of April eighteenth, saying "We don't really know
what can be done for the large number of Vietnamese who do deserve
evacuation, except to advise them to head towards the coast and
try to rendezvous with the Seventh Fleet." Well, for a city-dwelling
Saigonese to make the land trip, much less figure out how to get his
family into a small boat and get up alongside a Seventh Fleet vessel
seemed to us to be total abdication. And that was the real precipita-
tor of our decision. We had suggested earlier that an element of the
[State Department] Task Force be sent out from Washington to
take charge of evacuation in Saigon. That was rejected, so we knew
that if we'd ask to go ourselves, that would have been turned down
as well.

*Rosenblatt and Johnstone went AWOL from the State Task Force
and flew to Saigon on their own.*

When we arrived we decided we'd try to look as French as we could.
We borrowed a 1940's Citroen from a friend until we got vans, which
were much handier for transporting refugees. And on our first trip
down to the square where the main cathedral and the Central Post
Office are located, we pulled up in our black Citroën and I hopped
out with a briefcase to meet with our first set of refugees. It all did
seem a little bit melodramatic. Their first questions were, "So we
have to decide right away?" There was an air of unreality [because
none of them] realized that there was nothing between the North
Vietnamese army and that square in downtown Saigon.

It wasn't only Vietnamese who had this unreal appreciation of the
situation. I remember being accosted by an AID official five days

before the end, who asked us "Well, gee, you guys coming from Washington might be able to give me some advice. I'm trying to decide whether to extend for another tour." We said he ought to wait and see how things worked out.

[It was not easy] to contact and organize evacuees. We were always keeping an ear on the American radio for "White Christmas," which was the signal that the end was nigh. The Citroën didn't have a radio, and every once in a while we'd [stop somewhere to] try to catch the station to make sure that the fateful notes weren't being sounded.

Eventually we borrowed a van from an American airline company and our driver was a young lady who took us to the fringes of Saigon without ever showing a note of personal concern. The refugees filled in their paperwork after we got them into the airport. I remember these folks trying to fill out forms in the back of the military bowling alley at Tan Son Nhut, under the pinsetting machinery with the pins in the up position, and under streetlights on the hood of a military truck. This was all done in the military athletic area at the airport, and the last step was to be mustered up on the tennis courts and then to board buses that took them to the aircraft.

One of the people we took out was a government official who knew no English. We communicated in my Vietnamese, which had become rusty. He said there was no question in his mind that he would be killed. His dad had been killed by the Communists some years back. And then, just before boarding [time] he said, "Lionel, I've decided I can't go through with this. I look around and almost everybody here is rich or talks English. I don't qualify and I'm worried I'll starve to death. What's going to happen to us in the States?" And I said, "I have no idea. Basically we're inventing as we go along. You may be in a camp for a long time, but you will survive. You won't starve to death." Then I took out twenty dollars and I said, "Look I don't have much, but here it is. And this symbolizes that I stand behind you in terms of getting you at any time enough to eat." He now is a machinist in Minneapolis, owns his own house. He and his wife speak excellent English and the kids are doing fine in school.

We left on a DC-3, on a typical, ninety-degree, April Saigon day. We were exhausted and there was absolutely no heat in the cabin and none of us was wearing anything warmer than a summer shirt. And already as we and the Vietnamese aboard took a last look at the rice paddies receding below, we were shivering, as if instantly Vietnam and the tropics were a thing of the past and we were into new and northern latitudes.

NANCY BENNETT *is the wife of Josiah Bennett, the last political counselor of the Saigon Embassy.*

I was the public relations person in Saigon for the Holt Adoption Agency [of Eugene, Oregon]. The South Vietnamese government didn't want it called an adoption agency. We were called, in turn, a feeding station, a care station, and then the Holt Children's Services, Inc. In the final month there was a rush to get orphans out. We had government approval to take [them] out despite their papers not all being in order. Some of the children were not spoken for.

The Army had this huge plane, a C-5A [which had flown in some artillery as part of a token military resupply]. My boss and I went to look at it. They were going to stack the babies in like boxes. Mrs. Holt always insisted we have our own escorts. She would ask a woman who wanted to be an escort "Can you go thirty hours without a drink? Can you change diapers? Are you willing to learn?" We normally used Embassy women and commercial people from Esso and other firms, all of them Americans. But for the C-5A the Army said "You will take *our* escorts." They were elegant Vietnamese women who looked down on our children. We didn't like the way the flight was being run, so we got a Pan Am charter instead. As a result, none of our children was on the C-5A when it crashed.

People saw the plane go down. Friends called and asked "Are any of your children on that?" It was big news—a planeload of orphans. The Ambassador sent me to the Saigon municipal hospital where the survivors were being brought in. It was a terrible scene, but the plane had gone down in rice fields and it could have been worse.

A month before the end the Ambassador asked the senior wives to stay in order to keep things looking calm for the reporters. Staying was not particularly heroic on my part. I knew there was a plane for the Ambassador's wife, with room on it for us. I had to appear normal—I went to lunch with my Vietnamese friends as usual. And Fox Butterfield [of *The New York Times*] kept saying, "Well, Nancy's still here."

There were others who had to stay, too. One of them was Peter Orr, who worked in the consulate. Every day there was a vast crowd around the consulate, and Peter had to work day and night. He sent Vietnamese-speaking officers out with American passports to track down the children of GIs. Last-minute messages were coming in from fathers who had gotten birth certificates and who said that their wives wanted the child and that they would adopt them. We would go out and look for these children. Some half-black children had been hidden. Some families denied they had the kids—and some even asked for money for the kids!

Peter himself had a problem. He was divorced, and he had his two boys, five and three years old, with him. I volunteered to [take care of] the boys so he could stay. I even signed a document saying I would keep the boys if he died. He was trying to keep them from his ex-wife. At a time like that, you do it! We lived next door and we kept the boys with us.

I left April 25 on a private executive plane that went to Bangkok. The Embassy no longer wanted us. Peter Orr's boys came out with us. When we took off, Thomas, who was three, said, "We're off! We're off on a vacation!" His brother Benjamin, who was five, said, "Don't be silly! This isn't a vacation. This is a plane!"

THOMAS POLGAR

This is what happened with the orphans. The Vietnamese foreign minister and Ambassador Martin and others pick up on the idea that shipping a lot of Vietnamese orphans to the United States would evoke great sympathy. Here are these poor little kids, they lost their father and their mother, and will generate an emotional response to the problem of Vietnam. Again it was hoped that this would trigger some kind of pressure on Congress. Well, as in other aspects in the final weeks in Vietnam, Murphy's Law was in full operation. It was decided to use one of the C-5As that was bringing in military equipment on the empty outward run by filling it up with orphans and female Americans for whom this would be a good opportunity to go back to the United States. So a lot of the female personnel working for or related to members of the Defense Attaché's Office were selected to get on this plane to carry the orphans, something like six hundred all in one fell swoop.

Well, it's a nice spring afternoon, the plane takes off, it has some problem with its rudder. It turns around and makes a crash landing into a swamp near Tan Son Nhut. The C-5A is a very big plane and its wheels and the lower deck get buried in the swamp so two hundred and six babies and thirty-five or forty American females traveling on the plane get killed. Nothing happens to anybody on the upper deck of the plane. It was completely a matter of fate—who was on the upper deck and who was on the lower deck. And then, of course, it turned out that not all the orphans were orphans and some people had used this opportunity to get their kids to the States. And it was another one of terrible blows that struck the consciousness and, in end effect, exactly the opposite happened from what was intended.

————————•————————

LA ANH TU

In 1975 I was private in Army but still playing music at base sixty kilometers away from Saigon in Lai Khe. Things were getting bad. My duty was to perform in Army band for soldiers, but two or three months before the end, they make us guard around barracks. One week later they make us walk further around circle of compound. They have curfew for soldiers. No one can get in or out of camp after midnight. Later, civilians are included in curfew, too.

Every day a truckload came back with wounded soldiers, and I was scared. A lot of friends said people start leaving Saigon. They can see every day helicopter go up and down, up and down, to pick up the people. I asked my boss, the major, to go to Saigon on pass. My excuse was I needed a better set of instruments. So I got a pass. The pass was good for thirty kilometers. He said, "If MP catch you, your problem." I have military officer friends. I rode with them in a jeep into city.

I deserted for one month till end. I was staying with my Belgian friend at the house of workers for the Air France city ticket office. I was going out in the street, watchfully. I would see my family almost every day. The family would come to where I was hiding.

Thieu's resignation I watched on TV in my hideout. The minute that happened, I think it was a sign we would have to leave soon. In the last days in Saigon, when I walk on the street, everybody was so silent. They walked like they were running, and nobody talked to nobody. It make me worry more. Normally, in spite of war, people in Saigon took time to enjoy life. If we fight, we fight for ourselves, because nobody seems to care for the war.

Boss from Lai Khe camp went to Saigon to see my family. He says, "Tell him come back. Situation is not that bad." My mother tells me this. I said, "Just tell him I don't care how good or bad it is. I know it's dangerous, I don't want to stay there." I didn't trust him.

My brother-in-law, Larry Pope, managed Tan Son Nhut American Officers' club. Thuy Anh said she wouldn't leave if we couldn't get out. He said he'd find a way. He told my family everybody have shirt and pants in one suitcase and be ready to leave. Khanh Ha [another sister] already left Vietnam. She had kid and French citizenship because she had been married to a Frenchman.

Larry can get in and out of airbase. One day he said, "OK, *Now*!

Tomorrow we going to go.'' They don't check Larry's car, so we go two of us in trunk, two or three per trip. We went to cemetery next to base. Lan Anh and Uyen get in, then my brother and his wife, then me with my mother. In the car trunk, Uyen was afraid. We were thirty minutes in trunk. He goes in and out to pick up another two. My mother, she was so scared, also so happy. We get into base and have to stay overnight. Next morning we drive to DAO. We wait outside eight hours in car. We are afraid MPs will catch us if we get out. People bring food to us at lunch. We still needed red tape. At last we make a false pass. I pretended I worked at DAO. Later on Larry and a Vietnamese friend typed one pass for us. We took a night plane, a C-130, to Clark AFB. It was packed with people, all on floor. The people were scared.

It is difficult to say feeling I had that day. I was happy I got out of a dangerous situation. But I feel so bad [when] I see the lights underneath, and I say this is maybe the last time I see Saigon.

———◆———

KHE BA DO

In February of 1975, my wife and I were [in a delegation] invited to observe the French education system. There we heard about the invasion. Bad news came so fast it caught everyone by surprise. I heard friends on the trip talking about not going home. To defect is not my line of conduct, not my philosophy, so we went home for what turned out to be one month. The situation became worse and worse. My students from central Vietnam were cut off from family financial support. A lot of refugees were coming in. The buildings of my university became a camp, and the Ministry of Social Welfare took over. I went to work every day, but I couldn't do anything. Refugees were on the dorm floors, in the lecture halls, cooking everywhere. It was a kind of chaos.

I had heard rumors about Danang and the evacuation. It was a very scary situation, but I still trust that America will help us. I did not know the full war picture. I had been *educator* all my life. I did not have friends in the army. They were regarded as uneducated people. Some people were talking about killing themselves if the Communists came because there was no way to flee the country. The government did not grant you an exit visa. My sister-in-law, whose husband was teaching at Berkeley, cabled us to leave the country. USC sent us work permits and job offers.

I didn't plan to leave. I asked AID friends to use their phone to call my sister-in-law in Berkeley and explain. I said there was nothing to fear, we are going to fight back. The USIS director, Alan Carter, had said do not fear. He said "Don't listen to rumors. (Graham) Martin is not packing." I told him later he deceived us. I did not want to leave even at the last minute. The Sunday before we left my son had Catholic confirmation in the Saigon Cathedral. It was a big family gathering, twenty-five people. After lunch in my apartment we discussed to flee or not, and we all decided no.

Two days later was a holiday so the schools were closed and my wife was home. She got a phone call from Nancy Bennett: "It would be good for you to leave. You're so close to the Americans." I was in my office in Saigon. My wife came, closed my door, and told me of Nancy's call. I decided to go home. After lunch we discussed the matter for hours in our bedroom. My son didn't know, or my mother-in-law, or the three maids, the chauffeur, my two bodyguards, or the cook.

I am sad because my family and close Vietnamese friends are very angry [that] I did not let them know. When we did go, I could not leak to other people. Some friends ended up in France. I keep writing them to explain. I get no answer! I am the only one in my family who got out. Still an older sister, who is seventy, and two younger brothers are there. I did not dare to write them for six years. When my sister wrote and asked me to petition under the orderly departure program, I started to write them.

Here is proof that I want to stay. Earlier [an American] friend proposed that I send my son to Bangkok for safety. I said no. The only thing I asked him to sneak out was my family photographs and send them to my three oldest kids in California. If we have to die, at least my children in California have something for the family. One night in the middle of April my wife and I close the bedroom door and stay up to peel off the photos from the albums and put them in a box. Our friend brought the box back to us at Berkeley.

———◆———

RICHARD ARMITAGE

In December of 1974 I quit and I came home to my house in California and told everyone who'd listen, "It's going to hell in a hand basket." I called Washington back and forth saying "Look, We've got to do something," and I got a lot of "Yeah, uh-huh. Thanks for your views on national security affairs." I then spent a very difficult, for me and for my family, three months in California worrying. In March I went back to Vietnam just by myself. I saw the deterioration in Danang and the rapid retreats, and I came back frustrated beyond belief, and on the twentieth of April or so, I called up a friend of mine in the Pentagon named Erich Von Marbod and I said, "Erich, I hope people are listening. It's over." And he said, "We've been looking for you. Come to Washington immediately."

I came to see Erich and he said, "If you're willing, you can go back to Vietnam. It's over. We realize it. We're going to have to save some of our assets." I flew in on the last Pan Am flight, on 24 April. Immediately I was charged with going to the Vietnamese CNO* and explaining that we should make preparations to evacuate naval units and equipment and people. We started to develop a plan but even at that time we did not realize that 30 April would be the drop-dead date. Even the Communists have said they thought it would be early May. We were basically planning to order all naval units to come to their home ports and gather their families in the bases, ostensibly to weather the siege. Very few of us knew the real reason for this would be to evacuate in a group once the order was given. We could not ever say that.

In the middle of that, on the morning of the twenty-eighth, Erich called me to join him at Tan Son Nhut, and he said, "We've got some equipment in Bien Hoa Airbase we want to get out of there and we're going to send you up to do it, and there are some Vietnamese airmen to help you." Well, we got up to the base and then couldn't get out. A helicopter dropped me in the morning and the base was then surrounded by NVA and they were shelling it like mad and coming in the wire. The Vietnamese airmen who had been helping me pack up some sensitive helicopter parts were shooting the NVA at the wire.

I called Erich and I said, "We've got a problem." And Erich got some fellows from Bird Air, the CIA contract. They flew in in the middle of the most horrendous shelling of Bien Hoa you've ever seen, spun around on the runway, we all ran out and jumped in the back. We went the fifteen minutes or so back to Tan Son Nhut, and stepped out on the tarmac to be greeted by the bombing by those four A-37s which had been captured earlier. So I was one of the few Americans to have been bombed in Vietnam. By the enemy. [*chuckles.*] Plenty had been bombed by our own planes.

I went back to Navy headquarters where I spent that night, the night of the twenty-eighth. It was clear there was fighting all throughout Saigon. I found out we were beginning the evacuation, so I told the CNO of the Vietnamese Navy "All right, I'll meet you at Con Son Island." I went back to Tan Son Nhut and got out on a helicopter to the *Blue Ridge.*

---

*Chief of Naval Operations.

They dispatched me with a couple of ships down to Con Son. The Vietnamese Navy, about thirty-one ships, had steamed out and anchored and I met up with them there and we went with twenty- or thirty- odd thousand people across to the Philippines. I might say Erich Von Marbod effected the retrieval of many of our assets. We sank many of our small boats, though not enough of them, and we got most of the large craft out and made it impossible for them to fall into the hands of the North Vietnamese, a small solace, but it was, nonetheless.

GRAHAM MARTIN

Von Marbod was a wonderful guy. I like him very much, but he's a bloody disaster area. He had no authority, but he finally persuades Ky of all people to get the planes out. But what happened as a result he damn near destroyed the [United States'] relationship with the Thai in doing that. He flew 'em out without checking to see who the hell was on board. A lot of the crew people didn't want to stay. They had to drug 'em in Thailand to put them on the ships, the planes to Guam. There were fifteen hundred or so that caused unshirted hell over there. They wanted to get back. It wasn't worth it in other words, risking so much. But they finally gave him a medal for recovering the bloody planes.

And then I can't prove it, but it was pretty obvious that it [precipitated the shelling of Tan Son Nhut]. They deliberately came down the line in front of the control tower and hit all the Vietnamese planes that were there. They weren't going to take those out [destroy them] if they could get them. All this crap about denying them to the other side was all well and good. I'm all in favor of that. But I'm not willing to pay but a certain price for that. In this case it wasn't worth it.

MAI PHAM

In March 1975, we were all getting very worried. I was still DJ-ing, but I mainly worked for Saigon Radio as a news announcer. The only thing I ever got to talk about was enemy casualties. I would have to constantly try to pump into people's mind that the *enemy* was getting killed. We heard about the abandonment of major cities and provinces, but I couldn't report it. Things were very tense. We heard news from people fleeing from Nha Trang and Pleiku. Even though I knew it was happening, it was very hard to accept it was really going on. At the loss of Danang, everyone was overwhelmed by the fact this was going to be doomsday for us as a race. We were afraid for our lives. It demoralized everyone. People were talking about "the running."

I remember my mother crying as she sewed by candlelight, lining cloth bags to stuff personal possessions in and wrap around our waists. Then Saigon started getting rockets at night. When things got really bad, we sandbagged an area on the first floor and hid there every night. Between the fifteenth and the twentieth [of April] my father had meetings at the house a lot. CIA people were talking about evacuation plans. The American CIA launched a big evacuation plan for its radio people, including my sister Denise. My father thought it was a good idea if all three kids went that way. On the twenty-second we were flown from Tan Son Nhut to Phu Quoc Island, where a big U.S. boat would pick us up. We camped out in some abandoned barracks with two hundred other people. We had no water or sleep for three days. The place was full of mosquitoes. Then a helicopter came with a message for my family to come back immediately. My brother and I looked at each other and said, "Let's go!" But Denise stayed till the boat finally came.

In Saigon the situation was *really* bad. None of us slept that night with the shelling. Next day we packed up. We ate a lot. We'd been told we would be traveling hours and days. My grandmother was knocking her head on our steel door in grief at leaving. We thought she was going to die. Neighbors crowded into the front yard, looking to see what they could take. We brought some rice cakes and went to the [CIA] motor pool. We had the password, "John Ward." Father saw us to the airport, but he wouldn't leave. He assured us he would be protected by our American friends and we would be reunited.

There were three families at our house waiting to leave. They were all skillful, high-risk families who could adjust easily to the U.S. The CIA told us they couldn't take all of us out that day, and would be back after the first busload. So we left. Their promise was never kept. We got a wire later in California, explaining that they tried to come back to the house to pick up my uncle and aunt, but the streets were blocked and soldiers were spraying bullets into moving cars. Because of circumstances, it was impossible to keep all their promises. But it was no small promise. It was a promise of life, which they never kept. My father's youngest brother, a captain, was jailed for at least two years and my other uncle is going blind in one eye. So we feel deep guilt because we told them someone was coming back to pick them up. That's why my parents are so quiet. We send them gifts—goods, not money. We hear the state keeps seventy percent of money.

On the bus to the airport everybody was tearing money, big bills— five hundred piasters [notes]—shredding them. The scraps were two inches thick on the floor of the bus. People said, "Why leave it for the Commies?" Everybody was sad or crying. We looked out and saw lovers walking hand in hand. Not everybody knew. Merchants were selling soup. We wondered, "Do they know that the end has come? Maybe they *shouldn't* know, if they're not going." My father got out on the thirtieth by helicopter and was taken by aircraft carrier to Guam. I saw him there in a soup line, and called out, "Dad! This is like *War and Peace!*"

———————◆———————

NGUYEN BUU TRUNG

Life went on almost the same. A little more worry. Broadcasting was not telling the truth. They say we win some battles, we kill some Communists. Only good news. When I heard the loss of Ban Me Thuot, I think we have to give this part to Communists for strategic reasons, let the Communists attack, kill all of them, the Communists move back to North.

But every day the Communists come closer and closer. We knew high-ranking military people and Secret Service. They were looking to get out also. I heard no fighting in Saigon. But a son in America called his father, Lap Huynh, a multimillionaire, owner of Olympia cabaret, when I was there. He saw map with Red advances every night on American TV. He say, "Daddy, you have to get out."

I saw people buying gold and dollars at banks. Everybody looking for gold and dollars. I had kept some money at home, but it was piasters. Last few days we can't take more than five hundred thousand piasters from bank. Every night people going past my house in big bus from Embassy, starting the day Thieu resigned. Every night I heard a lot of airplane come. The buses started only after curfew. They were trying to sneak people out. I saw my friends gone, one by one. Only then I realized people were fleeing.

And Thieu and Khiem, they fled. So we knew something happened. My wife's father urged us to go. He had been five years in jail in North. He was ex-Viet Minh, though a liberal. Even up to the day before we left I did not know whether to go or stay. Government was threatening to put fleeing people in jail, so I don't know what I should do. And my wife keep crying, crying, "We have to go." The last day we become panicked when I was looking around to try to get into airplane. At this time I was also the private doctor of General Cao Van Vien. I went to his office. I said, "I never ask you any favor, but today my first day. My wife is crying at home." He said he is not chief of airplane, but he would try to help. I went to port to look for a boat, but called home to check. My wife told me we have airplane.

My uncle, Ngo Cong Khanh, drove us to the airport. He said he would not escape. He had been engineer in Paris. He said Western life is hard, and no big change with the Communists. He advised us, "Don't go." One or two years later he tried to escape three times and was caught each time. He and his entire family committed suicide by cyanide.

At Tan Son Nhut we met chief of Military Police. He came from General Vien. Every night they have one plane for special people working with high-ranking Vietnamese officials. It was a "black flight," a secret flight. He opens door into American area. We got right on plane for Philippines. General Vien just gave me a few places in the plane. He did nothing for Lap Huynh. Lap had to go by boat on the last day. Even Saigon mayor had to go by boat on last minute of last day.

FRANK SNEPP

My overwhelming recollection of the final days is of unbelievable exhaustion. I was so tired I could barely walk. I was turning out a study a day, or more, on the military situation. I never had time to eat, and as the clock was winding down, our crutches fell away. There was nobody to polish your shoes or iron your shirts or make sure somebody brought in food. Fending for ourselves was alien to most of us.

Then something so awful happened that even today if I could change anything, I would change that. On April 27, I was typing an analysis for Martin, cursing because he seemed incapable of absorbing the seriousness of the military situation. Mai Ly, a very tall Chinese-Vietnamese woman—a good friend I had known for years—called and said, "I am going to kill myself and my child if you don't get me out." She said she had bought pills. I was so numb that I said "I can't help you now, I'm so busy. Call me in an hour." One hour later I was down in the Ambassador's office, when somebody gave me a message from Mai Ly: "I would have expected better of you.

Good-bye." I spent the rest of the day trying to locate her. I learned through a policeman friend the next day that she *had* killed herself.

Something snapped at that point. I changed so radically in the way I looked at things. I had been trying to get Martin to move, and I thought, "What's the difference between us? Both of us have got our priorities screwed up. I should have put down everything to go help this woman." I went home through streets that were mostly concertina wire and fell into bed.

The next thing—Bang!—the shelling early on the twenty-ninth lifted me out of my bed. My apartment faced the airport and I could see the explosions, like sheet lightning. As I was going out to my Pinto to go the Embassy, my Nung guard said, "You won't forget me, will you?" He was married to my maid. I didn't know what to say to him. The streets were strangely calm, but the rest of the day was waiting for Godot.

In the last hours, schizophrenia took over. I got a report the Communists were going to shell the center of Saigon, which could have been our death sentence, but Polgar was not interested: He told me to tell Martin. I found Martin on his hands and knees going through classified files he hadn't destroyed. He said, "Go tell Polgar." The halls were full of people. Polgar was drinking cognac with some of his Vietnamese contacts. There was a lot of boozing, waiting for the pickup. People were joking with gallows humor about getting killed. I was a little offended. There were a lot of Vietnamese outside the Embassy still not getting in. Over the radios in the situation room people were screaming "I am Mr. Hai! Please save me." The radio operator would cajole them off the line. I had soundmares afterward which kept me from sleeping for months.

Around eight-thirty Polgar said it was time to leave. I walked down the hallway with him and saw some Vietnamese stashed in the rooms, including a beautiful Vietnamese woman with a baby. I turned into the stairwell leading to the pad. On the roof the controllers in their huge helmets looked like insects standing on their hind legs. The chopper rose. I saw out the porthole the Kim Do Hotel, where I first lived. It banked and I could see toward Bien Hoa. It was a clear night between storms. I could see cars and trucks and tanks coming into Saigon.

Being there at the end was a little like witnessing a B-52 strike at close range. I had always had the consequences of my actions separated from the causes. In the end, the distance between cause and effect disappeared. The sights and the call from Mai Ly did something terrible to my perception of American right and light and might. I had a feeling we'd used our power badly. It had always been sort of an old men's war and a young men's tragedy, and the end was the same. The old men spent the last day still in illusion—Martin on his hands and knees, getting his classified cables destroyed. The young were the ones out on the walls who couldn't get the people over, or the ones at Tan Son Nhut who had to make life or death decisions on what families went out.

In many ways, the end was the war writ small. We had two Presidents during the last years who deluded themselves, and an ambassador who shaved the truth in order to get us to stand tight. We misread some of our intelligence, as was so often done during the war, and in the end the old men breezed through it with their rationalizations and the young men ended up with blood on their hands. I came out with the idea it was time for the young men to have their say.

———————◆———————

NGUYEN CAO KY

Everyone came to me, especially political groups and the military, saying, "You are the only one who can do something. Tell people not to flee." They all think that I would replace Thieu. I still have the Army with me. So to prepare the people, they organized a lot of meetings around Saigon and asked me to talk with the people, to stay and fight.

When Huong became president, I call him. I went to the palace to see him. "Make me chief of staff," I said. I need something official, so I can reorganize the Army. Again Huong said, "Oh, yeah, a few days. Let me think about it." But I said, "There is not *time* for thinking."

On the last day I made my last effort to do something. With my twelve men I fly into the Joint Staff compound on Tan Son Nhut. But it was empty—empty! So I went up to the office of the Chief of Staff. Only one general was there. He shrugged. "There is nothing left," he said. From there I again tried to call the commander of the Air Force, the head of the Navy. Nobody answered. They already left. About noontime, all my aides were with me, and they said to me, "It's time for you to leave, too." The problem with me at that time was, where do we go now? I never had a plan to leave the country. We had a short range helicopter without much fuel. Where to go? I said, "Just take off and go to the sea." In the air we SOS'd for help on the international emergency radio frequency. The signal was picked up by the *Midway*. They guided us to the ship. We landed about one-thirty.

What can I do? For the last four years Thieu kept me out. I was a private citizen. I had no position, no small unit under the military. I try my best until the last moment. But on last day I was like a million other Vietnamese, a private citizen. What do you expect me to do? To stay with my Colt .45?

Just a step ahead of the draft, LT. RICHARD VAN DE GEER *joined the U.S. Army in 1969 and learned to fly helicopters. He left the service in 1971 to go back to school, but in 1973 signed up for another military hitch, this time in the Air Force. Van de Geer flew out of the post-1973 U.S. headquarters in Nakorn Phanom, in northeast Thailand. He took part in the evacuations of both Phnom Penh and Saigon—and then was summoned to war one last time, during the mission to "rescue" the crew of the freighter* Mayaguez *from the Khmer Rouge, seventeen days after the fall of Vietnam. As he tried to put his chopper down on the beach at Koh Tang island, a rocket grenade scored a direct hit on his cockpit. Van de Geer and others aboard the chopper are officially listed as the last American combat casualties of the war. A few days before he died, Van de Geer made a tape recording about his experiences in the evacuation, for his friend and former Army pilot colleague, Richard Sandza, who had become a* Newsweek *correspondent.*

Whenever it was that the Cambodian situation became dismal, I left my humble hovel in the north to go to Phnom Penh. The part we played in the evacuation, at least as far as I'm concerned, is almost worthless to speak about. It is, of course, true that people were evacuated and it is true that the city was nearly surrounded by the enemy and it is true that the firefights were going on, and the airfield was being shelled because the Khmer Rouge was two miles from Pochentong [airport] at that point. But for me, it did not leave a lasting impression. It was simply a tedious job.

I returned from Cambodia the same day. What ensued thereafter is fairly humorous, in a way. My leave had been cancelled for the third time and I simply needed to get away. I was given a three or four day pass, so I went to Bangkok to the American Embassy-subsidized hotel. I went up to my room, opened the door and the first significant thing which I saw was the "No Smoking In Bed" sign, and a long list of regulations. Basically what I'm saying is that it was still organizational and what I needed was indulgence. So I showered and I left the hotel at about three AM, and incredible as it may sound, shortly thereafter, I found a driver and a Mercedes. I rented them both for the duration with the stipulation that he be available twenty-four hours a day at my call.

Once that was agreed upon, I started [looking for] a hotel. I chose the Siam Intercontinental and I rented the Presidential suite for a hundred and seventy dollars a day. I made reservations for a French restaurant for the evening at Chez Suzanne. When I first checked in, I was introduced to the manager and the manager assured me that if there was anything I wanted, I shouldn't hesitate to call. If I was going to play the part of an Arabian sheik, I wanted to do as much as I could in the little time I had to do it. I told the manager that I needed the best body massage Bangkok had to offer, and I wanted him to recommend a place and a woman. He said they didn't open until six o'clock, but that he would see what they could do. [A little later] he said the Siam Intercontinental had made a special request, and that a limousine would come and pick me up at four o'clock and that I would be taken care of.

I had not gotten any sleep by this time. I had been up about forty hours. I was still having flashbacks of Phnom Penh when I received a message, about two o'clock in the afternoon, that there would be a plane waiting for me at the airport at seventeen hundred [five PM] to take me back. Of course, it was hard to believe that there could be such injustice in the world, but be assured there is. So I ended up paying a little over two hundred dollars for using the room for about four hours. That's the humorous side.

I arrived back at my home base about seven o'clock that evening. They said I would be leaving the following morning at three A.M. for Utapao, on the coast. The next morning, which was a Sunday, I went to an intelligence briefing and they told me that I was going to fly my airplane to a Navy carrier.

But I didn't know that the goddamn carrier was five hundred miles away off the coast of South Vietnam. Well, obviously I did manage to find the carrier, the U.S.S. *Midway*, landed, and was quickly indoctrinated into the way of the Navy. I didn't like it one goddamn bit. We went to daily intelligence briefings and basically [were told] we were there to evacuate Saigon if the situation deteriorated to the point where they couldn't use Tan Son Nhut.

Now, of course, one could belabor the point of asking why would it ever become necessary to send a helicopter lift force into an area to evacuate people when the people themselves should be wise enough to realize that their shit is getting weak, and they should get out while the going is good. Well, I watched the Phnom Penh situation develop for two months and they waited until the Khmer Rouge were close enough to the airfield to shell it with forty-millimeter recoilless rifles. That simply means to say they were very, very close.

We had an intel briefing at ten-thirty the twenty-ninth and at that time they said the expected execution time for the operation was eleven o'clock. Now, of course, this came as a shock, because nobody was prepared for it to be handled so offhandedly. Nonetheless, we were strapped into our aircraft at eleven o'clock. The actual execute time came at three P.M. I got out of the airplane a little over fourteen hours later, after I had made four sorties into Saigon.

The situation with a hundred and fifty thousand NVA around the city, of course, was not the most salubrious. At this point it becomes difficult to talk. I could tell you about how real the fear was, since from the time we crossed the Delta we were over enemy territory. We were being fired upon by twenty-three, thirty-seven, and fifty-seven millimeter antiaircraft guns. It was in SAM* operating range. The electronic gear on our aircraft, which was radar detection equipment for the homing systems on guns, were lighting like Christmas trees. The VC had commandeered Air America Hueys and they were flying them around, which made a very interesting chess game. I mean, it was bad.

We thought that they were going to call off the operation when it became dark because we never expected them to send us into such a bad situation to begin with, even if it was daytime. But they continued the mission on until nearly five o'clock in the morning. The night sorties were the worst because we flew lights out, going inadvertently IFR† because of the cloud decks. The tracers kept everybody on edge. To see a city burning gives one a strange feeling of insecurity.

Let me throw a couple of facts your way which may conflict with what you have been reading in the papers. I call them facts in that I saw them happen. Number one, approximately nine o'clock on the morning of the twenty-ninth, about five hours before any American military aircraft went into Saigon, a Vietnamese Huey flew out to sea and found the carrier. It was nearly out of gas. This aircraft landed about fifty feet away from mine, and the man who got out was quoted as saying approximately a week earlier that any South Vietnamese that left the country were cowards and that everybody should remain in South Vietnam and fight to the bitter end. This very same man was the first person to arrive on the U.S.S. *Midway* and, to my knowledge, the first to be recovered by the Seventh Fleet. In other words, it was an unsanctioned recovery that we didn't engineer. They simply flew out in hopes of finding someplace to

---

*Surface-to-Air Missile.
†Instrument flight rules.

land that was not South Vietnam. This man was General [Nguyen Cao] Ky.

Now, I really don't have any personal feelings about the war over here. But I did find myself feeling that I wish he had been shot down. He, along with Thieu and Lon Nol. You probably heard that they chartered a Scandinavian airliner to take out what they termed to be personal belongings. Scandinavian Airlines turned them down when they found out that it was seventy-two million dollars in gold.

I really don't know what other facts to tell you. It's like taking a pin and trying to poke a small hole in a water balloon. You just can't start because you won't be able to stop. I guess you'll have to forgive me if I don't go into more of the details as to what happened. We pulled out close to two thousand people. We couldn't pull out any more because it was beyond human endurance.

We finally prepared to return to Thailand off the carrier, [but] half an hour before launch time we were cancelled and delayed a day. The rumor was there was another operation going on. This was incredible to my ears because I couldn't think of anything else we could possibly do. It turned out to be a race with the Viet Cong for American fighters that had been flown into Thailand. In the same way that Hueys had been commandeered, the jet jocks had commandeered F-5s and A-37s, Gooney Birds,* A-1s, and other types of aircraft and flew them into Thailand. And Thailand, wanting to be as unantagonistic as possible to the newfound power in Indochina, said, "We will give the airplanes to anybody who wants them." The VC made immediate claim, so it was our job to get them out of Thailand as quickly as possible, and the way we did this is that we sling-loaded the aircraft for three days out to the *Midway*, which was standing off the coast.

I got back today. I am in bits and pieces. Fairly incoherent only because its been so fast-paced. I assure you that I am in one piece. It could very easily have been a different story, though I may have told you before that I am somewhat fatalistic about believing that I shall never come to serious harm in the military. I want to get off the entire subject now of military, [but] let me only say again that some of this information is very sensitive and, you know, if someone pocketed the cassette and listened to it, they could do the whole Ivan Denisovich† thing to me. Anyway, fuck 'em.

---------◆---------

*C-47 Dakotas.

†*One Day in the Life of Ivan Denisovich*, by Alexander Solzhenitsyn, was the first revelatory novel published in the West about political imprisonment in the Soviet *gulags*.

JAMES SCHLESINGER

On the day of our final withdrawal, I was told that I would have to
get out, as I recall, about nine hundred people. We snaked these
helicopters up the river, and as you know the Ambassador was busily engaged in holding back Americans and putting aboard Vietnamese
that he wanted to rescue. Meanwhile I'm getting calls from the White
House, when am I going to finish this operation, and I said, "They
keep giving us Vietnamese rather than Americans." By the time it
was over, I think we'd flown sixteen or eighteen hundred people
out by helicopter. And I was forced to send a message saying "Mr.
Ambassador, the last chopper is going to be at a certain hour, and if
you are not there, we are going to leave without you." That was
the only way I could terminate this operation, in which he was trying
to evacuate all of the people of Southeast Asia.

Logistically it was a harum scarum operation. That mission went on
a hell of a lot longer than it should have. The pilots were under terrible strain. They'd come in and sack out for thirty or forty minutes
and get back in their helicopters to try and haul more people out of
Saigon. Happily there was no attempt by the North Vietnamese seriously to embarrass us. I think they had sufficient residual fear of what
we would do—they really didn't have a good reading on these strange
chaps—that they thought, quite rightly, that a national humiliation
directly administered was not in their interests. We had some contact with the Soviets and the Soviets I think explained that to them.

All through that evening and the next day, as the North Vietnamese
approached Saigon, they were very slow because they didn't want
to tangle with us. I had given the order that we were to be prepared
to fire if fired upon, if it was not stray shots. We were not going to
use sniping as an excuse for heavy retaliation, but if there was a
concerted effort to get at our people, we were prepared to respond.
I think we had a couple of machine-gun bursts, but there was really
no attempt to go after the Americans. And we were scrupulous in
our adherence to the law.

That was the collapse. It was a rather sad day in American history I
think. I sent out my final message to the forces that day, saying that
whatever the differences about policy that one should remember
that American forces had never been defeated in the field, and that
they should be proud of the actions that they had taken in response
to higher command authority. I got in some trouble with the left for
praising our military people—breathing defiance to the end.

GRAHAM MARTIN

There wasn't any way in which I could come out of what was going on in Saigon without enormous criticism. And this in a way completely removed any pressure on me to do some goddamn fool thing just to avoid criticism. So I might as well do it right. And I said, "The other thing you've got going for you is my coolness and my judgment and so you just better back off." And they did.

I dealt with the President, and Kissinger basically left me alone. In the end I didn't get quite what I wanted but that wasn't really their fault, it was a screwup out in the Fleet. I wanted more lift than we finally got; I'd been promised more lift by the White House. Based on that I then made certain plans about the people in the compound. And when finally they decided to turn it off, without giving me about the fifty additional chopper flights that I had originally been promised, that sort of tore the thing up. We could have evacuated the compound. There were two or three hundred people left there. Most of those did get out, they came down the river and we picked them up.

Everybody over in the White House situation room I understand was just raising unshirted hell. "You got to close this off before he gets us into a disaster!" They wanted to get the Americans out as soon as possible. But you get the Americans out and you're through, aren't you? It was not so. Sitting back there we had Father McVea of Catholic Relief Services, who wasn't going to leave without his Vietnamese employees. How was the President going to explain to his good friend Cardinal Cooke back in New York that we left his friend, the father? That threw them for a loop, when I told them that. Really threw them for a loop.

You see, I called the White House and told them I was ready for the helicopters. They had told me that the minute I made that decision, I'd have the first helicopter within an hour. Actually, it took five hours before the first chopper showed up. Daylight hours. I expected the first one to be there not later than eleven o'clock and it was after three before it came in. I kept needling the White House: "What the hell is going on here? I told you we've moved to it [the helicopter extraction] and nothing happens. What gives?" They didn't know. They were checking with Honolulu. Honolulu [was] checking with the Fleet. Whether he *had* to do that or it was just something he'd rather do, I don't know.

But everybody did pretty well when they got started. So I didn't do any public complaints about the five-hour delay. It didn't change anything. I couldn't get the five hours back. I have an absolute, total distaste for this "I didn't do it, he did it" crap. [But] if they had come in, all the later anguish about getting people out of the compound would have been totally alleviated. There would have been nobody there. In other words, I had it figured right.

————————•————————

He likes to joke that "I became commander of United States forces in Saigon—for a very brief time." In April 1975, MAJ. JAMES KEAN, who ran the Marine security detachments at twenty-three U.S. embassies in the Far East, was hustled to Saigon to help in the evacuation. He had already served two thirteen-month combat tours; for superintending the dissolution of the last American outpost in Vietnam, Kean won a Bronze Star. He retired in 1983 as a lieutenant colonel, by then thoroughly turned off on the subject of U.S. intervention abroad. He now lives on suburban Mercer Island in Seattle and is an executive of a farm machinery exporter.

In March CINCPAC teams had come in to look at the reality of getting out in difficult circumstances. They came up with Frequent Wind—you got sufficient armed men, helo support, and communications, and you got people out of there as quickly as you could. The plan had called for two lifts off the Embassy roof of no more than twenty-five souls at the end. When the panic hit, we just made it up as best we could.

The attack on the palace by the A-37s created a sense of panic throughout the city. Immediately there was a curfew, and then it became a real new ballgame for us. A massive crowd came to the Embassy—conservatively, ten thousand people. We didn't know *who* was outside the walls. There were rumors of assassination teams in the crowd. People started trying to come up over the wall. The Embassy detachment was sixty-two Marines, and I got another hundred from the DAO compound at Tan Son Nhut by copter on the last day. They had come in from the Seventh Fleet for security out there. We set up four machine-gun locations for grazing fire down the top of the wall, and put out sodium nitrate burn barrels to create a wall of flame. [*Neither was ever used.*]

My Marines had been in Saigon for some time. They had seen a lot of these people. A young Marine corporal would sign his name to get every friend he had in Vietnam home, regardless of consequences. One kid from Danang married his girlfriend on the last day, without my permission. She found her own way down from Nha Trang. As soon as he found her, he married her. He knew he was going to be punished. I fined him five bucks.

The helo evacuation started late. I set up in the parking lot as ground control man to bring the copters in, load them, and get them out. The CH-53 is an enormous vehicle. It had to make a seventy-foot vertical descent. One bird put eighty-three people on. Normal capacity was thirty combat troops. The pilot would pull back on the cyclical. If he could lift off the ground, he would say, "Put some more on."

The initial word was that the lift would stop at dark, but the Ambassador got authority to continue. The Seabees put a big *H* on the compound parking lot with luminous paint. We parked all the Embassy vehicles around it and turned on the lights so they could see the landing zone. Early in the evening, before dark, the Ambassador said, "Shall we lower the colors?" I recommended that we wait till after dark, and he agreed. It was done with dignity—a Marine security detail went out, ran down the flag smartly, folded it up, and presented it to the Ambassador.

The choppers came in at ten-minute intervals and went out as fast as we could handle them. A bevy of young Ph.D.-type aides helped to marshal people and limit access to the copter area, one load at a time so we didn't have people grabbing the skids. Then Seventh Fleet wanted the lift to stop by eleven P.M. The Ambassador appealed to the President, but the President limited the operation to twenty more lifts.

About four A.M. Wednesday there was a lull. The Ambassador took off, and General Carey, the commanding general of the Marine Amphibious Brigade, ordered me to pull inside the building and get out of there. He said, "The President's words are that only U.S. personnel are to be evacuated from here on out." I knew we were on the speaker in the war room on the *Blue Ridge* [the Seventh Fleet command ship]. I made him repeat it, because people would be left.

I passed word to start breaking up and form a circle around the doors. As soon as we backed toward the door the gates gave way. A lot of my men had to scratch and crawl into the Embassy. We didn't want to use weapons or punch people, so a big Seabee picked up a piece of timber, held it under his arms behind his back and whirled it around. The Marines inside were grabbing guys by the collar and yanking them in the doors. The doors were mahogany, with, inside them, an electric drop gate. After everybody was inside we put the door bolt in place, but the screen froze halfway down.

We sent the elevators to the top and locked them, and then we went up the stairs floor by floor, sealing each one and dropping tear-gas canisters down the stairway. People drove an Embassy fire truck right through the front door to come in after us. The passageway from the top floors to the roof had heavy fire doors at each end with small windows in them. We jammed the corridor full of huge fire extinguisher bottles on carts and wall lockers, and sealed it off.

On the roof, CH-46s [helicopters] were loading twenty-two people per lift, and taking off. I had the Marines drop all their gear, just take the rifle and go. Finally, only a dozen of us were left—me and [Master Gunnery Sergeant Juan] Valdez [the NCO in charge of the Embassy detachment] and ten very trusted sergeants and corporals. We laid down flat and waited it out. Very few people even knew we were there.

The crowd broke through the grill gates and destroyed everything we had put in their way, and were coming. One kid, Steve Bauer, stayed in that passageway, shooting Mace through a window in the fire door at them. One guy scaled the wall of the embassy like a human spider. He was almost up to the top before he got bumped off and fell almost six stories. The Embassy was being looted. There was a tremendous collection of sidearms on the political section floor and people were getting hold of them. Random shots were being fired. One guy across the street from the Embassy in a third-floor apartment was shooting at everything, including the helicopters.

We laid up there two more hours with no radio. We had faith. "The Marines won't forget us," we kept telling each other. We just knew they were coming back. When dawn broke we were a bunch of tight assholes. It was mayhem down below. The Embassy compound looked like it had undergone a nuclear attack. Paper and weapons were strewn everywhere. Crazy drunks were starting up cars and driving them until they crashed. We saw Big Minh's motorcade come down the main drag with riot police in front, firing on looters to clear a path.

Finally, at eight in the morning our bird appeared and we ran all twelve at the copter as soon as it was down. I told the kids to open their [tear] gas canisters. No one had masks and we gassed ourselves and the pilot. Gas was billowing out from the top of the embassy. The pilot later got the Distinguished Flying Cross for flying more than twenty hours straight.

After we lifted off the radio buzzed and a voice said "What kind of pizza do you want in Manila?" Everybody was so exhausted we just laughed and cried at the same time. We landed on the U.S.S. *Okinawa* and just fainted in bed. When I woke up after six hours, a helicopter was waiting to fly me to General Carey at the *Blue Ridge*. I had to borrow a uniform. I had come out wearing a Ben Hogan golf shirt and blue slacks. I carried a beat-up old cigar and a briefcase. We left everything else.

Saigon law professor and politician NGUYEN VAN CANH *and his large extended family left North Vietnam for the south in 1954. He rose to be deputy dean of the Saigon University Law Faculty. Though he had American connections and was a likely target for persecution after a Communist victory, he was among the forgotten. Nevertheless, he managed to get his entire family—his wife and seven children, his mother, an elder brother with a wife and three kids, a younger brother, and two sisters—out of the country on his own. Canh now directs an occupational training center for Indochina refugees in San Jose, California, and runs a Vietnamese restaurant on the side.*

Every night in April I listen to BBC and Voice of America. It was the only reliable source. I heard of Danang and panic in Nha Trang. But they tell lies about true size of forces. One program said there fifteen Vietnam Communist divisions besieging Saigon. I *know* it is not true, especially after the Tet offensive when the Party and its forces were *beaten*.

I felt danger. I was born in North Vietnam and escaped. My mother was a hostage in a concentration camp before she escaped late in 1954. More important was that my family was classified as landlords, bourgeoisie. That was two strikes against us. There was another strike, too. I got a Ph.D. at the Saigon faculty in public law and political science. I did my thesis on Communism in Vietnam and strategy and tactics for dealing with it. I was anti-Communist, and secretary general in Dai Viet party. The party was fighting the French *and* Communism. I ran for senator in 1970 at the head of my party list. I was a professor at the National Defense College and the Command and General Staff College. We had been wealthy in North Vietnam, professionals, but we had just enough to survive in the South. We had a car. We had a cook.

On April fourteenth, one of my professors, a woman, came to my office [at the Saigon Law School] and said American advisers at the Faculty of Medicine already took the professors out. "Here you do nothing," she said. We met that day and decided we have to go. They appointed me to make contact with the Americans. I wrote Ambassador Martin asking help. I wait. Nothing happen. On the twenty-first, one professor contact the Embassy. They said the Ambassador is not available. Then we contact Alan Carter of the USIS. They give us appointment on the thirtieth. This was the only contact with America. I was there still working, even Saturday and Sunday, in case the Embassy called me.

On April 29, I knew that the situation was very desperate. There were a lot of defeats. I knew Americans set up an office to get out Vietnamese at Tan Son Nhut and one at USIS. Many people say they have to give money to Americans in order to get out. In the morning I came by scooter to the Catholic church near Tan Son Nhut. One of my friends, Dinh Thach Bich, editor of a Vietnamese paper in San Diego now, was there, and Hoang Xuan Tuu of my Dai Viet party, vice-president of the senate, who died in concentration camp in North Vietnam in 1979. I told them they had to leave. Generals were escaping. The military situation was confused. Tuu said if he tried to leave, the secret police would arrest him. I told him Thieu left on the twenty-fourth, the secret police disbanded.

After I go home a neighbor came in and said "Oh, Professor Canh, I am just back from Saigon Pier Number Three. A U.S. ship is picking up refugees. Please go right away." I did not believe it. You have honor to live with. I was very high-ranking officer in Saigon Faculty of Law, involved in politics. Many people knew who I was. I dare not do such a thing. If South Vietnam does not collapse, everybody will remember you tried to escape. So I stay home. At three-forty he came back. He said he went back to the pier and the ship was still there. He told my mother. You *have* to ask Dr. Canh to leave. My mother urged me to go. The whole family all there, waiting for me—eighteen people, ten of them children. We went to Pier Three but people said the ship left some time ago.

We decide to wait for another American ship, but none came. We saw a lot of helicopters coming in from the ocean. With each wave, an American jet was leading the way. On the river, ships from the South Vietnam Navy went out in a file—twenty-nine of them. We know they are going away. My younger brother, Dinh, was very bitter. "You taught at National Defense College. Your students were generals and high-ranking Air Force officers. Now *they* go out, and the professor stay back!" We sat all night with no sleep. Next morning we saw no more helicopters.

I thought how I used to eat at a restaurant in Nha Be [a river town south of Saigon]. There were a lot of fishing boats there. I said a fishing boat is risky, but if you survive, you must take chance. But when we tried to go a man said, "Last night Viet Cong took over. They will arrest you as refugees." So we go back to Pier Three. Then a big commercial ship that had been in the middle of the river moved to Pier Five. It was crowded with people and we decide to go on. But it began pulling out before we could all get on, so we had to climb down. My mother said, "Let's go home." She was tired and we had not eaten since yesterday. But from someone's transistor radio we knew the Viet Cong already were in Saigon. We went back to Pier Three.

On the dock I saw friends walking back and forth: Le Van Tai, a high-ranking secret agent for Ngo Dinh Nhu, Nguyen Hoang Cuong, a professor at the National Institute for Administration and Nguyen Huu To. Under Diem, To was a navy lieutenant commander. Le Van Tai saw me. "Hi, brother Canh," he said. "Come on, sit by my side." Cuong urged people to go to another boat. He said its motor was running. He told a lie to the people because our boat was too crowded.

To knew how to steer. He came on our boat and told someone to untie the rope. Our boat slowly move out. We left the dock at three-fifteen and reached Vung Tau when it was darkening. Some PT boat machine guns tried to shoot our boat so people could get in. To ordered women and children to stand up. The military saw and quit. In the dark, we met an American LST. He told us to wait for daytime, and someone else would pick us up. We met a Taiwanese LST, and it took women and children. One hundred seven men had to stay on board. The Taiwanese gave us food and we followed them slowly to the Philippines for six days.

RUSSELL MOTT

When I got back to Saigon [from Danang] I tried to avoid the Embassy. I was burned out, walkin' around with a thousand-yard stare, but determined to stay to the end. A couple of us got together and made up a plan to get a few thousand people out by sea. We knew eventually the Communists would close the airport. Everybody had lists of Vietnamese they wanted to get out. We were going to use the Newport dock. Barges would take them down the Saigon River to the fleet and the Philippines. There was plenty of shipping available.

Mel Chatman [another AID official] and I found eight or ten people we'd known in Danang and Hoi An, and told them we would get their families out right away if they would stay to help and then go out with us. Mel found an apartment near the Khanh Hoi docks and we put them there and got weapons from the Embassy stores.

On the last day, when the airport closed, an ARVN unit took over the area of the apartment for a bivouac. When I got there, concertina wire was strung around the entrance. I hadn't shaved for three or four days and I was carrying my Swedish K over my shoulder, and when I went in I met two troopers on the landing between the second and third floor. They stopped me and called their lieutenant upstairs. Everybody was armed and nervous. I was thinking about how ticklish the situation would be if they saw the arms in my apartment, so I decided to be straight. I told them about the plan and invited them to come. I said all I'd need is a couple of megaphones and the arms and clips. The rest of the stuff in the apartment you can have, and any trooper can go on the barge.

Finally eight of us armed up and jammed into my jeep. Word had gotten out that the evacuation was heading that way. We had to abandon the jeep in the crowd and walk to the dock. The barges showed up from upriver, with an Australian named Lombardo driving the tug. There were four barges, with room for twenty thousand people, but after a big initial rush there was nobody on the dock. The plan we had to spread the word didn't activate, or people didn't believe it was over. There was nothing resembling Danang. I later heard some rumors that police were stopping people at the gate unless they paid them. We left with five or ten thousand people at two P.M. on the twenty-ninth. The river meanders through Saigon and we could see the helicopters landing at the embassy.

I was pissed off—angry because we were leaving. I felt almost as if, all of a sudden, the whole thing didn't make any sense. I thought a lot about John Paul Vann. I was pissed that we'd called off the war. I remember weeping as we left. I knew it was the end, the last chapter of something that I didn't see as completed. It was a cornucopia of reactions. All of a sudden somebody calls you up and says, "Game's over, time to go home."

CHAPTER FOURTEEN

Aftermath

W HEN a war ends badly, it is the little people who find themselves caught in the backwash of their leaders' grand mistakes.

In Vietnam, a dispiriting defeat was followed by a disquieting peace. The Communist field army that marched into the newly renamed Ho Chi Minh City on May 1, 1975, stunned the Saigonese with its youth and its naivete. In turn, the residents of what had the day before been the capital of an independent country greeted the conquerors with indifference and disdain. These were country boys with dirt on their trousers and mud in their toes, for whom the sight of a great, Westernized city full of restaurants and nightclubs, refrigerators and motorbikes was an experience to take the breath away. Privately, the South Vietnamese wept to think they could have been conquered by an army of such hicks. Publicly, they held their peace and waited for the axe to fall.

And fall it did—though by no means with the bloodbath that anti-Communist propagandists had predicted. The troops retired to barracks, to be replaced by a yellow-uniformed Peoples' Police of authoritarian whistle-blowers and spies. The National Liberation Front and its ragged divisions of Viet Cong, in which many Western opponents of the war had misplaced their hope for an independent South Vietnam, disappeared as though swallowed by a whale. The Southern Viet Cong cadre, with whom many non-Communist Vietnamese had maintained contact over the years, were unceremoniously shoved aside by flinty Northern apparatchiks bent only on consolidating the conquest. No plan that proposed to build on the existing foundations, that failed to overturn the economic order, that sought to enlist the cooperation of the former middle classes, never mind the elite, could be accepted. Those who pushed were rebuffed; those who pushed hard were jailed.

"Reeducation" became the order of the day. Thousands of former soldiers and officials were incarcerated in camps that became a Vietnamese gulag archipelago.* Under the impact of rigid socialist principle, an economy that had grown progressively weaker since the heyday of French colonialism was soon in an uncontrollable tailspin. And at last, when the new rulers concluded that their control could only be solidified by getting the entire bourgeois class out of the way, there began that exodus which came to be known as the saga of the boat people. With no convenient land border to cross because of the holocaust in neighboring Cambodia, a million or more Vietnamese chose to vote with their hulls, so to speak. Jammed into small boats, they risked death at sea and an uncertain reception on foreign shores, rather than endure the looking-glass absurdities dictated by the politburo from Hanoi.

In Cambodia the Khmer Rouge victory, far from creating peace, unleashed a spasm of violence far worse than the blackest predictions of the anti-Communist ideologues. Two events immediately after the fall signaled what was to come. Three days after the collapse of Saigon, the remnants of the non-Communist diplomatic corps and the handful of American journalists who had remained in Cambodia, sheltered in the French Embassy, were trucked to the border town of Poipet and unceremoniously expelled into Thailand. Their tale of the forcible mass evacuation of Phnom Penh and of the visible misery in the countryside through which they had traveled provided the first eyewitness evidence of the Orwellian character of the new regime.

Ten days later, Khmer Rouge patrol boats seized the American container ship *Mayaguez* and its forty-man crew, when the freighter passed within two miles of the island of Poulo Wai in the South China Sea. Phnom Penh was even then waging war with its fraternal socialist neighbor for control of the offshore archipelagos (as well as of disputed lands ashore), and the *Mayaguez* had obliviously sailed into a combat zone. The United States, faced with a perceived challenge by a fifth-rate power to a real strategic interest—freedom of navigation—responded by ordering a military operation in which forty-one American military men were killed,† scores wounded, and the Cambodian port of Kompong Som leveled by American bombers. But the crew and the ship were retrieved and the net effect was to restore some measure of public confidence in the efficacy of American arms.

In the following two and a half years, Cambodia became a vast slave-

---

*The name given by Russian novelist Alexander Solzhenitsyn to the Soviet system of slave labor camps for political prisoners.

†Most of them in the crash of a helicopter-load of Marines in Thailand, en route to the action.

labor camp. By many estimates, between a quarter and a third of the entire population was slaughtered in a vain effort to eradicate every vestige of foreign influence. Finally Hanoi, wearied by the worsening border confrontation and worried about the way Khmer Rouge behavior was blackening the name of Communist ideology, occupied the country and installed a puppet regime that was still ruling in the autumn of 1986.

For Americans, the exit of the *Mayaguez* from Cambodian waters marked the onset of amnesia. A soldier's pay, as William Faulkner observed in his novel of that name,* is to have his suffering ignored by those for whom he sacrificed. Never more so than for the veterans of America's first unmistakable defeat. The men who had fought in Vietnam did not mind the absence of ticker tape and marching bands, but they were stunned to find their honor and courage suspect—and worse, themselves feared and reviled as violent animals who threatened the peace of ordinary people. Even the wealthy and the powerful, who felt their leadership had been threatened in some vague way by the social turmoil that accompanied the war, did not want the old wounds reopened. Only a decade later, with the revival of American martial spirit and the dedication of the Vietnam Memorial—a black granite descent of the dead into Mother Earth—did that begin to change.

PAUL VOGLE

In the last days there was a terrible fear among the Vietnamese. They felt, "If they have to take us by force there's going to be a bloodbath before they have a chance to cool down their tempers." It wasn't that they were going to search out names and execute people. It was [that the Northerners would feel] "Boy, finally we've won and we're going to show them who we are," sort of like a locomotive that's built up steam and can't stop at the end of the line.

Every day Radio Hanoi and the Viet Cong Radio in the South was saying that the Americans must leave. Before surrender or anything else, it was: Americans get out. They wanted them to know that they were not welcome there, but they didn't want to get them so riled up that they were going to come back in force again. Viet Cong officials told me later that that was a big concern of theirs. I myself was personally convinced that there was no way that could hap-

---

Soldier's Pay, Faulkner's first novel, published in 1926, was the story of a southern town's disdain for a shell-shocked veteran of World War I.

pen. But the Vietnamese, both Communist and not, kept saying, "Oh, the Americans will come back."

I tried to get out on the twenty-ninth along with everybody else, but I got chicken trying to get into the Embassy. People were trying to get over the wall, and I boosted up two UPI people, but there were mobs of Vietnamese around, and some of them knew me and were shoving these papers at me. "You're not getting out of here. We go. We have permission." I figured it was safer to just turn around and go back to the office.

On the morning of May first I was standing on the roof of the Majestic Hotel watching the liberators walk down Tu Do street. That's when it hit, and for the next few days I was in a state of numbness. They were mostly in trucks. Some of them were walking down the street in groups. Then they went and camped in little parks and along the riverbank. There was no cheering. Nothing. This all happened in absolute silence.

We went around and tried to talk to these guys, but we were a little bit fearful of approaching them. We'd see a group sitting around eating or reading or just lying in their hammocks, and we found out they were afraid of us, too. Ninety-nine percent of them had never been in a city before, let alone Saigon. I got the impression that they thought the people were going to come out and cheer them, and that when they didn't, that kind of threw them. But after a while the ice would break a little bit and there'd be giggles and little signs. Here it was—the great conquering army—and they were bashful and shy.

For a while they treated me very well. One day, even, a group of North Vietnamese and Viet Cong came by the office and suggested that we get some weapons because of the looting going on in the streets. But at the end of May I was invited to the Foreign Ministry one day, and this committee there told me I was invited to leave the country. I said, "Can I appeal this invitation of the committee?" And the official I was talking to said, very calmly, "No. We are having a revolution. We are starting everything new and getting rid of the old. You belong to the old." So I said, "Well, what did I do wrong? Why are you throwing me out?" And he said, "You haven't done anything wrong. You don't belong here, that's all. We are asking you to leave. We are not kicking you out. Don't ever tell anybody we threw you out."

There was no overt friendliness between the North and South Vietnamese on that day the NVA marched into Saigon, and that continues to this day. They don't mix. They are much farther apart than the Americans and the Vietnamese used to be. The last time I was in Saigon, which was in '82, the [Southern] Vietnamese I knew were talking about "us" and "them."

And I saw Viet Cong officials that I knew from before. And they would tell me "We are the losers," meaning themselves. "You guys were lucky. You got out. We've got to live with these Northerners." They're bitter. That's one of the myriad of problems the North has now. The old VC were led to believe they were going to be part of the new leadership, and they're not. The kids in the South make up nursery rhymes, and they change the lyrics to anti-Communist, anti-North Vietnamese, anti-regime, anti-government. And they sing them in the streets. I don't see any change. I keep in touch with some of the people coming over here from Saigon, and the most recent ones say the same thing. It's as though time stood still in Saigon beginning in May of 1975. No progress at all. It's really very, very sad.

———————•———————

TRAN VAN DON

When the North Vietnamese soldiers came into Saigon, my friends who stayed behind said that our soldiers cried when they saw their young faces. They asked: "How could we be defeated by these children?" As a military man, I can say that we should not have been defeated like that. We were not weak. Of course, we knew we needed ammunition. But what we really needed were military leaders who would stay calm. Our military leaders panicked weeks before the fall.

We were badly hurt by the American side [in another way as well]. How can you explain why our division, regimental, even battalion commanders had their families evacuated by the Americans one month before the end. When our military leaders arrived in Guam, they already had their families there. How can you explain it? Why did they do it? No one is stupid enough to fight once the families have been sent out.

Thieu should be blamed for resigning, but he is not the only one to be blamed. When he resigned, his devoted people in the Army and the administration did the same: They walked away from their jobs. It was complete disorganization. Without the Army's general command and the administration, what can you do? I didn't like Big Minh's policies, but you can't blame him for surrendering. He had no choice. There were no more people in command. What could he have done? You have to be frank and fair and say there was plenty of blame on our allied side.

When we had to leave our country, we thought we were defeated.

We had made mistakes and our allies, the French and Americans, had made their mistakes, too. We thought the North Vietnamese had won because they were better than us. If you are the loser, you have to accept. I thought that despite their Communism, the North Vietnamese would reunify Vietnam and make a great and independent country. Now ten years have passed and what we see is the contrary. They didn't improve anything. They continue to fight both inside Vietnam against people who still do not accept their domination and outside of Vietnam in Cambodia. They are controlling Laos and fighting the Chinese as well.

The most important thing for any country is economic progress. The economic situation is unbelievable. In Hanoi and the North, things haven't improved at all. In fact, the North is worse off. In the South there is no comparison with what we had before. I am not talking about politics or the lack of freedom. I am talking about the lack of rice. Vietnam is now a country worse off than Bangladesh. It has slipped that far.

For the past ten years, we Vietnamese who were defeated sat abroad watching. If the Communists had done well, we would have admitted: "Yes, you were right to have won the war." But they did not know how to manage the country. They have proved themselves incompetent. The Communists must ask themselves if they have reached the goal of giving happiness to the people. They have failed. I believe they are patriots though, so it must be very difficult for them to ally themselves so closely with the Russians.

———◆———

DOAN VAN TOAI

In Cambodia at the last minute when the Communists took over, Sirik Matak, president of Congress, decided to stay and was executed. In South Vietnam no top leaders decided to stay. This made people like me very angry. And government people were angry. My army friends, a colonel and a major, said if they had the power to kill Thieu or Ky they would. They were very ashamed about the regime. If *these* people escape, I tell myself, I have no reason to escape. Better dead at enemy's hands than to flee.

The [Nam Do] bank closed three days before the end because of the curfew, so we stayed home. Big Minh was in power. I met some student-movement and politician friends—moderate, good people in South—to learn their forecasts and argue about the future. All were optimistic. Even Tran Van Tuyen. He was a prominent moderate anti-Thieu man, leader of the Nationalist party, head of the opposition bloc in the lower house. He was a northerner of the Ho Chi Minh-Viet Minh cabinet. I met him two or three days before the end. One of his daughters married a Korean diplomat who could arrange a flight, but he refused to go. He would rather die in his country than joining with the corrupt people who run away.

I met with Nguyen Van Huyen. He was chairman of the Senate and became Big Minh's vice-president. He said things were under negotiation with Viet Cong. The first time we met he said the situation was not bad. Then on the twenty-ninth night—his house was one wall from my house—he said the situation was worse. He encouraged me to flee. He said he would die here. He did not want to join the "cowardly people." I talked to every side to learn about the situation. The more I contacted, the more I lost optimism. Yet I did not leave. Even the worst situation I can accept, to build the country. Because we have peace. If government is bad, I will be against them again.

On last day, my brother—he is only a businessman, not a politician, he was with Viet Minh in 1940's—decided to go. His friend had a boat. He told me, "Let me take your wife and children out." I said, "No, they stay with me." Then he said, "I'll stay with you." Luckily I was wise enough to tell him, "We are two brothers. You get out. If one dies, the other can survive." With his family and friends and many people, they went to sea in a fishing boat of twenty meters. They met a U.S. boat and they were saved. He is now a farmer and raises vegetables for Chinese market of Fresno.

On April thirtieth I and my friend drive around city to see Communist troops coming with tanks. We would like to watch the reaction of the people and the reaction of the newcomer troops. We went to Tu Do Street, not far from my house. Some people waved a welcome, some looked indifferent. There were not very big crowds. I think the people were curious. Some young men who joined with the troops had red bandannas on and climbed into cars and held weapons. Later, people called them "Thirtieth Revolutionaries." Both real Communists and the people *hated* them.

The way the soldiers behave surprised me and a lot of Saigon people. Everything I knew of Communist movement was from my friends who joined the VC. I never see Communists from North. Before we thought that liberators must be bright, clean, and optimistic. Of course they were dirty. They were living a long time in the jungle. But their eyes did not look like victors but look like person who come into a *surprise*. So I found out that Communists were instructed that South city people were poorer than people in Hanoi. When they came into rich city with good building and saw well-fed people, they looked surprised. So Saigon people disdained the liberators. The more they talked with them they found they are young, naive, and deceived by the party—except some commanders and politician.

So in order to hide the perplexity, most of Hanoi troops lie and exaggerate situation in the North. It became very funny. All their life they never see a refrigerator and Honda scooter. And Saigon people ask them, "Do you have in North?" So they say, "Yes, every house have that!" Someone ask, "Do you have Brigitte Bardot in north?" Communists thought it was name of something or other. They say, "Oh, a *lot* of Brigitte Bardots in North!" But looking at their ignorance, I was very sad and hurt. I think that whole generation was destroyed by Communists, and if the Communists control the South like that, next generation will be like that. So I love these people, and I felt very sorry for them. I think future of Vietnam is ruin. Generation of my children and younger is ruin under the Communist rulers. The revolutionary who devote their life to a cause, how they can support situation like that?

I have two uncles, one major, one engineer-politician, who joined North in '54. They came to Saigon two or three weeks after takeover. I ask to them, "What you sacrifice, devote *for*?" They give excuse, the war. With peace, everything can improve. But they complained about things in North. They embraced hope that "We Southerners will now build the South." Either I escape to protect myself and future, or I stay to try to convince and change things somehow, along with other people.

Before the fall of Saigon, most people were very indifferent about the situation. But events after April thirtieth shocked them. Collapse of South Vietnam Army, few people were shocked. That's natural. Generals and leaders run away, Communists come in, that's natural. They were not shocked. But when Communists repress the people, that's shock. And arrest former soldiers, that's shock. And some former soldiers who kill themselves, that's shock.

I was very lucky. My wife had French nationality. She left Vietnam when I was in jail. With papers from France and help of friends in government—and some bribes—I got a visa to France. I had the first press conference to denounce the new regime for violations of human rights. I provided documents of prison system and published my first book, *The Vietnamese Gulag*. Articles about the book got Joan Baez and Jane Fonda into a fight.

One sister is teacher. She decided to stay to teach and lived with my father. She cannot survive. In 1980 she left by boat, disguised as ethnic Chinese when Vietnam wanted Chinese out. My father died in Vietnam in 1982.

TRUONG NHU TANG *is the author of* A Vietcong Memoir, *a detailed account of his years as a Viet Cong leader—and subsequently, as a boat person. He now lives in Paris.*

I wasn't in the jungles of Vietnam in the months preceding the collapse of ARVN. From December 1974 I was on the road as an itinerant ambassador. I didn't return to Hanoi the hard way, on foot, like so many fighters, but in the luxury of a limousine along the Ho Chi Minh Trail.

My first ambassadorial task was as leader of the Provisional Revolutionary Government delegation to Algiers at ceremonies there commemorating the anniversary of Algerian independence. I remember noting that our embassy, the embassy of the southern Provisional Revolutionary Government, was far more luxurious than that of Hanoi, and had more means at its disposal. The reason was that the Algerian government, and not Hanoi, financed all the expenses. From Algiers I flew to Moscow and then to Budapest, then to Tirana, Albania's capital, where I met Enver Hoxha, then to Bulgaria and Syria, returning to Hanoi in mid-January 1975, with the final offensive already gathering strength.

We were briefed every day on the progress of the advance and I remember being told that the watershed of the campaign was the surprise attack on Ban Me Thuot, compelling Thieu to pull his forces back from the Central Highlands and regroup on the coast. From that moment onward he was lost and the morale of the South Vietnamese collapsed.

In Hanoi, we were shown newsreel films of the collapse of Danang and the panic-stricken civilians and soldiers trying to flee. I took off for Algiers once more on April fourth, to represent the PRG at a conference of the International Association of Democratic Jurists. I was elected vice-president of the conference as a token of esteem for the Vietnamese people and for our impending victory, and given a standing ovation.

Then I had to go to Peking to represent the PRG at the funeral of Queen Kossamak, Sihanouk's mother, and didn't get back to Hanoi until April twenty-eighth. Then began an around-the-clock vigil listening to the radio news, culminating with the sound of Big Minh telling all soldiers to lay down their arms. Everyone embraced everyone else in the room. Out in the streets, it was pandemonium. The whole of Hanoi was out celebrating, cheering, singing, sobbing, exploding firecrackers.

I was, of course, impatient to get to Saigon as soon as possible but we were told to wait—our security was, apparently, a problem. Finally, on May thirteenth, our PRG party boarded an Ilyushin in Hanoi and returned to a wild reception at Tan Son Nhut. It really was a spontaneous mass demonstration, with a welter of PRG [Viet Cong] flags in the crowd.

I was overwhelmed but my personal affairs were far from happy. When I phoned my aged mother from the Hotel Miramar where we were housed, she broke the news of my father's death, my wife's divorce, and the fact that both she and my daughter were living in the United States, and my son was in France. "My son, I simply can't understand you," she said when we finally met. "You have abandoned everything—a good family, happiness, wealth—to follow the Communists. They will never return to you a particle of the things you have left. You will see. They will betray you and you will suffer your entire life."

But at least, on May thirteenth and fourteenth, the cheering masses of people on the streets were some comfort. Then came the victory parade, on May fifteenth. President Thang made a moving speech: "All Vietnamese are now the victors. Anyone with Vietnamese blood should take pride in this common victory of the whole nation. You, the people of Saigon, are now the masters of your own city." But as soon as the military parade began, I knew that a major change had occurred. It consisted exclusively of troops from North Vietnam. At the very end of it came a few straggling companies of Viet Cong units, unkempt and ragtag in comparison. And they flew the red flag with a single yellow star—the flag of the Democratic Republic of Vietnam—not the Viet Cong flag which had been so much in evidence on the streets two days before.

I turned to General Van Tien Dung on the podium. "Where are our Divisions Three, Five, Seven, and Nine?" I asked. He replied: "The Army has already been unified." I said: "Since when?" He just smiled. I knew then that something was dreadfully wrong—and subsequent events only bore me out.

———◆———

NGUYEN VAN HAO

The young troops, they were very humble, very polite. They wait to be invited to come in. And we are very pleased. This can offer a hopeful attitude. I think the first contact quite surprising. But to get control of a city or town, the Communist people work through police, not army. And when troops go to the barrack and replace with the People Police with the yellow uniform, quite different. They are very arrogant. The way they look the people in the street, I never believe it. Just they whistle at you, they never look at you, just to know if you stop and go to him.

The way they organize, every thirty people gonna have one policeman. Basically day and night he have nothing to do but go around the thirty and see what happens. He looking for what you did every day. You go out from your home what time and you go back what time. If you go one day at eight, next day seven, next day at nine, could be a problem. You don't have a job. And if you go home one day six, another day four another day ten o'clock P.M., they gonna ask you "Okay, my friend. What you did? Where did you walk? Where did you go? From what time to what time were you there?" And they check it. Because for them, they would control every life. Something happens wrong, they know about. And who goes in and out of your home. If stranger, you must have a permission to accept him. If you stay one night my home, I have to ask to the policeman: "Today I have one guest." He say: "What is the name? Where he come from? Where is his permit?"

They never asked you to go to a reeducation center?

Never.* Everyone [else] had to go, except a few members of the opposition people against Thieu. And many of them stay a long time. Once I ask why, and this fellow tell me in a moment of excitement: "We have cheat to get the Americans out, number one. And number two, we have cheat to get the officer from the Army of the old regime, and all the civilian minister of the old government to go to reeducation, because for us if they don't go there we cannot guarantee our victory. If these people from the old regime out of our control we will never have any peacetime."

I got my flesh goose. I never consider this kind of argumentation could be come from the human being. Okay you accuse, I disagree with you. But sometime could be friends. I fight you for one moment, but I don't become your enemy forever. We never consider the Communists, the North Vietnamese is our *enemy* enemy forever. We always think might be one of these days, South Vietnam and North Vietnam have to live together, economically, commercially, might be diplomatically. We are two part of one country. We speak same language. We have same land. We have same customs. We have same civilization. I never consider the North Vietnamese is my *enemies*. But they consider the regime of South Vietnam is the worst enemy they have to eliminate, exterminate. After the Communists

---

*According to Snepp's book, there are allegations that Hao's refusal to send South Vietnam's two hundred twenty million-dollar gold reserve abroad was at least partly motivated by a desire to curry favor with the Communists.

won they still *believe* all the sources of the devil come from the officer in the Army. So they have to isolate them, put somewhere under control, not to contaminate them.

Counting my fortune, they always treat me very well. I didn't have any official title. I just working as a consultant. They create for me a private office. They ask my thinking, I give them. I tell them other countries, they go only by one way. They develop. We have to go two ways: rebuild, and develop. And if we are interest to close our rank with Americans, *maybe* we can export to Americans again, because they feel some kind of guilty. If save the face of Americans, I would say they could be a lot [of help] again.

They read it, but at that time they think they don't need it. Because after the Vietnam war they think Vietnam is like a crucial point of the humanity. They considered they defeated you. My view is quite different. I say the Americans is not defeated, just the South Vietnamese. The Americans just go home. And years after years I discussed a lot with fairly important people. But they never bring me to Hanoi. They bring only people they are sure that they one of them. They know that I am very independent.

They did try to solve economic problems, but it is very difficult for them to do. How you can develop economically if all your resources are mobilized to the defense? Every young people go to the army and all the financial resources go to defense. Nothing left for economic development. And because of the system, too. The system is unproductive. It couldn't provide any motivation for the people to work.

When I talk to the Communists, I discover something very interesting. I discuss with one of them, "Okay, what is the priority now you have the power." He say, "Once we got the power, number one priority is how to keep power. Because if something throw you away nothing will help you. And next priority will be how to consolidate power." I say, "But what is next, after that?" He says the next number three priority after that is to *extend* power" [laughs]. It goes on and on, expand, consolidate, expand, consolidate. I say, "How about economic development to improve the condition of people?" The answer very simple. "If you got the power, even if you cannot improve the conditions of the economy you still have power. If we cannot [have] economic development today, in our generation, let the *next* generation take care of."

Do you regret having stayed?

I would regret *not* to have stayed, but I regret to have stayed too long. After four years I know already what I have to know. I didn't have the usefulness to these people. I work by motivation, not by money. I feel satisfied when the government is consider me a human being, ask my advice. When I decide to go, first I asked in 1979 to let my wife and my two boys go, and they accept. In 1980 I asked "Okay, now let me go to Paris to see my wife and children for three months. Afterward, I come back." They don't believe me. They said no. From that time I stop working.

They treat me in a way, very fair, because they consider nobody force me to stay Vietnam. I stay because I can be of use to the country and because of the system they cannot use me. I am too much independent, not a party man. So they keep me exactly like the way I live before.

I survived because of my books. Might be I got the most beautiful private library in Saigon. Almost fifteen hundred books. I could bring just only eighty, just only books talking about China history, how China develop, how China deal with forces. The history of China is one of the best. How you become a man, how you become a leader, how to become good king, how you should be act in order your enemy respect you, and how you survive if you are defeated. I read number two a lot of religious book about Buddha, Confucianist and Lao Tze. They get me the internal strength, just keeping my dignity intact.

In '82 when I left, the people when they know that I leaving, say "Okay, you are lucky Hao." Is mean to them the people stay behind is condemned, and everybody else is free.

———◆———

Charles Benoit

Let me tell you a story about a guy. I can't tell you his name because it would be dangerous for him. Back in the late sixties when I was working for AID, we had a program to develop future leaders for Vietnam by picking out bright high school students and sending them to the United States for a good college education. Well, this guy was one of the people we picked out. He went to a big eastern university. He became very much a part of campus life and he became involved in the fight against racism in the United States.

Well, he graduated and went back to Vietnam, and the racism he saw there—of the Americans toward his own people—so revolted him that he turned into a dedicated Communist. He had a job in the government, and during the final offensive he simply could not wait for the NVA to arrive. He was looking forward very much to being part of the new regime.

I later heard that when the new government came in, he was put into one of the reeducation camps. Not so unusual, because a lot of former Saigon officials were put in them. But then came 1979 and *Geo* magazine sent me over to Southeast Asia to do a story on the boat people. I made my way from Hong Kong to Indonesia on a coconut boat and we ended up on these little baby islands in the South China Sea that didn't even show up on a map, just sitting there with all these refugees, from the North and South, all mixed up. It was a fantastic experience.

And then one day another boat floated onto the island. And as that boat came up on the beach, we all ran to it. And in the boat was this guy, this former student who had turned into a dedicated Communist. He looked terrible. He had spent three years in the camps. And one of the refugees who'd been sitting on the beach with me knew this guy, remembered him, and he turned to me and said, "If a man like this leaves, then there is truly no hope."

Do Duc Cuong

I got back to Saigon and on April twenty-fifth I find my father. He said quickly to find somewhere to living, change whole life before the Communists come. He would be in danger! He and I go to pick up dead-body ID, to street in Bien Hoa with lot of dead bodies because of artillery attack. I looked for dead guy like me, took his ID, exchange my picture for his on his document. My new name is Nguyen Hoan Quan. My father tried to call me loudly, "Quan!" At first I did not answer quickly. "You must try to remember your new name!" he shouted. His new name was Nguyen Hoan Doanh.

Both of us went back to Vung Tau to be close to sea, in area most of people are Catholic. We went around outside city looking for a house. People were trying to flee. We saw a police captain taking a suitcase to a car. We ask him, "You want to sell your house?" He thought this was funny. He say, "You want to *buy* it?" "Why not? How much?" my father says. "Whatever you have," he says. I emptied my pocket. Police captain signs blank paper and my father pulls out a notary stamp he had seized from a local government office. We paid one hundred thousand piasters.

It was a wood house, ready to collapse anytime, two rooms, very close to ocean through jungle. We dated paper to 1965. We went to church and told Catholic father truth. We asked for Catholic family certificate. He said it was against Vatican law. My father said, "I am Catholic, too. Give me one." He filled it in to match sale document. It said we were living in that area ten years.

Cuong went back to Vung Tau and joined with a pickup unit of mili-

*tary stragglers trying to hold off the Communists while thousands
of fleeing civilians tried to get out to sea. On April 30, he heard a
broadcast of Duong Van Minh's surrender order.*

I cared nothing for this order. I got a numb feeling all over my body.
I just changed clothes and go back to see my father in new home.
First I bury M-16 in backyard. Next I become country man, wearing very old shirt, black pajamas, barefoot and dirty. Every day,
we go to cut wood in jungle, carry home, bring to market for people's cooking. We do it for Communists, something normal like very
poor person so they do not pay any attention to me. Always they
think the very poor people are on their side.

But my father says we will have problems because Communists are
checking backgrounds. People very friendly to us there, I tell them
witness for me living here ten years. They do this, but they couldn't
tell Communists where I born, grandmother, grandfather, and so
forth. Communist Bible says the wrongly killed is better than wrongly released, so Communists send me to camp in Long Khanh. I got
released from camp one time but they recalled me because I could
not sew up the evidence of my background. I spent one year in camp.
I felt I would *die*. I am lucky because they paid little attention, they
think I am *stupid* guy. I was not often beat or pressured. Others
were killed and beaten. One time I was picking peanuts. One guy
next to me was hungry. He picked up and ate one peanut. They
beat him to death.

One night we were heading back to camp after day of labor. We
have shooting and blowing-up around camp. We did not know why.
I ran into jungle. In 1976, Communists were shooting artillery back
to jungle because they couldn't control. I got more shrapnel in back,
not too bad. I kept moving two days, got to highway and stopped a
bus. Driver ask me for money to Vung Tau. I had none. Nam [now
his wife] was on bus, and paid for me. We got talking. I find out she
worked at U.S. Embassy, her father was a major. She was going to
Vung Tau. We became best friends and planned escape together.

I must hide all time. I was living in jungle. My neighbors knew I
was still around, but no one discover me. My father and Nam buy a
fishing boat. Then I am captain of that little boat. Thirty-one days
and nights from Vung Tau we are at sea, using blankets to catch
rainshower. With me on boat were one young man neighbor who
now lives in Denver, Nam, my father. Nam was seven months preg-
nant. We avoid Thailand and pirates and arrived in Indonesia in
August 1977. We reach the U.S. in 1978.

I never sleep well. Every night I wake up anytime. I still hear the
gunfire. Until now, I'm still a soldier to myself. Sometimes I still

hear the terrible noise of the artillery shell, the sound of the tank. Most difficult thing is to concentrate the mind on job and to sleep.

Americans think they were wrongly involved in a civil war. Fifty thousand GIs die. American people, they turn their back. That's unfair. GIs were very good fighter who followed order of their government to do their duty and lost their life, not to protect President Nixon or President Thieu but protect the people living in freedom. Those people who died in our country is my hero. I try to pay them back. My ideas may give to Americans some jobs. I try tell young people here, "Don't be upset about America." It is most wonderful country in world. You never smell freedom. You never recognize what a wonderful thing you have in your hand in freedom. You recognize the value of water only when you are really thirsty.

———————————•———————————

EDDIE ADAMS

[In 1977] a friend of mine in the Embassy in Bangkok told me there were a lot of people escaping from Vietnam on boats. The United States was trying to keep it quiet. The term boat people wasn't even used yet. But he said, "If you could get on one of these boats escaping the country, it would be quite a story." So I went to the chief of the National Maritime Police and got the okay to go. The Thais were just putting a rope on a boat to tow it back out to sea—they weren't accepting any refugees—so I made them hold it up. They didn't have any fuel left, so I bought a hundred dollars' worth and jumped on board. I couldn't believe what I was doing. The Thai pirates were attacking boats in the area.

They welcomed me aboard. They knew if they landed at some other point and I was with them, they would be accepted because I'm an American. I was on the boat a day—Thanksgiving Day. There was no place to lie down—forty-nine people in a thirty-foot fishing boat. The Vietnamese—it was very funny—had one umbrella aboard, and they had someone stand next to me and hold the umbrella over my head because it was very sunny and very hot.

To give you some background, when you photograph children in disaster areas or refugee camps, there can be ten or twenty bodies stacked up, and the children will stand around the bodies and smile at the camera. They smile because they see a camera. It's not what you're looking for in terms of pictures. But on this boat there were forty-nine or fifty people, and not one of them smiled. So I called it "The Boat of No Smiles." Later in the day the Thai Maritime Police came back and ordered me off the boat. Finally they raised their guns, so naturally I went.

I wrote a story and released the pictures, and they were page one all over the world. And the State Department asked the AP for the pictures to be presented to Congress. This is when Carter realized what was happening, and he said "Let them come to America." A few days later, the boat pulled in on another section of Thailand. People from the U.S. Embassy were waiting. They were brought immediately to the United States. Now this doesn't happen to you every day, but if you can do that with a picture, it gives you a lot of satisfaction.

You went back to Vietnam in 1983. What drew you back?

Actually, I didn't want to go back. I thought I hadn't really left anything there. But when I got back, I was all wrong. I left a lot of myself. The feelings that came over me. Everything was wrong. At Tan Son Nhut, there were only two airplanes. During the war it was the busiest airport in the world. It used to take half an hour to forty-five minutes to get into Saigon. Now it takes ten. There isn't any traffic.

I was very uncomfortable. I found that in the South around Saigon, I wasn't treated as well as in the North. In the South I got this feeling "You left us here. You deserted us." I felt more comfortable in Hanoi. Your mind gets all messed up. I was in the Mekong Delta, I sat down to have coffee, and all of a sudden all these people started gathering around me and just staring, not saying a word. I asked some people why is it? I didn't realize some of these kids weren't around during the war. They hadn't seen whites. "Yeah," I said, "but they must have seen some Russians." They said most of the Russians stay in their compounds. They never go on the streets.

I also saw Cung, the guy I wrote about in my *Parade* story. That was frightening. I remember him having a rich, black moustache. When I went back in '83, it was all white. He really wanted to embrace me. He came running over. I felt really warm. Then he jumped back away from me and started looking around to see who was watching us. He backed off. I said, "It's okay. I won't talk to you." He was very frightened. I never saw him again while I was there.

———•———

JAMES SCHLESINGER

Did the military's impulse to get back on the tar baby, as you put it, play a role in the Mayaguez?

No, the *Mayaguez* was a decision taken by the senior civilians. Don't blame that on the military. That was driven by myself and Kissinger and the President, and by the perceptions that were left over from Vietnam: That here was this not even second- or third-rate, this fifth-rate state seizing our vessels, contravening what we regarded as freedom of the seas. And if the great stabilizing force in the world, the United States, because of these perceptions of weakness that had come out of Vietnam, could be defied by such a pathetic little regime as that in Phnom Penh, what standing would we have? I think we might have negotiated longer if it hadn't been for that perception.

The night here that the aerial bombardment, the first wave, was supposed to go off, I moved from the Pentagon over to the White House to attend a state dinner for the Dutch, and I discovered that in my brief transit the first wave had been cancelled. I was simply nonplussed by that. Kissinger came in and said that they had said on the Phnom Penh radio that "We are willing to discuss things." We had formed our plans, and I said "Henry, you can't be serious. You're cancelling the mission on the basis of some comment on the Phnom Penh radio? The only thing that we have that will persuade them to give up our people is the capacity to lambaste them on the mainland."

And he thought about it for a few minutes and he briefed and persuaded Ford, who needed no persuasion—it was Henry who did. And I talked to the NMCC, which was just overcome with the volatility of their civilian overlords, and said, "Put on the second strike," and pretty soon, to use the phrase of the current President, the Cambodians cried "Uncle" and delivered the crew members to the ship. That was a much more rewarding affair.

I have never seen a more hostile gathering of the press corps than that evening of the *Mayaguez* rescue. The press room over there, half those people, at least half the vocal ones, were eager to see the United States lose, and they were frustrated and disappointed.

———•———

KEN BEREZ

It was only after I got back to the States and was in the hospital that I really began to think about the war. Getting shot in the back does wonders for your political awakening. I spent almost a year in hospitals. I happened to be in Walter Reed during the November Moratorium march in '69. When you're that age and your body is blown apart, you really want to believe it was for something. In my case, I started to read, looking for a thread of evidence that would've made my sacrifice worthwhile. And the conclusion I came to was that it wasn't. As more and more evidence came in, the Pentagon Papers, My Lai, whatever, I began to see that Vietnam was a gross, gross mistake.

I lived with it for a long time internally. I didn't befriend other Vietnam veterans at first. I didn't become politically active. It was just bitterness. I was paraplegic for almost a year, and then I began to get some return because my spinal cord was bruised and bruising can heal and come back, and I got return on my right side. It took me almost two years to become physically independent, and then I lived quietly with my family, not doing much of anything. Time is a healer, but it took me a good number of years just to come to peace in my own mind, and it wasn't until the late seventies that I went back to school and got active in VVA.

And even though in a sense I'm a professional vet working for a vets' organization, all this that I'm saying to you now about my personal experiences in Vietnam, I don't dwell on it from day to day. Sometimes I raise the question in my own mind that if I didn't get shot that day, would I have survived the rest of the year? Maybe I would have gotten it right between the eyes five days later. And maybe for that reason I really don't think about it too much. I work in an organization where I deal with veterans almost every day who *do* have problems. I guess if there is anything I'm still bitter about it's that after fighting and bleeding in a war, people point fingers at me because I'm involved in an organization that's political, and say to me sometimes that I'm less than patriotic. And it isn't just the crazies, either. If it was only the crazies it wouldn't bother me. It's people who are in power. That gets me angry, more angry today than I ever was about getting hit.

And what attracts me to VVA is that it has a political agenda to make sure that Vietnams in other places in the world do not happen again—so that the public and the next generation are educated, so that we can make decisions for the right reasons, not out of ignorance and not follow like sheep.

———◆———

BOBBY MULLER

What radicalized you?
Let's say a couple things that need to be said. A lot of people said I wound up speaking out against the war because I got crippled. And I would say to those people, "Don't you understand? Because of what happened to me, it's *harder* for me to speak out against the

war." I've got guys in the hospital, not paras like me, but quads.*
Guys that will never ever move anything except their fucking head.
They were married, some of them. They had kids, some of them.
They got nowhere to go and nothing coming down the road except
more staring at the ceiling. And what do they do? They console themselves by the thought that goddamnit, it's a bitch but that's what
you got to do to fight for freedom, for democracy. They wrap themselves up in that they paid the price for America and what we all
believe in. And when you go to that guy and say, "Hey, pal, guess
what? You lost what you lost for nothing. There was no purpose,
no reason, and what happened to you is a total, fucking waste,"
well, that's a bitter pill to swallow.

And like I said, I never had a political discussion in Vietnam. It was
irrelevant. The day I got shot, I was assaulting an enemy position. I
wanted them. People would say, "If you thought the war was wrong,
why did you kill, why did you keep going?" And I said, "It's like
when I was on the hospital ship and a psychiatrist came by and I
asked him was there something wrong with me? He said, 'Why?' I
said, 'Why could I sit down, which I was doing a day or two ago,
and chow down with bodies around me? Am I inhuman. Is there
something wrong with me?' And he said, 'Your mind is an incredible organ. You've got defense mechanisms to protect you. Because
of where you were, your mind made adjustments to let you do what
you got to do. I guarantee you a year from now, you're back in New
York and you see a cab hit somebody on the street, you're going to
get as sick as anybody else.' "

That hospital ship was extraordinary. Tremendous, compassionate
people. And when I came back I was in St. Albans Naval hospital,
in Queens. And it was [also] a tight ship. While I was in St. Albans,
a guy from the VA came by and started throwing out forms and I
asked him, "What's that for?" He said "We're going to be giving
you money." I said, "For what?" And he explained, "Because you
got injured." I swear to God I didn't expect that. I figured, that's
your bum luck; you do what you got to do. If you get smacked,
they got to do everything they can to put you together again. That's
what I expected. But instead of getting quality medical care, I got
all this fucking money.

I went from St. Albans and spent a year in Kingsbridge VA hospital
in the Bronx. Kingsbridge was constructed in the eighteen hundreds
and it was a decrepit, dilapidated, run down facility. I was there for
a year, and being a veteran and getting cast into a welfare insti-

---

*Paras, or paraplegics, can use their arms and hands. Quads, or quadriplegics, are paralyzed
from the neck down.

tution—a glorified nursing home full of impoverished, geriatric, alcoholic drifter types—was a nightmare. Basically, here we come, young guys, acute medical care needs plus active rehabilitation requirements, getting dumped into a really depressing environment. And that's where the anger came from. Simple things: The therapy clinic was two guys. There were, many times, twenty-five of us in wheelchairs, hanging around for one of them to have time to work with us on motion exercises to keep the joints limber, on building upperbody strength, on chair control, on how to pop a curb in a wheelchair.

Life magazine did a cover story in May of 1970 using my ward as the centerpiece and it was the second-largest-selling issue they ever put out. That story triggered congressional hearings, a lot of national press, a whole lot of furor. After that I brought twenty-five guys in wheelchairs into the administrator's office, and we said, "Why don't we have another set of parallel bars? Why don't we have steps that we can learn to negotiate? Why don't we get a whole lot of obvious things—all of what you need to be independent in life." And they said, "Well, we don't have the money." And I said, "I don't want to hear you don't have the money."

I did a lot of network shows—*Today, Dick Cavett, David Susskind, Phil Donohue*—and my rhetoric was real simple. "I called in hundreds of thousands of dollars to kill people. I get shot in the process and come back and you tell me that you don't have the money to put me together again?" And a week before the election in 1972, Nixon vetoed the Veterans Medical Care Expansion Act, calling it fiscally irresponsible and inflationary. That's when I went in the streets, Times Square in New York, and went crazy. To put money into the VA hospitals was fiscally irresponsible and inflationary when you're spending the money we did to kill people? Gimme a break. You can't lay that shit on me. That was my rage.

Later on I got an invitation to a retired Marine officers' luncheon at Sardi's. Why not? I'm a retired Marine officer. So I go to the luncheon and I was the only guy under sixty. A general gives a presentation on the Corps. Any questions? So I get up. "Our motto, Semper Fidelis—always faithful—is something I believed in. Our guys fought and died believing that. So why did I and a lot of other Marines spend a year in a veteran's hospital and get a lot of national publicity about the atrocious conditions and never once did anybody from the Marine Corps come by to say, 'How are you guys doing?' That old Semper Fidelis—it doesn't carry over when we can no longer carry a rifle? You've made a mockery of what my guys died believing in."

Now you asked what radicalized me. It was a slow process. When I started doing my stuff some guys from Vietnam Veterans Against the War came in and said, "Look, man, you're saying a lot. You ought to know what we're up to." And we started to talk. Okay, it may be an organization that people disparage today, but back in '70–'71, VVAW was legitimate. I thought Bobby Muller had had a unique experience in Vietnam, but it turned out all these other guys had stories to match mine. The war was insane. The ARVN weren't fighting for shit. The NVA and VC were determined people. The level of violence we were pouring out was only getting more anger built back up at us. And as I talked to more and more vets, everything I had believed in began to unravel. That's when I started asking "How did this begin? Why did we get involved in the first place?" And then all of a sudden you start to hear about the French and the history of the place and the whole thing fucking unravels.

And so from being the mouthpiece at the hospital, [I went] to working with VVAW, to doing some speaking and getting attacked, being spit on, being called a coward and a traitor, and this wasn't a joke. People gave us the finger and called us names. I went to Clark High School in Long Island the night after we'd held a weekend of Winter Soldier hearings where vets gave testimony about what they'd done in Vietnam, and I'm recounting some things that weren't pretty about guys freaking out. So I talked and this woman stands up and says, "I object to your use of obscenity." I said, "What did I say?" A guy said, "You used the word bullshit." I said "You know it's amazing, I'm talking to you about the obscenity of war, about wholesale atrocities as a matter of policy and what you relate to as an obscenity is the word bullshit. What would you do if I said, 'Fuck you.'" This was in a full auditorium. It was great. Once in your life you got to do it. It was total pandemonium. In the aisles, ranting and raving. Boom. You know, ahhh!

So VVA grew out of VVAW?

No, VVAW was taken over by the Revolutionary Communist Party. It went whacked out and I just saw through the bullshit. VVA started out to be just a lobby. I came here in January of 1978 with a friend, a secretary, and myself, three of us. I had a meeting with Phil Geyelin who was running the editorial page of *The Washington Post*, and we put together a caucus of Vietnam Veterans in Congress, and banged away. That first year we had probably thirty-five editorials and columns on the Op/Ed page. At the end of the year, Geyelin said he had never conducted an editorial campaign [like that] and the response had been total silence. He said "I'm convinced you've got to talk about Vietnam not in terms of vets' benefits but in terms of what it did to trust in government, institutions, and leadership, what it did to our spirit and so on. He introduced me to Winston Lord, who was then president of the Council on Foreign

Relations, and Lord hooked us up with McGeorge Bundy, the president of the Ford Foundation.

Bundy and Lord cosponsored a luncheon at Ford with investment bankers, corporate representatives, big-shot journalists, a whole bunch of fucking powerful people. And we went for two and a half hours about the need to look at the Vietnam experience, not for purposes of pointing fingers of blame but to ask what went wrong? What did we learn? At the end Bundy said, "What you're doing is deserving, meritorious, righteous but you're not going to get support from your normal philanthropic sector—your corporations, your foundations." He said, "You're the symbol of that war and that war causes powerful people in this country to be uncomfortable and because of that they're not going to support you. It's a very negative area." And he didn't say that to be mean at all. He was just giving us the lay of the land.

What Bundy said was true, Vietnam made people feel very uneasy. Around that time I gave a speech at City Hall which got a tremendous response. What I said was "You people ran a number on us. Your guilt, your hangups and your uneasiness made it socially unacceptable for us to mention that we were Vietnam veterans. Whenever we'd bring it up, you'd walk away." It wound up on the front page of the *Times* as the quote of the day. [New York Mayor Ed] Koch was there and it was the first time anybody could recall him being speechless.

But the thing that turned it around, and it is black and white, night and day, was the return of the hostages from Iran and the ticker-tape parade in New York. The day of the parade I was in the office, and the phones didn't stop ringing. The first time ever, ever, ever that, unsolicited, we got calls. People were saying, "Not to take it away from the hostages, but I want you to know I'm thinking about you." My mother called from Houston, Texas, and she was outraged. She said, "One of the hostages came from Houston. They gave him a Cadillac and free passes to the ball games. What did anybody ever give you? Nothing." And the contrast between America going gaga over the hostages and they never did anything for the Vietnam Vets was so great that they were compelled finally to try and balance the scales.

And maybe even more important, the hostage crisis provided the emotional opportunity to the American people to talk about how we relate to the world. What is our role as a power broker? What *do* you go to war for? What are the values? What are the interests? Do you go to war because of a Khomeini? And as you get into those kinds of discussions, what's the basic reference point? The last time you went to war: Vietnam. *The New York Times* and *The Washing-*

ton Post ran articles and said that for the first time at cocktail parties and at social functions, Vietnam was being openly discussed as the reference point on the basic issues of the day. And I think that was the key—the understanding that we do have adversaries out there, like it or not, and we got to define how we relate to those folks. That put us on the agenda for public discourse.

And that was followed by the dedication of the National Memorial, which provided its own catharsis, and was the first time that tens of thousands of Vietnam Veterans had come together since the war. And that whole week, guys were coming in and checking things out, and Poof! with the reunions and people being on the street and down at the Wall, and the emotion and camaraderie a re-established sense of brotherhood [was] clearly, clearly being brought out. Look, we shared something that was powerful, and it shouldn't be forgotten. What it means differs to different people but it rekindled that sense and gave the beginning of, it's okay to be a Vietnam vet—you don't have to be ashamed or embarrassed.

———————◆———————

JOSH CRUZE

I came back and I was totally a mess with drugs. Before I had gone into the service if I'd taken two tokes on a jay and maybe a glass of wine to get a buzz, that was a lot. I came back two years later and these cats were doing a list of shit on the street corners. They had long hair. The music had changed radically. The Beatles in '65 had a beat. When I came back, it was na-na-na-na-na. This stuff was hard. I'd heard some of it in Nam, and I wasn't sure I liked it. I came back and all my buddies said, "Where've you been, man? It's like you've been asleep. Now you've got to get in with it."

Then there were so many things that came into play. Free love, girls burning their bras, feminism. There were so many things coming up, challenging things. And it wasn't like I'm thinking about this but it's not right. It was like, I'm thinking about this and I'm going to experiment with it and see where it leads me.

A lot of pain. I had to cope with the realization at one time in my life that if I didn't see somebody I was going to off myself. That's what it came down to. It was a very big decision for me to say, "Look, you have to see somebody because there's something screwed up." I didn't want to believe that. [But finally] I had to go to the VA and say, "Look, I'm either going to jump on the subway tracks or get a gun and blow people away because of the way I'm feeling. I want some help. I'm afraid. Please help me."

Prior to Vietnam I always saw myself as someone in control. Then came a point when I felt like I was in a void falling, and I couldn't grab onto nothing. If I saw a doctor and he said, "You're going to be all right." I said, "You're lying to me." If he said, "This pill will help, that pill will help," I wouldn't believe anything. "Just give me something to put me out 'cause I don't like the way I'm feeling." It's scary. I always say, "I wouldn't wish these feelings on my worst enemy." But I had to go through a lot of crying and telling people my experiences and about the guilt, to be able to feel good about myself.

It sounds to me as if simply doing Tracers *has done a lot for you.*

Definitely. I would not have been talking about Vietnam anymore if it hadn't been for those vets. My mind was just "Bury that. Put it somewhere where you never have to deal with it again." I was afraid of opening up this Pandora's box. I met John for the first time, before I was even cast. He walked into the room and I felt this trust. Trust is very important. I felt that if I came up with all this stuff, he would be there for me. If I broke down, no matter what happened, I could hold on to him. Not only did I have him, but when I was cast I had eight guys in a circle. If something happened, I could hold onto them because they understood exactly where I was coming from. That's what got me by.

I didn't want to talk about these stories before. It was like another life. It was a whole different human being that had done this sixteen years ago. I divorced myself from the reality, as if it didn't happen. But when that thing in Lebanon took place, that explosion, it was like I was back, seventeen years ago, seeing that building a shambles. I cried like a baby. I told my wife, Peg, "I can't believe that this is happening again." I felt like kicking in the TV, I felt like going to Washington and taking Reagan and just choking the son-of-a-bitch and saying, "Goddamn it, when are you going to learn, for Christ's sake? Those are young kids you're dealing with, man. It's the youth of our country and you just piss it away like it's nothing. Sure you're sitting up there in the White House and what the hell do you give a damn? Your son is a ballet dancer. Who gives a shit?" And yet to see those families that week being interviewed by the news media . . . it tore my heart apart. I thought, "Keep yourself calm."

———•———

JOHN DIFUSCO

I went through some kind of craziness because somehow, mythologically, you expected acceptance when you come back. We didn't get it. We get it from the show now. When we first did the show in Los Angeles, people would say, "What is this show to you?" And I would say, "It's a parade." But it's a special kind of parade. This idea of a ticker-tape parade is nice, but Vietnam is not a ticker-tape parade kind of war.

When the play was running in Los Angeles there was a hunger strike at the VA hospital. One day about six or eight guys arrived and set up tents in front of the hospital. Then day by day it grew and grew, and the guys there who were obviously observing that situation were stereotypes with dark glasses and after a while they just got to be treated like one of us. My involvement in the hunger strike was really just a support thing. I would go down every day, bring juice, hang out with the guys.

There was a guy named Jim Hopkins who drove a military jeep through the doors of the VA hospital in Westwood, Los Angeles. He ordered everybody out of the lobby and filled [it] full of bullet holes with two rifles he had. He shot up all the pictures of Presidents and generals, claiming he had an Agent Orange problem and a delayed stress problem, and he couldn't get any help.

His case became tied in with this hunger strike thing. Going through the litigation and trying to decide whether this guy should be put in jail or in the hospital, he was found dead in his home in Malibu. Ron Kovik, he was a very heavy political activist and one of the founders of Vietnam Veterans Against the War, was organizing this thing. He called me up one night and said they were going to do this funeral at the VA Hospital. They're going across the street to the VA cemetery. [Hopkins] had some kind of problematic discharge so that the Marine Corps wouldn't give him a color guard. Would the *Tracers* cast be a color guard and bring the weapons? It was cleared through the sheriff's department. We loaded the weapons into my old Pinto station wagon and drove up to the VA and a very polite sheriff's deputy checked out the M-16s to make sure they weren't functional. Then we marched out to the cemetery.

One of the most fascinating things was listening to the cameras click. In two or three hours I probably had my photo taken more than in the rest of my life. I had a big peace symbol on the back of the fatigue shirt. Everyone loved taking photograph of the M-16 coming up over my shoulder with the big peace sign on my back.

———◆———

Not all American POWs in Vietnam were well-educated flyboys. Some were plain farm kids like DANNY HEFEL, *reared in the limestone hills of northeast Iowa. Hefel was a door gunner with the 101st*

*Airborne Division in Vietnam when his chopper was shot down in
1970, leaving him with a broken back and other wounds. Unable to
move, he was taken prisoner, held in the jungle for a time and later
in the Hanoi Hilton. By the time he was released in 1973, he had
spent eleven hundred and forty-three days as a captive. He learned
to walk again, but is disabled and survives on a pension. Hefel, who
owns a big Harley, lives in a relative's house overlooking the Mississippi River east of Sherrill, Iowa.*

Everybody wanted to welcome Dan home at the airport. That's
where it ended. I get enough to live on, but I can't gain. I've got
about what I possessed when I came back home. My back's not
much better, and now my legs go to sleep all the time too. I can't
get married or buy a house. All I need right now is mortgage payments, insurance payments on a wife, insurance payments on a kid.
The old popularity ain't what it was twelve years ago. All the time I
meet people who never heard of Dan Hefel. They look at me with
these big eyes and say, "Wow, that happened? I didn't know shit
like that could happen!"

I watch the big shots argue about the war on television. I think,
"*Now* you're telling us what we should have done!" That war should
have been over before I left home. I was going over there to do
something. It didn't work out that way. I didn't mind going. I was
going to kick some ass for two years and get out, let somebody else
kick some ass. They got the best part of my years. Everybody always
wants this, everybody wants that—but nobody ever wants to give
nothing. When you're a soldier, you get sent off to do what somebody else wants done. But you'd better be ready to come home and
hold your pride up, because nobody else will. Here I am, just surviving. I can keep myself supported and keep a roof over my head,
but that's all I can do. Shit happens to you in life. That's my attitude: Shit happens.

I don't get the big, scary dreams anymore. Sometimes I get talking
about it, how I was locked up in that goddamned camp, my freedom gone. That's when I dream. I wake up in the middle of the
night, rolling around my water bed. Being in camp is what I remember. Just being locked up, unable to walk, with all those thoughts in
my head.

I wouldn't give up the medals and ribbons. Mom won't let me take
them off the wall. I think she still has the little blue uniform the
Vietnamese sent us out in. I've still got no love for those people.
I'll go to a Chinese restaurant and eat Oriental food. Just so there
aren't too many of them around.

I've still got my box of clippings. Sometimes I take them out and read them. I look at my invitation to the big White House presidential dinner, too. They invited me and my mom but not my dad so I wouldn't go. When I see that invitation, I get pissed and throw it back in the box.

I don't belong to the Vietnam Veterans group here. Those guys are fighting for the right things, but I'm just going to sit back. I'm tired of hollering at the government. The World War II guys are starting to get a little closer to the Vietnam guys. When I'm down in the VA hospital in Iowa City, I can talk to those older guys. Things are changing.

The future? Forget it. If it weren't for Vietnam, I'd be a heavy equipment operator, working construction. Probably would have married that girl. Now I'll just go through life fucked. Like the song says, "I don't want a pickle; just want to ride my motorsickle."

CHAPTER FIFTEEN

The Legacy
of Vietnam

IT is an article of conservative faith that the legacy of Vietnam was an era of American retreat. At home three Presidents—and a Congress tired of war—cut defense spending with a vengeance. Inflation and the end of the draft pushed the costs of buying weapons and paying troops to levels never imagined in the fifties, and there was no political will to keep pace by approving higher budgets. The armed forces shrank by half: the Army from 1.5 million men to 700,000, the Navy from 900 ships to 450, the Air Force from 7,000 warplanes to 3,500. Together, the war and the budget cutback cost the Pentagon the 1985 equivalent of half a trillion dollars in procurement—literally thousands of planes, tanks and ships that never entered the forces.

Abroad, the United States withdrew from armed struggle for influence in the Third World. Having legislated an end to Vietnam, Congress also forbade a barely begun secret intervention in Angola. The U.S. declined to support Somalia's war of aggression to wrest the Ogaden desert from newly Marxist Ethiopia. Jimmy Carter proposed to withdraw from South Korea, though he later relented, and he maintained U.S. neutrality between the Sandinista rebels and Nicaraguan dictator Anastasio Somoza. At the end of the decade, American purpose seemed absolutely frustrated by events in the Near East: The Soviets invaded Afghanistan; the Shah was toppled in Iran; the U.S. Embassy staff in Teheran was held hostage for 444 days; the beginning of the Iran-Iraq War brought on a second oil shortage and another massive jump in prices; and the U.S. military bungled an effort to take back the hostages by force. Small wonder that Americans suddenly felt powerless in a hostile world, and elected Ronald Reagan, who promised to make them strong again.

On reflection, however, that feeling may have been a classic case of failing to see the forest for the trees. As William Sullivan, Stephen Solarz, Eugene McCarthy, and others point out, the seventies were nothing like the disaster for American foreign policy they were made out to be. The doors to China and Egypt, pried open by Richard Nixon and Henry Kissinger, turned out to be wide gates onto broad boulevards. Three years after the fall of Saigon, the "Communist monolith" of Russia and China had dissolved, and Peking was behaving like an American friend, if not an ally. In Egypt Anwar Sadat not only sent home his erstwhile Soviet helpers but made peace with Israel. In Western Europe Communist advances were rebuffed in Spain, Portugal, Italy, and Greece; in the East, Poland, Hungary and Rumania all seemed to loosen their ties to Moscow. Southeast Asia's weakling dominos turned into powerful economic dynamos. And perhaps most important for the long haul, revolutionary Communism, having shown itself to be both a second-rate economic engine and a dehumanizing political system, began to lose its appeal among the European intellectuals who had long believed it superior in every way.

Nonetheless, Ronald Reagan set out in 1981 to restore American military strength by ladling out hundreds of billions of dollars and large dollops of patriotic spirit. And he did succeed in rebuilding the image, at least, of power. It is no small irony, then, that Reagan himself turned out to be a most unwarlike president. When his political counselors told him the country was in no mood for war, and his military advisers argued that before committing troops to combat the U.S. government had to have a clear purpose, strong political support and a determination to win quickly, he listened.

The necessary circumstances occurred only once in the first six years of his presidency. In 1983, the Marxist prime minister of Grenada was murdered in a radical coup. Administration officials feared the new rulers might make hostages of a thousand American medical students on the island. The United States invaded with 7,000 soldiers and Marines, overran the local militia and its 700 Cuban supporters, rescued the students, and restored democratic rule. The military bungled some parts of the operation, but it was hugely popular at home. Coming just after the loss of more than 250 lives in the Marine barracks bombing in Beirut and six weeks after the Soviets had shot down KAL 007, it also helped the Reagan Administration slide past what might well have turned into yet another period of self-flagellation over American military ineptitude.

But elsewhere, Reagan tended to talk loudly and carry a small stick. Presented in Lebanon with a serious military challenge that had long-term implications for U.S. policy in an important area of the world, he pulled back without hesitation. The U.S. was drawn into Lebanon in 1982 when it moved to stop Israel from occupying Beirut and making war on Syria. The Marines landed in Beirut first to guarantee the safe withdrawal of Palestine Liberation Organization guerrillas, and then returned as a "peacekeeping" force to allow the Israelis to disengage south of Beirut. In addition the Marines were to help prop up President Amin Gemayel, by rebuilding the Lebanese Army. It was that role which got them in trouble.

In the summer of 1983, Syrian President Hafez Assad, outraged over a U.S.-sponsored agreement that promised an eventual peace treaty between Lebanon and Israel, ordered an assault on the Gemayel government. Moslem militiamen coached by Syrian regulars attacked Souk al Gharb in the Shouf Hills overlooking south Beirut. The town, which guarded a back-road supply corridor into the capital, was defended by a battalion of Lebanese regulars who were armed, trained, and advised by the Marines. The attack on Souk al Gharb brought orders from soon-to-be National Security Adviser Robert McFarlane to use Marine artillery at Beirut Airport and the naval guns of the U.S. Sixth Fleet to support the Lebanese. The Syrian-backed forces replied by shelling the Marines at the airfield and hitting them with guerrilla attacks, culminating in the suicide truck-bombing of the barracks.

The United States spent the rest of the autumn and early winter licking its wounds. U.S., French, and Israeli intelligence officers soon thought they knew who was behind the bombing—Iranian-led Shiite Moslem terrorists based at Baalbek in Syrian-controlled eastern Lebanon. French and Israeli warplanes bombed the Baalbek camp, but proposals for a U.S. air strike were batted down by Gen. John Vessey, Chairman of the Joint Chiefs of Staff, with strong backing from Defense Secretary Caspar Weinberger. The Pentagon feared being drawn into a cycle of retaliation that could well lead to even worse reprisals against a Marine force already too small to defend itself. The other military option floated by the National Security Council staff was a massive infusion of troops to try to pacify Lebanon. But heading into a presidential election year, that was a nonstarter, and so Ronald Reagan simply opted out. In February the Marines scurried out of Lebanon across the same beach they had scampered in.

The Pentagon's reluctance to get involved in Lebanon evoked a thinly veiled attack by Secretary of State George Shultz in the spring of 1984. Shultz worried that the United States was too reluctant to use force to back its goals abroad. Weinberger struck back in the fall, saying that U.S. troops should not be committed to combat without a visible national security interest, strong public support, clear and attainable military objectives, a determination to win, and enough force to do it quickly. That began a running debate in and out of the

Administration over the proper uses of power. The debate evoked some hand-wringing by commentators and former officials about whether Weinberger wasn't setting conditions under which American forces could never be used short of a major war.

Military attitudes changed slightly after Vessey was replaced by Adm. William Crowe. American warplanes were used to intercept an Egyptian airliner bearing the hijackers of the *Achille Lauro*, and later to launch an air strike against Libya in reprisal for its support of terrorism against Americans. The Defense Department also seemed prepared to take a more active role in Central America, where large-scale construction in Honduras was creating a network of bases much like those that had once made Thailand a vast rear area to support the war in Vietnam.

But the problem for the Reagan administration, and any successor that might be tempted to make war, was that in the absence of an overt threat to U.S. security interests, the use of combat troops abroad would meet stiff domestic opposition. However he might be denounced, Weinberger's statement of the conditions that needed to be met before the United States could go to war again seemed to express with great precision the real legacy of Vietnam: Having watched four administrations fritter away 58,000 lives and hundreds of billions of dollars on a losing enterprise, Americans were not prepared to see it happen again without good reason. At bottom they seemed to have settled where one might say they should have been all along—on the notion that wars which cannot be justified to the people who have to go fight them, ought not to be fought at all.

———◆———

THOMAS POLGAR

Was there a big debriefing after you got out?
Not then, not in Washington, not since. The first guy who talked to me in any detail about what happened in Vietnam was David Butler.* You are the second one. There was no Agency end of action report on Vietnam. The Agency has never written any kind of a definitive history on Vietnam or who did what, why, what did you do right, what did you do wrong, what have you heard. That's CIA.

The military was a little better. They asked people who were going to war colleges to do studies. And Congress never held any hearings. After Pearl Harbor we had five or six commissions that chewed the thing over again and again and again. But in Vietnam, nothing.

———

*A former *Newsweek* writer, and author of a 1985 book on the fall of Saigon.

There's never been any effort made to really synthesize this, not a single place where you can go to get a truly authentic version of what really happened. The American political and military consciousness has not digested the reasons for the defeat.

WILLIAM SULLIVAN

This may sound Panglossian, but a Vietnam had to happen to us sometime. This war was a very tragic event. It tore the country apart. It had consequences politically, socially, and economically from which we are still suffering. But it did draw a line under the prevailing sense of omnipotence and omniscience that the United States postwar generation had developed. When we came out of World War II we were artificially strong. We had a monopoly on nuclear weapons, the strongest conventional military forces, the most resilient economy, a vibrant political system. The rest of the world was in ruins, but it was bound to come back.

And, of course, this is the thing that is so hard to explain to the rednecks. I sometimes do lectures for the Council on Foreign Relations in places like Wichita. Why, they want to know. "Why can't it be like it was then? Goddamnit, we could snap shit and people would pay attention!" A lot of yahoos in this country never accepted that things had inevitably changed. And eventually, just by sheer force of decibels, they got us around to the point that we were prepared to behave like John Wayne and sort of knock their teeth out, knock 'em back, put 'em back in their box, blow 'em back to the Stone Age, whatever phrase you want to use. Sooner or later we were going to run into a place where we tried to do that and it didn't work.

So the Panglossian part is that just in terms of not having suffered the ruination of the country, we were damned lucky it happened in a place that didn't really matter all that much, like Indochina. Had we taken a stand in a place like Hungary, it could have blown up the world, including the United States. Fifty-eight thousand lives is too many to pay for a lesson, but it's probably smaller than we might have paid had we gone into Czechoslovakia in '68, or done something else that would have led to a direct confrontation with the Soviets or with the Chinese. So Vietnam was a tragedy but it may have been the tragic price that American hubris needed somewhere along the line to get back to reality.

Looking back on Vietnam, the supreme irony of it is that four Presidents took the United States into combat in Vietnam because they were convinced that the strategic balance in Asia was shifting against us and our friends. It wasn't just the Lao Dong* moving down into South Vietnam; it was also the Chinese operations in Thailand and Malaysia and the Philippines and above all in Indonesia. What they saw was a vise tightening across the sea-lanes connecting Japan to its energy sources, isolating Australia and New Zealand, and the whole of Southeast Asia becoming Communist.

Now, that didn't happen, but I think the point that all the commentaries that were written on the tenth anniversary missed is that while we didn't win the war, *had* we won, we would have had to keep troops in South Vietnam. And had we kept troops in South Vietnam, the North Vietnamese and the Chinese would have had to patch up their differences to some extent, and the Soviets and the Chinese would have had to give them logistic support. The whole thing would have stayed glued together even though it was palpably inconsistent. Once we pulled out, everything changed. The Chinese were able then to vent their true feelings about the Vietnamese. The Soviets moved in with the Vietnamese in a way that's concerned the hell out of the Chinese. And what you got was the Chinese making this enormous change and reaching an accommodation with the United States.

And the consequence was a cosmic shift in the geostrategic position. Although the Chinese are not our allies, they act in concert with us, in intelligence and other things. We've changed our whole outlook as a result. We no longer think in terms of fighting two and a half wars; we think in terms of one and a half wars. The *Soviets* have to think about two and a half wars. It's the Chinese who keep pounding on the Soviets and the Vietnamese in Southeast Asia, and it's the Vietnamese and Soviets who keep the Chinese in check. Had we plotted it and planned it this way as Machiavellians, it couldn't have come out better.

The fact is, we stumbled into it by what turned out to be an enormously costly, traumatic national experience for the United States— not only fifty-eight thousand people killed, but also the disruption in our own society. Now I think that disruption in some milder form would have come anyway. Vietnam was not a catalyst so much as an accelerator of changes that were inevitable in our society: the civil rights movement in the South, the women's revolution, the youth revolution, the black revolution. Because it all came at once it was somehow or other in our minds associated with Vietnam. But all those things, it seems to me, have obscured the fact that in its own unintended way, the Vietnam operation turned out to be one of the master strategic strokes of the century. Lyndon Johnson would nev-

---

*The Vietnam Workers' [Communist] Party.

er believe it in his grave but this is so. And when the historians finally get around to it, I think a lot of the pain and the trauma that went with the sixties will be put in another perspective.

It's very easy, particularly for those who philosophically oppose these changes, to attribute them all to Vietnam and to, essentially, a failure of American will. The great right-wing myth is that the military had that war won, but the damn civilians and the press and the fuzzy intellectuals snatched defeat from the jaws of victory. You know damn well we didn't have that war won and the supreme irony is, aren't we lucky we didn't, because we've now got an equilibrium in the Pacific which is probably the best that has prevailed there since the sixteenth century.

ROBERT KOMER

There is one thing on which I am very clear, and that is the loss of the strategic real estate that was Indochina had only a very modest impact on our global geostrategic position. All this domino crap is just that. Yes, if Vietnam went, Laos and Cambodia inevitably went too. But Thailand is still there, and stronger than it was in '75; Malaysia is still there, Singapore is a lot stronger, and Indonesia has adopted an increasingly Western orientation.

One can make an argument that the anchorage at Cam Ranh Bay is very useful to the Soviets. But basically if a war came we drop some mines in the mouth of the Bay and our carrier task groups launch a few strikes while they're on their way from Subic to the Indian Ocean, and it's not a problem. What really interests me is that our geostrategic position was not undermined at all by the loss of the Vietnam war. I don't want to argue about zero versus two percent, but the U.S. is still perceived as a superpower. The Soviets are still more impressed by our technological superiority than they are by the fact that we got winkled out by a regime of sixteen million hard noses up in Hanoi.

What did hurt us was the enormous cost of what started out as a quite minor, limited war. On top of the fifty-eight thousand lives we lost, when you look at the price of Vietnam in today's dollars you find that the war itself cost us on the order of a third of a trillion. You have to add to that third of a trillion the substantial cutback in defense spending as we expiated Vietnam, and in today's dollars, that's another hundred and fifty billion. You add those and you come out with about a half trillion dollars of defense resources down the drain for a war we lost. In my judgment most of that came out of procurement—all the bombers, tanks, guns, ships, and planes that we didn't buy in the '65 through '76 period. So you could argue that the Vietnam war cost us perhaps a decade of defense modernization.

Now what were the strategic consequences of that? It seems to me that in terms of the overall balance of power between us and the Soviet Union, this was an enormous cost. A half a trillion bucks is a lot of dough. And you have to add another factor, which is the loss of American nerve: the Vietnam syndrome, which is maybe in an attenuated form, but with us still. This administration is trying to do everything about Nicaragua in order not to find itself down the road in a situation where there are pressures for American troop intervention. It knows that that would *really* be unpopular. So helping the Contras in Nicaragua, military and economic aid to Duarte in San Salvador, these are really as much designed to prevent another Vietnam staring us in the face. The administration inflicts on itself a fifty-five advisor ceiling in Salvador. The Congress picks this up and says that any more than fifty-five will be a sign that we are hell-bent on the road to intervention.

THOMAS POLGAR

Why did we lose in Vietnam? I don't pretend that I know every aspect, but on paper we should have won easy. And there are a lot of reasons. There's an old saying among traveling salesmen, you got to know your territory. You cannot go into a foreign war without knowing the geography of the country, the history of the country, the psychology of the people, the language of the people, and above all with the assumption that they are going to act like you would. I think we were totally ignorant of what we were up against.

The second thing, the time-rotation principle I think is the undoing of any military effort. Nobody wants to die before his time, so when you tell the troops "You got to go to Vietnam but you only got to stay one year," you get yourself a military [man] that becomes very conscious that with every day that he has evaded combat duty he is one day closer to getting home safely. We didn't do that in World War II. In World War II, you gave the troops rest periods, but the idea was you stay until the job is done.

Thirdly, I have basic problems the way the Army today is organized and we already saw that in Vietnam. In the old days you had the Texas National Guard, you had the Fighting Irish from New York, and you had a unit pride. In Vietnam they were brought together from all over and until they met there they didn't have anything in common.

Fourthly, we had this silly business where each officer had to get his ticket punched in different kinds of jobs so you can show you are versatile and you can be promoted. Now, when you know that you are not going to be with the unit in six months, you have two desires: First, create something that will make you look good for these six months, and second, get out and never mind if your successor has to eat all the shit subsequently. "History starts when I take over and ends when I leave, and never mind what comes after." You had a lot of officers with that attitude.

Also if you're going to only be there for a very limited period of time, you have absolutely no incentive to learn the language, And that's a fifth problem. We had only one general who could speak Vietnamese, and he was not fluent. It's a difficult language but it can be learned. But that's not only the military. CIA and the State Department weren't much better either. State Department made a real effort to teach some officers Vietnamese. CIA followed the example of the military, [and] really made no effort at all.

Sixth, there is something about every army where they try to fight the last war. The U.S. Army came into Vietnam very much influenced by the war in Germany, and we developed a regular routine. First we would fly the air strike, then we would have the artillery support, and then we would send in the armor and then would come the infantry. Well, in this war by the time the infantry came, they could never find any Communist soldiers because as soon as the bombers came they knew "The infantry is going to come so let's get the hell out of here." And not only that. The North Vietnamese took trawlers out into the China Sea and the bombers would fly over them and they would pick them up on radar and say, "Ho, ho! The bombers are coming," and everybody had a couple of hours' warning.

We disregarded the enemy's ability to adjust his tactics to what we were doing. We called them slopes and gooks and totally underestimated them—and this is not a new trait, either. Let me give you some famous last words. [*Reads from a book.*] "The Hawaiian Islands are overprotected," says the former chief of U.S. Naval Intelligence in 1941—in 1941! "The entire Japanese fleet and Air Force could not seriously threaten Hawaii." Famous last words. Here's Josephus Daniels, former U.S. Secretary of the Navy. He says, "Nobody fears that the Japanese fleet could deal an unexpected blow on our Pacific possessions. Radio makes surprise impossible." Major George Fielding Eliot—he was considered for a long time the best North American military authority: "A Japanese attack on Pearl

Harbor is a strategic impossibility." Secretary of Navy, Frank Knox: "No matter what happens, the U.S. Navy is not going to be caught napping."

———◆———

WALT ROSTOW

I did not envisage 1975 as inevitable and I don't think historians will treat the ending in '75 as inevitable. I think they will say what the London *Economist* said, that we snatched defeat from the jaws of victory. The South Vietnamese defeated the North Vietnamese in 1972 with the help of U.S. air and naval power. And I think there's a fair chance that they would have continued to be all right if they'd had the aid that was promised to them. If we hadn't walked away, South Vietnam might very well have been another South Korea.

But 1975 was a very different time than 1965. We and the Southeast Asians used those ten years so well that there wasn't the panic [as Vietnam went down] that there would have been if we had failed to intervene. Since 1975 there has been a general expansion of trade by the other countries of that region with Japan and the West. In Thailand we have seen the rise of a new class of entrepreneurs. Malaysia and Singapore have become countries of diverse manufactured exports. We can see the emergence of a much thicker layer of technocrats in Indonesia. I don't have the figures in front of me, but if you check, you will see that the rise in the proportion of the twenty- to twenty-four-year-old age group who have higher educations is staggering.

There is no question that they are still politically fragile. You know, all God's chillun got problems. But the rise in living standards and the creation of broad middle classes throughout the region should help to keep them stable. All through the area now, they are of pretty good heart. The one exception to this is the Philippines. The dynamism of Asia is now a tremendous reality, to which is added the coming dynamism in China.

The one thing that could destabilize Southeast Asia again is renewed military pressure from Vietnam and its Soviet allies. The presence of the Soviet fleet in Cam Ranh Bay and Danang has clearly shifted the military balance in the area. The number of days the Soviet fleet can stay at sea in the area is seventy-five percent higher from Vietnam than it was when they were operating exclusively out of Vladivostok. And they are directly across the South China Sea from our bases in the Philippines.

Would we be better off cutting a deal with the Vietnamese to get them to scale down the Soviet presence?

You've got to get the map out to see what a Vietnamese-occupied Cambodia looks like to the Thais. It would be a terrible blow to the ASEAN countries* if we made a deal that left the Vietnamese Army on the Thai border. So we first have to get Hanoi to give up its occupation of Cambodia. You know, the Vietnamese remind me a little bit of a story that LBJ used to tell. It went something like this: The Widow Brown had been the wife of a farmer down in Texas, and after he died people thought she would sell out. But instead of that, she turned out to be a very effective farmer herself and made very handsome profits. And whenever a piece of land next to hers would become available, she'd buy it up, and gradually her farm got bigger and bigger, until people started to worry that she was going to own all the land in the neighborhood. Well, finally, they sent a delegation to call on her and ask what her intentions were. And what she said was, "I don't want to own *all* the land. I just want the land that's next to *mine*." Well, that's the Vietnamese. They don't want *all* the countries of Indochina. They just want the ones that are next to *them*. Hell, let them go home and grow some food and send their kids to school like everybody else. Until they do that, nothing will be settled and we can't let down our guard in Southeast Asia.

———

A member of the post-Vietnam, post-Watergate "Class of '74" elected to the House in a Democratic landslide, STEPHEN SOLARZ of Brooklyn has made himself a considerable influence on American foreign policy in the space of a decade. As chairman of the House Foreign Affairs subcommittee on East Asia and the Pacific he was the author of legislation to provide U.S. aid to the Cambodian resistance, and a supporter of American help for the Afghan guerrillas fighting Soviet occupation. But he also bitterly opposed aid to the Contras, and played a key role in uncovering the financial scandals that helped bring down Ferdinand Marcos in the Philippines. Solarz was reelected to a seventh term in 1986.

I don't think we are crippled by the Vietnam experience. We are much more likely to be prudently cautious about the commitment of American troops to combat abroad, but I don't think we're incapable of doing so when our national security is involved. It is important to distinguish between small-scale involvements for which the reasons may not be entirely clear, and the will of the United States to honor its treaty commitments to its allies in Europe and Asia if they become the victims of aggression. There is no doubt in my mind whatsoever that if NATO, Japan, Korea, Australia, or any of our other allies were attacked that we would respond with whatever means were necessary to repel the aggression.

To the extent that Vietnam has had any impact at all on the will of the American people, it relates to the will to use force in the Third World. And there the Vietnam experience was I think salutary in the sense that it made us much more cautious and careful in situations where vital U.S. interests were not involved. But even in the Third World, where there are real threats to the vital interests of the United States, we are capable of dispatching troops to protect those interests. It's only that as a result of Vietnam, we are much less likely to use force gratuitously.

People argue that because our hands were tied by the Vietnam syndrome in the 1970's, a number of small countries such as Ethiopia and Angola fell into the Soviet orbit, and the Soviets felt free to invade Afghanistan.

That phenomenon had significant implications for our relations with the Soviet Union, because it contributed to a feeling on the part of the American people that detente was a one-way street and that the Soviet Union was on the march around the world. But I think that is a misreading of those experiences. In Ethiopia there was a revolution that was neither stimulated nor organized by the Soviet Union, but was due to the inadequacies of the ancien régime. In Angola there was a civil war among various factions that were contesting for power. These were unique situations in which the Soviets benefited from indigenous circumstances which they exploited but did not create.

And in the meantime, there were a number of other strategic shifts that were far less favorable to them. One was the movement by Egypt out of the Soviet orbit. A second was the successful transition to democracy on the Iberian peninsula, and the defeat of Communist efforts to seize control after the fall of Franco in Spain and Salazar in Portugal. A third was the emergence of ASEAN as a dynamic, coherent group of non-Communist nations in Southeast Asia, forming a significant counterweight to the Vietnamese. A fourth was the withdrawal of Somalia from the Soviet sphere of influence because of Ethiopia—although I acknowledge that in the trade the Russians got the better of the deal. And fifth, the normalization of our relations with China, has been a factor immeasurably helpful to the West.

Now, in Afghanistan we had a real interest in helping the freedom fighters in the resistance movement. The only hope for a political settlement there is if the resistance exacts a sufficiently high price from the Soviet Army for the occupation, so that they become willing to consider reaching an agreement for withdrawal. And even if there is not a settlement, we have an interest in making the Soviets pay as high a price as possible, to dissuade them from trying to gobble up pieces of Pakistan and Iran.

That is the same reason I proposed that we should give five million dollars to the non-Communist Cambodian resistance. The intention in a nutshell is to enhance the prospects of persuading the Vietnamese to withdraw, while keeping the Khmer Rouge out of power if they do withdraw. We want to induce the Vietnamese to leave, and it is clear they will not leave of their own will. There is no resistance in Laos, but they still have fifty thousand troops there.

CASPAR WEINBERGER

There's still a very strong feeling against any kind of United States involvement in actions that require military force. That's one of the legacies. To my mind the principal lesson learned is that we should never go into combat if it isn't important enough to our national interest. It should be a major national requirement that we achieve certain objectives or stave off certain happenings, such as an active attack, by the use of military force. But then when you do that you have to apply military force in sufficient numbers and with sufficient skill and determination and resolve to win.

I think in both Vietnam and Korea we committed military forces without an intention to win, and indeed with a feeling that we could achieve some of our objectives simply by having some men there who would participate in limited kinds of activity, but in the case of Korea *told* not to win, and in the case of Vietnam clearly without the intention of applying the degree of force necessary to win. That's a very terrible thing to do to military people—to ask them to go into extreme danger, but in effect to have a decision made that it's not important enough for us to win.

A corollary to that is that there's got to be some reasonable assurance that there *is* the necessary degree of sustained public support to enable you to commit forces and maintain them with this national resolve to win. We had it in World War II without the slightest question. It was clearly absolutely essential to our national survival, and we went to war with a total national commitment to win. And in Grenada on a tiny scale compared to that, we had exactly the same thing. And that's vital. That's what was missing in Korea and Vietnam.

We went to Grenada and it was essential to do it. You had a thousand American students there. We had the shadow of a Teheran, four hundred-day detention of our people happening again. We were begged by the neighboring countries to go in. There was total anarchy and a twenty-four-hour curfew on anybody seen walking around. We had no alternative, and every requirement that we go in, and we did. But we went in with sufficient force to win, and we did what we could in the limited time available to let the people know why we had to do it. And we stayed in long enough to win and we won, and now as the final remnants are being taken out we're meeting a very strong local resistance, not "Yanks, Go Home," but "Yanks, Please Stay." And that's a novelty.

But this is not a doctrine or a set of rules or anything that would prevent us using force. It's to prevent it being used lightly or ill-advisedly or in situations where it isn't necessary. The military should be committed to combat only as a last resort. We have economic, we have political, we have diplomatic pressures and powers, and these should all be used first. I don't understand that there's a great deal of disagreement with that. There are some people who disagree with everything you say, and they immediately said, because we talked about reasonable assurance of public support, that I thought we had to take a Gallup poll or have some sort of a referendum before we went to war. That is not true. That is not my definition of reasonable assurances of support. If you have a thousand Americans who may be killed if they're seen walking around the street, who may be taken prisoner and kept for over a year, I think that then your attempts to deal with this have reasonable assurances of public support.

Things might not have been so simple if the Cubans and the Grenadians had been better armed.

Well then you have a different set of rules. Instead of putting in pieces of a couple divisions we would have put in pieces of four or five. That's what I mean by sufficient force to win and win quickly. One of the problems in Grenada was that with less than forty-eight hours' notice, we didn't know how many [enemy] were there really. And my contribution to that, so to speak, was to double the number of troops that [we] put in. If we had known for example that there were ten thousand troops there and we had a thousand American citizens to rescue we probably would have done a few things differently. We would certainly have had different tactics, and we would certainly have had a very large number of additional troops. You've got to size the force to do the job.

That was the problem in Lebanon. We had a battalion, reinforced, to do a very specific job, which was to be part of an international force intervening between withdrawing forces that had been locked in combat, Syrian and Israeli. They didn't withdraw, and this force then was not able to interpose itself and give them confidence that they could withdraw. So the idea of trying to have a force sized and sent there for a specific purpose do something very different, is an example of something that wouldn't work.

Vietnam was a very traumatic experience for the nation. We went in in an incremental way. We were told that it wasn't a war, that we didn't have to curtail domestic spending, that we could continue to do all the things that we wanted to do, that we would be finished with it in two weeks and four weeks and a month and six months; that we only needed ten thousand more troops, we only needed five thousand more troops, we only needed fifteen thousand more troops until we got up over a half a million and more, and there were heavy losses. And that did cause a lot of anger and unhappiness and vows of never again.

———◆———

RICHARD ARMITAGE

How did the Vietnam experience shape the way we maneuvered to get rid of Marcos in the Philippines?

Several things went into our calculations. One was Ngo Dinh Diem. A Diem-type outcome—an assassination—in the case of President Marcos would have been unacceptable. Second, we saw the need to have a viable alternative. When Diem was assassinated, the alternative to his government wasn't very well formed in the mind of Henry Cabot Lodge or anybody else. Not that Americans in the Philippines shaped the alternative but we understood that there had to be [one]. That's one of the reasons that the Administration resisted, earlier on, congressional pressures to walk away from Marcos. To do so would have been very easy and very popular with our Congress but it would have left no formed alternative to the Marcos government.

Another thing was the necessity of having a military that was worthy of continued support. In Vietnam, when we left and security assistance was turned off, the will to fight was also turned off. You'd have enough bullets for tomorrow and the day after and the next day, but there was no long-term supply. You find in Cuba, you find in Somoza's Nicaragua, that what brings people down is the lack of support. It's a psychological downfall much sooner than a military downfall—the feeling "Who is going to support us in the struggle?" Batista's memoirs talk about the single blow that brought him down was not the fact that he didn't have more troops and more bullets than Castro. His soldiers lost the will because there was no security assistance. So in the Philippines we wanted to maintain, tried to maintain, some security assistance, at the same time pushing the armed forces as much as possible towards reform.

We realized that if a year and a half ago we had had happen what happened [in 1986], the Army would have turned on itself. But as reforms developed we got to a situation where the Army did not fall upon itself. They had to the largest extent, made up their own minds that the best thing for the country was reform and that was what avoided bloodshed.

Another thing that comes to mind is we didn't do to Marcos what we did to Diem—we didn't pull the rug out. Marcos had a choice. He could reform or he'd have to go eventually. We kept steadily turning up the heat. But had he made those reforms in the political and social and economic and the military, he'd be there today. He didn't, but he had the choice.

Lastly, we wanted to avoid absolutely the introduction of any U.S. forces. We don't want to go ever where our people aren't welcome— where there's not large popular support both here and there for it. And so consequently we had in the back of our minds that the most important thing was to try to keep ever from the introduction of U.S. forces. And all of those things come out of the Vietnam experience.

Would we have been as successful in the Philippines if it was not an English speaking country that had a long and very intimate relationship with us?

Well, we wouldn't have had the influence we had. We wouldn't have had the strategic relationship that we had, so, I think probably I would say no. But I don't know, I can't think of any situation that would ever be like the Philippines. It's very unique. It is sui generis. You can't apply just the lessons of the Philippines to other parts of the world. Some people think, "Oh, We ought to do just what we did in the Philippines with Korea." The same. The differences are enormous.

First of all there's a live, real, and serious military threat to the survival of the Republic of Korea. Number two, you do not have a long association with democracy in Korea. You had at the turn of the century, a feudal kingdom, brutal by anyone's standards, followed by occupation for forty-odd years by the Japanese. The liberation in 1945 was followed immediately by a civil war which rent the country. And you've had an experiment with a very limited democracy for forty years. It does not have the association our colonial heritage with the Philippines gave us, with a long, close tie to a democratic country. And it's Confucian. There are also enormous economic differences. It's a poorer country in terms of natural resources, but it's richer because they've [channeled] their very energetic populace into durable high-tech goods. And there is a major political difference. People look at Korea and talk about repression, but when was the last political murder in Korea? You do not have that. So the violence that was associated with politics in the Philippines is absent from politics in Korea.

RICHARD HOLBROOKE

Has Vietnam really changed American foreign policy?

Profoundly. We live with recent historical myths. When I grew up the central myths were Munich and Pearl Harbor. Munich, because we wouldn't have appeasement, and Pearl Harbor, because we wouldn't be caught by surprise. Today the enduring myths are Vietnam and Iran—and we can add the Philippines because that could be the right sort of myth, that American influence can be used to improve the lot of people and restore democracy. It remains to be seen, but I'm hopeful.

Is every crisis Vietnam all over again? Of course not. Is there a Vietnam angle to most of our crises? To the extent that any policy involves the possible use of American forces, Vietnam always comes up. Every one of the present adminstration's flirtations with force in places like Libya and Nicaragua is an attempt to push back the limits that Vietnam has created in their minds on the American public's willingness to tolerate involvement overseas.

It's certainly good that policymakers think twice before putting American lives at risk. But it would be a great tragedy if the only lesson of Vietnam was that the American public will not support foreign activities. I don't think that is the lesson. I think one of the lessons is that the public will support anything which is successful very quickly, like Grenada. But whether they will support something protracted when they don't believe our vital interests are at stake remains to be seen. It's interesting that in the Reagan administration, the man most gun-shy of Third World interventions is also the very man who is most belligerent in relation to the Soviet Union—Mr. Weinberger. Weinberger's view has a certain logic to it: It is in the direct confrontation of the Soviets that we have to be toughest and we weaken ourselves by mucking around in these gray areas. It's also true that all of our involvements since World War II have come in these Third World areas. But it's the State Department that wants to risk lives for limited diplomatic objectives. It's Weinberger who doesn't, because he and his uniformed services are carrying very deep scars,

Isn't Weinberger's argument that to get involved you need a political support base that won't go away, and enough force to get the job done quickly?

Those two points come precisely out of his understanding of Vietnam. He wouldn't have thought of those two things twenty or thirty years ago. Now they carry great weight and he raises them to argue for limits on involvement. The one area we haven't mentioned is Lebanon. In Beirut, our most conservative, hard-line President made an instantaneous decision to pull out in the face of a deepening involvement. And because of his political skill he got away with it without any political consequences. Was he right?

He was not right to send the Marines in; he certainly was right to pull them out, and it showed an extraordinary ability to make quick tactical turns. Everyone knows that whatever the horrible price, three hundred Americans dead, it would have only been the beginning had we stayed. The number could only go up, the chance of achieving the objective could only recede. And having recognized the profound error, he found a way to get out and survive politically. Nixon could not do that in 1969.

I cannot tell you how strongly I feel about this subject. We're going to be having the same discussion fourteen years from now in the year 2000, when we'll be celebrating the twenty-fifth anniversary of the fall of Saigon, instead of the tenth. We'll be doing it the rest of our lives. This goddamn war was the American Civil War of the twentieth century fought twelve thousand miles away in the worst terrain. Some things just don't go away and it will take us a long time and perhaps even some other transcending national event, comparable to World War II or the Depression, to get us beyond it. The once optimistic hope that we would learn what the lessons are, absorb them and never make the same mistakes, is impossible. Every argument of 1963 and 1975 will still be fought out in the year 2000. The sides may shift, but we'll get into the same argument.

But the aspect of Vietnam which concerns me most today is not finding a final historical answer. What I want to see is an end to the poisonous political division which Vietnam put in our society. Normal dialogue has been heightened to venomous levels where the right accuses other people of being unpatriotic and treasonous simply because they argue certain positions. That is grossly unfair, particularly when it is the right, the pro-Vietnam hawks, who actually weakened the country.

I'd like to do whatever I can to make people understand why Vietnam really didn't work and the most important thing for people to know is that we *couldn't* win. And the second most important thing is that that is not an anti-American or defeatist statement. That is a statement of somebody who believes that American power should be used in ways that do not diminish it.

JAMES SCHLESINGER

This was a time when the American people felt failure—perhaps the first time. This is a country that believes "Conquer we must when our cause it is just." It's a country that has a tendency to believe that if it's losing, it's because we've done something wrong. We're immoral. We had a lot of those problems back then. Now we're in a recovery, but you must understand it's a partial recovery, because it goes in two directions. The public instinct is that we'd better not get into that kind of situation again. But the public also wants a restoration of faith in the country's invulnerability. And these two forces are playing one against the other in our society today. "By God, once again America is supreme and second to none; on the other hand, let's not get involved." You could see that in Lebanon and you could see it in the joyous reaction at Grenada. That was taken to be confirmation of that thesis that the United States is triumphant.

Very few people, I think, understand this. The Administration really would like to believe that the era of apparent American omnipotence has been restored. It hasn't been, but it would like to believe that. And at the same time they know that if they do anything that will seriously involve the United States, public support is going to disappear very quickly.

I think that's an important point that Cap Weinberger is making. Where Weinberger is wrong is that nobody can guarantee in advance that you're going to have a continuing consensus in support of a war. The military establishment is paid, at considerable cost, to go off and fight when the president thinks it's necessary. No one can guarantee that they're going to be beyond criticism. No military establishment has been in history. It's that part of it that is wrong. Cap seems to want an advance guarantee that it's going to be a popular winnable war, that the consensus is going to remain in support of the forces. That is in practice a formula for saying that we're never going in anyplace. And you can't tell your possible opponents what you're not going to do. And in that respect Shultz is quite right.

When we went into Vietnam, we *had* a national consensus. We had agreement. It's just that it fell away. There is no stability in these matters. And when Cap demands a guarantee, he is renouncing the use of the military instrument unless in effect American forces are directly attacked. In this connection he is by and large representing the military, but he is overstating something that is down there in their viscera. No military person would I think put it quite as baldly as Cap has. And the fact of the matter is that the American public is not paying out three hundred billion dollars a year for a military establishment so that its commanders can tell you all of the places that they don't want to fight.

So there are two clear lessons that may collapse into one lesson. The first is that the United States has neither the prestige nor the power to sweep all before it. We had that for only a brief period after World war II. And therefore we must be very careful in thinking through where and why we are prepared to use force. We should not respond simply with an injured reaction to an emotional appeal. It has to be carefully thought out in advance where we will deploy our forces and whether or not the objective is worth the cost involved. And secondly, if we do decide to go in, then the United States must use its resources with great tactical and strategic skill, understanding the nature of the conflict, the terrain and the peoples of the region, and not seeking to impose our own preconceptions upon the contest. In other words to use our military resources, once they're engaged, with economy and skill. These two lessons may simply collapse into one, which is that if we indeed are to use our power, we should not be prodigal with it.

———◆———

ALEXANDER HAIG

We failed in Vietnam in two ways. First, by departing from classic geopolitical considerations in the conduct of conflict, and second, by our failure to analyze carefully the emerging differences between China and the Soviet Union. The first had been underway for some time, and it continues to plague us. There was a distortion which crept into American strategic thinking early in the Kennedy years, because of the spectrum of threats we faced. We were overwhelming in the nuclear area. In conventional forces, we had work to do but the job was going along well. Insurgency, however, was a gray area. And the belief was that through the so-called hearts and minds struggle we could contain insurgency at its cutting edge. But that was a specious distortion of our national power. It put us in the position of having to win in an area where the ability of the other side to pile in assets was open-ended, and where the democratic character of our side made it impossible for us to fight forever.

So we should have taken the steps that General Johnson recommended. We should have understood that when American blood was going to be shed, we had to be prepared for the consequences that would follow. In a nuclear age you cannot be trigger-happy, but if you are unwilling to take those risks, it is best to stay out of conflict entirely. But in 1965 we had in effect overreacted to the experience of Korea, and that deprived us of the judgments that should have been made about the conflict between Moscow and Peking. That was so even much later. After my first meeting with Chou En-lai in Beijing [in 1971], which lasted two and a half hours, it was very clear to me that they did not want us either to lose or to withdraw [from Vietnam]. When I conveyed that on my return to Washington, however, I was accused of taking leave of my senses.

Now, we Americans are constantly lurching from one set of extreme perceptions to another. The paralyzing consequences of Vietnam, which dominated our perceptions in the seventies, we've shed now and we're on the path to a more balanced view of the world. Lebanon, it's true, was built on some of the same perceptions. But there were different considerations that caused the failure there. My view is that the introduction of our Marines into West Beirut was only in the context of a multilateral policy mechanism to insure that an agreement was abided by. But it would only be abided by if we had permitted Israel to continue with the highly successful military operations it was carrying out at the time. In short, the Syrians were beaten up already, and all we had to do was send them a message by letting the Israelis continue on. Instead, we sent them the reverse message. We told them through the Saudis that we would not permit that. So the heart of the misjudgment was the conditions under which our forces were put in there in the first place. Once that had been done, the conclusion was foreordained.

Weinberger's six points all clearly go back and draw on the Vietnam experience. They are a centerpiece of how we deal, for example, with Central America. Why Central America has importance for us is not that it's a social and economic struggle, but that it's an external intervention which is dangerous to our vital interests. But there are also a number of imponderables. One is the real intention of the Soviet Union at a time when that country itself is in deep trouble. Another is how Fidel Castro reads the risks that the Soviet Union will take or will be able to take physically in supporting him.

What we shouldn't do is take the course of incrementalism we took in Vietnam.

BRENT SCOWCROFT

I think there is a very definite legacy from Vietnam. It really changed what had been an attitude of confident realism that we had now learned to use measured force in pursuit of our national objectives, and that we could deal in a sophisticated way with the problems of the world. Our first reaction after Vietnam was to withdraw and in a sense be the way we had been for the first hundred and fifty years of our existence. There was a difference, though. We used to withdraw because we thought we were too good for the world; After Vietnam we said "No, we're not good enough. We've failed. We supported a corrupt regime."

We've come partly out of that, but the overhang still invests discussions about issues that have very little relevance to Vietnam. When we talk about Nicaragua or Salvador we often say "No more Vietnams." Carter in the first part of his term wrapped us in national guilt. But there were two distinct phases to his presidency. Carter in his last year, with Afghanistan, and since then Reagan in various ways have exorcised it to some extent. And so we're kind of halfway in and halfway out now. I think in the abstract we're much more prepared to use force than we were in '77 or '78, but in practical terms probably we're not.

Let's just suppose for example that the President comes to the conclusion that the only way to settle the Central American situation is to go into Nicaragua. He might be able to go in but I don't think he could complete the job. My assessment is that anything we can do in three days or five days, before the opposition mobilized, we can do. But if he launched an engagement that would take as long as Nicaragua would take, I think he would absolutely be cut off at the knees. A Grenada we can do. Nicaragua would be a far different case.

And I think that is unhealthy. To me one of the most telling examples of the inhibitions we still have [is] Cap Weinberger's six conditions for intervention. Absolutely appalling. It would take us back to the worst days of pre-World War II, where the only time you get in a war is if it's a national crusade. What Cap was saying was that you have to have a Hitler before you can use force. And that almost guarantees that by the time you do get into a conflict, it's a big one. Under his conditions you can't ever act in the incipient phase where there is some chance that with the modest use of the military you can turn the situation around. That is very debilitating to us.

Now, to a large extent, what Weinberger said reflects the thinking of the Joint Chiefs. I have heard the military talk in terms of these six points many many times. And in a sense, it is more understandable coming from the Chiefs than it is from the civilians. After all, the Chiefs are naturally reluctant to apply force when they may become the scapegoats. Their attitude is "Sure, the President launches us into some foreign adventure, but *we're* the ones to catch it when it doesn't work out." It is not fundamentally the role of the military to integrate diplomacy with the use of force. So in a sense you could say that the military have become the doves of our time, yes.

THOMAS POLGAR

If you today turn to Central America and to Nicaragua, do you know what our objective is? I don't. You do not want the spread of Communism but what is it that you *do* want to accomplish? Central America is very different from Vietnam in many respects, but there are enough similarities to make you think that, too, can be a quagmire. You know, every time the President speaks on Nicaragua, he has different objectives. To my way of thinking what we should have done in Vietnam is first have a concept of policy—what is it that we want? And once we have a policy then you've got to figure what is it going to take to implement that policy. And the third question is, are you prepared to pay that price? Is it worth it?

But you take Nicaragua. First, when the Contras came into being, the Administration said "We want to stop the infiltration of arms into El Salvador." Now it's conveniently overlooked, of course, that Nicaragua doesn't have a common frontier with Salvador. Honduras is in between. So if you want to bring pressure, you bring pressure in Honduras, where the stuff goes through. Then they start talking about hurting the Sandinistas. Then we end up by mining, in violation of international law, the harbors. Then we are called to account for that and we say we don't recognize the jurisdiction of the international court. Only a couple of years ago we were raving mad because the Iranians wouldn't recognize the international court when we complained about them. Now the President says we've got to have fourteen million dollars for the Contras. Well, we already spent maybe a hundred million. And if a hundred million didn't work, how can you believe that fourteen more will work? But once that is spent he will say "Now we need fifty more," and it goes on and on because we don't have a policy.*

If the President really feels that Nicaragua represents an unlivable threat to the United States, then he should go to Congress and say "I want to declare war, and we need an Army, which we haven't got now, so let's call up the Reserves or institute a draft." Of course, nobody is going to have anything to do with that because nobody can believe in his right mind that Nicaragua is a threat. Its about as fool an excuse for a country as there is. I've been there several times. It's nothing.

Now, if I may generalize, Americans generally do not have a sufficient concept of history and geography. [From the earliest days] virtually all our problems could be resolved through technology and therefore this is a very technologically oriented nation, and because of that, many Americans, including American politicians, have a problem understanding other societies which hold different values, and that your power with engineering resources may not necessarily resolve the question. When you read what was written in the 1930's about the Japanese—those little brown bandy-legged fellows will never be able to attack us and if they do we'll finish them off in three weeks—that racist attitude sort of leads you to the underestimation of the North Vietnamese and I think to the current underestimation of the Nicaraguans. When the President of the United States says "When they cry uncle we are going to let up on the pressure," he wouldn't talk that way about the Russians, because the Russians are also big and white.

Reagan's speeches give the Nicaraguans a wonderful excuse to go to Russian and say "Fellows, we need a hundred million dollars worth of antiaircraft missiles because this son-of-a-bitch is going to attack us. And the Russians have already got missiles up to the ceiling; they are going to give them. If America wants to have another little Vietnam in Nicaragua, the Russians would want to see that. Even if in the process, Nicaragua gets lost, hell, that's no skin off their ass.

---

*In the eighteen months after this conversation was conducted, the Reagan administration came back to Congress twice for more money to support the Contras—first for twenty-four million dollars, and again for one hundred million. Administration officials also let it be known that they planned to make an even larger request for funds in 1987, but the 1986 election results, which handed control of Congress to the Democrats, cast doubt on whether larger funds would be approved. Few military or political analysts in Washington believed that the Contras could mount an effective challenge to the Marxist government in Managua, which had one hundred thousand men under arms, Cuban advisers and pilots, and was receiving huge amounts of miltary supplies from the Soviet Union.

JOHN D. NEGROPONTE *was involved in Vietnam from 1964 to 1973,*
as a political officer in the countryside, as a liaison officer at the
Paris Peace Talks, and on the National Security Council. During
the Reagan years, as the U.S. Ambassador to Honduras, he watched
over the buildup of a sizable U.S. military presence and the cre-
ation of the Contra army that sought to overthrow the Sandinista
regime in neighboring Nicaragua. He was called home from Cen-
tral American in 1985 to become Assistant Secretary of State for
Oceans and Environment.

Does the Vietnam experience apply to Central America?
It would be a mistake to believe that an experience in one part of
the world is automatically applicable to another. The largest difference is the geographic proximity of Central America to the U.S.
Vietnam was literally halfway around the globe. Because of [that],
I think there is less debate on the proposition that what happens in
Central America really does impinge directly on U.S. interests. We
are linked to Central America through economic, ethnic, and social
ties that are impossible to evade.

The principal similarity between the two situations is that there was
an East-West dimension as well as a local dimension to both of them.
And the issue for the U.S. is how to deal with the East-West dimension. What this Administration and previous ones have sought most
to avoid in Central America has been direct U.S. military involvement. So while there is a recognition of the importance of prevent-
ing a Communist expansion into the area, there is also a great deal
of sensitivity to the way it is done.

The important point to make is that the Salvador guerrilla war has
lasted for more than five years now, and U.S. forces have not gotten directly involved. The progress that has been made in bringing
the situation under control would seem to me to demonstrate that
with economic and military assistance the local government is capable of dealing with the situation.

A Vietnam-style U.S. military intervention is an eventuality that
we are working very hard to avoid. If the necessary resources are
approved by the Congress for our policies in Central America, then
I don't see any reason why we should have to contemplate that
option. In both Vietnam and El Salvador we sought to encourage
them to democratize their governments and encouraged elections.
I wouldn't call what we did in either instance "propping up." We
provided both with economic and military assistance to survive and
be viable as a state.

Vietnam shaped our attitudes toward the way and the extent to which we seek to involve ourselves in those situations. It demonstrated that even for a country so wealthy and powerful as the U.S., there were costs beyond which it would be extremely difficult for us to go. I think it has had a moderating effect on our behavior, if you will, a tempering effect. I think the aphorism "No more Cubas, no more Vietnams" is very apt. We don't want any more Cubas, but we don't want any more Vietnams either.

————— • —————

CLARK CLIFFORD

Now, what lesson have we learned? An enormously important lesson: We must be absolutely certain, before we send troops to engage in armed conflict, that our national security is at stake. I think it would be very wrong to send armed forces down to Nicaragua. I don't think our national security is involved, though I think that we ought to watch with care to be sure that it doesn't upset ultimately the balance in that part of the world. I have grave doubts about the action of sending our troops into Grenada. It was something that the American people applauded. There's a macho element in our people. I suffered terribly though, that it took three days for seven thousand American troops to defeat six or seven hundred Cubans.*

Vietnam made us much more cautious as a people. They say Vietnam is the first war we ever lost, and I always get up on my hind legs on that, because I don't believe we lost the war. I believe we concluded that the situation wasn't what we originally thought and so we pulled out. But the American people, going back to the Spanish-American war, have thought they would always be the winner. Military actions from time to time seemed to be almost a way of life for the nation. And then came Vietnam. Most Americans today feel that Vietnam was a mistake. Millions of young people at the time thought it was a mistake. They had candlelight parades around the White House which you could watch from this window. Our confidence in our leaders was shaken considerably, and so the American people will demand a much clearer and more convincing presentation of the need for military action than they have before. And from that standpoint I think that the experience was a very valuable one.

————— • —————

---

*Clifford is referring to the clumsiness of the operation, which has been heavily criticized. In effect, he is saying that with such overpowering force, the U.S. should have won the battle in a day.

GEORGE BALL

I'm not always sure when I hear what comes out of the White House these days whether we learned any lessons or not. But I think that Congress, which reflects the mood of the people, demonstrated a commendable caution in, for example, Lebanon. And I think also it's serving as a kind of restraint in relations with Nicaragua. These things are useful. I think that for an Administration to engage in a war without the support of the country is very great foolishness. It ought to look far enough down the road to recognize that even though it may have support at the moment, war is going to involve such an expenditure of effort that it's going to lose that support if it doesn't achieve its objectives quickly. And in most cases when we're dealing with Third World countries, that's almost impossible.

If the Vietnam War had not occurred, on the whole the attitude of the country would be far healthier. Among other things in Vietnam, it seemed to me we sacrificed a number of our principles and we've been paying for it in a general degradation of the American spirit. I'm talking about our belief in a world of law. It seems to me we've abandoned that under Reagan. We mine harbors in neighboring countries. We conduct a Brezhnev doctrine in the Caribbean and Central America. We turn our back on the World Court. We attack the United Nations because it doesn't always do our will. All of these things represent an abandonment of American principle, which I think is extremely serious.

I don't say that Vietnam was the sole cause, but that, compounded by our special relationship with Israel, has led us to defend a great many actions which have been fundamentally contrary to our principles. The invasion of Cambodia and the use of Agent Orange for defoliation were offenses against the kinds of principles which I thought the country had always stood for. So are the denial of self-determination, the willingness to accept the idea that a nation can hold property seized by force, the violation of various Geneva conventions. Vietnam started us down the road of an easy acceptance of the abandonment of principles.

Vietnam was a lesson that had to be learned at some point. Unhappily, we learned it in the worst possible way: the dragged-on commitment; the eventual effect it had in causing the country to lose confidence in its leaders and the integrity of its government; the disruptive effect that it had on a whole generation. All of these things, I think were a very high price to pay for a lesson that we should have learned without it.

Armed with an MIT doctorate in economics, LES ASPIN went to work as one of Robert McNamara's Pentagon whiz kids in the mid-sixties. The experience taught him the difficulty of reform from within. He ran for Congress as a liberal Democrat from Wisconsin in 1970, was elected, and joined the Armed Services Committee. Using his insider's knowledge of the Defense Department, he made himself a gadfly with an unusually brutal sting. Liberals who wanted to rein in the Reagan defense buildup jumped him ahead of several senior Democrats in 1985 to become committee chairman. Aspin put reform of the military's top echelon, through reform of the Joint Staff and centralizing power in the Chairman of the Joint Chiefs, at the head of his priority list—and together with other members of his committee and Senators Barry Goldwater and Sam Nunn, managed to write it into law in 1986.

The one thing the country is most divided and in agony about is the use of force in gray areas, where there is no direct threat, but there is some kind of national security interest. We have no consensus on sending troops into that kind of action; before Vietnam we had a rather casual attitude about it. I don't think we should go back to that, but it would be nice if we could come down somewhere between where we were in the fifties and where we are today. In the fifties we felt the United States could do anything, and that is how we stumbled into Vietnam.

There are really two questions here: Are we domestically in a position to use force whenever we choose, and is it wise to use force in small conflicts? The answer to the first question is clearly no. It may now be more difficult to use force than is good for the country. Sometimes I wish we did not have all these specters and ghosts hanging over our heads, but that may be changing too. After all, who would have suggested beforehand that we would go into Grenada, and yet you can say there were some positive fallouts from that. And in Lebanon, it was very unlikely that the Administration as well as Congress would've wanted to go along with a major commitment. It sounded like a quagmire to everybody.

Secondly, when to use force is a very tough thing to know. There are a lot of these situations where the right-wingers would like to get us involved on the theory that the red blots are spreading across the map. But the Soviets move into a lot of places where they can't sustain themselves. They make themselves unpopular and then get thrown out again as happened in Egypt and Somalia. This is a very hard thing to analyze in the abstract, but one other thing in the background is that our forces are not configured well for small-scale operations. They're too muscle-bound. We are beginning to do some of the right things about that now, but it will be a while before we know whether they work.

In the meantime, I think the Soviet Union is nowhere near as aggressive in the eighties as they were in the late seventies. That has more to do with their domestic economic troubles than any change in their philosophy, but they have also found that their military adventures and their alliances in places like Afghanistan, Angola, Nicaragua, Vietnam, and Cuba are a big drain on their resources with a very uncertain payback. Clearly any government that invites them in can also invite them out.

———————◆———————

DANTE FASCELL, *a Florida Democrat, had recently inherited the chairmanship of the House Foreign Affairs committee after the death of Clement Zablocki, when he gave this interview in 1985. Along with Republican Jacob Javits in the Senate, he was a major player in passing the War Powers Resolution over Richard Nixon's veto in the spring of 1974.*

The biggest legacy of Vietnam is the change in the attitude of Congress with respect to military interventions and the conduct of foreign policy generally. The record is clear that in the period between the Gulf of Tonkin Resolution and the two pieces of legislation passed toward the end of the war—the Cambodian bombing halt and the War Powers Act—there came to be a greater determination by Congress to try to stay abreast of foreign policy decisions, and *not* to leave the field to executive decision-making alone.

When the Tonkin Gulf resolution came up, I think it was clear to people in Congress that the President was trying to buttress the basis for his actions in Vietnam, not just to get approval for the one incident. It was very, very broad language. Anybody who took time to read it had to understand that the President was seeking permission to take very broad actions.

When we started considering the War Powers Resolution, I was concerned with the need to institutionalize a system where Congress could have some say in the gray areas between instances that have been historically accepted such as the President taking action to save American lives, or a case where we had a full declaration of war. And in addition the War Powers Resolution gave Congress a point of reference from which it can say "Mister President, you should have done so and so." Then there is a basis for an argument or a dialogue and you can go to the American people.

We are hearing more these days about a return to bipartisanship in foreign policy, but you can't have bipartisanship if the President is not going to extend himself to *make* it bipartisan. And no policy will be really supportable in the long run if it is not fully understood by the American people and therefore by Congress. That is an essential part of the political process. I don't minimize the difficulty for any chief executive in carrying out his responsibilities under our system, but the mark of wisdom in the executive branch is to get Congress involved in the decision making process. Congress needs to be in on the takeoff of these things, not just the hard landing.

Administrations have been saying for as long as I can remember that Congress puts barnacles on their conduct of foreign policy, but I don't think that is true. The President as commander-in-chief has the right to move troops and to take any action he deems essential. It's only afterward that Congress can control him, and even then only by direct legislation or by control of the budget, and in either case he has the veto. I don't see that as a serious constraint on presidential action. As a matter of fact, in every serious case I can think of, Congress has said we are going to authorize what you want to do, or appropriate money for it—even in Central America. What administrations generally want is both money and authorization without any restrictions one way or the other. But Congress is not going to go for that. It never has.

———————◆———————

HENRY KISSINGER *was Richard Nixon's national security adviser and later Secretary of State to both Nixon and Gerald Ford. He conducted the Paris talks with North Vietnam, for which he was awarded the Nobel Peace Prize a year before Hanoi renewed the war and conquered the South. He is currently a consultant, author, and foreign-policy observer in New York.*

I think future challenges to the equilibrium also will come regionally (as in Vietnam), not globally. The challenges will not be unambiguous. We therefore have to get some national consensus. What accumulations of regional changes threaten our security? That issue requires some serious bipartisan effort which hasn't been made, and which had to be made prior to a crisis. If the effort is not made, the equilibrium will gradually be tilted against us.

If you can avoid force, you should avoid force. But there is no cost-free foreign policy. After Vietnam, answer this question: Is there anything in this world other than an attack on the United States that we will resist by force? If the answer is "no", we will gradually be pushed back into fortress America, by definition.

———————◆———————

He comes across as a nice Unitarian boy from Maine, slender of build, a trifle shy, with a serious cast of mind, not an overpowering presence, but a reassuring one, like a good family doctor. SEN. WIL-LIAM S. COHEN, *Republican of Maine, began practicing and teaching law in Bangor in the same year that Lyndon Johnson dispatched the first American combat troops to Vietnam. As a member of both the Intelligence and Armed Services committees, he has done some hard thinking about the circumstances under which he'd vote to send his own sons off to fight. He became vice-chairman of the Intelligence Committee in January 1987.*

Vietnam is still with us, although I don't think in a negative sense. We have learned something from it. Its lingering effect does not mean we won't send our sons to fight anywhere, but it *does* mean we won't send them to fight *everywhere*. If we're going to send them, it has to be clearly defined and clearly perceived as in the national interest.

One of the reasons there are no troops in Central America is that we have learned a very serious lesson, which is not to commit troops to any region unless the country and the Congress are convinced that the reasons are good. I don't think this Administration or any Administration can commit troops in the absence of widespread public support. So you can say that fundamentally it is not *Congress* that is a restraining force in this; it is the people themselves.

I kept a journal in 1979 when the renewal of the draft registration laws was under consideration, and I recorded my sensations on the sixteenth birthday of my oldest boy, and when I looked at it again the other day I saw that what I had talked about was that in two years he could either be off to college or off to war. I have two sons, and I could very well be in the position of voting to send young men off to die. As a father, I want to make sure the cause is really worth the possible loss of their lives.

———————◆———————

It is a pair of small ironies that SEN. GARY HART *of Colorado, who entered politics through the antiwar movement and managed the 1972 McGovern presidential campaign, made it a point not only to join the Armed Services Committee but to take as his area of spe-*

cial interest the U.S. Navy. Hart, who ran for the Democratic presidential nomination in 1984, left the Senate at the end of 1986 to pursue the 1988 nomination full-time.

We don't have to get involved in wars in the Third World just because, as the hawks argue, a number of countries went Communist in the seventies. The key word there is went. It's like the debate over who lost China. We don't "own" other countries. They are not ours. To use words like "lose" and "went" tilts the equation. Threats to our alliances we have to meet, but those are easy situations. The hard ones are the grays and the plaids. Angola and Central America fit in that category.

Right now there are four areas that worry me, South Africa, the Philippines, South Korea, and Central America. In each case we have a choice—either to side with the indigenous democratic forces, or to sit back and watch a bloody slide into repression. And in some of those cases we are making the wrong choice. We are, for example, providing military hardware to the Contras, and that I think is going to come back to haunt us.

Is there a military legacy from Vietnam?

It is true that defense spending went down. The Reagan administration now interprets this as a sign that we lost our will. But that is not true. We spent three hundred fifty billion dollars in Vietnam, and undertook a tremendous military buildup. But defense spending should be a continuum, not a series of peaks and valleys. Critics of the war said in the long run it would weaken us—and it did. When the war was over, the American people, not just Congress, wanted military spending to go down. That's a common reaction in the wake of wars. People like the Reagans of this world who wanted us to get involved in Vietnam should remember that when wars are over there is bound to be a sag in military spending.

EUGENE MCCARTHY

In light of what's happened in Vietnam and especially Cambodia, was there some justification for our being there?

If we had stayed out of Cambodia, I don't think things would be as bad as they are. We really just tore up, in Vietnam and to some extent in Cambodia, the whole government and social structure. Really, you figure that we put two or three million men through a community that had only a couple of million women and we just left it in chaos. And having done that, you have to expect the disorder—even more serious disorders than they otherwise might have had.

Whether we learned a lesson from it, I don't know. They say we'll never get in another war like Vietnam, and I guess we never will. But they also say "Well, we're never going to get into a limited war." So you say "Well, God, it'd be better to be in a limited war like Vietnam than to be in an unlimited war." It's a leap of logic, but that's sort of the implication of it.

I read into the very limited commitment in Lebanon a kind of lesson from Vietnam. Not that it was the same situation either militarily or geographically, but that was the kind of a place where you could have gotten deeply involved, with the Russians supplying the Syrians and having us fight in an area far away from home. It came at the beginning of a political year, and Ronald didn't hesitate to get them out, so whether it was a good thing to hang in or not, it indicated that they weren't going to.

Where does that leave us when the other guys are playing hardball in Afghanistan and Ethiopia and Angola?

I don't know. We haven't really been tested, I don't think. The Russians have gone as far as Afghanistan, but that's about it. Ethiopia? Well, the Russians used to have Somalia and we had Ethiopia. And now they've got Ethiopia and we've got Somalia. They had Egypt and now we've got Egypt. We never had Afghanistan. We're better off with China than we were ten years ago. They got Vietnam—well, give 'em a few more like that. Even Cuba.

You know, I only saw Kosygin once, but that was when they had Egypt and he was talking about how things change. And I said, "Well, you know we ought to trade allies about every five years. You take ours and we'll take yours." And he said, "I'll give you China for France." And I said, "I won't give you Israel for Egypt." We sort of laughed at that. But I kept it in my mind, and when Sadat came in he said "We want the Russians out." And they went out like the next morning. The Russians couldn't wait to get out. They said "Good-bye. We're not wanted here. We're gone." And Sadat said "Well, I wanted you out but I didn't want you to go quite so soon." So you can argue about who's on our side, but if you count China in, more or less, we're in pretty good shape.

———•———

J. WILLIAM FULBRIGHT

Look, it's very unpleasant to even talk about this [Vietnam]. It has no significance any more. The country didn't learn a damn thing for it. They're doing right now as bad or worse in Nicaragua, intervening, throwing their weight around like the big bully they are. We oughtn't to be intervening except in a place where it's of real importance to us. We have no business going about the world thinking we can tell every small country how to run their business. It's a form of escapism. Because we don't want to bother with our own problems, we go off and bother with somebody else's.

We can't do anything about our own budget and our own deficit and the imbalance in our trade. We just treat that with the back of our hand. Our public facilities and our education are going to pot, but we're *all out* for Nicaragua and the Middle East, Qaddafi and so on. Anybody who disagrees with them is a Communist. And they just make up the evidence to suit whatever their objective is. I don't believe hardly anything the government says about affairs of this kind.

We're very busy all around the world. We're intervening in Angola and Good Lord, I don't know, Afghanistan and where have you. I don't know why we are unwilling to let anybody struggle with their own problems. They undoubtedly know much more about it than we do. You leave them alone and they won't be any more happy with the Russians. It's just like Egypt and Guinea and a lot of others. After they have a little dose of it they throw them out themselves.

These people come in from Hollywood and think they can do anything, just like John Wayne. They feel that it's a big country with lots of power, and they've got to use it. Our duty. This idea that because we're the leader of the free world we have to intervene everywhere, I think is bad and dangerous for the country.

———————◆———————

JOAN BAEZ

My perspective is a pacifist perspective. I don't have any favorite wars. As a Quaker, we give up the right to take other people's lives. So my work started before Vietnam and continues long after. When I was approached by some boat people in 1979 about human rights conditions in Vietnam which were bad and terrible, it wasn't surprising to me, because I feel as though we really fertilized the ground for more violence. The Japanese did it. The Chinese did it. The French did it. And we did it. I think we had a massive share in creating chaos. The Vietnamese people are suffering and, of course that was proven with the exodus of the boat people. Vietnam is not an open society. It's a totalitarian state. It saddens one. On the other hand, I would not retract anything I did in the sixties. We had no business being there. And as we're about to do the whole round again in Central America, one wonders if, in fact, we did learn anything.

The other night after a concert a girl—she was sort of wired-up like a disk jockey—said to me, "Oh, I can't believe it. You lived in the sixties." I said "Yeah." She said, "Oh God. I mean it's so fantastic. Out of sight. I mean . . . " I tapped her on the shoulder and I said, "You know how many Americans died in the sixties? About fifty-eight thousand." She skipped that and she said, "That means you were at Woodstock, too." I said, "You're not listening to me. Want to know how many Vietnamese were killed?" Finally I just kind of shook her a little bit by the shoulder and I said, "You're acting like a goof ball. That's not really what the sixties was all about. It wasn't just the Beatles and flower children and Woodstock." I don't think she ever did click into what I was saying.

I think it's a fact that the pendulum swings back and forth; it's not even on the graph right now. They say "Well, Ms. Baez, where's the Movement?" It's very difficult in the shock waves of the pendulum which just flew off the graph to say what the Movement *is*. They call me a do-gooder, and I smile and say "That's interesting. It could be worse." But I find it just creepy as hell to have a business-school student who's twenty-four years old say to me "I don't know what this do-good crap is about. I don't see why you're so preoccupied. Those guys know what they're doing. Nobody's going to push that button." Maybe ignorance is bliss. Let's just all hope for a direct hit.

A sixteen-year-old recently put it to me perfectly. He was a very thinking young man. He had just taken a course from Colman McCarthy on nonviolence and he said, "In the sixties you guys had it all. You had a cause. You had the music. You had the momentum and you had each other. We don't have any glue." He thought he was speaking for his age, but he was really speaking for all of us who feel that our glue is not the technological society. Our glue has to be more profound, and more meaningful and more far-reaching. We don't feel connected [any more].

I think at the moment this country is going through a very myopic stage of new patriotism. We have to feel invulnerable. We have to feel "good about ourselves." This is a phenomenon I think is very dangerous and I think it's very shallow and I think the optimism is projected by the Administration and bought by the people. Which is in my opinion why Reagan was elected. Everybody's so anxious to find an escape and Reagan provides it with a genuinely buoyant personality and a smiling face.

Unfortunately I think what he's leading us to is absolutely murderous. That's the insanity of that office. I get frustrated when I hear that children get their lunches taken away so we can build more unusable weapons. And he believes that by doing that we're making the world safe for democracy. I don't know *what* he believes. But I don't think it's that guy that makes the difference; it's the office. There's a quote from Kissinger in Stanley Karnow's book on Vietnam: "What interests me is what you can do with power." That's what it turns into. Can you imagine that position as the "most important figure in the world?" So we know what he needs is to take his guidance from us. But if you have three quarters of the population on vacation from the thought process, he can just do with his Commies what he wants. How do you wake up the population? That I don't know. That has to do with the people and their desire not to think.

———◆———

BONNIE BERTRAM

What legacy did the Vietnam era leave?
I still like listening to the music. People like Neil Young really express intensity, vulnerability, and frustration. The street people that still live in Berkeley are fragments of a time of confusion and frustration. They were all participants in that time. Mostly they are drugged-out vets or students that have nowhere else to go. Otherwise, I think the common use of drugs is inherited. When you're involved in anything that you want to ignore, drugs are the perfect escape. We also inherited the idea of free sex since the draft proved that you have no control over your body anyway.

[But] student protest has become almost a cliche and now, whenever students get together to protest foreign policy, it always seems like an echo of the sixties. When the government is not going to listen, there is really nothing you can do. That could explain why we appear to be so uncaring. My generation sees that opposing the government may not be the most effective way to get your point across. Sometimes working within the system is better because people will listen. Otherwise, you are easily written off as just another agitated student.

Politically, Vietnam left me with a distrust of the government and a curiosity to know beyond what the media says. You know that what you are receiving is piecemeal. When I hear people speak on campus that have actually been in Central America, I realize that the media is not giving a complete or accurate picture of the situation there. I think that my generation learned a lesson from Vietnam: Don't trust the government.

We express that as widespread apathy. My generation is full of frustrated protesters because we have been shown that the government doesn't really care. It's like we resent the sixties generation because they had a cause to fight and they fought it incorrectly. And so, we know that no matter what we do, it won't make any difference. My roommate is a healthy eighteen-year-old male who is scared to death of being called up to fight in Nicaragua. He doesn't agree with the fight that is being waged there, but he feels that any protest on his part will be meaningless. Reagan is not going to halt his war on account of some eighteen-year-olds who resist being just disposable little soldiers.

If you were called to fight, would you go?

It would really depend what we were fighting for. The government's policies don't always coincide with my views. If I were to be sent to Nicaragua, I wouldn't go because I think the government has been lying about the situation there all along. It's not so much a sense of nationality but a sense of justice that would motivate me to fight for my country. But I think that with my family's political connections there would be ways that I could get out of it. Really, I can't see laying down my life for any of the foreign situations that we are involved in now.

———————◆———————

KEN BEREZ

Is there any way you'd support this country going to war again?

The world is very complex today, and yes, obviously the United States is a great power and it has responsibilities. But I think we should be very cautious on where we spend our blood. And in a democracy, the public has to know the cost of involvement, up front. When, tragically, those two hundred and fifty Marines were lost all in one day in Lebanon, people started to get scared. They were surprised that men got killed. But if you ask Marines to go off into a hostile environment and be exposed to fire, you should not be surprised that they got shot at and eventually many of them got killed. The question should be asked whether they should have been there in the first place. But once they were there, that's what an army is about. It's meant to fight.

And if [the country] is not willing to spend that blood and energy and treasure, then let's not get involved. Otherwise, it's a great deception. That's one reason—and I'm *not* speaking for VVA here—that

I believe in a universal draft that's equitable. We've always had a professional Army, Navy, and Air Force, but the people who actually fought the war—the grunts, the privates, and the corporals—were basically citizen soldiers, whose main thought was to get home. And I think that's the greatest rein on the military—that those who fight want to get out as quick as possible. I think a mercenary army is a danger in a democracy, and beyond that, I think just on principle, a democracy should ask everyone who's healthy to serve when necessary. It is an irony that because of the scars that existed after Vietnam, the legacy of it, that political leaders are afraid to ask everyone to spend time in the service today.

An important part of my work is to try to educate the public that was of age and conscious of the war and also the new generation just coming of age who really know very little of Vietnam. I speak before a lot of schools, and kids will say to me, "That's history," and I resent that. I'm flesh and blood. I'm not history. And I think it's really important to let people know what Vietnam was about, because there is a segment in our society that would like to redo the story. And I'm afraid there are powerful people who want to in some way get involved in Central America or the Middle East just to prove that Vietnam was the right cause.

I guess what I also resent is that the Dean Rusks and the McNamaras to this very day have never gotten up in front of a microphone or on a podium and simply said "I'm sorry." I don't want to try them as war criminals, but these were the architects of our policy in Vietnam. Just let them say "I'm sorry. I didn't have all the answers and we made the wrong decisions." They have yet to do that.

CHAPTER SIXTEEN

Epilogue

DuRING the negotiation of the 1973 Paris Accord, Richard Nixon and Henry Kissinger secretly promised Hanoi—in writing—that the United States would provide nearly $5 billion in postwar reconstruction aid. That pledge was almost as foolish as their vow to Nguyen Van Thieu that the United States would reenter the fighting if Hanoi breached the peace. Even had Nixon survived Watergate, America's desire to be done with the war, the continued violations of the cease fire, and Hanoi's refusal to account for more than twenty-five hundred American servicemen missing in action made a congressional vote for massive aid as unlikely as one to lift the ban on further military action. Hanoi's conquest of the South with a full-scale invasion in 1975 made it less likely still. Even so, there was a brief flurry of hope after the election of Jimmy Carter in 1976 that the United States might come to terms with the new Indochinese reality and make peace with the Communist government. But that was not to be.

The Carter administration twice held out the olive branch in 1977, but Hanoi, still thinking its supporters in Congress held the whip hand, foolishly surfaced the Nixon letter and demanded a commitment to aid before it would talk about anything else. Instantly, a firestorm of protest led Congress to tie Carter's hands so that even if he had wanted to negotiate, he was forbidden to do so. It took a year and a half for the new American reality to percolate into the Politburo's consciousness, and by then it was too late. Hanoi was preparing an invasion of Cambodia that deeply worried America's non-Communist allies in ASEAN, and the U.S. had decided, rightly, that a full restoration of ties with China, which supported the Khmer Rouge, was worth far more than anything Vietnam had to offer.

Hanoi clearly did the world a service by kicking Pol Pot and his

gang out of Phnom Penh in 1979. But the precedent it set by install-
ing a puppet regime and establishing an open-ended occupation of
the country made it impossible for the act to bring any Western
reward. Worse yet, with its avenues to the capitalist world closed
off, Vietnam had only the Soviet Union to look to for help—and
Moscow's price was a major new military position based on the wartime port and airfield complex at Cam Ranh Bay. From a handful of
destroyers in 1979, that presence grew by 1986 into a fleet of twenty-
five warships, accompanied by squadrons of maritime bombers,
reconnaissance planes, and fighter-interceptors. The Soviet presence threatened south China, and menaced the sea-lanes from Europe
and the Persian Gulf to the Far East. The Vietnamese also followed
the Soviet model in economics—and managed to convert a once-
prosperous economy into an Asian basket case.

Not until the mid-eighties, when the generation of revolutionaries
began to pass from the scene, did Hanoi seriously rethink its position. In 1984 Vietnamese officials began signaling that they wanted
to negotiate both a solution in Cambodia and a normalization of relations with the United States. The Reagan administration was in-
trigued, but it bluntly told Hanoi that there was no sense even talking about those two issues before it had produced a full accounting
for the MIAs and possible POWs. In 1985, Hanoi set up a two-year
timetable to settle that problem, and it even arranged for American
teams to dig into some aircraft crash sites in Vietnam and Laos to
retrieve any remains that might be there. The politburo also brought
in a reform-minded technocrat, Vo Van Kiet, to take charge of the
economy, and talk began to circulate that the country might emu-
late the Chinese model of development. Thus there seemed a possibility, as 1986 drew to a close, that it might fall to the Reagan
administration to write the last chapter to a long, sad saga for both
countries—and for the Vietnamese to join the modern world at last.

RICHARD HOLBROOKE

*We seemed near to a rapprochement with Hanoi in '77–'78. Why
didn't it happen?*

During the 1976 campaign Jimmy Carter said he'd send a delegation to Hanoi to talk about the MIAs. Carter wanted to be a President of reconciliation and establish full diplomatic relations with the
countries we didn't recognize. High on that list were China and Vietnam. Lower down were Angola, Cuba, Outer Mongolia, and so on.
So we sent the Mansfield-Woodcock mission to Hanoi. They got

some movement, and we agreed to go to Paris in May of 1977 for [broader] talks.

President Carter made me head of the delegation. My opposite number was the Vice Foreign Minister, Phan Hien. In 1968, when I was a junior member of the Paris Peace Talks delegation, I had been assigned to cultivate Phan Hien during the coffee breaks. Nine years later we were representing our countries and there was a kind of symmetry to it. He was asking where Phil Habib was and was he still eating so much, and about Governor Harriman.

Now, the Nixon-Kissinger-Ford position on Vietnam had been "We will veto your membership in the United Nations and we will not discuss cooperation or recognition until you give us a full accounting of MIAs." We thought that was self-defeating. In the formal meetings I told the Vietnamese we would no longer vote against them. We knew we would lose anyway, just the way the UN had overridden U.S. objections to China's membership, and we didn't want to invite a defeat. The second thing we said was that we needed a full accounting of the MIAs. And thirdly that if they moved toward a full accounting, we would be willing to move toward full diplomatic recognition.

Phan Hien then made a decisive mistake. He pulled out the Nixon letter of February 1, 1973, and he said "Fine, Now give us the four point seven five billion dollars that President Nixon promised us." I said "I'm sorry, that letter has no standing. It never went to Congress. It was done by a President on his own authority when he didn't have that authority." But Phan Hien stuck to his guns. The next day he repeated his request and I rejected it again. And then I got a call from Washington telling me that he had held a press conference and publicly called for the U.S. to honor the Nixon pledge—and that amendments were starting to be put on the floor of the House prohibiting aid. So I called up Phan Hien and I said, "If you've given a press conference calling for this stuff, you are going to pay the penalty. The United States is not going to be able to give you any aid." The Vietnamese had failed to appreciate that Jimmy Carter was offering them a very good deal.

Of course we knew about the letter, since Sonny Montgomery* had revealed its existence. Prior to that no one in the United States government except Kissinger and Nixon knew it existed, and they weren't *telling*, for obvious reasons. Nixon and Kissinger issued strong denunciations, saying there was a codicil making it subject to the approval of Congress. Now those words are not in the actual

---

*A Mississippi Democratic Congressman who was interested in the POW-MIA issue and had traveled to Hanoi.

document. The North Vietnamese had been persistent and Kissinger had been willing to move that out of the text. And second [Nixon and Kissinger] said that it had been overtaken by the Vietnamese violation of the agreements. But whatever their attempts to justify it, they had made a bizarre commitment. Even if the North Vietnamese had honored every bit of the agreements of 1973, Congress was never going to give four and three quarter billion dollars in aid to Hanoi. Never. And you want to tell me that that wasn't understood by President Nixon and Doctor Kissinger when they wrote that piece of paper? No way. I agree that North Vietnam's invasion of '75 obviated any validity that had. But I'm convinced that at the moment Kissinger and Nixon agreed to it, they knew it was just words to get out of this thing.

I went back to Paris in June of '77 for another series of talks with Phan Hien. He took me aside during the break and he said, "Just tell me privately what kind of aid you'll give." I said, "I'm sorry, Mr. Minister. You don't understand. I cannot promise you anything. I will have to go back to Congress in two days, and I will have to tell them the truth. And the truth will be that I did not make any aid commitment." And he went back to Hanoi very disappointed.

Now the point of this story is that Hanoi came to Paris in 1977 living off a decade and a half of viewing America as a country run by a hawkish President driven by a dovish Congress. They had not understood that Jimmy Carter was going to make them the best offer they would ever get, and if they didn't take it, it would vanish. A year and a half later [Vietnamese Foreign Minister Nguyen Co] Thach accepted it in toto. But by that time the boat people were being driven into the South China Sea, Vietnam had eleven divisions on the Cambodian border massing to invade, and we were deep in negotiations with the Chinese. There had been that dreadful spy case in which their ambassador to the United Nations had been implicated and we had thrown him out. And the window had closed.

They lost that opportunity at a time when ASEAN had saved them an empty seat. They could have been peaceful participants in Southeast Asia. Instead, driven more than anything else by the deep enmity of China, they made a historic decision to cast their lot with Moscow. That's how it happened.

It struck a lot of people when the Vietnamese invaded Cambodia that they were doing the world a favor. Why didn't we see it that way?

I agree completely that the removal of the Khmer Rouge from Phnom Penh was a favor to the people of Cambodia and therefore a favor to the world. We understood that completely, and nothing I did, nothing Cy Vance did, was ever designed to either prevent that from happening or to restore the Khmer Rouge to power in Phnom Penh.

But once Hanoi was in control of Phnom Penh we decided that what the Vietnamese had done was not a precedent we wanted to accept. And on that narrow grounds we voted, and continue to vote to this day, for the Cambodian seat in the UN to go to Democratic Kampuchea or its successors and not to the DPRK which is the Vietnamese-backed regime.

Nothing I did in four years as assistant secretary of state has troubled me personally more, and yet I'd make the same decision again. I despise the Khmer Rouge; they perpetrated a version of the Holocaust on their own people. But the night before the first vote, Vance called me in and asked me whether or not we really had to vote this way. He'd received a message through the so-called "dissent channel," in which junior officers could argue directly with the Secretary against a policy, and he was troubled, too. I remember vividly the sun was setting on a beautiful Washington day and he looked out the window and he said, "Let's go through it one more time." And I did and he said, "Well, you're right. I know it. We'll have to vote."

Reagan attacked us in the campaign for that vote, yet he repeated it. It has to be understood against the background of our relations with the rest of the region—ASEAN, China, Australia, New Zealand, and Japan, all very strongly not wanting to legitimize the Vietnamese invasion because of the precedents. So whenever we made that vote, we would state we were voting for it on narrow grounds and not to support the Khmer Rouge.

Given Vietnam's decision thereafter to allow a large-scale Soviet military presence, was it a good idea regardless of the precedents?

The Vietnamese decision to cast their lot with Moscow was made no later than the spring of 1978, and it probably was inevitable given the enmity between Vietnam and China. The Chinese had cut off Russian resupply by rail of Hanoi as early as '69. There was a split over who supported whom in Phnom Penh. These were signs, I might add, that the Nixon and Ford administrations completely failed to understand. Witness Kissinger's endless requests to the Vietnamese in Paris in the early seventies to discuss Vietnam and Cambodia together. The Vietnamese kept saying "We can't. It's an independent movement," and Kissinger wrote in his memoirs that this was nonsensical Communist propaganda.

But in the spring of '78 Hanoi joined COMECON,* and on November second, Brezhnev and Pham Van Dong signed a friendship and cooperation treaty. Brzezinski will tell you that the move towards relations with Vietnam was stopped by Carter on his advice because

---

*The Communist East-European equivalent of the West European Common Market.

we were negotiating with China. And that was Zbig's primary motive. Yet I made the same recommendation for very different reasons—the exodus of the boat people and the impending invasion of Cambodia. Does that mean I didn't want the Vietnamese to get Pol Pot out of there? Not at all. But you end up sometimes with conflicting principles, and here was a classic case. I believe the policy we articulated was the one that was in the strategic interests of the United States.

If I had been a simple private citizen at the time, I might have been appalled. But as assistant secretary of state, I had to make a recommendation to the Secretary and the President of what was in America's national interests. To do otherwise would have created an intolerable dislocation of our relations with ten major governments in that part of the world. So I am comfortable with the way we turned out.

———————◆———————

NGUYEN VAN HAO

You asked me about the prospect of Vietnam. I think Vietnam still a very interesting country. The proof, now even after ten years, you as Americans, you like to know more about Vietnam. Vietnam is not a backwater country or represent the past. It's still present, and maybe capable to have some future. From view of history, the Vietnam people have proved two of the most natural characteristics of a country. They are survivors and have capability to adapt difficult circumstances.

I think the number one problem of today is the image of Vietnam. After '75 the international opinion looked on Vietnamese as something fantastic. It be David-Goliath, and David come out something stronger. And after ten years what happen? The situation become very difficult. A lot of people just flee Vietnam. They prefer to risk their life not because they don't love Vietnam, but to have a better future for their children. So image now is not very attractive.

What happened? Why changed? Before Vietnam always present a constructive image, and now become we just know only one thing to do, is to make war. We don't know how to construct a country. Our *specialité* is making war. You know during all the time of war the people in Hanoi launch a business, it's a professional full-time job, nothing to do except making war. But you know sometime in order to overcome such trouble, specially in economic, we have to solve some political problem.

So first, maybe, we have to make peace with China. China represent a big problem for Vietnam not only today, not only in the past, but in the future too. China is too big, close to us, and they know our mentality. And for China time is not a problem. They have eternity to solve the Vietnam problem. To make peace with China it not represent that we have to capitulate. We always independent but need to be friendly too.

Number two, I would say we have to normalize relations with the U.S. sooner or later, because U.S. can help a lot and can do harm a lot. In the history of Vietnam we always make peace with the enemies. If we can consider U.S. as the enemy, according to our tradition, make peace. We have done that at least six times in our two thousand years of history with China. And why is there any reason we don't do it with the U.S.?

Number three we have to find some solution with the Cambodian problem. Not just neighbor relations but important for military problem too.

And sooner or later we should have some way to make some reconciliation with almost a million people fled Vietnam. These people represent a human resource. I never saw any country can develop with lack of human resource. This represent I think a lot of asset for Vietnam. So now if we have some intelligent policy to make peace between Vietnam and the people who flee Vietnam, would be fantastic.

List of
Participants

For the reader's convenience, this is an identification list of the people who contributed to this oral history. The names of the interviewers and the approximate time of the interview appear in brackets. The interviews were conducted in February and March of 1985, and between February and May of 1986.

EDDIE ADAMS is a photographer who covered the war for the Associated Press. His most famous Vietnam photo showed the National Police chief executing a Viet Cong on a Saigon street corner with a bullet to the head. [Anne Underwood, 1985]

RICHARD L. ARMITAGE is the assistant secretary of defense for international security affairs. He served several tours in Vietnam as a Navy officer and later as a civilian in the Defense Attaché Office. [Kim Willenson, 1986]

REP. LES ASPIN, Democrat of Wisconsin, is chairman of the House Armed Services Committee. He was one of Robert McNamara's Pentagon whiz kids in the mid-sixties. [Kim Willenson, 1985]

JOAN BAEZ is a folk singer who became an icon of the Vietnam protest movement. She appeared at dozens of antiwar rallies and traveled to Hanoi during the Christmas bombing of 1972 to visit the American POWs. [Patricia King, 1985]

GEORGE BALL, a Wall Street lawyer and investment banker, was the government's leading internal dove as undersecretary of state in the Kennedy and Johnson administrations. [Steven Shabad, 1985]

NANCY BENNETT is the wife of Josiah Bennett, the last political counselor of the Saigon Embassy. [Martin Kasindorf, 1985]

CHARLES BENOIT was an AID worker and later chief of the Ford Foundation in Saigon. He served in Vietnam from 1967 to 1975. He is now a businessman. [Richard Manning, 1985]

KEN BEREZ was an infantryman in Vietnam, where he was wounded in the spine. He is associate director of the Vietnam Veterans of America Foundation. [Kim Willenson, 1985]

BONNIE BERTRAM was a student at the University of California, Berkeley, majoring in English literature. [Allison Levin, 1985]

PETER BRAESTRUP, a combat correspondent in Vietnam and the author of *Big Story*, a critique of press coverage of the Tet Offensive, edits *The Wilson Quarterly*, journal of the Woodrow Wilson Institute in Washington. [Kim Willenson, 1986]

SAM BROWN, a leader of the antiwar movement, organized the Vietnam Moratorium in 1969. In the postwar years he had a fling at politics in Colorado. He is now a businessman. [Jeff Copeland, 1985]

NGUYEN VAN CANH, deputy dean of the Saigon Law Faculty, escaped by boat with his family on the day Saigon fell. He runs a refugee training center in California. [Martin Kasindorf, 1985]

ALAN CARTER, the last U.S. Information Agency chief in Vietnam, is a vice president of the Experiment in International Living in Brattleboro, Vermont. [Richard Manning, 1985]

CLARK CLIFFORD, a Washington attorney and Democratic power broker for fifty years, succeeded Robert S. McNamara at the Pentagon, and persuaded Lyndon Johnson to de-escalate after the Tet offensive of 1968. [Kim Willenson, 1985]

SEN. WILLIAM . COHEN, a liberal Republican from Maine, is vice-chairman of the Senate Intelligence Committee and serves on Armed Services as well. [Kim Willenson, 1985]

WILLIAM COLBY is the former director of the Central Intelligence Agency and was involved in CIA operations in Vietnam throughout the war. He is a lawyer in Washington. [Kim Willenson, 1986]

WILLIAM CORSON, a retired Marine colonel, spent much of his career fighting Indochina's secret wars. He is a Washington-based editor for *Penthouse* magazine. [Kim Willenson, 1986]

WALTER CRONKITE, the *CBS Evening News* anchorman throughout the war years, is now retired but still does occasional documentaries for his network. [Steven Strasser, 1985]

JOSH CRUZE joined the Marines at seventeen and fought as an infantryman in Vietnam, where he was wounded by a mine. He recovered, and later became an actor in *Tracers*, a critically acclaimed play about the war. [Anne Underwood, 1985]

DO DUC CUONG, farmer's son in northern South Vietnam, became an ARVN intelligence officer. He escaped by boat two years after the end of the war and is now an engineer in California. [Martin Kasindorf, 1985 and 1986]

LEON DANIEL, a correspondent in Vietnam for United Press International, wrote a memorable account of the looting of Snuol, Cambodia, by American troops. [Kim Willenson, 1986]

JOHN DIFUSCO served in the U.S. Air Force in central Vietnam. After the war he conceived, directed, and acted in *Tracers*, a critically acclaimed play about Vietnam. [Anne Underwood, 1985]

KHE BA DO was vice-minister of education in Saigon from 1971 to 1974. He escaped in the American evacuation. He is a dean at American River College in Sacramento, California. [Martin Kasindorf, 1985]

TRAN VAN DON, a retired general, was a leader of the coup against Ngo Dinh Diem, and was later elected to South Vietnam's Senate. He works at a travel agency in Virginia. [Ron Moreau, 1985]

REP. DANTE FASCELL, a Florida Democrat, is chairman of the House Foreign Affairs Committee. With the late Republican Sen. Jacob Javits, he helped pass the War Powers Act over the veto of Richard Nixon. [Kim Willenson, 1985]

SEN. J. WILLIAM FULBRIGHT was chairman of the Senate Foreign Relations Committee when the Johnson administration hustled the Tonkin Gulf Resolution through Congress to lay the basis for war in Indochina. He practices law in Washington. [Kim Willenson, 1986]

ALEXANDER HAIG was a military aide to Robert McNamara, Richard Nixon's last chief of staff, Supreme Commander in Europe, and Ronald Reagan's first Secretary of State. He is a perennial candidate for the Republican presidential nomination. [Kim Willenson, 1985]

MORTON HALPERIN worked for Henry Kissinger on the National Security Council and was among the Nixon administration's first wiretap victims. He directs the Legislative Office of the American Civil Liberties Union in Washington. [Kim Willenson, 1986]

NGUYEN VAN HAO was Nguyen Van Thieu's economic czar in 1974–75, and stayed on as a consultant to the Communist regime until 1982. He now works in Africa for the United Nations. [Verne Smith, 1985]

DAVID HARRIS went to prison for refusing the draft during the war. His book on the experience, *I Shoulda Been Home Yesterday*, was published in 1976. [Gerald Lubenow, 1985]

SEN. GARY HART, a Colorado Democrat, is a veteran of the antiwar movement. He ran for the Democratic presidential nomination in 1984 and quit the Senate in 1986 to try again. [Kim Willenson, 1985]

JOHN HASEK, a Canadian infantry major, headed a regional Canadian ICCS team in Vietnam in 1973. He is retired from the military and teaches at York University in Canada. [Kim Willenson, 1986]

DANNY HEFEL, a farm boy from Iowa, was captured after his helicopter was shot down in South Vietnam in 1970 and spent more than three years in prison camps. Disabled, he lives on a military pension. [John McCormick, 1985]

RICHARD HOLBROOKE worked for AID in Vietnam, served in the Johnson White House, wrote a volume of the Pentagon Papers, and became Jimmy Carter's assistant secretary of state for East Asia. He is an investment banker in New York. [Kim Willenson, 1986]

MICHELL JACOB spent three years in the Mekong Delta for a private aid group, International Voluntary Services, helping farmers breed better pigs. He is an agricultural consultant in Washington. [Ron Moreau, 1985]

MARINE MAJ. JAMES KEAN superintended evacuation of the U.S. Embassy in Saigon and, with a dozen Marine enlisted men, was aboard the last chopper out. He is a trade executive in Seattle. [Martin Kasindorf, 1985]

LARRY KIEWIT, of Milwaukee, went AWOL from the Army and defected to Canada rather than go to Vietnam. He is a house painter in Surrey, British Columbia. [Martin Kasindorf, 1985]

ROBERT KOMER for a time ran LBJ's White House office on Vietnam. In 1967, he went to Vietnam to run the pacification program. He was deputy defense secretary in the Carter years and is now a Rand Corporation analyst. [Kim Willenson, 1985]

NGUYEN CAO KY commanded South Vietnam's Air Force and was premier in Nguyen Van Thieu's first government. He is now a businessman in Southern California. [Martin Kasindorf, 1985]

GARY LARSEN served in Vietnam as a Foreign Service officer from 1969 to 1973. He is chairman of a bank in Long Beach, California, and has traveled to Vietnam on behalf of an international relief group. [Ron Moreau, 1985]

JOHN LINDSAY reported on Congress and politics for *Newsweek* for more than twenty years and was intimately involved in covering the Watergate scandal. He is semiretired. [Kim Willenson, 1986]

CHARLES LITEKY, a U.S. Army Catholic chaplain, won the Congressional Medal of Honor in Vietnam. Later, he became an antiwar activist. He is now campaigning against U.S. involvement in Central America. [Kim Willenson, 1986]

GRAHAM MARTIN was U.S. Ambassador in Saigon from mid-1973 until the collapse. Earlier he had been Ambassador to Thailand during the Vietnam buildup. He is retired and lives in North Carolina. [Verne Smith, 1985]

LARRY MARTIN grew up in San Diego and fled the United States in 1969 to avoid the draft. He is a social worker in Vancouver, British Columbia. [Martin Kasindorf, 1985]

SEN. JOHN MCCAIN, Republican of Arizona, son of Adm. John McCain, then the U.S. Commander-in-Chief, Pacific, was shot down over North Vietnam and spent five and a half years as a POW. [Kim Willenson, 1985]

SEN. EUGENE MCCARTHY launched the challenge from the left that helped bring down Lyndon Johnson. He is a director of Harcourt Brace Jovanovich publishing company's Washington office. [Kim Willenson, 1985]

Marine LT. COL. EDISON MILLER, ret., a POW for five years and four months, was censured by Navy Secretary John Warner for his alleged behavior in Hanoi prison camps. He is still appealing the decision. [Martin Kasindorf, 1985]

CHARLES MOHR, Southeast Asia correspondent for *Time* magazine in the early sixties, was in the middle of a dispute over the character of the Saigon press corps during the Diem years. He is now a *New York Times* national security correspondent in Washington. [Kim Willenson, 1986]

MAJ. GEN. ROBERT MOLINELLI was a much-decorated helicopter commander in Vietnam. He now directs Army research on combat support systems. [Debbie Seward, 1985]

RUSSELL MOTT, an AID official in Vietnam from 1968 to 1975 under the name Robert Lanigan, helped to organize the evacuations of Danang and Saigon. He is a photographer in Las Cruces, New Mexico. [Martin Kasindorf, 1985]

BOBBY MULLER, a Marine lieutenant in Vietnam who came home a paraplegic, is the founder and president of Vietnam Veterans of America. [Kim Willenson, 1986]

JOHN D. NEGROPONTE served as a political officer in Vietnam, was on the Paris peace talks delegation, and was a National Security Council aide from 1963 to 1974. He is now an assistant secretary of state. [Joe Contreras, 1985]

DON OBERDORFER covered Vietnam for the Knight-Ridder newspapers and the *Washington Post*. He is the author of a striking book titled simply *Tet* and is diplomatic correspondent of the *Post*. [Kim Willenson, 1986]

GEN. BRUCE PALMER, ret., was William C. Westmoreland's deputy and later commanded the U.S. Army in Vietnam. Palmer wrote *The Twenty-Five Year War*, an authoritative history of the Indochina conflict. [Kim Willenson, 1986]

MAJ. GEN. GEORGE S. PATTON III, son of the famous World War II general, fought in both Korea and Vietnam, where he served three tours between 1962 and 1969. Retired, he is a farmer in Massachusetts. [Anne Underwood, 1985]

MAI PHAM, daughter of a Vietnamese intelligence official, was an Armed Forces Radio personality and sometime newswoman in Vietnam. She is now a TV anchor in Sacramento, California. [Martin Kasindorf, 1985]

DOUGLAS PIKE was the leading U.S. public analyst of Vietnamese Communist affairs during the war. He now heads the Indochina Archive at the University of California-Berkeley. [Gerald Lubenow, 1985]

THOMAS POLGAR was the CIA station chief in Vietnam from 1972 until the fall of Saigon. He is now an international security consultant in Maitland, Florida. [Verne Smith, 1985]

LIONEL ROSENBLATT was an adviser in Vietnam from 1967 to 1969. In 1975 he and a colleague flew to Saigon on their own to try to rescue some of their friends. He is now at the State Department in Washington. [Steven Shabad, 1985]

WALT WHITMAN ROSTOW was Lyndon B. Johnson's national security adviser. An unreconstructed hawk, he teaches economics and history at the University of Texas in Austin. [Kim Willenson and Dan Pedersen, 1985]

GEN. BRENT SCOWCROFT, retired, was Gerald Ford's national security adviser. He is a consultant in Washington and a Reagan administration adviser on defense and foreign policy. [Kim Willenson, 1985]

JAMES R. SCHLESINGER, JR., has been a cabinet officer under both Republican and Democratic presidents. Secretary of Defense when Saigon fell, he is a counselor of the Center for Strategic and International Studies in Washington. [Kim Willenson, 1985]

COL. GEORGE SHINE, ret., and his wife, Helen, are the parents of four children who served in Vietnam. One was killed, a second badly wounded, and a third is still missing in action. [Anne Underwood, 1985]

FRANK SNEPP, the senior CIA analyst in Saigon when Vietnam fell, set down his recollections in *Decent Interval*, a book that stung Washington to the quick. He now teaches at Long Beach State University in California. [Martin Kasindorf, 1985]

REP. STEPHEN SOLARZ, of Brooklyn, was elected in the post-Watergate Democratic landslide of 1974. He has specialized in Asian affairs and made himself a considerable influence on U.S. foreign policy. [Kim Willenson, 1985]

JEFF STEIN was a U.S. Army intelligence operative in Danang. He is a writer and magazine editor in Washington. [Kim Willenson, 1986]

ADM. JAMES B. STOCKDALE, ret., a Navy pilot, was an eyewitness to the Tonkin Gulf incident and led the first major air strike on North Vietnam. Shot down in 1965, he was the senior U.S. POW for seven and a half years. [Pamela Abramson and Kim Willenson, 1985 and 1986]

RETIRED AMBASSADOR WILLIAM SULLIVAN, a career diplomat, was involved in the Indochina conflict from beginning to end. He served in Vietnam and at Geneva, but principally in Laos during the American "secret" war. He is retired and lives in Mexico. [Steven Shabad and Kim Willenson, 1985 and 1986]

TRUONG NHU TANG is the author of *A Vietcong Memoir*, a detailed account of his years as a Vietcong leader—and subsequently, as a boat person. He lives in Paris. [Edward Behr, 1985]

DOAN VAN TOAI was a student antiwar activist who stayed in Vietnam to work with the Communists, only to be jailed in the same cell in which the Thieu regime had held him. Now living in California, he has written several books on Vietnam. [Martin Kasindorf, 1985]

DR. NGUYEN BUU TRUNG was a Vietnamese military doctor who became the country's leading practitioner of reconstructive hand surgery. He is a doctor in Los Angeles. [Martin Kasindorf, 1985 and 1986]

LA ANH TU evaded the South Vietnamese draft and, with his brothers and sisters, formed a pop-music band that played for American officers and others from the late sixties until the last days of the war. He and the band perform in California. [Martin Kasindorf, 1985]

LT. RICHARD VAN DE GEER, a helicopter pilot, participated in the evacuations of both Phnom Penh and Saigon. He tape-recorded his experiences for friend and fellow pilot, *Newsweek* correspondent

Richard Sandza, just before he was killed by a Khmer Rouge rocket during the *Mayaguez* incident.

PAUL VOGLE, originally a U.S. Army linguist, later a correspondent, was an eyewitness to the war from 1956 through the Communist victory in 1975. He was expelled six weeks after the fall of Saigon and is now an editor for UPI in Detroit. [Richard Manning, 1985]

COL. JOHN WAGHELSTEIN served in Vietnam with the Special Forces and later with a line regiment. In the early eighties, he helped train Salvadoran troops in counterinsurgency. He is commander of the 7th Special Forces Group at Fort Bragg, North Carolina. [Steven Shabad, 1985]

CASPAR WEINBERGER served Richard Nixon and Gerald Ford as director of the Office of Management and Budget, and later as Secretary of Health, Education and Welfare. He is Ronald Reagan's Secretary of Defense. [Kim Willenson, 1985]

BARRY ZORTHIAN headed U.S. Information Agency operations and was, in effect, press relations czar of the U.S. Mission in Vietnam from 1964 to 1968. He is an adviser to the Embassy of Oman in Washington. [Kim Willenson, 1986]

Index

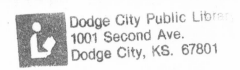